STUDIES ON CHINA

A series of conference volumes sponsored by
the American Council of Learned Societies.

Re-Drawing Boundaries

This volume, and the conference from which it resulted, was supported by the Joint Committee on Chinese Studies of the American Council of Learned Societies and the Social Science Research Council.

Re-Drawing Boundaries

Work, Households, and Gender in China

EDITED BY

Barbara Entwisle and Gail E. Henderson

UNIVERSITY OF CALIFORNIA PRESS

Berkeley   Los Angeles   London

University of California Press
Berkeley and Los Angeles, California

University of California Press, Ltd.
London, England

© 2000 by the Regents of the University of California

Library of Congress Cataloging-in-Publication Data

Re-drawing boundaries : work, households, and gender in China / edited by Barbara
Entwisle and Gail E. Henderson.
   p.   cm.
Includes bibliographical references and index.
   ISBN 0-520-22090-0 (cloth : alk. paper).—ISBN 0-520-22091-9 (paper : alk. paper)
   1. Labor—China—Congresses.   2. Sex discrimination in employment—China—
Congresses.   I. Entwisle, Barbara. II. Henderson, Gail, 1949–
HD8736.5 .R43   2000
331.4'133'0951—dc21

                                                      99-047587

Manufactured in the United States of America

09 08 07 06 05 04 03 02 01 00
10 9 8 7 6 5 4 3 2 1

CONTENTS

v

PART TWO · RECENT TRENDS IN GENDER AND INEQUALITY

PART THREE · GENDER AND MIGRATION

PART FOUR · HOUSEHOLDS AND WORK

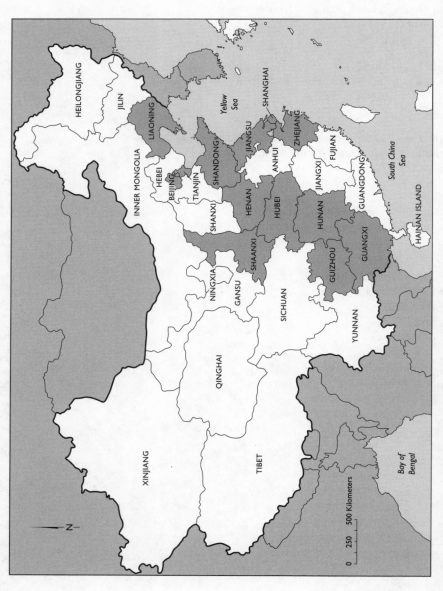

Map 1. Provinces included in studies by contributors.

PREFACE

This volume is based on papers, commentary, and discussion from the conference "Gender, Households, and the Boundaries of Work in Contemporary China," held in Chapel Hill, North Carolina in October 1996. Four conference sessions were organized around four questions about work, households, and gender in China; this structure underlies the four sections of this volume. The specific questions addressed were:

1. What is work? What are the views of social science scholars? What are the views of Chinese men and women?
2. How have gender inequalities in work changed over the course of recent history in China?
3. How has migration affected interrelationships among households, gender, and work?
4. How do families and households influence and how are they influenced by the organization of work?

The conference was multidisciplinary, as is this book. Participants represented a variety of disciplinary perspectives: anthropology, demography, economics, history, and sociology. Why did we design the conference in this way? As we looked at the literature on gender, households, and the boundaries of work in China, we found scholars in different fields applying theoretical and interpretive models to certain types of data with certain methodologies and communicating their insights and results to audiences already familiar with these same models, data, and methodologies. An explicit goal of the conference was to bring together scholars from a variety of disciplines to improve communication; to discuss the strengths, weaknesses, and complementarities of their approaches; and to compare the results of their work.

Diversity in disciplinary perspective is reflected in the variety of data and methods used. Approximately half of the chapters are qualitative in orientation, basing their analyses on historical documents, participatory field research, in-depth interviews, key informant interviews, and focus group discussions. The other chapters take a quantitative approach, using social survey and census data. The chapters report on diverse study sites as well, as shown in map 1. Included are the three metropolitan provinces—Shanghai, Beijing, and Tianjin—and urban and rural areas in ten other provinces and autonomous regions: Guangxi, Guizhou, Henan, Hubei, Hunan, Jiangsu, Liaoning, Shandong, Shaanxi, and Zhejiang. Links between chapters largely involve thematic issues of work, households, and gender rather than data or methods per se, although there is some overlap in this regard for some chapters.

Shared topical focus and strong unifying themes help counterbalance this diversity. The conference generated a genuine sense of excitement about the topic and collegiality among participants. Part of the reason it worked so well was the innovative format, which assigned a larger than usual role to discussants and is reflected in the organization of this volume. The format for the conference emphasized both in-depth discussion of individual papers as well as more general and integrative discussion of papers in relation to one another. During the first morning, participants in each of the four sessions met separately for small-group discussion. Discussants provided detailed critiques of individual papers at this time. Authors also commented on each other's papers, which they had been asked to read in detail. These discussions were lively, interesting, and generative. All conference participants met together in the afternoon of the first day, and for the remaining one-and-a-half days of the conference. A half day was devoted to each of the four sessions. Papers had been made available in advance of the conference, so authors limited themselves to short, ten-minute summaries. Discussants followed, bringing out important perspectives and findings of individual papers and emphasizing general issues and unifying themes for the session. We include these remarks in the present volume at the end of the relevant section. One of the benefits of attending a conference is the opportunity to hear the discussant as well as general discussion. Authors have incorporated the detailed suggestions made by the discussants in the revised versions of their papers. The more general commentaries of the discussants are provided so that all can benefit from their larger view and insights.

ACKNOWLEDGMENTS

This volume and the conference that preceded it were made possible by support from many sources. Both are the culmination of a research collaboration between us, which in turn was part of a larger five-year project, funded by the National Institute for Child Health and Human Development (P01 HD 28076), to study work patterns, child nutrition, and reproductive behavior in the context of rapid social change in China. We came together initially because of our association with Barry Popkin, another collaborator in the larger research project. Graduate students Jill Bouma (now on the faculty at Berea College) and Susan Short (now on the faculty at Brown University) contributed importantly to the research effort. For us, the conference represents the social science research and commentary that we wish had been available at the beginning of our work.

Plans for the conference were first formulated in a planning meeting and workshop held in Chapel Hill, North Carolina in February 1995. Yanjie Bian, Mary Brinton, Elisabeth Croll, Denise Hare, Gail Hershatter, and Zhai Fengying attended, and we would like to acknowledge their helpful ideas and suggestions, many of which were incorporated into the subsequent design of the conference. The University Center for International Studies and the Carolina Population Center provided support for the planning meeting. Travel expenses for some of the attendees were covered through their participation in the Triangle East Asia Colloquium (TEAC).

The Joint Committee on Chinese Studies of the American Council of Learned Societies and the Social Research Council, the Chiang Ching-kuo Foundation, and a grant from the Mellon Foundation to the Carolina Population Center provided support for the conference and the preparation of this volume. We want to acknowledge and express our gratitude for this support.

We would also like to acknowledge and thank the many individuals whose help was vital. Chief among them is Amanda Brickman Elam, graduate student in sociology, who expertly handled all of the details for the conference itself, including correspondence with authors, arrangements for the conference site, preparation of materials, scheduling, and many other management activities. Amanda Elam was also central to the conversion of the conference papers into a publishable volume, again handling correspondence with authors and tracking papers as they were reviewed, revised, edited, and checked. We would also like to thank Lynn Igoe and Leslie Cornell for verifying references in the unified bibliography and for other editorial assistance; and Debra A. Donahoe, Allison Greene, Brad Hammill, Marion Hughes, and Guobin Yang, who served as graduate student notetakers at the conference. Final manuscript preparation was ably handled by Shea Farrell.

Barbara Entwisle
Gail E. Henderson

Introduction

Gail E. Henderson and Barbara Entwisle

China is an especially interesting context for studies of work, household, and gender. During the past fifty years the Chinese have experimented fundamentally with both the meaning and substance of work. Notions of how work should be organized, where it should take place, and who should be doing it were redefined in the transition to socialism after 1949 and again in the shift to "market" socialism following the economic reforms of the late 1970s. As described and explored in this volume, this experimentation has had implications for households and gender as well. The volume is organized into four parts: 1. Perspectives on Work; 2. Recent Trends in Gender and Inequality; 3. Gender and Migration; and 4. Households and Work. This introduction provides an overview of each part. First, however, we explore the social, economic, and political context of China.

BACKGROUND

At the end of the twentieth century, China has emerged as the world's fastest growing economy. This is a breathtaking achievement. During the century prior to the Communist revolution, China was a poor, war-torn peasant society. The fall of the last dynasty in 1911, prompted in part by increasing economic encroachment by Japan and Europe, left the country without an effective central government until 1949. During this time, the nation experienced protracted regional conflict, fragile unification under the Nationalist regime led by Chiang Kai-shek, military aggression by Japan before and during the Second World War, and a four-year civil war. The Communist victory in 1949 finally established a secure and stable political order.

To create a socialist society China's new leaders set about transforming most of its social, economic, and political institutions. Work was collectivized, and private ownership was gradually eliminated. Marxist ideas about equality through labor played a central role in the redefinition of social relations in the areas of gender, family, urban-rural residence, work, and politics. The role of private household and family activities was diminished, and the personal and work lives of Chinese citizens in both urban and rural areas became increasingly subject to state control. In the countryside, after land reform redistributed farmers' plots, farms were gradually collectivized and then organized into larger communes. These communes promoted socialized agricultural labor and limited private activities such as sidelines, private gardening, and small household-run businesses (Parish and Whyte 1978). In the villages, Party cadres took control of many aspects of rural family and work life previously under clan and patriarch authority (A. Chan, Madsen, and Unger 1984; Huang Shu-min 1989). In cities, commerce and production were socialized and private enterprises gradually disappeared. The Party exercised authority over daily life through neighborhood residential committees and through urban workplaces, *danwei* (Henderson and Cohen 1984; Walder 1986; Whyte and Parish 1984).

The institution of the urban and rural household registration system in the late 1950s permanently linked welfare and employment opportunities to both household and place of residence and enabled the government to enforce migration restrictions. One of the world's strictest systems of population control thus reinforced and deepened the boundary between the nation's urban and rural populations. Successive political movements were launched to overcome this division—most notably the Great Proletarian Cultural Revolution (1966–1976), which relocated almost 20 million urban people to learn through labor in the countryside. Today, despite relaxed regulations that have encouraged the migration of over 100 million rural residents, the urban-rural divide remains China's largest social division (Griffin and Zhao 1993; Potter and Potter 1990).

Another great social divide China's new leaders addressed was the one between men and women. In 1949 the majority of Chinese women lived in the rural households of husbands, fathers, or sons. Regardless of where women lived, gender differences in educational attainment and employment opportunities were substantial. After the Communist revolution, legal reforms such as the Marriage Law of 1950 were enacted. Yet during the Maoist period (1949–1976), gender inequalities in work, education, marriage, and family relations were only intermittently the subject of political or legal campaigns (Andors 1983; Croll 1978; 1983; M. Wolf 1985). For the most part, the new Chinese government maintained the view that true gender equality would come hand in hand with socialism. Practically speaking, improved gender relations were to be enforced by the socialist organizations that controlled most aspects of daily life.

The exhortation to behavior reflecting the values of socialism was everywhere in evidence—in the media, in the small group political discussions held in all workplaces (Whyte 1974), and in the propaganda of Communist Party teams that investigated the implementation of various policies at the local level. Mao Zedong's assertion that "Women Hold Up Half the Sky" was reiterated throughout this period and inspired women labor models—"Iron Girls"—and one of the highest levels of female labor force participation in the world. At the height of radical Maoism, exemplified by the political excesses of the Cultural Revolution, the Communist worldview dominated everyday categories of discourse. When this state discourse was repudiated, following the death of Mao in 1976, individuals and communities reexamined and retold personal and local histories of the period. A major conundrum of post-Mao scholarship thus involves disentangling state rhetoric about equality between men and women, reconstituted versions of events, and the realities of lived experience.

The post-Mao reform era began officially in 1978. The leadership set out to transform China's lagging economy through introduction of market reforms; modernization of science, technology, industry, and agriculture; and opening China's markets to the global economy. The goal of increasing agricultural productivity spurred rapid decollectivization of communes in rural areas, returning control—though not ownership—of land to farm households. In urban areas, reform of state-run enterprises was more gradual, yet over time market forces have encouraged substantial organizational changes. The transition from a centralized, bureaucratic allocation system to a market-oriented economy has not been painless, as the rising unemployment figures, increasing number of failed state enterprises, and increasing urban-rural income inequalities attest. However, privatization and industrialization have created diverse opportunities and have changed the nature of work in contemporary China.

Certainly from the view of the household, much has changed over the past two decades: the rise of private sector activities (agricultural and non-agricultural, household-based and non-household-based); the industrialization of the countryside; the migration of workers within rural areas and between rural and urban areas; the "feminization" of agriculture, including activities once almost solely the province of men; continued gender wage differentials; and reports of discrimination against female industrial workers as enterprises are pressured to compete in the market place.

The motivation for this volume began with questions about how Chinese households were responding to these changes and how these responses were affecting the location and organization of work, especially in relation to gender. The "open door" policy of the 1980s also opened the door to social science research by both Chinese and foreign scholars. Many scholars were drawn to examine the social and economic consequences of such profound change. In addition, during the 1980s gender and gender inequalities became legitimate subjects of officially sponsored research (Croll 1995). The Chinese Women's Federation was commissioned to support investigations of unequal treatment, including female infanticide, the selling or kidnapping of rural women, and employment practices that discriminated against women workers. Despite these trends, documentation of the impact of the most recent economic changes on gender work patterns has been incomplete, as has description of the work patterns themselves.

The goal of the conference on which this volume is based was to rectify this deficit in the literature. More important, we sought to generate a comprehensive framework that would allow us to move beyond description and link work, household, and gender in an analytic model. To develop this framework requires: first, clear concepts of work, household, and gender; second, a detailed and nuanced understanding of recent changes in gender and work in China; third, a clear understanding of the ways in which Chinese families and households affect the organization of work and the work opportunities of individual members; and fourth, a well-specified model of individuals, families, and households within rapidly changing social and economic contexts.

In many ways the chapters of this volume contribute to achieving these objectives. Yet as the chapters describe and examine the interconnections between work, household, and gender, they also reveal the major theme that emerged at the conference: Clear concepts of work, household, and gender, which are necessary for conceptual and empirical research, are also elusive. What counts as work, what counts as household, and what constitutes properly gendered behavior are constantly shifting categories, and their boundaries are constantly being *re-drawn*. This is particularly evident in a time of rapid social and economic change, such as the period examined in this volume.

The chapters do address a number of basic questions about the nature of work, household, and gender in the reform era: What are the different categories of work, and how are men and women distributed across them? Do men or women predominate in private sector jobs, in household-based work activities, in migration for new employment opportunities? How do individuals interact with the resurrected household economy and with the collective and state-run sectors? This volume takes two approaches that are combined in each section. The first is straightforward and substantive. To fill in the many gaps in our knowledge, we draw together studies by scholars from several disciplines, using a variety of data and methodologies, to define and describe work patterns in contemporary China. The second approach is to contextualize these descriptions with historical and other qualitative accounts, challenging some of the accepted wisdom about work and the place work occupies in and between households, and offering both new accounts and new questions with which to address these topics. One way or another, each of the chapters illustrates the logic of the volume's subtitle: the interconnectedness of work, household, and gender.

PERSPECTIVES ON WORK

The goals of part 1 are to problematize the definition of work: to show that definitions change over time and to explore ideas about how who does what kind of work and where vary over time and stages of economic development. The theme of boundaries is introduced in this part and revisited in all the other parts.

Part 1 opens with a historical review by Susan Mann of work in imperial China, focusing particularly on the rise of households as units of production and the division of labor within households. Mann describes the origins of the still-common attitude about gender and work in China that associates women with activities done inside the household and men with jobs outside (e.g., "men till, women weave"). She provides the context of work as China underwent industrial and then socialist transformations, and work activity was increasingly shifted outside the household. Her chapter elegantly demonstrates that it is impossible to understand the nature of work without considering where it is done and who is doing it.

Chapter 2, by Gail Henderson, Barbara Entwisle, Li Ying, and associates, also takes up the question of the meaning of work, as well as the relationship between the meaning of work and its location and characteristics. In this case, the authors report on data from recent focus-group interviews with village and town residents in Hubei province. The particular concept explored is *gongzuo,* a term used during the Maoist era to mean permanent formal-sector employment—a "real job" in a state-run work unit. Whereas the authors find that a job is less likely to be thought of as *gongzuo* if it is private, household-based, low paying, temporary, and agricultural, they also find considerable diversity of opinion; and this diversity is not tied to any easily identified predictors, including gender and other background characteristics of the observer. Perhaps not surprisingly, the study shows that at a time of changing employment opportunities and shifting boundaries between private and public, household and non-household, and agricultural and nonagricultural activities, there is substantial ambiguity about what a "real job" is.

Rachel Rosenfeld provides a framework with which to consider these results, with comparative perspectives from the social sciences on work, household, and gender. She presents a simple two-by-two table, laying out categories and boundaries that invite explication and debate. Two cross-cutting dimensions—remuneration and work location—create four categories: (1) paid work outside the home, (2) paid work within the home, (3) unpaid work outside the home, and (4) unpaid work inside the home. Rosenfeld considers linkages between these categories for individuals, households, and economies, and shows how work may shift across the boundaries of household and pay, with changes in perceptions, values, and rewards.

The final chapter in part 1 is the discussion by Stevan Harrell. It addresses the ways in which arguments about labor—about what is work and what is not, about the proper kinds of work for men and women, and specifically about the differences between household- and non-household-based labor—have evolved as part of the broader discussions of what a post-collectivist Chinese society should look like. He describes the virtual elimination of household-based production in the socialist era, whether compensated or not, and the movement away from a gendered division of labor to an ideological denial of the gendered division of labor—where women were still at a disadvantage because they still had to do those things formerly defined as women's work. He concludes with a discussion of the blurring of distinctions between household- and non-household-based work, and the rethinking of the gender division of labor during the reform era.

RECENT TRENDS IN GENDER AND INEQUALITY

Part 2 shifts the focus from work to the meanings of gender and to gender inequality in work during the Communist and reform eras. These chapters examine the boundaries of gender as well as differences in the returns from work experienced by men and women in China since the revolution. The first two chapters rely on historical data to explore events in rural areas during the 1950s and 1960s, highlighting the ways that changing expectations about work for rural and urban women affected the meanings of gender. The second pair of chapters present results from survey data about factors related to specific types of gender inequalities in education, income, and job opportunities.

Gail Hershatter's chapter draws on documentary research and field interviews to tell the story of Cao Zhuxiang, a labor model in rural Shaanxi during the early 1950s. She brings us into the lives of rural women when the reorganization of agricultural work was just beginning. We learn about this process from the perspective of several women praised for crossing boundaries of household and work. Hershatter argues that by this process the state did not create a new, ungendered division of labor as much as it valorized and propagated one that already existed among many poor households in rural Shaanxi. State intervention in the form of visiting cadres, agricultural technicians, and Women's Federation officials was crucial in the emergence of labor models as recognizable revolutionary icons; in the process, some aspects of the gendered experience of these women were emphasized but others were ignored by state officials and by the women themselves.

Emily Honig explores gender and work during the Cultural Revolution through the experiences of "Iron Girls," young women who crossed traditional gender boundaries in the division of labor and were featured for doing so in media reports of the era. Challenging received wisdom about the Cultural Revolution, Honig finds that rather than sponsoring contestation of gender roles through promoting the Iron Girls, it was far more common for the media to emphasize women's general participation in the paid labor force and to honor their achievements in female occupations such as textiles. Her analysis of the personal memoirs of urban youth "sent down" to the countryside demonstrates that the assumption of male occupations by Iron Girls never represented cultural norms about appropriate roles for women and that the gendered dimensions of work during this era were far more complex than has previously been recognized.

Shifting the focus to urban employment, Yanjie Bian, John R. Logan, and Xiaoling Shu present data on the work lives of Tianjin residents over the last half-century from a 1993 survey. They examine gender disparities in urban wages, which despite rapid changes in the economy and class structure as a whole, have persisted relatively unchanged. They find five key reasons for this persistence, the most important being the policy that requires working women to retire ten years earlier than working men. Other factors include differential access to higher education, Party membership, administrative and market-potential jobs, jobs in state versus collective work units, and the fact that women change occupations and work units less often than men, and when they do, it helps them less.

In a companion essay, Ethan Michelson and William L. Parish examine the sources of men's and women's educational and economic success in the countryside, using data from the 1991 wave of the China Health and Nutrition Survey, a survey of eight provinces. They find that patriarchy matters, with parents devoting more resources to sons and employers continuing to favor men over women. Yet they also find that patriarchy is weakened by economic development. Women who live in more developed communities appear to enjoy distinct advantages, including better education and better jobs. Initially, single women in these communities benefit. However, at higher levels of development, where nonfarm work in a community exceeds 60 percent, even married women enter the nonfarm labor market. Finally, Michelson and Parish find that family connections still count. When it comes to staying in school and to finding a good job, scarce social capital is expended more often for men than for women.

The discussion chapter for part 2, by Martin K. Whyte, unites these accounts of gender and work with a review of the complex issues involved in attempting to reach summary conclusions about gender inequality in China. He observes that it is especially difficult to assess the possible impact of the economic reforms on gender inequality when comparable baseline data from earlier periods are lacking or are of questionable objectivity. Furthermore, even if such evidence were available, it is unlikely that there would be a simple answer about whether women's situation relative to men has improved or deteriorated in the reform era. Examining recent claims about gender inequalities, including increased job discrimination against urban women, a rise in the abduction and sale of rural women, and a new rise in female infanticide, Whyte concludes that the picture is mixed.

GENDER AND MIGRATION

Part 3 turns our attention to work, household, and gender in a special context—the recent phenomenon of rural migration of individuals and/or households in search of new work opportunities. Like parts 1 and 2, this part includes chapters that employ different types of data and methodologies, namely, census data, social surveys, and ethnographic observations of a community of unofficial migrants. The term "official migrant" in China refers to those with an official change of household registration and includes students, those with official job transfers, and (mainly) women who move for marriage. "Unofficial migrant," a relatively new category, includes people who move for economic or family reasons but do not change their household registration.

Chapter 10 sets the stage with a description of Zhejiangcun, a settlement in Beijing populated by unofficial migrants from Zhejiang province, near Shanghai. Li Zhang's powerful essay explores the interconnections between gender relations, social space, and the meaning of work in this migrant community. It highlights the relationships between power, work, and the construction of gendered spaces, especially spaces "inside" and "outside" of households. Two arguments are made: First, the migrant or floating population is a highly stratified and diversely situated social group, and accordingly, migrant women occupy various social positions and encounter changes in gender relations in very different ways. Second, the increase of migrant women's economic status or participation in economic activities does not necessarily go hand in hand with their empowerment. Zhang finds that wives in middle-income households share a more egalitarian relationship with men than do women in the wealthiest households, but interestingly, she also finds that their work, though indispensable, tends to be devalued because economic production is domesticated, that is, performed at home.

Chapter 11 contextualizes Zhang's portraits of migrant women by presenting data on migration from Zhejiang province. Using 1990 census data, Xiushi Yang compares men and women in their propensity to migrate, reasons for migrating, and characteristics associated with migration. He finds that regardless of type of migration (within or between provinces, official or unofficial), men are more mobile than women. Further, men are more likely to migrate for economic reasons than women, although for official migrants economic reasons dominate for both and the gender difference is relatively small. Also examined is the connection between rural out-migration and female participation in agricultural production (the "feminization" of agriculture). Like Michelson and Parish's observations in chapter 8, Yang's results suggest some female substitution for male labor in agricultural production, mainly due to rural industrialization.

Sidney Goldstein, Zai Liang, and Alice Goldstein present data on migration, gender, and work between 1985 and 1990, based on an analysis of census data for Hubei province. They find that men are more likely to be unofficial migrants and women to be official migrants. Men make official moves most often for schooling and job relocation, whereas marriage and family reasons account for most official moves made by women. "Business" was the reason given by most unofficial migrants, male or female. Citing survey data, the authors report that women who migrate for economic reasons believe that migration has enabled them to benefit from economic change and has provided them with a degree of autonomy not possible at their place of origin.

Wang Feng closes part 3 by posing and responding to three sets of questions about the relationship between gender and migration. Asking who benefits from migration, Wang reports that while males predominate among official migrants who move for economic reasons, females are better represented among the temporary or unofficial migrants. Next, he asks whether women are "associational" migrants, meaning that they move with their family and mainly for family-related reasons. The answer appears to be no, the majority of female unofficial migrants move for other reasons. Lastly, Wang raises the fundamental question of the effect of migration on women's work and gender equality. As the other chapters in part 3 demonstrate, the answer is complex. Migration offers increased work opportunities for women, but that work seems to be concentrated in a few sectors. Moreover, even when working in the same industries, women migrants are less likely than men to occupy positions of power and high salary. One issue, Wang concludes, is that, compared with urban women who are official residents or official migrants, unofficial migrant women lack the institutional support or intervention that might promote gender equality.

HOUSEHOLDS AND WORK

The chapters in part 4 examine the household in urban and rural contexts, asking how the emerging economic and political systems of the reform era have challenged or altered its role. Deborah Davis opens part 4 with a chapter on the critical role scarce housing has played in the configuration of Shanghai households. With parallels to Zhang's attention to social space, Davis provides a fascinating account of how housing strategies pursued by Shanghai residents during the early years of the regime have been challenged by the recommodification of residential space in the 1990s. Prior to the reform era, issues of property ownership were generally irrelevant because, legally, parents only retained "rights of occupancy" to their apartments. After 1991, as apartments became available for purchase to current household heads, coresidence became equated with co-ownership, generating the potential for conflict between coresident and non-coresident children. Describing the housing arrangements of 75 Shanghai female retirees and their 157 married children, Davis shows that in a more marketized urban economy, the norms of patrilineal succession have emerged as a salient parameter of coresidence and the boundaries of household membership have become more explicitly gender-specific.

Chapter 15, by Barbara Entwisle, Susan E. Short, Zhai Fengying, and Ma Linmao, asks a different set of questions about household strategies, in this case, strategies about economic activities. Positing that one way for households to minimize risk during times of economic transition is to diversify across activities, they document patterns of household diversification using data from the 1989 wave of the China Health and Nutrition Survey. They examine the extent to which households bridge three major dimensions of economic structure and change: occupation and industry (agricultural or not); mode of production (household-based or not); and employment sector (private, or state/collective). Specifically, they ask whether the diversified or specialized economic activities of household members reflect coordinated activity, or even an explicit household strategy. Despite the expectation that households would diversify, the authors find that there is less diversification and more household specialization observed in the data than expected.

Nan Lin's discussion chapter for part 4 interprets these findings and those of Davis as evidence of constraints imposed by structural factors and evidence of new opportunities arising when the constraints changed. Household strategies are a response to the impact of structure (economic opportunity, state policies) on the household organization of work activities. Lin focuses on factors that lead to the placement of social actors—individuals, families, and households—in a system of social inequality and associated rewards. As state policies change, not only will the types and extent of structural constraints and opportunities change, but the meaning of social context will change as well.

Re-Drawing Boundaries concludes with a chapter on boundaries by Barbara Entwisle and Gail Henderson. The essays in the volume illustrate the interrelationships of work, household, and gender in China. The familiar "inside/outside" dichotomy encapsulates this interconnectedness spatially and socially. Drawing on the other chapters in this volume, this concluding chapter traces the varying understandings of what counts as work and what does not, the spatial and social boundaries of households, and gender in relation to both. It shows how concepts of work, household, and gender presume the drawing of boundaries, and that not only is the movement across boundaries of interest, but so are the boundaries themselves. Furthermore, what counts as work, what counts as household, and what constitutes properly gendered behavior are also all in flux. As argued in this introduction, the "inside/outside" boundary is no more than a starting point. The boundary is not a given, but rather should be problematized as one among many potential influences on social arrangements.

PART ONE

Perspectives on Work

ONE

Work and Household in Chinese Culture

Historical Perspectives

Susan Mann

Classical notions of work in China focused on the household as the basic unit of production. Household members were supposed to be interdependent, with women working "inside" and men "outside" to provide for the needs of the whole. In this classical discourse on work, an individual's labor was subsumed by the collective household economy—usually managed by women, whom McDermott (1990) has called "domestic bursars." The household so conceived was a kin unit and the basic unit of domestic organization, encompassing both production and reproduction of goods and labor. In late imperial times, the ideal household was a joint family, comprising at least three generations under one roof.[1] To be economically successful, the household constructed an elaborate division of labor according to age and sex, based on each member's understanding of his or her roles and responsibilities. The larger the household and the more elaborate the division of labor, the better the chances for success.

As this chapter shows, the classical ideal and its historical transformations differ in important ways from contemporary understandings of work as a job (*gongzuo;* see chap. 2). China's earliest classical texts recognized work as one of the defining characteristics of free persons—a mark of respectability and a sign of social status. At the same time, work was construed as a collective, not an individual, activity. Philosophers and statesmen imagined work in the context of household production units laboring to serve their own interests, and in so doing, constructing the social division of labor in society as a whole. Writ large, work was a visible manifestation of a harmonious social and cultural system where "those above" labored with their minds and "those below" labored with their hands. Writ small, work was the everyday activity of every person in every respectable household. Individual subjects did not work for the commonweal, nor were they expected to labor for some abstract concept of a greater social good, much less to earn an individual living wage. Instead, people worked hard for their families. Members of every household saw themselves as part of a patrilineal descent group in which the labor of present generations repaid a legacy from the ancestors and built a foundation for successful progeny.[2]

The household itself emerges as a unit of production in the earliest Chinese classics. Imperial statecraft situated each household in the larger context of an occupational division of labor (the "four classes" of people, namely: scholars, farmers, artisans, and merchants). Thus the economy was construed as a complexly interdependent layering of specialized occupational groups, each composed of the basic building blocks organizing all labor: commoner households. To illustrate this in historical perspective, this chapter is divided into three parts. The first explains the earliest philosophical understanding of households as production units within a complex division of labor. The second shows how these early classical notions were implemented in the statecraft and political theory of the early empire (through the thirteenth century). The third part describes the late imperial system of production that flourished on the eve of the twentieth-century revolutions.

CLASSICAL MODELS OF THE HOUSEHOLD
AS A UNIT OF PRODUCTION

The organization of work in commoner households is prefigured in the Chinese classics. Early Confucian philosophers and statesmen (551–c. 233 B.C.E.) understood that people labored primarily to eat—in other words, to feed and clothe themselves—but they never conceptualized labor as an individual human activity. Instead, they talked about work in the context of a division of labor: as part of a household production system, as part of an occupationally differentiated society, and as part of an economy of exchange. Although these same philosophers and statesmen were concerned about mobilizing labor for the state, almost all of them argued that a skillful ruler should mobilize the labor of his subjects only for projects dedicated to the common good. Similarly, rulers were cautioned to exercise restraint when making demands on people's labor. Every household had to be free to work so that it could meet its own needs before taxes.[3]

The same philosophers and statesmen praised human qualities that made good workers: diligence, frugality, and skill. Although there was no classical term for efficiency, strategies to increase labor efficiency continually focused on the division of labor—among the people by occupational groups, and within the household production unit by gender. Classical writers also stressed the need for accessible markets to encourage local and regional specialization and to level regional and seasonal fluctuations in the supply of goods.

Labor defined and displayed social status, and classical writers deplored its absence (as leisure or idleness). Work meant not simply labor, moreover, but a respectable calling. In the third century B.C.E., Mencius (372–289?) drew his famous distinction between "those who labor with their minds" and "those who labor with their hands":

> Xu Xing, in search of benevolent rule, travels from the state of Chu to Tang, where he pledges his service to Duke Wen. After some time in residence in the Duke's kingdom, Xu Xing is heard to complain that the Duke is not the benevolent ruler he purports to be, because a benevolent ruler is one who "tills the fields and eats together with the people" *(yu min bing geng er shi)*. Plainly, Duke Wen was an oppressor and not a benevolent ruler at all. After all, he maintained granaries, treasuries, and arsenals, all financed from levies he exacted from the people. When a visitor asks Mencius about Xu Xing's complaints, Mencius responds with a series of questions of his own. Does Xu Xing make his own clothes? Does he forge his own tools? Does he fire his own pots? No, concedes the interlocutor, Xu Xing exchanges his grain for these things. Well, says Mencius, there you have it: "Great men have their proper business, and little men have their proper business. . . . Hence, there is the saying, 'Some labor with their minds, and some labor with their strength. Those who labor with their minds govern others; those who labor with their strength are governed by others. Those who are governed by others support them; those who govern others are supported by them.' This is a principle universally recognized." (Paraphrased from Mencius 3A.4/4–6; translated in Mencius 1960, 249–50)

Noticing that he's made a leap in logic, Mencius goes on to elaborate by noting that the great sage-king Yu could not possibly have gone out to cultivate crops while he was in charge of clearing fields, diverting floods, and opening up land to cultivation for his people. The same was true of the mythic Minister of Agriculture, who taught the people to sow and reap and cultivate the five grains—how could he have done that while working as a farmer? Duke Wen's work as a ruler, Mencius concludes, is not to farm, but to protect his people and provide for their welfare by storing weapons and food, and by filling a treasury to pay for it all.

Mencius and Confucius (551–479 B.C.E.) return often to this concern about the division of labor between those who rule and those who are ruled. Confucius, like Mencius, understood work to include moral and ritual activities as well as manual or physical labor. He never saw it as an isolated activity, but rather as something done for someone else. He used the term "work" *(lao)* to talk about labors performed by a filial son for his parents, for example (*Analects* II:8 and IV:18; see Confucius 1938, 89 and 1979, 74, respectively). He also used the verb "work" *(lao)* as a transitive verb, as in "to make others work hard," acknowledging the fact that those above command the labor of those below them, but stressing the mutual obligation of those above and those below (*Analects* XX.2; see Confucius 1979, 159). In chapter 19 of the Confucian *Analects,* for instance, the disciple Zixia says: "Only after he has gained the trust of the common people does the gentleman work them hard, for otherwise they would feel themselves ill-used" (*Analects* XIX.10; see Confucius 1979, 154). Rulers themselves must work hard to win this trust: when Zilu asks Confucius about government, he replies: "Encourage the people to work hard by setting an example yourself." Zilu asks for more detail, and Confucius adds: "Do not allow your efforts to slacken" (*Analects* XIII.1–2; see Confucius 1979, 118). The ruler who truly loves his people will make sure that they work: "Can you love anyone without making him work hard?" (*Analects* XIV.7; see Confucius 1979, 125). In other words, rulers make people work hard for their own good: people who work hard will have enough to eat *(zu shi)* and a stable source of livelihood *(heng chan).*

Notice how this early work ethic brings to the fore the people's livelihood and checks the state's power to extract labor. Rulers trying to make the people work hard had to be careful that their own demands would not interfere with every household's need to provide for itself. Even Xun Zi (fl. 298–238 B.C.E.), who is sometimes considered the earliest proponent of "Legalist" thinking (which stressed the absolute power of the state and its need to control labor and production), agreed with Mencius that taxes and labor service extracted from the people should be minimized, for the same reasons (see the discussion in Hsiao 1979, 187).

The classical work ethic, on occasion, even spoofed or expressed skepticism about the value of scholarly or mental work, as opposed to manual labor. The *Analects* include a story in which one of Confucius' disciples appears as an effete intellectual who is humbled in the presence of an honest laboring farmer. The story concerns Zilu, who loses his way one day and encounters an old man weeding in the fields. When Zilu asks the old man if he has seen Confucius, the reply is dismissive: "Your four limbs are unaccustomed to toil; you cannot distinguish the five kinds of grain *(siti buqin, wuliang bufen)*—who is your master?" (*Analects* XVIII.7; see Confucius 1960, 335). Mencius, too, squirmed when he confronted the problem of the scholar's labor and its value, as we see in his conversation with Peng Geng. When Peng Geng asks Mencius about earning a living, he inquires whether the "superior man in his practice of principles" is earning a living just the same way the carpenter and the wheelwright do. What, in other words, is the superior man's purpose? Is it simply to get by like everyone else? Mencius replies, somewhat testily: "What have you to do with his purpose? He is of service to you. He deserves to be supported, and should be supported" (Mencius IIIB.5; see Mencius 1960, 270).

Mencius's interest in the division of labor and the mutual obligations of those above and those below is also reflected in his keen interest in markets. No household was expected to be completely self-sufficient, and early statesmen understood that rulers must provide a market economy to stimulate the exchange of goods and services. Mencius himself viewed the orderly and regular exchange of grain for commodities as a hallmark of good government (Mencius IIA.5/2; see Mencius 1960, 199). He was also not concerned about merchant greed or about the trader's quest for profit, but was more worried about the marketplace as a lure for idlers. Like the most famous classical economic theorist, Guan Zi (d. 645 B.C.E.), Mencius believed it was the ruler's job to balance the interests of farmers against those of merchants so that all of the "four kinds of people" could, in Guan Zi's words, "exchange skills and trade the products of their work, so that the profits of their year-long labors will not allow any one of them to gain unfair advantage over the others. Thereby the people's labors will be combined and they will all gain equitable benefits."[4]

These early ideas about work also specified gender roles. The most vaunted kinds of work in classical texts—scholarship and farming—excluded women.[5] Significantly, too, men who ruled might labor with their minds, but all women, regardless of status, were expected to perform manual labor, especially spinning, weaving, and needlework. Womanly work *(nü gong)* was one of the "four virtues" of a respectable woman, first canonized by Ban Zhao (d. 116 C.E.) in her book, *Nü jie* (Instructions for women). Early texts make it clear that womanly work means spinning and weaving, and that sericulture *(sang)* was the counterpart of agriculture *(nong)*—the former, women's work "inside," the latter, men's work "outside." The ideal gender division of labor, with men working in the fields and women weaving in the house, was also described by Mencius, who urged his ruler-advisees to exhort every household with five *mu* of land to diversify production, planting mulberry in the space beneath the walls around family compounds so that women could rear silkworms and the elderly could be clothed in silk (Mencius VIIA.22/2; see Mencius 1960, 461).

In genteel families, a woman working at her loom was the complement not of the farmer but of the scholar poring over his books. The trope of the weaving woman and the studying man may date to a story about Mencius and his mother. Early illustrated copies of the book, *Lienü zhuan* (Biographies of women) by Liu Xiang (77–6 B.C.E.), show Meng Mu brandishing her scissors in front of her wayward son. By slashing the cloth on her loom, she shocks Mencius into realizing the cost of his wasted talent. Chastened, Mencius reforms—to become China's greatest philosopher (Liu Xiang 1983, 15–16).

In sum, philosophers and statesmen writing in the classical age developed clear ideas about what kinds of work were legitimate and how the division of labor in society should be organized. They viewed hard work as a natural activity of ordinary commoners striving to feed and clothe their families, care for elders, nurture young, and improve their lives—an activity the government should nurture, encourage, and protect. Finally, they assumed a division of labor in society between the four occupations (scholars, farmers, artisans, merchants), whose mutual dependence would be expedited by trade, and a division of labor within the household between men and women, whose complementary functions would support tax-paying families.

THE RISE OF INTENSIVE HOUSEHOLD PRODUCTION BEFORE THE THIRTEENTH CENTURY

Statecraft writings of the early empire focus on the broad division of labor in society as a whole, rather than on individual households. The oldest economic treatise in the Chinese historical record, the "Treatise on Food and Money" in the *History of the Former Han Dynasty,* explains that the "four kinds of people" each have their proper occupations *(simin you ye):* "Those who study to attain their status we call *shi* (scholars); those who cultivate the soil to grow grain we call *nong* (farmers); those who by their cleverness produce implements we call *gong* (artisans); and those who circulate wealth and trade in commodities we call *shang* (merchants)"(Ban Gu 1983, 532). The hierarchical order of this list echoes Mencius (e.g., Ch'ü 1957, 245–48). The superior form of labor was "mental" labor (study), followed by "manual" labor (plowing, planting, and harvesting; and manufacturing—including toolmaking, carpentry, woodcarving, ceramics, spinning, weaving, and embroidery). Though trade and business came last, merchants were not always at the bottom of this hierarchy. The *Guliang zhuan* (Duke Cheng, first year, 589 B.C.E.) lists merchants right after scholars but before peasants and artisans. Moreover, pejorative judgments about the value of merchants are hard to find in discussions about the four kinds of work. Instead, merchants are simply supposed to limit their profit taking; or, better still, the government is supposed to intervene to prevent undue disparities of wealth between rich and poor. Fierce competition was the norm, as we learn from resigned complaints like the following, written by the Song scholar Ye Shi (1150–1223): "The four kinds of people and the hundred arts flourish by day and subside by night, each vying with all their might, each pursuing their own interests, fearless in the face of danger, insatiable in the face of abundance" (Ye 1961, 1:164). Some early texts propose a hierarchy of occupations. For instance, criticism of merchants and their work begins in

Han times (206 B.C.E.–220 C.E.) with complaints about profiteering.[6] Han writers also argued that "cleverness" *(qiao),* the gift of the artisan, was less desirable than the farmer's ability to grow grain. By exclusion, the "four peoples" discourse in Han times also marginalized other types of work: military service and the religious activities of priest, monks, and nuns. On the other hand, early imperial governments did not identify "polluting" kinds of work nor did they stigmatize certain occupations as "base" *(jian).* The work of butchers and *yamen* runners (messengers, guards, policemen, and other menials employed by county magistrates), which marked them as pariahs in late imperial times, was considered merely humble during the Han period, when even butchers and yamen runners were permitted to enter official careers (Ch'ü 1972, 126–27).

Regardless of occupational hierarchies, work as an essential activity of free persons separated the "four kinds of people" doing respectable work from slaves. During the Han period, slaves labored in mining, manufacturing, farming, handicraft work (including spinning and weaving), domestic and military service, and even entertainment (Ch'ü 1972, 135–59). The Han government also employed slaves, while frequently accusing them of idleness and sloth and of living off the labor and tax revenues supplied by ordinary commoners.[7] The government made clear its preference for laborers conscripted from free commoner households, or even (anticipating a contemporary debate) convicted prisoners.[8] As a result, conscript laborers—or even convicts—and not slaves made up the bulk of the public works labor force, with soldiers playing an important role in peacetime.[9] And despite the obvious importance of corvée labor to the government's vast mining operations and public works projects—including water control, post stations, canal transport, wall construction, and other state-funded construction and service[10]—conscripted labor had to be acquired with minimum cost to individual households whose members were respectably employed. Han political theory, following classical teachings, stressed the need to ease the burden on farm households so that they could perform labor at a level sufficient to support themselves. Dong Zhongshu (179?–104? B.C.E.) echoed his predecessors when, in his critique of the problems of the first Qin empire (221–206 B.C.E.), he called on the government to "reduce taxes and levies and lessen labor services, in order to give freer scope to the people's energies" (Hsiao 1979, 502).

A final form of labor organization during the early centuries of empire was monastic production. Like conscript and slave labor, monastic labor was marginalized in policies and political theories about work. Most schools of Buddhism disdained manual labor in any case, especially agricultural labor, which was forbidden to monks by religious law. Monks relied on tenant farmers and on novices for agricultural labor on the Buddhist estates that flourished in the early part of the Tang dynasty (618–907). The exception was the Chan sect, which rejected this tenet of Buddhist law. The Chan master Huaihai (720–814), who led the movement to promote manual labor in Buddhist monasteries, insisted on working together with the laborers on his monastic lands, popularizing the aphorism: "One day of no work, one day of no food." Huaihai described manual labor in the fields and gardens—including chopping wood, cutting grass, digging wells, tilling the soil, carrying human waste for fertilizer, and so on—as a universal calling *(puqing).*[11] For Huaihai, manual farm labor was not a purely physical activity but one of the essential spiritual activities binding the monastic community:

> In . . . *puqing,* all should exert equal effort regardless of whether the task is important or unimportant. No one should sit quietly and go contrary to the wishes of the community. While performing his duties, one should not indulge in ridicule or laughter, or boast about one's talents or ability. Rather, one should concentrate his mind on the Dao, and perform whatever is required by the community. After the task is completed, then one should return to the meditation hall and remain silent as before. One should transcend the two aspects of activity and nonactivity. Thus, though one has worked all day, he has not worked at all.[12]

Devout Chan Buddhists were expected to work without attachment to the action itself or to the rewards it would bring. Nevertheless, the high productivity of monastic estates of all kinds created a vast pool of wealth, much of it tax-exempt, which threatened the state's control over labor and resources. The mid-ninth-century campaigns that destroyed the Buddhist monastic establishment put a permanent end to large-scale monastic production (Dalby 1979, 666–67).

With slave and conscript labor marginalized and monastic production suppressed, farm families and landholding households emerged as the model workers of the early empire. The Mencian household production unit had become more than a philosophical ideal. Records suggest that throughout this early period, most Chinese farm labor was performed by individual households, as tenants or freeholders. In Nishijima Sadao's words:

> [T]he typical rural community during Han was the hamlet, consisting in theory of a hundred families, all of which owned small amounts of land. . . . It must be noted that the rise of great landholdings during Han did not necessarily imply the development of large-scale farming, except in the few cases where slaves were employed to work estates. Tenants of these landowners cultivated their holdings on an individual and small-scale basis and this, due largely to the lack of sufficient slave labor and the intensive nature of farming, continued to be an important feature of Chinese agriculture. (Nishijima 1986, 559)

Similarly, in his study of Han agrarian technology, Hsü concluded that

> intensive care of each individual plant had been brought almost to the level
> of gardening. . . . Such farming demanded a concentration of labor and was
> associated with smaller farms. Also the farmer's incentive was crucial to guar-
> antee the thoroughness of the field work, which made extensive use of slaves
> or contract labor unreliable. All these factors help to explain the maintenance
> of independent farmers in the Han period and the preference of large land-
> holders for tenancy rather than slavery. (Hsü 1980, 127)

Hsü (127–128) emphasized that even as early as the Han, the most successful farming depended on the combined efforts of all household members, including women and children.

HOUSEHOLD PRODUCTION, SONG (960–1279)
THROUGH QING (1644–1911)

The contemporary scholar Kang Chao, while agreeing that the farm household was the most important labor unit in the history of Chinese agriculture
(1986, 194), points out that the intensive farming practices developed in
late imperial times were probably not "necessary" or even "widespread" in
China until the twelfth century, despite the availability of techniques of intensive farming since at least Han times. Chao (1986) locates the shift from
extensive to intensive farming in the Song period, identifying three of its
most important characteristics: multiple cropping, reclamation of fallow
lands, and intensified fertilization along with higher-yield strains and crops.
Champa rice, introduced into the Lower Yangzi by Emperor Zhenzong in
the early eleventh century, triggered the shift to intensive cultivation, ush-
ering in "a new era of agrarian history in China" by promising "a higher total output by absorbing more labor" (Chao 1986, 200–201). By the end of
the Song period—the thirteenth century—the household, whether gentry
or peasant, had emerged as the basic unit of agricultural and protoindus-
trial production in the Chinese economy.

The Song dynasty was a crucial period in the development of a discourse
on work in households. Ebrey has pointed out that instruction books like
Yuan Cai's, printed for gentry families seeking to take advantage of the
Song's new economic opportunities, paid unusual attention to work:

> What most distinguished [Yuan Cai] . . . was his unconcealed admiration for
> those who worked honestly and diligently to ensure their families' security.
> Whatever the importance of ethical strengths, he did not think one should
> ignore the need for productive property [chan] or wealth [cai], or an occupa-
> tion or other heritage that brought in income [ye]. (Ebrey 1984, 78)

Ebrey (1984, 121) stresses that Song gentry families conceived of themselves as a "unit of political economy, not simply a group of relatives," whose survival depended upon the successful use of property and, one might add, on the successful management of labor. Yuan Cai was clear about the importance of an "occupation" *(ye)* for everyone, regardless of status:

> People with no occupation, and those with occupations who are too fond of leisure to be willing to work, will get used to indecent activities if they come from rich families and will become beggars if they come from poor families. (Ebrey 1984, 268)

Yuan offered his own assessment of the most desirable kinds of work for men in respectable gentry families in this order: scholarship (studying for the exams and winning office or, if that fails, teaching), clerkship (handling documents), tutoring children, teaching medicine, practicing Buddhism or Daoism, "gardening" (genteel cultivation), and commerce. All these, he suggested, could "provide support for your family without bringing shame to your ancestors" (Ebrey 1984, 267). At the same time, and in keeping with the philosophical views of early Confucians, Yuan Cai was unapologetic about dodging corvée labor service. The main problem he saw with corvée dodging, in fact, was that if you failed to pull it off, you were caught and punished (Ebrey 1984, 309–10).

After the thirteenth century, households that had intensified production by cultivating double-cropped rice found incentives to increase efficiency still further, as cotton cultivation spread from the southeast coast to the Lower Yangzi region. The labor required to prepare cotton fibers for spinning—including ginning, fluffing, straightening, and sorting—was easily organized in the context of a joint family unit, with its attendant servants and multigenerational workforce. Like hemp and silk, cotton absorbed the labor of women, who could work respectably in the home, where we see them in paintings and drawings from the Song period onward.

Meanwhile, the crowded commercial cities of the Song period (960–1279) and women's prominence in the commercial and service sectors provoked a strident moral discourse on cloistering women that gained wide currency in Song gentry families. A study by Quan Hansheng (1935), which explores expanding work opportunities for Song women, shows women working in all aspects of the urban economy: as proprietors of teashops, fancy restaurants, and herbal medicine stores; as peddlers hawking candy or tea, or selling Buddhist paraphernalia; and as tailors and weavers. Nuns sell jewelry, clothing, caps, hair ornaments, and other kinds of female adornment, all made by hand, at temple fairs. On the farm, women pick mulberry leaves and rear silkworms; in the marketplace, they tell stories, juggle, do magic tricks and acrobatics, sing, dance, and perform opera. Song women worked at all kinds of menial labor as maids—cooking, hauling water, lighting stoves—and as prostitutes and courtesans they served every class of the male consumer population. As if to deny these arenas for womanly work, one of the most famous early genre paintings, the *Qingming shanghe tu* (Going upriver at the Qingming festival), shows only a few women on the streets of twelfth-century Kaifeng, even on a holiday. Noting this, Ebrey (1993, 21–44) observes that the separation of the sexes into "inner" and "outer" spheres was a powerful moral value in Song gentry writing and that women's work "inside" became a mark of status in gentry households. The woman who could avoid labor outside the home (especially hard farm work, but also tea-picking, fishing, and other lowly pursuits) was a symbol of her family's prestige. A cloistered lifestyle, Ebrey suggests, was also conducive to the embrace of another status symbol, footbinding, by women of the upper classes.

On the eve of the late imperial period, then, intensive household farming had become the norm in China's most productive regions. During this same period, the boundaries of work also hardened to celebrate and enforce the confinement of female labor inside the home.[13]

THE HOUSEHOLD AS A UNIT OF PRODUCTION IN LATE IMPERIAL TIMES: THE MING (1368–1644) AND QING (1644–1911) DYNASTIES

The late imperial fisc depended on land and labor taxes collected not from individuals but from registered households. Late Ming and Qing rulers promoted what we would call Confucian family values to support household production through campaigns targeting ordinary commoners. Universal marriage and childbearing (especially bearing sons to continue the patriline), wifely fidelity, filial piety, and ancestor worship were touted and rewarded by the state through government-endowed shrines, imperial certificates of merit, and even cash prizes honoring chaste widows and filial sons. Through laws enforcing partible inheritance, through policies protecting tenants and freeholders from excessive taxation, and through legislation limiting the purchase and sale of slaves, late imperial governments also provided an economic environment that favored freeholding peasant households and encouraged them to accumulate resources through labor.

Largely because of these supportive central government policies, the peasant household was the dominant unit of production and reproduction by the seventeenth century, as serfdom and "serflike tenancy" all but disappeared from China's core regions. One hallmark of the success of late imperial policies promoting household labor is the attention paid to "women's work" *(nü gong)* in the statecraft writings of the late imperial period. Women working respectably at home, as spinners and weavers, began producing for the commercial economy as cotton cultivation spread after the fourteenth century. By the late Ming period (after 1550), cotton's low cost and versatile uses had produced a thriving consumer cloth market that helped to drive the Ming commercial revolution. Household production units—where "men plow" and "women spin and weave" in the classical Mencian formula—supplied the bulk of the commodities circulating through late Ming rural markets (Xu Xinwu 1981). The late imperial ideal of "men farming, women weaving" *(nan geng nü zhi)*, celebrated in illustrated texts, statecraft writings, and family instruction books of the late Ming and Qing periods, became a cornerstone of family values in Chinese popular culture. Meanwhile even the emperor and the empress took up the theme and displayed it in the ritual cycle at court, where the emperor annually engaged in a ritual ploughing of the fields, while the empress led the sacrifices honoring the patron goddess of sericulture (see Mann 1992; 1997, 143–177; Kuhn 1988).

In an economy that celebrated workers in households, unattached hired workers—especially single men—were suspect and carefully screened. Landlords looking for hired labor tell us clearly the sorts of qualities they prized—and what they sometimes had to settle for. Zhang Lixiang, a seventeenth-century landlord, advised: "In general, the best is the docile and diligent worker; second best, the skilled and alert one; next, the incompetent but honest one; worst is the one who is cunning, deceitful, talkative, and lazy." An employer who wanted to keep a good hired worker had to act in loco parentis, providing not only a good wage but also adequate supplies of wine and food (see Wiens 1980, 20, 21, citing observations by the scholar Zhang Lixiang [1611–74]). Meanwhile, local officials strove to anchor every able-bodied person securely in a household economy. The imperial government reserved special praise for officials who expanded opportunities for work in their areas and who looked out for the needs of ordinary peasant householders (Brokaw 1991, 198–99). Officials were expected to encourage and introduce new modes of production, new seed strains, and new technologies whenever possible to improve household productivity. This effort sometimes worked at cross purposes with the government's need to mobilize corvée labor for public works, as peasants loath to divert labor from their own households to the government, sought tax protection from wealthy gentry families, creating a continuing labor shortage for state projects.[14] Dodging corvée service in the interests of one's own household was different from laziness, as Yuan Cai noted. To be lazy was often defined not simply as idleness, but as engaging in unseemly work— and was the mark of a lowly person. Thus women who "neither spin nor weave," including prostitutes and other women in subethnic groups of "mean people" *(jianmin)*, were stigmatized as pariahs.[15]

In these and other rhetorical signs from late imperial texts, we see how normative ideas of respectable work were firmly lodged in the context of the household. From the imperial court down to the commoner household, the boundaries of work in late imperial China divided men's and women's labor. Men worked outside in the fields, women labored inside at the loom. So powerful was this ideal, and so successfully was it promoted, that the ideal household as labor unit was still visible in rural China during the 1920s, when Buck (1937, 292) found to his surprise that men performed 80 percent of farm labor, women only 13 percent, and children 7 percent.[16]

If the Chinese government and Chinese political theory promoted the household as the basic unit of productive labor, and other factors created a hospitable environment for household-based production,[17] we still must ask what made householders so responsive to government policies. Folk sayings attest to the extraordinary work ethic of Chinese farmers. Arkush (1984), surveying hundreds of proverbs from North China commonly in use before the twentieth century, observes that most stress the importance of and returns from hard work. Besides hard work, he notes, other moral qualities are essential: frugality; skill in selecting proper inputs of fertilizer, seed, and so forth; ingenuity to tap all available sources of income, including sideline industries; knowledge (of farming, in particular); self-reliance, or cooperation within a small group; and anticipation of income. A few sayings point to the significance of the household as the production unit. Buck (1937, 307), for instance, recording adages in praise of human farm labor, found one that links it to filial piety: "The filial and obedient couple will be fortunate, the well-tended fields will bear grain" *(xiao shun ye niang you fu qin li tianchang you gu)*. All of these values were recognized in early classical statecraft and philosophy, and all can be traced through records of imperial policy and family practice from earliest times.

Western observers of China in the early twentieth century echoed the sentiments of China's own folk wisdom: Chinese people work hard, even in the face of very low returns, and they are constantly on the lookout for more productive outlets for surplus labor.[18] As Tawney put it, "The first sensation of a visitor to a Chinese city is one of suffocation beneath a torrent of human beings, straining at manual labour or clamouring to be given it" (1932, 119).[19] Studying farm labor at about the same time, Buck remarked: "The amount of man labor in China is almost unlimited and one of the great problems is the discovery of enough productive work to keep this vast human army profitably employed" (1937, 289).

But hard work alone does not explain the success of farm families, as Buck emphasized. The reason why profitable farm employment had been expanded to the maximum was its efficient division of labor. By Buck's estimates, farm work per se occupied the full time of only about two-thirds of the farm population, with sideline industries occupying one-eighth and a combination of farming and sideline work employing another one-fifth. These sideline occupations (called "subsidiary work" in Buck's study) were

mainly home industries like spinning and weaving, hog and poultry raising, and bee culture—women's work in the household economy (Buck
1937, 298).

This is the same women's work vaunted in late imperial statecraft, which
emphasized the need for skill not only in performing tasks but in creating
opportunities for productive labor wherever they could be found.[20] At the
women's festival on Double Seven (the seventh night of the seventh month),
when women and girls used to "beg for skill" (qi qiao) from the stellar Weaving Maid, the goal of every young petitioner was more than skill with the
needle. Skill prepared her for entry into a productive household as a valued
member. Not only would a talented seamstress make a better marriage; she
would also please her mother-in-law, ensuring a less stressful life in the
household into which she married.[21]

The importance of skill inculcated through training and disciplined by
high motivation, the high returns from intensified labor in the rural workforce, and the centrality of women's work in a gender division of labor
where women work "inside" while menfolk labor "outside"—all were key
aspects of a household production system supported and protected by
China's earliest rulers and statesmen. In this production system, workers—
male and female—were motivated by complex incentives far more compelling than an individual wage. In late imperial China, political, economic,
social, and moral incentives all rewarded couples who kept their married
sons together and trained the next generation to work hard in a household
economy.

WORK IN CHINESE HOUSEHOLDS AT THE TURN
OF THE TWENTIETH CENTURY

What implications does this historic legacy of household labor have for
modern China? Recently the traditional gender division of labor has been
the subject of attention, as scholars speculate that norms confining women's
work to the household reduced the supply of female workers available for
China's factories during early industrialization. Huang (P.C.C. 1990, 111),
for example, has argued that the "cultural constraints against women venturing outside the home, plus the logistical difficulties of managing female
labor that came with those constraints" created a crucial shortage of female
labor for light industry, slowing the pace of industrialization in the early
twentieth century.[22] Hershatter (1986, 55–56) found that in Tianjin, women
were only 9.14 percent of the cotton mill workforce in 1929 (as compared
with over 70 percent in Shanghai mills), a factor she attributed partly to the
role of women in the rural economy of the North, which confined women
almost exclusively to work inside the home. Honig (1986, 64–65), by con-

trast, noticed that much of the early female labor force in Shanghai's textile mills was recruited from women who could no longer earn money from household handicrafts but who expected their menfolk to continue farming. Either way, women's expectations about factory work and its importance to the household income were shaped by their participation in household production units, manufacturing home-spun and home-woven goods on the eve of industrialization and scorning farm work outside the home.

The early Communist government's attempts to reconfigure ideas about work overrode these historical household-based motivational systems. In the Maoist era, work was organized collectively or communally, partly by appealing to classical notions of sharing returns from labor and stressing the mutual obligations between "those above" and "those below"—managers and workers, or technicians and manual laborers. But collective labor was never wholly successful. It violated long-held assumptions about the boundaries of work (women "inside," men "outside"). It closed down the marketing systems on which households had depended to exchange their surpluses. It overrode the specialization of crops and tasks that maximized the diverse capacities of regional and human resources. And it destroyed the motivational system oriented backward toward the ancestors and forward toward descendants that for centuries had fueled China's renowned work ethic.

The astounding success of the return to household production units after 1978 during the post-Mao reform era at first glance appeared to confirm that household production units still motivated workers better than collectives did. The household responsibility system in China's countryside tapped ideas about gender, household, and work that have a long and remarkably coherent history. Ironically, the conviction that work inside the home is women's work also seems to have survived intact from late imperial times into the contemporary reform era—pretty much unscathed by egalitarian campaigns like the Great Leap Forward and the Cultural Revolution. The boundaries of the household as a production unit appear to be the strongest and the most difficult to penetrate of all the structures of work inherited from the past.

Despite the resilience of the household as a unit of production, however, the modern concept of work as *gongzuo* (a job) has continued to erode classical boundaries of gender, household, and work, drawing women outside the home into a legitimate public workspace where modern "jobs" abound. In the 1990s, with increased incentives for individuals to pursue their own career goals without regard for their family obligations, the boundaries promised to erode still further, as they have in Taiwan, Hong Kong, and overseas Chinese communities (Whyte 1996). Even less durable, it appears, are other historical ideas about work in China: the long-standing critique of the leisured class, radical celebrations of the importance of shared labor, and the moral conviction that those who labor with their minds should justify their position before those who labor with their hands.

NOTES

1. See Cohen (1976, 57–85) on the collective character of the family economy.

2. See Harrell (1985). The problem with this reification of the household, of course, is that it ignores the ambiguous relationship of women—especially unmarried women—to the patriline. See, for example, Greenhalgh (1985). Exploration of this topic lies beyond the scope of this chapter, which focuses on the boundaries of the household itself.

3. The so-called "Legalists" took a different view, arguing that the ruler should command the labor of his subjects solely for the purpose of increasing his own power. This line of thinking was discredited in mainstream Chinese political theory, which (rhetorically, at least) deferred to Confucian "benevolence."

4. Translation, slightly adapted, from Hsiao (1979, 357).

5. Of course women always worked in farming and, especially after the seventeenth century, they were visibly engaged in scholarly activities, but the imperial government's policy and political theory reserved recognition in both arenas for men alone. Farm women were honored for sericulture, spinning, weaving, and needlework, but never for laboring in the fields.

6. Ch'ü T'ung-tsu (1972, 117, 118) comments that "In pre-Ch'in times we do not find any historical evidence to indicate that there was discrimination against merchants. On the contrary, it seems that their social and political status was rather high. . . . Merchants in Ch'ing times also enjoyed a superior social status." He dates the earliest discrimination against merchants to a law dated 214 B.C.E.

7. See Ch'ü (1972, 144–145). He quotes the following comment from the Han dynasty "Debates on Salt and Iron" *(Yantie lun):* "The common people are not free from work from morning to evening, whereas (government) male and female slaves idle about with folded hands" (145).

8. Scholars have generally concluded that the hardest government labor was reserved for convicts and conscripted laborers, not slaves (Ch'ü 1972, 145). This view is shared by Lien-sheng Yang (1969, 29) and C. Martin Wilbur (1943). In fact, Yang emphasizes that "Altogether, government and private slaves did not play any significant role in public works, even in those relatively early periods of Chinese history when slaves are supposed to have been fairly numerous" (210). See also Watson 1980a, b.

9. L. S. Yang (1969, 210) notes that idle soldiers were judged a waste of government resources.

10. Examples of the mobilization of forced labor under the early empire include the 700,000 convicts employed to build the imperial mausoleum and palace of the First Emperor (221–209 B.C.E.), and the 146,000 men and women drafted to build the city of Chang'an in the early Han (206 B.C.E.–220 C.E.) (L. S. Yang 1969, 202). Massive water conservancy projects on the Yellow River employed hundreds of thousands of conscripts in Han and Sui (599–618) times (203). Construction and re-

pairs on the Great Wall demanded labor forces ranging from 300,000 to 1.8 million (203). The largest conscript labor force ever assembled for a single project, according to Yang (204), was the 2 million people who built the city of Luoyang in the Sui. During the Song dynasty (960–1279), most public works were staffed by military labor rather than conscripts. Yang (211) noted that "this division of labor between civilians and soldiers freed the common people from both the bulk of military service and most of the labor service. This government policy was praised by contemporary scholars as highly beneficial."

11. Literally, "everyone is invited," translated by Ch'en (1973, 148) as "collective participation."

12. See Ch'en (1973, 148–50). Translation slightly adapted from Ch'en (150). Ch'en (151) views this Chan teaching as an "accommodation to the prevailing Chinese work ethic."

13. For differing interpretations of the significance of women's textile production in peasant households during late imperial times, see Mann (1997, 143–77) and Bray (1997, 173–272). Both recognize that women's work in the household economy, especially spinning and weaving, was valorized in the late Ming and Qing periods by government policies celebrating women's work in the home. Bray sees this as a shift that marginalized female productive labor by removing it from the higher skilled, higher paying shops in towns and cities dominated by male labor. Mann notes that in many areas the spread of spinning and weaving technologies in peasant households increased female labor productivity. Both agree that norms confining female labor to the home were strikingly effective in removing female labor from the fields in China (as compared with other rice economies, for example in Japan and Southeast Asia).

14. According to Huang Liuhong, the late seventeenth-century magistrate whose advice book became a classic reference for generations of officials, a county official might need conscript labor for the following jobs: repairing the city walls, working on the Yellow River or Grand Canal water conservancies (including damming, dredging, diking, planting willow trees on river banks), towing government barges, repairing guest houses maintained for visiting dignitaries and officials, and so on. (See Huang Liu-hung 1984, 227–33).

15. Cole (1986, 65–72) describes the *duomin* ("lazy people") of Shaoxing, a local pariah population whose work marked them as polluted. *Duo* ("lazy") is a homophone for *duo* ("fallen"). Courtesans and prostitutes likewise were scorned as pariahs because they did not do "womanly work" (Mann 1997, 121–142). See also Honig's (1992) study of Subei people in Shanghai, which shows that a reputation for clumsiness, slowness to learn, or lack of skill all barred Subei workers from respectable kinds of employment.

16. Buck (1937, 292). Buck acknowledged that these figures varied by region and that the largest proportion of farm labor done by women was in the double-cropping rice areas. He also noticed that hired farm labor was overwhelmingly male.

17. Scholars have noted several features of late imperial society that made it especially conducive to household-based production. These include the rice economy and its capacity to reward intensive labor, a flourishing marketing system, a fluid stratification system, open marriage markets, and a joint family system. On the rice economy, see Bray's (1986) analysis of what she calls "skill-oriented" technologies;

on access to markets, Skinner (1964–65); on stratification, Ho (1962); on marriage markets, Mann (1992). The joint family system favored particular strategies for reproducing labor and for deploying male and female labor inside and outside the home: early marriage, large offspring sets, and multigenerational residence permitting an efficient division of labor by age and gender (Greenhalgh 1988).

18. Arthur Smith (1894) devoted an entire chapter of his book on Chinese characteristics to praise of "industry," conceding that "there can be little doubt that casual travelers, and residents of the longest standing, will agree in a profound conviction of the diligence of the Chinese people" (27). King (1973, 16), who was far more impressed with the moral fiber of East Asian farmers than was Smith, professed amazement at "the magnitude of the returns they are getting from their fields, and . . . at the amount of efficient human labour cheerfully given for a daily wage of five cents and their food, or for fifteen cents, United States currency, without food."

19. Tawney's list of work includes coal and iron ore mining and iron smelting ("nearly one-half" of the pig-iron produced, he estimated, was made in charcoal furnaces with bellows worked by hand or water power); cotton spinning (some in factories, but some, along with most weaving, still done at home or in small workshops); and finally metalworking, potting, tile-making, building, carpentry, furniture making, painting, shoemaking, hat making, tailoring, tanning, woodcarving, lacquer making, silk reeling and weaving, woolen weaving, tapestry making, rope making, and myriad artisan crafts producing housewares, ornaments, jewelry, and "artistic products"—all of the latter "still much what they were five centuries ago" (1932, 111).

20. Bray (1986) calls rice economies skill-oriented (rather than mechanical) technologies because they require ever-higher levels of skill to produce the rising productivity necessary for supporting more people on scarce land. Bray (155) stresses Thomas Smith's (1959) point that, unlike Western-derived development strategies, the Japanese model "is based on improvement in the application of human skills rather than the substitution of machinery for labour, and requires a low level of capital investment."

21. As late as 1988, female informants in my interviews in Shanghai recalled vividly (and sometimes painfully) the humiliation of failing to pass their mother-in-law's test of their skill in needlework, the first rite de passage of the young bride after her wedding night.

22. Schneider's work on Sicily (1985, 81) posits in a similar vein that "cultural patterns making female labor unavailable for income-producing activities have impeded agrarian transformation and economic development." Describing the early factory labor force in British India, Morris (1983, 644) remarked that "among the less expected features of the factory labour force—at least, as compared with the early experience of other nations—were the relatively small proportions of female and child labour and the stability of those proportions." The total proportion of women and children combined never rose above 22 percent or fell below 20 percent between 1892 and 1928. See also Gadgil (1965) and Morris (1965, 65–69). These figures are almost exactly in line with China's, with a similar family system and comparable constraints on women going out to work.

TWO

Re-Drawing the Boundaries of Work

Views on the Meaning of Work *(Gongzuo)*

Gail E. Henderson, Barbara Entwisle, Li Ying,
Yang Mingliang, Xu Siyuan, and Zhai Fengying

Work is an ambiguous concept everywhere, but perhaps especially so in contemporary China, where economic reforms implemented in the 1980s fundamentally changed the landscape of employment opportunities. Before the reforms, state and collective-run firms accounted for virtually all urban employment. This was still largely true in 1990, when 94 percent of urban employees worked in the state or collective sectors (see table 2.1). The state and collective sectors continue to dominate employment in urban areas, but the degree to which they do so is beginning to slip, together accounting for 83 percent of urban employees in 1995. Employment in the private sector, previously at zero, has mushroomed. By 1995, foreign or jointly run enterprises accounted for 5 percent of the urban labor force, domestic private enterprise *(siying)* 3 percent, and individually or household run businesses *(geti)* another 9 percent. Distinctions between what does and does not count as work have likely become muddied with the weakening of employment guarantees, the growth of contract and temporary labor, and the reemergence of the household as a focus of economic activity.

Changes have been even more pronounced in rural areas. Within agriculture, the "household responsibility system" replaced collective agriculture, shifting agricultural activities from the collective to the private sector and under household control. Privatization of sideline and other domestic activities also redefined the boundaries between "inside" and "outside" work. At the same time, industrialization of the countryside led over 200 million people to leave agriculture for work in industry, trade, and services during the first 15 years of reform. Table 2.1 shows that the number of employees in TVEs (township- and village-run enterprises, *xiangzhen qiye*) doubled between 1985 and 1995, and by the latter date accounted for 29 percent of workers in rural areas. Employment in private enterprises *(siying qiye)* and

TABLE 2.1 Urban and Rural Employees in China

Percentatge Distibution of Employees by Employment Sector

	Total Millions	State	Collective	Other [a]	Private	Individual
			Total Urban			
1985	128.08	70.2	26.0	0.3	——	3.5
1990	147.30	70.2	24.1	1.1	0.4	4.2
1995	173.46	64.9	18.1	5.2	2.8	9.0
			Hubei Urban			
1995	8.97	65.0	15.5	4.5	2.2	13.3

Percentage Distribution of Workers by Employment Sector

	Total Millions	TVEs [b]	Private	Individual
		Total Rural		
1985	370.65	18.8	——	——
1990	420.10	22.1	0.3	3.5
1995	450.42	28.6	1.0	6.8
		Hubei Rural		
1995	18.10	36.7	1.2	12.7

SOURCE: State Statistical Bureau, 1996. *Zhongguo tongji nianjian 1995* (Statistical yearbook of China 1995). Beijing: Statistical Publishing House of China, pp. 90–91.

[a] Includes jointly owned economic units, share-holding economic units, foreign funded economic units, and economic units funded by Chinese from Hong Kong, Macao, and Taiwan

[b] Township- and village-run enterprises.

household businesses *(geti hu)* rose to account for 1 and 7 percent of rural workers, respectively. Diversification of employment thus has taken place along three dimensions—sector (private/state and collective); occupation (agricultural/nonagricultural); and mode of organization (inside/outside the household)—with likely consequences for how different kinds of economic activities are viewed and valued.

Within the context of these changes, our goal is to understand how boundaries are drawn between what counts as work and what does not. Our approach is "emic"—to ask people themselves what they think. Because economic transformation has been most dramatic in the countryside, we direct our attention to that context, drawing data from 12 focus group interviews conducted in two villages and two towns. Focus group interviews are guided group discussions on prespecified topics (Stewart and Shamdasani 1990). Developed initially as a marketing tool, focus group interviews have been used by social scientists to gather qualitative data in a wide variety of settings (e.g., Knodel et al. 1990). For our purposes, group interviews were preferred over individual interviews because we were interested in the discussion of work and its meaning, the points of agreement and disagreement. The focus group interviews were conducted in Hubei province in October 1995. Individual and household businesses and TVEs are more common in Hubei than in China as a whole, as table 2.1 shows. This is an advantage, given the purpose of our qualitative research: We want to investigate the concept of work in a context in which work itself is changing.

The particular concept we explore is *gongzuo,* which can be translated as job or work.[1] We chose this concept because it is frequently used in survey data collection. The China Health and Nutrition Survey (CHNS), for example, a data source used by several contributors to this volume (chaps. 8 and 15), asks whether each person in the household "has *gongzuo*"; occupation, employment sector, and other information is collected for those household members who do. *Gongzuo* encapsulates a modern view of work focused on individual activity outside of household contexts (see chap. 1). During the Maoist era (1949–1976), the term *gongzuo* was restricted to work for wages in the formal sector in a work unit *(danwei),* for which urban household registration was required. This type of work, especially in a state-run work unit, topped the job status hierarchy at that time (Walder 1986), perhaps corresponding to the idea of "a real job." As we will show, there is considerable ambiguity about the meaning of *gongzuo* now.

FOCUS GROUP INTERVIEWS: DESIGN

In the focus group interviews, a vignette was used to generate discussion about work *(gongzuo).* Participants were told that a long-lost relative of the Feng family, Mrs. Chen, was coming for a visit and "we would like you to help us describe their activities to Mrs. Chen." Then the activities of each of three Feng brothers and their wives were described, followed by two questions: "If Mrs. Chen asks him (her), 'What do you do?' *(Ni zuo shenma?)* what will he (she) answer?" Then, "Does he (she) have a job/work?" *(Ta you mei you gongzuo?).* Table 2.2 lists the activities of the Feng family members as they were described to the focus group participants in the town and village interviews.

We predicted that in the present time of economic transition, there would be considerable variation in whether or not someone's activities were thought of as *gongzuo.* Focus group participants' attitudes might depend on characteristics of the activity, such as locus vis-à-vis the household and whether and how it was remunerated (cf. chap. 3). They might depend on the gender of the person performing the activity. Women's contributions might be less visible than men's, even when the work they do is the same. We also hypothesized that response to the Feng family vignette would vary

TABLE 2.2 Activities of the Feng Family in Focus Group Vignettes

	Town Interview	Village Interview
First brother	Private transport company with 4 men; then seasonal fieldwork	Grows cotton, family garden; then seasonal fieldwork
First brother's wife	Cooks, cleans, washes clothes, small garden; then large garden, expensive mushrooms to sell	Cooks, cleans, washes; seasonal fieldwork
Second brother	Full time in collective farm tool factory; then only two month's salary	Runs family transport business
Second brother's wife	Cooks, cleans, washes clothes, family dry goods shop; then opens bigger store outside home, 6 days/wk	Cooks, cleans, washes clothes, family garden, raises chickens (made 800 *yuan*); then chickens die (makes 100 *yuan*); then job in local textile factory
Third brother	Permanent but only part-year in large joint-venture beer factory; then full time, permanent	Helps second brother with transport business; then factory subcontract for transport, good money
Third brother's wife	Job at neighborhood-run day care center	Cooks, cleans, washes clothes, family garden, few chickens and pig; then helps in family dry goods shop

depending on the characteristics of the people in the group. That is, the gender and age of the focus group participants, and whether they resided in a village or town, or in a wealthy or poor county might be related to their views of work and what activities would count as *gongzuo*.

The vignettes were carefully structured to allow us to compare and contrast reactions to characteristics of the activity and to the gender of the worker. The village interviews allow for comparisons between (1) agricultural and nonagricultural activities (a man operating a farm versus a man operating a family transport business; a woman with a chicken business versus a woman working in a family-run shop selling dry goods), (2) year-round and seasonal activities (in agriculture), and (3) pay (a woman who makes a lot of money selling chickens, a woman who makes only a little money selling chickens, and a woman who raises chickens for home consumption; a man who helps his brother with a transport business versus a man who arranges a lucrative subcontract for the family transport business).

The vignettes used in the town interviews allow for comparisons between (1) activities in different employment sectors (a man working in a collective factory versus a man working in a joint venture factory; a woman employed by a neighborhood-run day care center versus a woman who works in a family store), (2) seasonality (a man with year-round versus a man with seasonal work in a small private transport company; a man with half-year versus a man with full-year employment in a large joint-venture beer factory), and (3) pay (a woman with a small garden versus a woman with a large garden that produces expensive mushrooms to sell; a man with a job in a collective factory versus a man with the same job who only gets two months' salary; a woman who works in a small family shop in the home versus a woman who works in a large family-run store outside of the home). We constructed these comparisons to highlight one particular aspect of work and to control for other aspects, including gender of the worker.

Other comparisons were designed to see whether the gender of the worker makes any difference. The vignettes used in the village interviews allow for comparisons between men and women involved in year-round agricultural activities, seasonal fieldwork, and a family-run business. Those used in the town interviews allow for comparisons between men and women running a family business, and men and women with employment in the state or collective sector. The goal was to be able to examine the gender of the worker independent of the characteristics of the activity.

Our focus group interviews are somewhat more structured than is typically the case. It is not unusual for moderators to be given no more than a list of topics to cover in an interview, leaving up to them the order, exact wording, follow-up questions, and probes. In contrast, we asked moderators to follow particular question sequences and to use specific terms and language when asking about activities. We wanted to examine each interview as a whole, but we also wanted to be able to compare the ways the different focus groups regarded work or job characteristics (e.g., sector of employment, degree of permanence, level of remuneration), especially in relation to the gender of the worker. A common set of "stimuli" was important for making comparisons between interviews. Also, since our interest was in understanding the meaning of *gongzuo* and the factors affecting people's views of it, controlling how and when moderators used the term in the course of the interview was important.

Twelve focus group interviews were held—the total number determined by the resources available. Separate groups of mothers, fathers, and grandmothers were interviewed in two town neighborhoods and in two rural villages in Hubei province.[2] The differences in group composition offer important opportunities for exploring the meaning of *gongzuo*. Comparing the views of mothers and fathers allows us to see whether interpretation of this concept varies by gender of the observer as well as by gender of the person performing the activity in the vignette. Comparing the views of mothers and grandmothers allows us to see whether interpretation varies by generation.

The sites for the focus group interviews were selected for their potential to generate contrasts. We selected two pairs of town neighborhoods and rural villages. One pair was located in a relatively developed county, Fu Xian, the other in a relatively poor county, Han Shan Xian.[3]

Fu county seat is a town on its way to becoming a city. It is full of commercial and industrial businesses, including department stores, restaurants, hotels, textile factories, a joint-venture feed factory, gravel transport, and lumber companies. A large hospital has also opened recently. In contrast, Han Shan county seat is not marked by the dust and dirt of construction seen in Fu county seat. There is barely a building that rises above three stories. The town is characterized by one resident as having "not much money, not much of an economy." Whereas the neighborhood in Fu county seat selected for the interviews is very close to the town center, the one in Han Shan county seat is a village annexed by the town where many people continue to farm in the adjacent fields, despite their urban registration.

The two villages also differ, although not as dramatically. Residents of Fu county village are engaged in intensive, profitable vegetable gardening. There are a number of private household businesses, including duck raising, dry goods stores, and a clothing store, but there are no village-run enterprises. (Several were attempted but failed.) Residents who work outside the village go to factories run by other villages or towns. Han Shan county village, however, has its own village-run factories, whose enterprises include stone-cutting, flour grinding, brick-making, and tree-cutting. As in Fu county village, there are family-run businesses, restaurants, and various small vendors. While the Fu county village focuses on growing vegetables, in Han Shan county village agricultural products include rice, wheat, sweet potatoes, peanuts, cotton, tobacco, and soybeans, and many families raise chickens and pigs. Despite this apparent economic diversity, people in Han Shan county village consider themselves and their village to be poor, reporting a per capita income that is only about 25 percent of that of Fu county village. Many of the houses have mud floors and are made of mud bricks. While Fu county village does not look very different, all of the houses have electricity, half have televisions, and a few people are building new homes.

In textbook applications, focus group participants are strangers to one another. Such a plan is not well suited to the social realities of life in the rural villages and town neighborhoods that make up the Chinese countryside. We expected that participants recruited from the same village or neighborhood would already know one another, and we verified that this was true at the beginning of each interview. The conversations that took place within the focus group interviews thus occurred within a social context that pre- and postdated the interview itself. For this reason, we took great care in the design of the interview to avoid placing participants in potentially embarrassing situations. The vignettes especially helped in this regard, providing a venue for participants to express their opinions about social relationships and work activities without having to discuss the particulars of their own situation or that of anyone else they knew. The benefits of recruiting participants from the same neighborhood or village are many and include practical considerations as well as the opportunity to account for contextual differences in responses.

The focus group interviews were conducted by staff members of the county, provincial, and national Epidemic Disease Prevention Stations. Residents of neighborhoods and villages that were already part of the China Health and Nutrition Survey were recruited with a letter that described the topics of the focus group interviews and requested their signed, informed consent. This consent procedure was repeated verbally at the start of the interviews. The groups consisted of six or seven participants. The interviews took about one and one-half hours. Instead of tape recorders, two trained note-takers were used. The note-takers combined their versions, and translation was done immediately. The analyses described below are based on the Chinese versions and English translations of the focus group interviews, the comments of the moderators, and our own observations.

THE INTERVIEWS: OPINIONS ABOUT GONGZUO

The Feng family vignette elicited a variety of opinions about *gongzuo*. In some groups, virtually all activities in the vignettes were labeled *gongzuo,* while other groups were much more conditional or restrictive in their approach. Participants of some groups quickly came to a consensus view, whereas in other groups there was dissension. Our goal here is to describe the focus group interviews in such a way that some general conclusions can be drawn from the details of the discussions. In the following paragraphs, we review the evidence that supports four conclusions about *gongzuo* and its meaning for the focus group participants: (1) *gongzuo* has diverse interpretations; (2) differences in views about this term and the general concept that underlies it are not tied in any obvious way to gender or generation of the participants, or to their urban-rural location or its economic context; (3) rather, classification of particular activities as *gongzuo* or not depends on employment sector, degree of permanence, pay, and nature of the activity; (4) gender of the worker (in the vignettes) matters, but only a little bit.

1. There is no common understanding of gongzuo.

This first point is easily made by considering the totality of the focus group interviews. Many of the specific activities we asked about drew a mixed response. For example, discussing agricultural fieldwork, some focus group participants said, "Farming is *gongzuo*. It earns money. Whenever you do that, you have *gongzuo*." Others said, "It isn't *gongzuo*. It's not a job. He works on a farm." Likewise, with respect to agricultural sideline businesses, some participants commented, "She has *gongzuo*. It's a household sideline. If you plant cash crops, it's *gongzuo*." Others said, "Sideline production is not *gongzuo*." Regarding family-run nonagricultural businesses, some said, "She's running a store, contributing to the family finances. She has *gongzuo*." The contrasting opinion was: "She works for herself, but it's not *gongzuo*. *Getihu* (private household business) is not *gongzuo*."

Focus group participants did agree that permanent, full-time employment in a *danwei* (work unit) is *gongzuo*. In five of the six town focus groups, participants were unanimous in their view that the Feng brother with a job in a collective factory manufacturing farming tools has *gongzuo*. There was complete agreement about the third Feng brother's wife, who works in a neighborhood-run day care center. All thought that she has *gongzuo* too. Similarly, in all six village focus groups, participants agreed that when the second Feng brother's wife goes to work in a local factory making cotton clothes, she has a job. One of the fathers from Han Shan county village remarked, "Definitely she has *gongzuo*, because she works in a unit." However, there was little agreement about household-based activities in the private sector, including fieldwork, household sidelines, and running or working in a family business.

2. Interpretations do not depend on focus group composition.

Whether or not particular activities are classified as *gongzuo* does not depend very much on the composition of the focus group. This finding comes from an examination of the focus group interviews one by one, and is particularly well illustrated by the four focus group interviews of fathers. One of these groups expressed a broad concept of work, two groups offered restrictive definitions, and the final group took a conditional approach to the classification of the various activities. As evidence, we provide a brief summary of each of these interviews.

The Fu county village fathers were vocal about their beliefs that *everything* is *gongzuo*. Six of the seven fathers had completed lower middle school and one was a high school graduate; four were farmers, two drivers, and one did interior design. They all felt that *all* of the Fengs' activities should be considered *gongzuo*. Fieldwork, whether seasonal or not, is *gongzuo*. "You can earn money from farming." "Even if it's just in the fields, it's still *gongzuo*."

"Seasonal fieldwork is *gongzuo*—making money is *gongzuo.*" Everyone agreed that the first brother's wife, who works in the fields at planting and harvest times as well as cooks, cleans, and washes clothes, has *gongzuo.* Operating and even helping in a family transport business counts as *gongzuo.* "It depends on whether there is money coming in." Raising chickens (even when most of them get sick and die) is *gongzuo.* "Of course," going to a local factory is *gongzuo.* This group was equivocal only when it came to classifying the activities of the third brother's wife, who takes care of a few chickens and a pig, works in the family garden, cooks, cleans, and washes clothes. But most agreed that doing housework is also *gongzuo* work. "She has an occupation. She has *gongzuo.*" "If you live in a village, you are a farmer." When in the vignette the third brother's wife joins her mother-in-law in a family shop, all agreed that she has *gongzuo.* "She changed from being a housewife to doing a business."

In contrast, the fathers in Han Shan county village were hesitant to say that *anything* outside the formal sector was *gongzuo.* The occupations of these fathers were comparable to the fathers in Fu county village (three were farmers; one was a driver; the others did construction or technical work), although their education was a little lower (ranging from less than primary school to middle-level technical school). Most agreed that the first Feng brother, engaged in agricultural fieldwork, does not have *gongzuo,* although one father dissented: "Whenever you have a thing to do, you have *gongzuo.*" Opinions did not change with seasonal fieldwork. Running or helping out in a family transport business does not count as *gongzuo* either. It only becomes *gongzuo* when the third Feng brother arranges a factory subcontract. For the fathers in Han Shan county village, the Feng wife engaged in fieldwork does not have *gongzuo,* nor does the wife selling chickens for 800 *yuan.* They were divided about the wife helping the mother-in-law in the family shop.

The fathers in Han Shan county town were also fairly restrictive in their classification of work activities, though not as restrictive as the fathers in Han Shan county village. The seven fathers in the Han Shan county town group included three farmers, three blue-collar workers, and one in *getihu* business; two were primary school graduates, four had lower middle school degrees, and one was a high school graduate. This group tended not to rate activities outside the state and collective sectors as *gongzuo,* although there were exceptions. Work in a *getihu* transport business is *gongzuo,* as long as it is not seasonal. These fathers were divided about the second Feng brother's job in a collective factory, particularly when in the vignette the salary is reduced to two months' pay for a year's work. This was the only focus group that questioned whether collective factory employment counts as *gongzuo.* These fathers were also mixed about a temporary job at the joint-venture factory (as were many of the groups), but agreed that permanent, full-time

TABLE 2.3   Contextual Variability in Definitions of *Gongzuo*

Broad Definition		
Fathers	Village	Rich county
Mothers	Village	Poor county
Grandmothers	Town	Rich county
Grandmothers	Village	Rich county
Grandmothers	Town	Poor county

Restrictive Definition		
Fathers	Village	Poor county
Fathers	Town	Poor county

Conditional Definition		
Fathers	Town	Rich county
Mothers	Town	Rich county
Mothers	Town	Poor county
Mothers	Village	Rich county
Grandmothers	Village	Poor county

work there constitutes *gongzuo*. As for their opinions about the Feng wives, most felt that housework is not *gongzuo*, although one or two changed their opinions when the first brother's wife's sideline business selling mushrooms was profitable. In contrast to their attitude about the transport business, the fathers in Han Shan county town did not consider working in a family shop, even if it is a large store, to be *gongzuo*. "She has no *gongzuo*. She just has a small store with her family." "A *getihu* is not *gongzuo*."

In contrast, the Fu county town fathers tended to label activities as *gongzuo* when the hours increased from part- to full-time, when the enterprise grew, and when the pay increased. They agreed that the first Feng brother's work in the family transport business qualifies as *gongzuo*, even when seasonal. Collective factory work is also *gongzuo*, though according to one father, receiving only two months' salary is not. All but one father said that temporary work at a joint-venture factory is *gongzuo*, but that father shifted his opinion when the factory work becomes full-time. Wives doing housework and raising animals for family consumption do not have *gongzuo*, according to the Fu county town fathers. However, when the first brother's wife has a cash crop garden and makes money, "then she has *gongzuo*—she runs a specialized household." The fathers' opinions were split about whether running a small family shop is *gongzuo*, but all agreed that it is *gongzuo* when the shop turns into a large store with full-time employment.

It would be difficult to identify a "fathers' perspective" from these four interviews. Similarly, evaluating each of the twelve focus group interviews according to whether a broad, restrictive, or conditional definition of *gong-zuo* was expressed, no obvious pattern emerges related to the different groups (see table 2.3).

Two of the fathers groups were the only ones to convey a restrictive definition, while a third fathers group expressed a broad definition and the fourth, a conditional one. Mothers and grandmothers groups expressed both broad and conditional definitions. Town and village groups are evenly distributed among the possibilities. No specific definition of *gongzuo* is associated with Fu (rich) and Han Shan (poor) county groups. Thus, the meaning of *gongzuo* expressed by each focus group as a whole appears to be unrelated to the group's gender, generation, urban-rural residence, or economic context.

3. Whether an activity is gongzuo *work depends on the nature of the activity, the employment sector, degree of permanence, and pay.*

Whereas virtually everyone in every focus group agreed that nonagricultural work in the state or collective sector is *gongzuo*, there was disagreement about other forms of activity. Take agricultural work, for example. Two of the six village groups felt that fieldwork does not count as *gongzuo*, and participants in one of the other village groups could not agree among themselves. One of the village groups was unwilling to classify a lucrative chicken business as *gongzuo*, and there was disagreement in another group. Although none of the town groups was completely unwilling to classify gardening—even growing expensive mushrooms for sale—as *gongzuo*, there was considerable disagreement in three of the six groups. What is it about these activities that raises doubts in the minds of the focus group participants? Is it agricultural activity per se? Or is it some characteristic of agricultural work, such as its seasonality, or generally low level of remuneration?

In the village focus group interviews, we asked participants to consider the first Feng brother's small farm and the second Feng brother's small transport business. Five groups classified the small transport business as *gongzuo*, and some participants of the sixth wanted to do so. Only three groups thought that the farm work qualified as *gongzuo*, two groups thought not, and there was disagreement in the other. We also asked participants in the village interviews to think about the chicken business of the second Feng brother's wife and the small shop in which the third Feng brother's wife worked. Four groups considered activity in either type of business as *gongzuo*, and there was disagreement about both types of business in the fifth group. But opinions in the sixth group changed: the chicken business was clearly not *gongzuo*, while the shop clearly was. Evidence from the village interviews suggests that, holding constant the size and household nature of the business as well as the gender of the person working in it, nonagricultural activity is more likely to be seen as *gongzuo* than agricultural activity. This distinction seems less relevant in urban areas, based on a comparison of reactions in the town interviews to the mushroom business of the first Feng brother's wife and the shop run by the second Feng brother's wife.

Initially, we thought that the seasonality of agricultural work might be one reason for ambiguity about its classification. The village focus group interviews asked explicitly about this, in connection with the first Feng brother and his wife. We were surprised to find that opinions about the fieldwork done by this couple were mostly the same, regardless of whether the fieldwork was seasonal or year-round. Remuneration, however, did make a difference.

In the village interviews, the relevant comparisons begin with the second brother's wife, who works in the family garden, cooks, cleans, washes clothes, and raises chickens for sale. Initially, the chickens bring in 800 *yuan*. To put this amount into perspective, according to interviews conducted with village officials in 1995, per capita income in Fu county village was 4000 to 5000 *yuan*, and in Han Shan county village, 1000 *yuan*. Four of the six village focus groups described the second brother's wife as having *gongzuo*, the fifth group said that she does not have *gongzuo*, and the sixth group could not agree. Then, according to the vignette, her chickens get sick and many die. She now makes only 100 *yuan*. This change in economic circumstances had little effect on the opinions expressed by the focus groups. A grandmother in Fu county village commented, "It's hard to say. She has *gongzuo*, but she does not have very good fortune."

But if we compare opinions about the second brother's wife with opinions about the third brother's wife, the importance of an income is clear. The only difference in the activities of these two wives is that the second brother's wife makes money raising chickens, whereas the third brother's wife raises them for home consumption only. Fu county village fathers thought that the second brother's wife has *gongzuo*, regardless of the amount of money the chicken business brings in, but their opinions were mixed when chickens are raised for consumption. Similarly, the Han Shan county village fathers began with mixed views about the second brother's wife, but agreed that raising chickens for consumption only is not *gongzuo*. The opinions of mothers and grandmothers were less influenced by income, with one curious exception. Fu county village mothers said that the third brother's wife has *gongzuo* but that the second brother's wife does not. It is difficult to know what to make of this. In the debriefing, the moderator wondered about the comprehension level of the mothers in this group.

Thus, in the village interviews it appears that if an activity generates some income, it is more likely to be seen as *gongzuo*. Level of remuneration does not seem to make much of a difference beyond that. In the town interviews, however, level of remuneration does matter. In these interviews we find the same general pattern: if a sideline business generates some income, it is more likely to be seen as *gongzuo*. When the first brother's wife enlarges her garden and starts to make a lot of money selling the mushrooms she now grows, opinions shift. The two town groups in which all participants agreed that cooking, cleaning, washing clothes, and tending a small garden do *not* count as *gongzuo* no longer held to this view when the garden produces income and so some portion of the wife's activities begins bringing in money. In the words of one of the mothers in Fu county seat: "She has *gongzuo* because she earns money." This was not a unanimous view, either in that focus group, or more generally. Three of the focus groups agreed that when her gardening activities produce a large income the first brother's wife has *gongzuo,* but there was disagreement in the three other groups. Even when participants disagreed, however, the income associated with an activity was identified as a relevant consideration. For example, one of the fathers in Han Shan county seat remarked, "Although economic conditions are better, it can't change our perspective."

To sum up the discussion so far, ambiguity about whether agricultural activity counts as *gongzuo* appears to stem from the nature of the activity per se and also from its level of remuneration. We now turn to private sector activity, asking a similar set of questions. We noted earlier that employment in a *danwei* clearly is work according to the focus group interviews, whereas there was less agreement about household-based and private-sector activities. Why? Is it because *gongzuo* is a designation that has been reserved for formal sector—state and collective—employment? Or is it because of the low level of remuneration associated with some jobs in the private sector, or because of their temporary, seasonal, or unstable nature? We need to say at the outset that we can only answer these questions for nonagricultural work. All of the agricultural activities we asked about in the focus group interviews were household-based and in the private sector. Indeed, very few agricultural workers can be found in the state or collective sector nowadays.

In the town focus group interviews, two comparisons are specifically relevant to employment sector. The first is between the first Feng brother's private transport business and the second Feng brother's job in a collective factory that manufactures farming tools. The focus groups responded similarly to these two jobs—that both are *gongzuo*. The second is between the dry goods store operated by the second Feng brother's wife and the job of the third Feng brother's wife in a neighborhood-run day care center. Here, we see more of a difference in response. Although four of the six groups classified both as *gongzuo,* the other two groups did not. Mothers in Fu county town could not agree about working in the dry goods store, although most thought that this is not *gongzuo*. "She works for herself, but she does not have *gongzuo*." "*Getihu* is not *gongzuo*." None of the fathers in Han Shan county town were willing to count work in the dry goods store as *gongzuo*. "She doesn't have *gongzuo*. She just has a small store with her family." But everyone in all groups agreed that a job in the day care center is *gongzuo*.

Doubts about private sector activities become even more evident when the vignette points out their low level of remuneration and temporary, seasonal, or unstable nature. Consider first the town focus group interviews. Whereas the first brother's job in a small private transport company with four other men counts as *gongzuo* for everyone in five focus groups and for most everyone in the sixth, this is no longer true when the moderator changes the work to seasonal—whenever the harvest comes in. There is now disagreement in two of the groups, and in a third no one is willing to label the activity as *gongzuo* because it is "unstable." Similarly, when the third brother's job in a large joint-venture beer factory changes from six to twelve months a year, doubts expressed about calling it *gongzuo* in two of the six focus group interviews disappear.

Indeed, level of remuneration is important even for jobs in the state and collective sector. When the second brother, who works in a collective factory that manufactures farm tools, receives only two months' salary rather than a full year's salary for his work, opinions shift in three of the six town focus groups. Five of the six groups were unanimous that he has *gongzuo* on full salary, but only two thought so after the salary cut. Comments in those two groups included: "No. Can't change the answer. He has *gongzuo*." "He still has *gongzuo*, just no wages." "We think he has *gongzuo*." "He has *gongzuo*, but the benefit is not much." Comments on the other side included: "It's hard to say." "He doesn't have a job." "He doesn't have *gongzuo* now."

In summary, in village and town focus groups, whether or not an activity is viewed as *gongzuo* depends on its characteristics. If it is agricultural, it is less likely to be seen as *gongzuo*. Agricultural or not, if it is seasonal, temporary, or unstable, it is less likely to be seen as *gongzuo*. If it is located in the private sector, especially if it is household based, there will be ambiguity about its classification. If the activity does not generate much of an income, it is less likely to be seen as *gongzuo*.

Consider what these tendencies mean for how the typical activities of men and women are viewed. Men are more likely to operate year-round non-agricultural businesses, especially in rural China, while women tend to oversee seasonal agricultural sidelines. We should not be surprised if the men are more likely to be seen as having *gongzuo* than the women. In urban areas, men are more likely than women to have stable state-sector jobs, and so again we should not be surprised if men are more likely to be viewed as having *gongzuo* than women. Of course, in addition to the characteristics of the job, the gender of the worker may affect people's views. We conclude our analysis of the focus group interviews with a consideration of this question.

4. Gender of the worker matters, but only a little bit.

The focus group interviews were designed to allow conclusions to be drawn about the gender of the worker independent of the characteristics of the work. In the town interviews it is possible to compare responses to the first Feng brother, who operates a private transport business, with responses to the second brother's wife, who runs a large dry goods store across the street from where the family lives. The responses were the same in five of the six groups. Fathers from Han Shan county town, the sixth group, felt that the brother with the transport business has *gongzuo* whereas the wife working six days a week in the store does not. "She doesn't have *gongzuo*. She is running her own store *(getihu)*." A second comparison is also possible between the second Feng brother's job in a collective factory and the job of the third brother's wife in a neighborhood-run day care center. Virtually everyone agreed that both have *gongzuo*.

Three comparisons are possible based on the village interviews. The first involves year-round fieldwork. Four of the six groups responded the same way, whether a Feng brother or his wife did this work. A fifth group, grandmothers from Han Shan county village, thought the Feng brother has *gongzuo* but not his wife. "He has *gongzuo*. Farming is *gongzuo*." "She does not have *gongzuo*." "She is a farmer and a housewife." A sixth group, mothers from Fu county village, held the opposing view. In the debriefing following this interview, the moderator noted that these mothers were emphatic that Feng women doing fieldwork have *gongzuo*, but Feng men doing fieldwork should "go out and get a real man's job." A second comparison involves seasonal fieldwork. The results are similar to those for year-round fieldwork, except that one of the fathers from Fu county village was unwilling to describe the seasonal fieldwork of the first Feng brother's wife as *gongzuo* but expressed no doubts that her husband doing that same work does have *gongzuo*. A third comparison possible with the village focus group interviews is between the third Feng brother, who helps the second brother with the transport business, and his wife, who helps her mother-in-law run a small shop. One group, the grandmothers in Han Shan county village, distinguished between helping with a transport business and actually running it; they felt that running the business is *gongzuo*, while helping is not. These same grandmothers thought that the wife who helps in a family dry-goods store does have *gongzuo*, though. The other five groups did not differentiate between helping with and running a business, whether the comparison was between two brothers or a brother and his wife.

Overall, the focus groups showed a tendency to classify men's activities as *gongzuo* more often than women's, but the tendency was slight.

IMPLICATIONS

Whichever way we organize our data, we find ambiguity in the meaning of the term *gongzuo*. Participants in 12 focus group interviews agreed that full-time, permanent, formal sector, *danwei* employment is a job; they disagreed about other kinds of activities. Interestingly, focus group participants used the same justifications to explain opposing views: "She doesn't have *gongzuo*—*getihu* is not *gongzuo*." "She has *gongzuo;* a *getihu* is *gongzuo*." Clearly, and perhaps in contrast to the pre-reform era, the term *gongzuo* has different meanings for different people. Views depend to some extent on characteristics of the work and to a lesser extent on the gender of the worker, but even so, there is no common definition of the boundary between activities that count as work and those that do not. Nor, given a boundary, is it sharply drawn. At least for focus group participants, the typology presented by Rosenfeld (chap. 3), which distinguishes work activities according to their household basis and remuneration status, identifies only the ends of continua between work and not-work. As Harrell (chap. 4) notes, the middle ground is contested territory. That is, formal-sector, paid work outside the household counts as *gongzuo,* and unpaid work inside the household does not, but the classification of other kinds of activities generates discussion and disagreement.

How work is viewed depends partly on its characteristics—the nature of the activity (agricultural or not), relationship to the household, employment sector, degree of permanence, and pay. If a job is agricultural, it is less likely to be seen as *gongzuo*. To some extent, this is because such work is seasonal, is organized by households, and tends not to produce much income. If a job is seasonal, temporary, or unstable, it is less likely to be thought of as *gongzuo*. If it is household-based, or located in the private sector, there is more disagreement about its classification. If the activity does not generate much income, it will be less likely to be seen as *gongzuo*. Even if we take these specific characteristics of agriculture into account, however, comparing small farms and agricultural sidelines with other kinds of household businesses, agriculture is still less likely to be viewed as *gongzuo*. These results suggest that the nature of an activity—whether it is located in the agricultural sector or the industrial or service sectors—affects how it is viewed, independent of remuneration or its location vis-à-vis the household. This is a pattern that may well characterize rural economies around the world (cf. Dixon 1982).

Holding the characteristics of work constant, we find a slight tendency to take women less seriously than men. However, the characteristics that typically define the work matter a lot. Consider a permanent job in an urban *danwei*. Everyone in the focus group interviews agreed that such work counted as *gongzuo*. Men are more likely than women to hold such jobs (e.g., chap. 7), and while the evidence tends to be anecdotal, men may be more likely to keep them (Jacka 1990). In urban areas, men and women have found work in newly created private businesses in urban areas, but the proprietors are likely to be men (Sabin 1994, 963). Providing assistance in a household business is less likely to be seen as work than running the business, according to our research. In rural China, men more than women have turned to nonfarm work (Entwisle et al. 1995; Parish, Zhe, and Li 1995), at least initially (chap. 8), leaving the agricultural jobs to women (chap. 11; Odgaard 1992). Not only are rural women more likely to do agricultural work than men, they are also more likely to combine different kinds of part-time and seasonal activities (Entwisle et al. 1994), many of them developed from traditionally female sideline activities ("courtyard enterprises"). Work characteristics make the work that men and women do differentially visible. Whether measured in relation to the nature of the activity, its location vis-à-vis the household, employment sector, degree of permanence, or pay, men are more likely to have work that is considered *gongzuo* than women.

The fact that different kinds of work are differentially visible has implications for monitoring economic change in China. In the cities and towns there is movement away from state and collective sector employment. Contract work and work that is part-time, temporary, and without guaranteed pay are increasing. Households have reemerged as an important base of economic activity. Based on our results, these are the kinds of activities that are *less* likely to be thought of as *gongzuo*. In rural areas, industrialization is shifting workers out of agriculture, into jobs that are *more* likely to be seen as *gongzuo*. To the extent that attempts to monitor economic change rely on respondent reports (as is the case with social surveys) there is potential for shifting attitudes about work to bias the picture.

One potential source of bias in survey-based monitoring appears *not* to be a problem, according to the focus group results. Interpretation of *gongzuo* is not predicted by characteristics of the focus group itself—gender, generation, urban-rural location, or economic level. Based on our results, no systematic bias is introduced by the person who reports on work activities. For example, the picture should be the same whether a husband reports on his and his wife's activities or his wife reports on her own and his activities. Gender differences relate to characteristics of the work and, to a lesser extent, to the gender of the worker, but not the gender or other characteristics of those classifying the activity. Similarly, urban-rural differences relate to the work but not to the views of the persons describing it. This is reassuring from the standpoint of social survey applications. Although there may be systematic error in the data collected about work, it does not appear to be related to the characteristics of the respondents or the site (the sampling unit).

Of course, these conclusions are based on only 12 focus group interviews in two county seats and two rural villages in Hubei province, and it is difficult to know how far the results can be generalized. Strictly speaking, they cannot be generalized at all. Focus group participants were not selected according to any probability method; interviews were conducted in only four sites.[4] However, our failure to find contextual variation in the interpretation of *gongzuo* may actually be a strength in this regard. We designed the focus group interviews explicitly to explore contextual differences in industrial and commercial development, and their consequences for attitudes about work. We did not find these effects. This is a weak result, but it suggests that *where* we conducted the interviews did not matter—the findings would have been the same.

NOTES

Funding for this research was provided by the National Institute of Child Health and Development grant P01-HD28076, the National Science Foundation grant #37486, and the Fogarty Center. In addition to the authors, our research team in Hubei included Susan Short, Jill Bouma, Lin Hai, Lu Bing, Li Dan, and members of the Fu and Han Shan County Epidemic Disease Prevention Stations. Susan Short generously made her fieldnotes from additional research work in Fu and Han Shan counties available to us as background for this chapter.

1. In early versions of this chapter we translated *gongzuo* as "work." Various readers of the earlier versions pointed out that *gongzuo* can also be translated as "job," and that by using "work" we insert a more evaluative tone than is appropriate. Because of this concern, we have chosen to use the term *gongzuo* in our essay rather than its various translations: "work," "activity," "job."

2. The larger purpose of the interviews was to explore work and child care, and for this reason we selected mothers, fathers, and grandmothers of children or grandchildren less than seven years of age.

3. The county *(xian)* names are pseudonyms, referring to the economic level of the counties. Fu means wealthy; Han Shan means cold mountain, implying poverty.

4. The focus group interviews were designed in relation to the China Health and Nutrition Survey. The four sites are sampling units within the larger survey, and as such, were selected as part of a probability design.

THREE

What Is Work?

Comparative Perspectives from the Social Sciences

Rachel A. Rosenfeld

A full understanding of individuals' lives in the context of social change requires a broad definition of work: effort resulting in some product or service for exchange or domestic consumption.[1] Work can be done in the
home (broadly defined)[2] or outside it. It can be done for pay (such as a
wage, a salary, or profit) or direct exchange or neither. In this chapter I use
these two cross-cutting dimensions—work location and returns—to organize discussion about work, gender, and households (see table 3.1). I consider the nature of the work shown within each cell; linkages between the
cells for the same individual, the household, or the economy; "movement"
of work from one cell to another; and, finally, some of the problems with using these dichotomies for work location and for pay. Examples come mainly
from the United States and Europe, although a few from China are drawn
from other chapters of this volume. A full application to the China setting
is undertaken by Harrell in chapter 4.

WORK LOCATION AND RETURNS

Work for Pay outside the Home

Industrialization brings an increase in formal wage jobs, with the timing
and context of this increase related to characteristics of the labor force. In
eighteenth-century America, where land was plentiful and labor was not,
the first factory workers in New England textile plants were farm daughters,
although the typical occupation for employed women then was domestic
servant. Women's participation in the labor force increased over time, especially with the growth of service industries and women's education, but

TABLE 3.1   Categories of Work

	For Pay or Profit	Unpaid
Outside the home	1. Wage Work Informal sector Self-employment	3. Volunteer work Community action Family business
Home based	2. In-home business Home-based employment Informal sector	4. Housework, child care Family business

men maintained their majority in the labor market into the end of the twentieth century: in 1870, women were 15 percent of the U.S. labor force; in 1960, 32 percent; and in 1992, 47 percent (Reskin and Padavic 1994, 25; Weiner 1985). In many developing countries that are part of the capitalist world system, industrialization first brought more industrial wage jobs for men. During the late 1960s and early 1970s, however, women—often young, single women—became the favored workers for transnational corporations as part of the "global assembly line." With the help of improved transportation and communication technology, as well as political agreements establishing export zones with low or no tariffs, transnational corporations could move labor-intensive parts of production (and later, of information processing) to Third World countries, where labor (especially women's labor) was very cheap (Ward 1988). While such jobs generally make up a small part of total and manufacturing employment, they have been the location of rising participation for women. Along the U.S.-Mexico border, for example, where the *maquila* (assembly plant) program was established in 1965, women comprised 80 percent of the workers in electronics, apparel, and other light industries by the mid-1980s (Tiano 1990).

Women's wage work outside the home has been higher in state socialist countries and in others with ideologies of gender equality based on equal labor force participation, such as Sweden, the former German Democratic Republic (East Germany), and China. But even in these countries, men's employment rates are somewhat higher. In the former German Democratic Republic, among those born in 1951–53 and 1959–61, 97 percent of men and 88 percent of women held jobs for pay in 1989 (Trappe and Rosenfeld 1998). In urban China, earlier retirement for women than for men explains some of the gender difference in employment (chap. 7). In rural China, gender differences in nonfarm employment are found among the married, although not the unmarried, population (chap. 8).

The boundaries between paid jobs outside the home and other types of work are not always sharp, however. Jobs in the former category are not just "regular" office, shop, and factory jobs, but also include paid work in agriculture and other primary industries. Industrialization, commercialization, and revolution can increase the relative number of agricultural wage and salary workers, as compared with unpaid family farm laborers. Outside jobs (cell 1) also include self-employment situated away from home, which describes about 60 percent of the self-employment outside of agriculture in the United States (U.S. Bureau of the Census 1998, tables 661, 662).

Two additional distinctions relevant in this context are those between contingent and noncontingent work and between informal and formal sector jobs. Polivka and Nardone (1989, 11) define a contingent job as "any job in which an individual does not have an explicit or implicit contract for long-term employment or one in which the minimum hours worked can vary in an unsystematic manner." American social scientists use the term "contingent work" to describe flexible work arrangements increasingly used by employers since the 1980s to control labor costs in the face of rising international competition, economic downturns, and rapidly changing markets. Migrant agricultural laborers, restaurant servers scheduled day-by-day or week-by-week, and college teachers hired "by the course" are examples. While some workers choose such jobs because they have alternative sources of income or are involved in additional activities (e.g., school, child care), for others it is the choice of these jobs or no jobs. Women seem to predominate among contingent workers, although according to recent U.S. statistics, the gender difference is most evident among the employed between the ages of 20 and 44 (Bureau of Labor Statistics 1995).

The informal sector is a somewhat related concept. Portes and Sassen-Koob (1987, 31) define the informal sector as "all work situations characterized by the absence of (1) a clear separation between capital and labor; (2) a contractual relationship between both; and (3) a labor force that is paid wages and whose conditions of work and pay are legally regulated. . . . The informal sector is structurally heterogeneous and comprises such activities as direct subsistence, small-scale production and trade, and subcontracting to semiclandestine enterprises and homeworkers." Researchers argue that this type of work is growing in contemporary advanced and developing economies as a result of globalization of the division of labor. "Capitalists and TNCs [transnational corporations] . . . use informal-sector workers, particularly women, instead of formal wage workers to avoid labor legislation and to keep labor cost low" (Ward 1990a, 2). This concept puts more emphasis on the vulnerability of the worker than on job insecurity and variable hours. Zhang (chap. 10) gives examples of exploitation of young unmarried women from rural areas working as wage laborers for small family enterprises in the near suburbs of Beijing.

Home-Based Business or Employment

One feature of industrialization is change in the location of work from farm or home workshop to factory, office, or store. In both industrialized and contemporary less-industrialized countries, however, the home can be a place for paid or income-generating work. The boundary between "work" and "nonwork"—spatially, temporally, and perceptually—can be very fluid in this case. In the early twentieth century in the United States, for example, because of norms and sanctions among many ethnic groups and employers against married women's employment outside the home, women earned money at home by taking in boarders, doing piecework, or producing crafts. Many of these efforts were not officially recognized as work (Bose 1984). In the United States, China, and elsewhere, there is a continuing tradition of agricultural and nonagricultural sidelines run by farm women that bring cash into the family (chap. 6; Entwisle et al. 1995; Sachs 1983). Even if not always recognized as results of "real" work, women's egg, butter, and vegetable sales can be crucial for the family economy (Fink 1986; Rosenfeld 1985). Under some circumstances, this lack of recognition of in-home work can have advantages. Margery Wolf (1985) discovered that because under some Chinese Communist Party (CCP) regimes rural women's sidelines were classified as housework, these women could earn private incomes sometimes greater than those of men working full-time on the farm collective.

Among nonagricultural households also, many small businesses operate from the home, and the informal sector often involves home workers. In industrialized societies, technological advances with respect to equipment size and communications may increase the proportion of workers who are paid for work they do at home. In 1997, 18 percent of workers in the United States did all or some of their work on their primary job in the home, with about a third of these self-employed (U.S. Bureau of the Census 1998, table 663). Some—but not all—of these jobs provide flexibility for workers and employers. Home workers in the United States tend to be either clerical and blue-collar contingent workers or high-status professionals in "regular" jobs to which they telecommute, blurring the line between home and office (Reskin and Padavic 1994; Tomaskovic-Devey and Risman 1993). In China, economic reforms have led to an explosion of family-owned small businesses, and often production activities take place in the same space as domestic activities (chap. 10).

Working for pay within the home seems more compatible with women's domestic work than work away from home. In the United States, however, there is not a large overall difference by sex (U.S. Bureau of the Census 1998, table 663). The proportion of those working at home who were self-employed rises with age and is especially high at 65 and over (U.S. Bureau of the Census 1993, 404), suggesting that those in life cycle stages other than child rearing find working at home convenient. In research on rural China based on data collected in 1989, Entwisle and colleagues (1995) reported that men were more likely than women to work in a small household business (although they did not distinguish whether the business was located in the home or outside it).

Work without Pay outside the Home

As discussed later, it can be difficult to draw the lines for work/nonwork in this cell, given the general definition of work I use. I include here unpaid family workers in businesses located away from home, and also organized volunteer work and other community efforts. Blau, Ferber, and Winkler (1998, 56) define volunteer work as "tasks, performed without direct reward in money or kind, that mainly benefit others rather than the individuals themselves or their immediate family." In the United States, the proportion of the population doing volunteer or more broadly defined community work seems to have declined over the last two decades. Women are somewhat more involved than men, although the types of volunteer work differ by gender (F. Blau, Ferber, and Winkler 1998). Among American farm families in 1980, men and women were about equally likely to be part of a community organization such as a church, PTA, or Rotary (57 and 61 percent), but men were much more likely to be part of farm-oriented organizations (Rosenfeld 1985). At least some of this unpaid work is done for pay by government or private workers in other countries.

Community action is often studied as political activity rather than as work and tends to be described in community case studies. In China one might put the efforts of "model workers" (e.g., chap. 5), neighborhood vigilance committees, and political activists in this cell, as well as "volunteer" political duties required by the Communist Party. Corvée and other kinds of forced labor might also fit here.

Unpaid Work in the Home

If a regular wage job is the "typical" job for nonfarm men in many settings around the world, unpaid work in the home or compound is "typical" work for women. Here the boundaries between work and nonwork, and among types of work, can be especially cloudy, with consequences for the recognition and value of women's activities in particular. Housework is often trivialized and neither considered "real" work (Hochschild 1989) nor given high priority. Work that can be viewed as domestic work is not valued or rewarded as highly as the same work done elsewhere (chaps. 2 and 10).

Everywhere, even in the most gender-egalitarian countries, women do most of the housework, child care, and elder care (F. Blau, Ferber, and Winkler 1998). There is, however, some variation in the unevenness of the workload across countries and among groups within countries. The division of household labor between employed spouses looks surprisingly similar in the United States and Sweden, for example, with husbands doing about a quarter of household tasks, on average, although Swedish men do somewhat less child care and slightly more household chores than American men (Kalleberg and Rosenfeld 1990). Entwisle and colleagues (1994) found that in China, among couples in which the wives were 20–44 years of age, about three-quarters of the wives did laundry and cooked the week before the survey, while three-quarters of the husbands did neither. Urban husbands did more of this work than rural ones, however.

Unpaid home-based work also includes other subsistence work, such as gardening, canning, sewing, and knitting. According to the 1980 U.S. Farm Women Survey, most farms or ranches had gardens or animals raised for family consumption, and three-quarters of the women said raising vegetables or animals for the table was a regular duty (Rosenfeld 1985, 57). In addition, women often work in family businesses, even though they do not receive direct pay for this and are not listed in surveys as "owner or operator." This is certainly true for farm and rural women in both the United States and China (Entwisle et al. 1994; Rosenfeld 1985). Zhang's fieldwork shows that among Beijing's "floating" population, women's labor-intensive production work done in the home can be viewed as "chores" rather than "real" work, in contrast with men's part of the production and marketing process, which takes place more often away from home: "In men's narratives of labor division and productivity, the roles of their wives and daughters as the primary producers and supervisors of production often fade away in the domestic background" (chap. 10, page 187).

LINKS AMONG TYPES OF WORK:
INDIVIDUALS, HOUSEHOLDS, AND THE ECONOMY

The boundaries between categories do not indicate mutually exclusive activities. The type of work a person does in one category of work can affect the work he or she does in another domain and have interconnections with the work of other household members as well (chap. 15). The most obvious linkage is between unpaid home work and work categorized in the other cells. Women's underrepresentation in market work, especially in "regular" wage or salary jobs, is often attributed to their greater responsibility in the home. As noted, women spend more time on domestic work and less on paid work than men in all countries for which data are available—more and less developed, capitalist and state socialist (F. Blau, Ferber, and Winkler 1998). What varies among countries are gender differences in total work weeks and the balance of paid work outside the home and unpaid work within the home. American women who are employed spend less time on domestic work than those not in the workforce, although it is only recently that employed women's husbands have increased the time they spend on housework.

Causality may also vary: Women may spend less time on domestic work *because* they are employed, or they may cut down their job hours because of greater domestic responsibility. In most Western countries, being female, married, and a mother make it more likely that one is employed part-time, although countries differ considerably in the proportion of the female workforce with reduced hours (Blossfeld and Hakim 1997; Rosenfeld 1993; Rosenfeld and Birkelund 1995). Reductions in job hours in order to care for young children, for example, are not always possible in the United States but have been part of public policy in Sweden and Norway, as well as in other countries such as West Germany (Kalleberg and Rosenfeld 1990; Trappe and Rosenfeld 1998).[3] Controlling for family configuration, spouse's employment, job characteristics, sex role attitudes, and demographic attributes, Kalleberg and Rosenfeld (1990) examined reciprocal effects between hours employed and participation in domestic work among those employed and married or cohabiting in the United States, Canada, Norway, and Sweden. They found no effects for men in any of these countries, but found that hours employed had a negative effect on housework participation for employed American wives—and effects in the opposite direction for women in Sweden and Norway.

As noted, in the United States the greatest sex differences in contingent work emerge in the childbearing ages. Women's informal work has also been described as allowing women to both care for their families and earn money. "Flexibility" and employment at home, however, do not always lead to this outcome. Piecework in the home at low per-unit rates can lead to very long work days and require the labor of other family members, including children (Ward 1990a). "Flexible" jobs can mean heavy work demands that do not fit with home responsibilities. Reskin and Padavic (1994, 160) cite Costello's (1989) interview with a home worker who processed insurance claims: "If you'd [unexpectedly] get six hours of work someday and you have two little kids at home and you only have three hours worth of TV, when are you going to get the work done?" (see also Rosenfeld 1996).

Implicit in much of the discussion about trade-offs between regular wage jobs and other sorts of work as a result of domestic responsibilities is the idea that there are other earners in a woman's family, especially a husband. Not all households have a husband, however, or a husband who has income, or other people who bring in money (Tiano 1990). Even when there are other earners, women's earnings are often important, especially when household income is low. Tiano's study of northern Mexico shows that women working in *maquiladoras* (foreign-owned assembly plants) and the service sector had jobs because of economic necessity, even when they were not the only ones in the household who were employed.

More generally, though, paid jobs can support the unpaid work of the same individual or others in the family. Off-farm jobs held by varying combinations of household members—depending on the characteristics of spouses in particular and on local labor demand—can help finance farm production (Rosenfeld 1985). At the same time, unpaid work in the home helps support other kinds of work. In the "two-person" career, a wife who entertains, does the husband's research and clerical tasks, and frees him from household chores can be important to a husband's career success (Pavalko and Elder 1993). Employees' gardening and other subsistence food production can allow Third World employers to offer below-subsistence wages (Ward 1990a). Fink (1986, 56) notes that in the United States "Farm commodity production did not stand on its own or pay its own bills during much of the period from 1880 to 1940; rather, it was subsidized by a subsistence economy that has been ignored because it was women's work."

Women's paid work outside the home can create opportunities for paid and unpaid work by others, both inside and outside the household. Household members other than the mother care for children. In the United States, in 1993, almost a third of the children five years of age and younger were cared for at least part of the time in their home by someone other than the mother, in some cases by a relative or friend without pay, in other cases by someone who was paid (F. Blau, Ferber, and Winkler 1998, 329). Some families take on shift work, so that one parent is always available to care for the children (Presser 1989). A mother who is a nurse, for example, might work the evening or night shift, while the father has a morning shift. There is a generational aspect to such combinations of paid and unpaid work. If women in the grandmother generation are still employed when their daughters are having their families (as is true among baby boomers in the United States), they may not be available to help with child care. On the other hand, the daughters may have to modify their own employment patterns to care for those in the grandparent generation (Rosenfeld 1996). In China, the changing ratio of children to parents and grandparents with the introduction of the one-child policy may have future consequences for such intergenerational exchanges of women's work especially.

Connelly (1992) demonstrates that in the United States women with children are more likely than others to run home day care centers—work that falls into cell 2. Byerly (1986), however, found that in southern mill towns white women employed as textile factory operatives would spend roughly a day's wages for an African American woman to stay in their homes caring for their children and doing other domestic work—informal sector work in cell 1. Such arrangements often depend on the presence of lower class and/or subordinate racial or ethnic groups with few alternative work opportunities (Glenn 1992). Before Equal Employment Opportunity legislation, no African American women—and only a few African American men—were hired in the mills Byerly studied.

For China, where there is little part-time employment in nonfarm wage and salary jobs, Entwisle and colleagues (1994, 36) found almost no difference in work patterns between young married women who did and did not report taking care of children. Interviews with two of the women are instructive. Neither mentions cutting down hours of work to care for young children: "Taking care of children is first priority, so you cannot reduce the time spent on this. But you can ask others to help you." "It is very important to go to work, but a person should not reduce time on child care for this reason. We would not ask relatives for help. We would hire a nanny." As Hershatter (chap. 5) discusses, however, 1950s labor heroines were not always in a position to be successful in caring for their children as well as fulfilling their duty to display their heroic virtues.

Linkages between demand for unpaid labor in the home and paid work in the labor market are not just at the individual or household level. Policies that try to help women balance home and job responsibilities, such as paid maternity leaves and reduced hours for mothers (and sometimes fathers), can affect the kinds of jobs to which women have access. In Sweden and the former German Democratic Republic, for example, women were steered away from jobs with higher earnings and authority because of the assumption that they would temporarily leave their jobs or reduce their hours when they had children, as allowed by state policy (Rosenfeld, Van Buren, and Kalleberg 1998; Trappe and Rosenfeld 1998).

Elsewhere, women are selected into jobs based on marital status and fertility. Tiano (1990, 217) states, "For many, particularly older, partnered [Mexican] women who occupy the most vulnerable sector of the female labor force . . . , jobs in the formal service sector are difficult to obtain, as are positions as live-in domestic servants. Thus, their main employment alternatives involve income-generating activities in the informal sector." Ward (1990a, 12) cites Enloe (1983) as showing, "In Puerto Rico . . . TNCs [transnational corporations] have encouraged increased investments in sterilization and birth-control programs to ensure a supply of women workers."

Unpaid work outside the home (cell 3) is another realm of work in which there are important links to other cells at many levels. In the United States, for example, unpaid volunteer work may be very important to one's job, both as a semiformal requirement (to fulfill "community service") and as a source of political and business contacts. For those not employed (students, men and women out of the labor force), volunteer work may provide experience that improves their chances on the job market later. Many volunteer activities, such as those in churches, schools, and youth groups (PTA,

Girl Scouts, 4-H), are related to child rearing and may involve extensions of domestic work (e.g., cooking for bake sales, sewing for school plays). Although volunteer work is an important part of the American upper and upper-middle class woman's role (in contrast with paid work, Ostrander 1984), and although—as already mentioned—the amount of volunteer work seems to have gone down as women's labor force participation has gone up, recent surveys show that employed people actually do more hours of formal and informal volunteer work than those not employed (F. Blau, Ferber, and Winkler 1998, 56–58).

Participation in unpaid activities outside the home can have a widespread impact on the structure of work and individuals' access to it. Work in cooperatives, political organizations, unions, professional associations, and social movements may lead to either change or preservation of existing economic structures and opportunities. Those taking part in the contemporary American women's movement, for example, generally seek to bring about greater opportunity for women in labor market work, as well as greater support for their unpaid domestic work (e.g., increases in affordable child care). Likewise, labor heroines in China were models for the propagation of new economic arrangements the CCP was trying to impose on rural areas (chap. 5). Many American farmers and their families, on the other hand, belong to organizations or do other community work to try to maintain the family farm and, implicitly, its traditional division of labor.

CHANGES IN WORK LOCATION AND REMUNERATION

Up to this point, I have discussed distributions of individuals among and within the four work categories of the typology I propose and linkages among types of work. There are also linkages among the four categories as changes take place in the relative opportunities for different types of work, with consequences for individual work patterns. Work may shift across the boundaries of household and pay, bringing changes in perceptions, value, and rewards.

As already mentioned, one of the biggest changes in the location and remuneration of work comes with industrialization, as more work is done for pay and away from the home or workshop. This has consequences for the division of labor in the household even beyond the linkages between wage work and domestic work discussed above. With industrialization, many of the products women made with unpaid or paid labor in the home, such as candles, cloth, and clothing, become factory-produced commodities. These factory products may be cheaper overall, but obtaining them requires cash. In some situations, women's ability to earn money at home or in the informal sector decreases as household items are manufactured outside the home. In China, for example, spinning and weaving, including producing .

textiles for the market, were part of women's domestic work before 1949, but this private production largely disappeared with the rise of centralized production and state-run factories (chaps. 1 and 5; Entwisle et al. 1995). Reform in China has meant a return to or increase in home production for some rural and urban families (chaps. 10 and 15).

At the same time, with increases in women's paid work away from home, more services that formerly were provided without pay within the home become regular or informal sector jobs. With fewer women providing unpaid work at home, the demand for organized children's activities, prepared or ready-to-prepare food, cleaning services, household appliances, and perhaps certain welfare services are likely to increase. Such demand can be fulfilled through small businesses located in the home and also firms of many sizes outside the home. As noted, where the firm or government has to provide these services for workers, it may discriminate against women.

Although not well documented, jobs involving activities also or formerly performed in the home may be especially likely to employ women (England, Chassie, and McCormack 1982). Overall, women are overrepresented in service industries and nondurable manufacturing, whether in regular or informal sector jobs. Women are more likely than men to be day care and primary school teachers, for example, or to work in the garment industry in many parts of the world. These industries also tend to pay less than others. Zhang (chap. 10) tells of a migrant woman in the near suburbs of Beijing whose husband made her close a profitable leather goods shop but allowed her to run a large day care center. At the same time, what is "masculine" and what is "feminine" varies over time and across cultures, depending on labor demand, characteristics of potential male and female workers, job structures, and the culture. In Europe, for example, where there is school-based dental care, many dentists are women, while in the United States dentistry has only recently increased its proportion of women (F. Blau, Ferber, and Winkler 1998).

PROBLEMS WITH THE FOURFOLD CLASSIFICATION OF WORK

Starting from the cross-classification of paid versus unpaid work and home-based versus non-home-based work highlights often-unrecognized work that women are likely to perform. Discussion of linkages among types of work also leads to consideration of the nature of individual, household, and national work patterns. The problems with this classification are to a large extent created by the very boundaries they demarcate, however, and examining these problems can provide further insights into the complexities of studying work.

One set of problems is that of measurement. The boundaries between categories are not always clear. Certain types of work can be done both inside and outside the home, such as informal-sector work and work in a family enterprise. This distinction may be relatively unimportant in some cases. If one is emphasizing various sources of family income and types of family labor, it may not matter whether such work is done physically in the home. On the other hand, if one is concerned with the extent to which women have activities outside the home and whether domestic tasks take place in the same location as work for pay or profit, then this distinction could be important. Of course at times, even if one wishes to distinguish between "home" and "outside" work, deciding where to put a particular case can be difficult (e.g., if the family business is very close to the residence).

The Chinese "inside/outside" distinction illustrates these tensions. Inside work was (and is) women's work: "men farm, women weave" (chap. 1). While this ideal of women's work as "inside" was sometimes taken literally, it masked the reality that women were also in the fields and at the markets (chap. 5). The contrast between the literal ideal and the actual location of activities is important. On the other hand, using the definition of for/ with versus outside the family, rather than physically inside versus outside the home, is very useful, especially in the Chinese context. This dichotomy helps conceptualize work in the last half of the twentieth century in China. Small, family-owned businesses, for example, would be "inside" regardless of where they were located, while new joint-venture employment would be outside. Zhang (chap. 10), though, shows that the physical location of the family business can make a difference in women's involvement. Further, seeing such a distinction as fixed would ignore the changes over time in what is defined as "inside" and therefore suitable for women, as compared with "outside" and therefore inappropriate for women. Zhang stresses how the boundaries of the spaces to which women are allowed free access in the different social strata of the "floating" population change, and how socially constructed spaces shape and are shaped by gender relations. It is not just the site where an activity takes place but also the meaning associated with that site that influences who does the work, in what way, and for what value.

Measurement problems also arise when a person does more than one task at a time. Child care is often combined with other tasks in the home or family business, making it hard to calculate time spent in child care. When there is a family business, determining where production for the family ends and production for pay or profit begins can be difficult. A woman making tamales to sell could also be making her family's dinner. Coleman and Elbert (1983, 3) interviewed one American farm woman who, "when asked to enumerate the hours spent in farm versus home tasks, opened the lid of her washing machine, revealing a common mixture of barn suits, children's jeans, and furniture covers all tumbling around in the soapy water." Someone with a large garden can sell off the "extra" produce without con-

sidering this a home-based business. The worker may see one activity or another as the "real" work at a given time (see also chap. 2).

What is done for "pay or exchange" is also not always clear. In his text on
the sociology of work, Hall (1994, 2–3) gives the example of his being a volunteer member of the ski patrol who gets ski lift tickets and discounts on ski
equipment. Even more difficult for classification purposes are situations
where people provide information, goods, or services without a direct reward. This is true in many community and political efforts, as suggested earlier, but in more private contexts as well. Could "neighborliness" be considered work—for example, helping an elderly neighbor whose family lives
in another state? This might be considered unpaid work outside the home,
even though there is no direct pay or exchange.

A second set of boundary problems involves the household. When considering different types of work and how they affect and are affected by the
work of other household members, what are the boundaries of the household? Does "household" refer to people who are in the same residence, regardless of whether they are family members and regardless of whether they
are paid for home-based tasks? Alternatively, is it better to talk about "families" rather than "households"? Davis (chap. 14) emphasizes the importance of distinguishing between families and households for understanding
what has been going on recently in Chinese urban housing markets. Family
obligations and rights extend beyond coresident units, and household
arrangements relate to understandings of such reciprocities. Davis shows
how family members redistribute themselves over households with changes
in marital status and apartment ownership.

Households may be formed by unrelated individuals. In the Philippines,
for example, groups of young factory-worker women living together to save
on living expenses often share chores such as cooking or getting water. On
the other hand, some households contain paid domestic help, hired hands,
or wage laborers (Byerly 1986; Fink 1986). These workers' earnings may
help support households other than the ones in which they live. Households can also subsidize the wage work of family members elsewhere. Diane
Wolf (1990) reports that in Central Java not only did daughters working in
factories and living away from home send back only a small proportion of
their wages, but families actually subsidized low factory wages by providing
daughters with food, household goods, and sometimes cash. At the same
time, savings and gifts from factory wages helped the families survive during
a crop failure. Again, simply using a "family/outside" distinction would miss
the importance of physical location and its meaning; concurrently, it is important to keep in mind family connections beyond a particular household.

A third set of problems is due to the fact that this classification system
does not go far enough in examining patterns and their variations. It sets

up overly strict boundaries around different types of work. Examining types of work separately can be useful for recognizing work that might otherwise be overlooked. For example, a more complete understanding of the family economy can be achieved by looking at a woman's work in the separate cells and then the linkages among the cells for her and other family members. Further, while individuals and households do often have the same general interests, this is not always the case, and power differences among family members can influence the particular household division of labor. Diane Wolf (1990) emphasizes that the factory work of the daughters she studied was not always something the parents controlled, nor was it always economically rational for the family in the short run. Focusing on the work of different family members individually makes it easier to study this (see also chaps. 10 and 14).

On the other hand, this classification scheme deemphasizes combinations of work activities. Entwisle et al. (1994) make a good case for considering sets of work activities and their variations. Women often work double or triple "shifts" made up of formal paid work, unpaid domestic work, and income-generating sidelines. But some women (and men) are likely to have fewer shifts than others, and there is variation among people in the content of each shift. "Indeed, it may be that these *combinations* rather than individual tasks are the object of negotiation, struggle, choice, and control within households. . . . Studying the implications of one activity for another runs the risk of confusing causality for joint choice" (Entwisle et al. 1994, 38–39).

Looking at the work patterns for the household as a whole is also worthwhile. The New Home Economics (Becker 1981) sees households as decision-making units striving to maximize a household utility function. Households are assumed to allocate their members' labor on the basis of relative skills, wages, opportunities, and substitutability. Men specialize in paid work because their time is more valuable than women's in the labor market (they earn more), and women specialize in home production for family consumption. Moen and Wethington (1992) note that such a theory is often applied after the fact, ignores power differences within the family or household, and misses "nonrational" allocation of family resources that are cultural or personal (as illustrated in D. Wolf 1990). It still emphasizes, however, the agency of the family or household in the face of its immediate or changing economic environment (chap. 15).

In general, households respond to changing circumstances—whether within the family or in the larger economic structure—by changing their consumption and production patterns, directly or indirectly. Changing the household allocation of labor is part of this. Lobao and Meyer (1995), for example, found that when there were work changes during the 1980s farm crisis in the United States, women in Ohio farm households tended to increase time spent on household tasks and off-farm work and decrease their farm involvement. When the men made any change, they also tended to increase their time spent in off-farm jobs, but they decreased time for household tasks and increased time overall on farm tasks. (Unfortunately, the results are reported separately for men and women, rather than by family.) Looking at the entire set of members and their work simultaneously is important in studies of household or family well-being and reaction to change, even if there is not a coordinated "family strategy" (Moen and Wethington 1992).

CONCLUSIONS

I defined work as effort resulting in some product or service for exchange or domestic consumption. Such activities can be done for pay or without pay, be home-based or performed mainly outside the home. Within each cell formed by this cross-classification, there are a number of different kinds of work. Paid work outside the home can be a "regular" office, shop, or factory job; self-employment; an agricultural wage or salary job; or some less regulated, less stable, and less secure work. Paid work within the home can be part of self-employment or can be for someone else. Unpaid work outside the home may be volunteer work, neighboring, or community or political action. Unpaid work within the home includes child care and other domestic work, but also working in a family business. Work in one category may be linked to work in another category at the individual, household, and national levels, as illustrated by the discussion of child care. Further, the same activity may become work in another category when there are changes in the overall work structure, as when many domestic tasks become paid jobs outside the home. While the cross-classification of location and pay highlights these processes, this model also raises problems of measurement, scope, and integration. At least some of these problems are the result of trying to force boundaries on different types and locations of work, insisting on dichotomies in the face of more complex realities. One value of examining the transition from Maoist to reform-era China is that, as with the "inside/outside" distinction, these boundaries are even more fluid than in many capitalist, advanced industrialized societies, where "work" is more—but certainly not completely—segregated as "household" and "nonhousehold."

This chapter is more conceptual than theoretical. It describes types of work and the linkages among them without pushing on to generalize about what leads to the development of various kinds of connections and how they affect individuals' lives. Some of this theorizing has been done in the women-in-development and informal-sector literature (e.g., Ward 1990a) and some as reactions to the New Home Economics. The discussion in this chapter has focused on the various dimensions of work and on definitional problems—and suggests the need for a multidimensional approach to comparative and longitudinal research on gender, households, and work. Further conceptual development, however, needs to be driven by theory about dynamics of the work patterns of individuals, households, and the economy.

NOTES

I thank Heike Trappe and the conference participants for their useful comments.

1. One textbook on the sociology of work adds that the effort or activity "is considered by the individual to be work" (Hall 1994, 5), emphasizing the subjective nature of this concept. It is not only the individual doing the task, of course, but also the perceptions of others that set the boundaries of activities considered to be "real" work and that potentially affect their value and rewards. I will not extend the definition to efforts to manage interpersonal relationships, such as "emotion work" or "expressive tasks" (England and Farkas 1986; Hochschild 1983), unless this is in the context of providing a formal service, such as psychotherapy or community mediation. Even this example illustrates how difficult it is to set boundaries on which activities are "work."

2. Home-based work can include activities that are part of domestic or income-generating work done mainly in the home, but that actually take place outside the home, such as shopping, doing errands, or distributing home-produced crafts or food.

3. Reduction in mothers' hours was part of East German family policy, although the regular work week there was 43.75 hours and the reduced hours 40 hours a week. Some women balanced responsibility in the work force and the home by temporarily taking a job for which they were overqualified (Trappe and Rosenfeld 1998).

FOUR

The Changing Meanings of Work in China

Stevan Harrell

All revolutions, including the industrial one, are in a sense about the division of labor—and, of course, the way it relates to ownership of property. But the Chinese revolution, beginning with the self-strengtheners of the late nineteenth century, continuing through the significant failures of the Republic and the grander and more significant failures of collective socialism to the partial return to household-based labor in the present Reform era,[1] has been particularly concerned with issues of who should do what kinds of work. This chapter is about the ways in which arguments about labor—about what is work and what is not; about the proper kinds of work for men and women, educated and uneducated, rich and poor; and specifically about the differences between household-based and non-household-based labor—have evolved as part of the broader discussions about what a post-collectivist Chinese society should be like. In doing so, this chapter draws on the materials and insights provided by the authors of the first three chapters in part 1, as well as on material discussed in later chapters.

As Rosenfeld points out in chapter 3, a useful heuristic device is to classify work done in any society in a two-by-two table, divided into work inside and outside the home, and work for compensation or not (see table 3.1 in chap. 3). This gives us four general types of work: remunerated labor outside the home (cell 1); remunerated labor inside the home (cell 2); unremunerated labor outside the home (cell 3) and unremunerated labor inside the home (cell 4). In any given societal arrangement of work roles, differential values will be placed on the four types of work, and different combinations of the four types will be considered appropriate for particular types of persons: men and women, old and young, noble and commoner, and so on.

A classification like Rosenfeld's is an appropriate starting point for trying to sort out how the proper relationships between work, gender, and household have been defined and contested through Chinese history, and particularly in the transition from the collective to the Reform era. I would make only one refinement, which Rosenfeld herself suggests: we should consider the division between household-based and non-household-based production to be at least as important as that between work that physically takes place inside the house or compound and work that takes place outside. We cannot, for reasons that will become apparent, shift our boundary frame all the way from the house to the household, but in order to understand the discussions about gender and household, we need to talk about the household organizational boundary most of the time, and consider the physical walls as the boundary only a little of the time. With this caveat in mind, let us examine how ideas about work have changed in relation to household and gender through the course of the Chinese revolution, and particularly in the transition from the collectivist to the Reform economy.

THE DIVISION OF LABOR IN PREINDUSTRIAL CHINA

Our historical baseline is conveniently provided by Mann, who shows in chapter 1 that all through the imperial era of Chinese history, scholars and officials thought of the proper organization of labor as household-based. The ideal empire was an accumulation of households that were primarily self-sufficient, though they might be dependent on markets to one degree or another. The role of the laboring individual was that of a partner in a household division of labor, in which those tasks that could be done without leaving the ideational space of the household itself—its house, fields, gardens, and, for some urban families, also its commercial properties— could be performed by the household's female members. Those tasks that required extensive forays into the wider world—into markets, trading centers, or official circles—were restricted to the males. In this division of labor, then, the "inside," or female domain, referred sometimes to the physical interior of a family's compound, whereas at other times and places it might also include farmwork. Agriculture stood somewhere between "inside" and "outside," so it was predominantly but not exclusively male, while such things as transport and politics were supposed to be done by men only.

This preindustrial ideal division of labor would place just about all activities into the two bottom cells of Rosenfeld's grid: household-based, whether remunerated or not. Ideally all work was household-based, because all property ideally belonged to households. The only exceptions were corvée, military service, officialdom, and quite unusual (and exclusively male) practices of hiring out for labor (usually in transport) and exploiting resources as a collective band (usually in mining). As Ebrey (1984) has shown, many household moralists thought it was perfectly acceptable to try to dodge corvée or military service, and long-term hired labor and mining partnerships stood conceptually on the lowest rungs of the social ladder, outside the four honorable occupations of scholar, farmer, artisan, and merchant. Thus most remunerated activities outside the household lay outside the normal division of labor. There were a few exalted bureaucrats and a lot of despised policemen, soldiers, and coolies who worked outside of the nexus of household ownership and management of resources. But certainly over 90 percent of the population worked in family enterprises of one sort or another.

Within the family enterprise, the distinction between work for direct compensation and not for direct compensation (between cell 2 and cell 4) was really not very clear. Fieldwork was mostly done by men, though how exclusively male it was depended on the region of the country and the season of the year; women in the south tended to go into the fields more than their northern sisters, and where strictures were relaxed, they were of course most often relaxed at planting or harvest time. Mostly male fieldwork combined with mostly female gardening and animal husbandry and exclusively female cooking, cleaning, and sewing to produce livelihood. One side could not exist without the other, as long as people needed to eat as well as have some place to live and someone to prepare the food. Quantitative analysis might have yielded some figures about whether men's or women's labor products were more or less likely to be exchanged rather than consumed directly, but my hunch is that this, too, varied according to the region. Men might have grown only grain exclusively for household consumption, or they might have also grown vegetables or tobacco or cotton for sale; women might have made cloth either to wear or to sell; they might have either cooked or sold the eggs from the family's chickens or the meat from its slaughtered pigs.

As Mann points out, there was one word, *lao,* that covered every kind of activity in this household-based production system, from the mind work of the scholar to the field labor of the ordinary male householder to the inside labor performed by women. Semantic distinctions of course were made, but there was no kind of productive activity that could not be accommodated under the general term *lao.*

CHANGES THAT CAME WITH EARLY INDUSTRIALIZATION

One of the most important changes that comprise the historical transition from agrarian to industrial societies is the transition from an economy in which almost everyone lives off of family property to one in which almost everyone lives off of a salary earned in a non-family-based enterprise. When industry and large-scale wage labor came to China's large cities in the beginning of the twentieth century, China was faced for the first time with the prospect of a system in which all four cells of Rosenfeld's table were possible and present. China thus needed new rules to guide the new division of labor—who should work in non-household-based enterprises, who should continue to work in the household, how should compensation be structured for different kinds of work, and what should be the prestige value of one kind of work relative to another?

It was conceptually rather easy to create new rules for male labor outside the household context. After all, even though hired labor was not part of the ideal model set forth in Mann's chapter, there were in fact always a fairly sizable minority of males who worked for wages. For women, the problem was somewhat more difficult. Of course there had always been women who worked for wages as servants (Pruitt 1967) or, among the poorest classes, as transport workers, tea pickers, and so on. But women working outside the household context ran into a double ideological barrier: not only were they, like their menfolk, violating the ideal of the household as a self-sufficient productive unit; they were also violating traditional norms of chastity and family honor that placed women inside the *house* as well as inside the *household*. Whereas men who worked for wages had the stigma of being poor, women who worked for wages had the added stigma of being immoral. Hershatter (1986) describes the reluctance of Tianjin families to send their daughters to work in the cotton mills at the beginning of the twentieth century because of the possibility of this stigma.

There were compromises to be made, however, as in so many countries in the early stages of industrialization (D. Wolf 1992; Ong 1987). One of the most important ones was allowing young, unmarried women to take low-wage manufacturing jobs (primarily in textiles) where they could earn supplemental income for their households and do so in a cloistered dormitory atmosphere where their chastity was somewhat less likely to be compromised than if they had been allowed to live on their own or if they had only worked 60 or 70 hours per week instead of the somewhat longer week they actually worked.

Still, by the end of the Republican era in China, the overwhelming majority of the population (probably nearly 90 percent) was still rural (Emerson 1971, 188), and most rural people were household-based farmers—either owners or tenants. Even in the largest and most modern city of Shanghai, in 1957, immediately before the large-scale socialist transformation, the urban work force was reported to consist of over 40 percent in self-employment or family-operated businesses, and about 60 percent in wage labor or salaried jobs (Howe 1971, 220). The trend toward wage employment was thus on its way by the time of the founding of the People's Republic , but was by no means complete even in Shanghai, and certainly less advanced elsewhere. The greatest changes in the division of labor still lay ahead in 1949.

THE SOCIALIST REVOLUTION

The Communists set out to change the division of labor fundamentally by making two kinds of changes. Production was to be moved out of the household into the public sphere, and all adults, male or female, were to take part in this public-sphere production. This was accomplished in somewhat different ways in the cities and in the rural areas.

In urban China, household-based production was effectively abolished. Family-owned businesses were confiscated, nationalized, or absorbed into collective enterprises, and everyone with a paid job (which, after 1958, was everyone who was not a child, a student, a disabled person, a pensioner, or an illegal migrant), became part of a state or collective work unit, or *danwei*. These work units not only paid almost all wages in urban China during this time; they also controlled access to many kinds of services that could not be purchased with cash, such as housing, medical care, and schooling (Walder 1986). In addition, women as well as men were expected to engage in wage labor during this time, so that there was no longer, in the ideology at least, a difference between the woman as the "inside" worker and the man as the "outside" worker. Both worked outside for wages—cell 1 of Rosenfeld's table. Cell 4, unremunerated household-based work, however, seems to have remained primarily the province of women, giving them a kind of two-shift existence (Hochschild 1989) similar to those in other industrial countries. In many cases this also kept women from rising to higher-paid or more responsible positions in their work units, because everybody knew they had to cook, clean, and take care of children. Work in cell 3, unremunerated activities outside the household, also became very important at this time, as people were required to engage in political meetings, neighborhood committees, and intermittently, in political campaigns.

Paradoxically, it was cell 2, household-based work to produce exchange value, that practically disappeared in urban China during the collectivist era. This had been the mainstay of the petty capitalist class that had been so important in the development of Chinese urban life for the previous thousand years and had also provided an important engine for China's early industrialization (Gates 1996). Now it was not petit bourgeois but just plain bourgeois to engage in any kind of family business, be it in manufacturing or sales, and commercial sales were taken over by large state stores and their smaller outlets.

The legitimacy of wage labor in state and collective enterprises was symbolized by the issuance of a *gongzuo zheng*, or work permit, to every worker or retired worker. This served as a personal identification card until universal *shenfen zheng*, or identity cards, were introduced in the late 1980s. The little red *benzi* (booklet), as it was unofficially called, served as the passport to all kinds of social services and even to such life necessities as the ration coupons that were necessary from the late 1950s to the 1970s to buy grain, cotton, and a host of other commodities. Working for wages in a state or collective enterprise, bureau, or educational or service institution was thus the basis not only of income but also of urban citizenship in collectivist China.

The household, of course, continued to exist in the collectivist era, and was in fact the basis for registration of the urban population (Cheng and Selden 1994). In addition, many people saw the family during this time as a "haven in a heartless world" (Lasch 1979), a place where one could retreat at least temporarily from the rigors of the politics that perfused life in public places, including workplaces. So the household in collectivist urban China stood in a paradoxical position. It was no longer the site of production or exchange activities, and its members depended on their work connections not only for income but for legitimate status as citizens. But at the same time, the state attempted to use the household as the lowest level of social control in the collectivist system: without an urban household registration, one could not obtain legitimate work, and without work or officially approved retired status, one could not obtain the ration coupons that gave access to life's material necessities. The household thus changed from a place of independent production and the organization of livelihood to a space for the local implementation of state control. This is perhaps best indicated by the fact that household-based work—the bottom half of Rosenfeld's grid—was no longer allowed (cell 2) or no longer respected (cell 4). That is, housekeeping was still necessary but was not considered enough to earn a woman full citizenship; for this she had to have paid, outside work, or *gongzuo*.

The household economy and division of labor fared somewhat differently in the rural socialist transformation, in which socialism was implemented through the development of collectivized agriculture. This began with the formation of mutual-aid teams in the early 1950s and proceeded to full-scale collectivization across most of the country in 1956 and the formation of people's communes in 1958. For the first time in Chinese history, agricultural production was not centered around the household.[2] Instead, agricultural workers were organized into production teams, consisting of 20–40 households each, and these teams worked their allocated land collectively, with tasks assigned to individual workers or teams of workers every day or every few days (Huang Shu-min 1989, 66–67; Siu 1989, 229–31). Individual workers were awarded "work points" *(gong fen)* for their labor contribution.

During the heady days of the summer of 1958, China proclaimed to a skeptical world (with no one more skeptical than N. S. Khrushchev) that it had skipped the intermediate stage of socialism and leapt directly forward into communism; all the activities that otherwise would be distributed among all four cells of the table were moved out of the household, and cooking, child care, and in a few places even residential arrangements were turned over to the collective, the better to liberate women's labor for production. This did not last long. Flaws in the incentive structure and the planning process led to possibly the largest famine in world history two years later (Banister 1987, 85). However, the lasting legacy of these failed utopian reforms was the presence of women in the fields, everywhere and at all seasons. As in the urban sector, women's compensation tended to be less than that of men (M. Wolf 1985, 97), because of the tacit recognition (once the extreme collectivism of the Great Leap had faded) that they would still be doing the uncompensated household-based labor of cooking, cleaning, and feeding the pigs and chickens. Their participation in labor for compensation was simply less than that of the men, not because they labored less, but because some of their labor was defined out of the sphere of work for compensation.

The greatest paradox of collective agriculture, however, was that it was in one sense still household-based. The work points that were assigned on the basis of each household member's work were in fact allocated not to the individuals themselves, but to the households to which they belonged, and the harvest was shared out each fall according to the number of work points accumulated by the household as a whole. And since, in contrast to the urban situation, members of production teams lived and worked side by side, the production team was in the end a collection of households, not a *danwei*. The distinction was made clear in the contrast between the two kinds of household registration—*nongcun hukou*, or farm-village registration, and *chengshi hukou*, or urban registration.[3]

It was very difficult to move from village to urban household registration because there was an implicit hierarchy. Not only were the farmers poorer and less educated on the whole, but in the system there was a built-in bias against farmers, despite all the ideological ballyhoo about going to the countryside to emulate the poor- and lower-middle peasants (Bernstein 1977). This bias was at least partially because the farmers were not entirely modern or socialist—that is, their work was, in effect, not yet wholly included in cell 1 of Rosenfeld's table (remunerated work outside the household). Farmers did not *gongzuo*—they did not work at paid jobs in state units. Their economy still bore the stigma of production that was partly household based. Even though their economy was socialist in the sense that the means of production were collectively owned, the fruits of labor were distributed to the household, and in other areas, such as support for education and for the elderly and disabled, farm families had to depend on their own resources. They had labor, *laodong*, and this was ideologically admirable, but they did not have wage jobs, *gongzuo*. This compounded with their poverty and ignorance to make them literally second-class citizens, and the household registration system kept them so. An occasional son or daughter of a farm family could obtain *gongzuo* by becoming a cadre, technician, or teacher, but according to division-of-labor criteria, the farm economy still belonged in the premodern era.

The socialist era thus produced a series of truly revolutionary changes in the division of labor. For one, the same criteria were applied to women's labor as to men's: if it was pursued outside a household-based context and produced social exchange value, it was compensated and valued. If it either was done in the home or did not produce exchange value, it was uncompensated and devalued. This kind of work (cell 4) had to be done anyway and, despite a few desultory campaigns to the contrary that were later discredited by linking them with the hated Jiang Qing, Mao's widow, everyone assumed that women would do it. This meant that women could rarely come up to the same standard of compensation or prestige in their work as men did, whether in a research institution or on an ordinary agricultural production team. In other words, China moved from a vision of a gendered division of labor, where some tasks were appropriate for women and others for men, to ideological denial of the gendered division of labor. Men and women were expected to do the same things, but women were largely incapable of doing them as well because they still had to do those things formerly defined as women's work but now not defined as anything in particular. Instead of men and women each having their own spheres, they now operated in the same sphere, but with women at a disadvantage.

The other revolutionary change was the radical devaluation and virtual elimination of work categorized on the bottom row of Rosenfeld's table, that is, household-based production. This change was only possible if the shift in the parameters of the gender division of labor occurred at the same time, since taking women out of their former role in household production would give them no socially useful role at all unless they also began doing non-household-based work for compensation.

DILEMMAS OF THE REFORM ERA

All this has been reconsidered, and to an extent repealed, during the Reform era. Collective agriculture was the first to go, with the land redistributed to households, in usufruct if not in fee simple, by the early 1980s. Once again, for a short time at least, most inhabitants of rural China were engaging in household-based agriculture. But the division of labor now is not what it was before the great socialist experiments. For one thing, women have not retreated to an "inside" existence, but have remained full-scale agricultural workers in the new family enterprises. For another, rural China did not remain agricultural. The township and village enterprises (*xiangcun qiye*) that were a small part of the rural scene during socialism now grew exponentially (Putterman 1995), so that by the early 1990s only about half the rural population was engaged in agriculture as a primary occupation (State Statistical Bureau 1995, 83–88). Moreover, the trends of the economy's retreat to the household level and development of local industries have combined, so there are now a large number of small- and medium-sized enterprises in rural China that are family owned and operated. Finally, the household registration system was allowed to loosen greatly, so that it is now possible for migrants from rural areas, such as those described by Zhang (chap. 10), to become a significant source of urban labor and rural remittance income (see also chaps. 11 and 12). Migrant labor seems to have its male (construction) and female (service and manufacturing) components, but this is a division of labor within cell 1 (remunerated labor outside the household), not a division between "inside" and "outside."

The cities have changed as much, if not more. Perhaps the most striking thing superficially is the profusion of family-owned stores and restaurants that now line the streets of every major and minor city in China. A large proportion—though still a minority—of labor for exchange value is once again based in the household, and cell 2 (income-generating activities within the household) is once again a prominent sort of labor. Aside from this, there has been a rethinking of the gender division of labor. The activities of cell 4 (housework, child care) continue to be predominantly female, but there is a growing sentiment that this is proper and ought to be recognized as such, that women do not really belong in public life. Women's involvement in the workplace is no longer an aspect of their liberation, as it was considered under socialism, but is a response to household economic needs. Thus we see in Zhang's chapter that among the wealthiest families of the Zhejiang in-migrant community in Beijing, women are once again secluded, if not behind the physical walls of the house, at least behind the conceptual walls of the household, reduced to an existence of *mahjong*, shopping, and ladies' lunches. Most women, of course, continue to work as a matter of necessity or personal fulfillment or both, but it is no longer assumed; traditional ideas about the gender division of labor, though ripped out of their earlier context, can be used to justify not working, and working for less compensation.

Ideas about household-based enterprise and about the gender division of labor are now in great flux. This is reflected in chapter 2, where Henderson, Entwisle, Li, and associates report on their ethno-semantic attempt to determine what people think of as work in two county towns and two nearby villages in Hubei province in the 1990s. In the socialist era, it was easy to define what was *gongzuo:* it was something that gave you a *benzi,* which only came when you worked for wages, and wage work was always, of course, outside the household. Uncompensated housework did not count; in fact it did not count to the extent that women could not get away with doing only that work unless they were retired. Farm work did not count either. It was too tied to the village, the household's livelihood, the necessities of a rural existence, where people did not know how much they would earn in a given year until the harvest came in. Farm families could dream of their sons or daughters going out to *gongzuo;* it meant no longer being a "peasant," a *nongmin* (Cohen 1994) and becoming something more prestigious.

But now these distinctions are breaking down. People clearly do different kinds of work (as reflected in the stories of the Feng family that Henderson, Entwisle, Li, and associates told to their focus groups), and they do them to different extents and for different employers, including their own households. There is no longer a clear line between *gongzuo* and household-based work; both can bring in money. And there is no longer a clear line between *gongzuo* and farmwork, especially since farmwork is increasingly commercialized. We could say that there are continua from the ideal types of salaried work or large-scale entrepreneurship on one end, to uncompensated housework on the other end of one scale or subsistence farming on the other end of another scale, but there are no clear divisions. No wonder there is disagreement in the 1990s over what constitutes *gongzuo.*

Whether or not a new consensus will evolve is unclear. Reform-era China has yet to reach agreement on the rules of enterprise, the division of labor, the nature of gender, or the obligations owed to the household or the family descent line. Socialism imposed a consensus, but it was quickly broken when the socialist economy was dispersed. My own guess is that China will go the way of the United States, where these issues remain in the public arena as points of contention between people with different political, economic, and moral views. Eventually, the term *gongzuo* may revert to something like its presocialist meaning of any kind of labor or profession. But I doubt this will result in general agreement over who should work where, for whom, or how.

NOTES

1. I use the capitalized term "Reform" or "Reforms" to refer to the specific policies known in Chinese as *gaige kaifang,* implemented in 1979, and to the era in which these policy changes have been carried out.

2. There had been other attempts by central governments to deprive households of property rights in land, notably the "equal field" system of the early Tang dynasty (Elvin 1973, 59–61). But as far as we can reconstruct the way in which this system actually worked, communal property was still allocated to households, who farmed it and paid a portion of the crop to the local treasury.

3. In small towns in southern Sichuan Province where I have conducted research, the common term is actually *danwei hukou* (work-unit household regisration).

PART TWO

Recent Trends in Gender and Inequality

FIVE

Local Meanings of Gender and Work in Rural Shaanxi in the 1950s

Gail Hershatter

Following the 1949 Communist victory, the Chinese party-state moved rapidly and forcefully to rearrange rural social relations and the categories through which they were understood. One of those categories was gender. Early accounts of land reform, marriage reform, and collectivization emphasized women's active participation in these campaigns and suggested profound discontinuity, even incommensurability, between rural women's lives before and after Liberation.[1] More recent scholarly accounts have introduced a chorus of skeptical footnotes to this vision of thoroughgoing change. They call attention to the party-state's limited conception of gender reform, centered mainly on Engels' dictum that women should be brought into paid labor outside the home; to its tolerance of patrilocal marriage, which kept women in a subordinate role in both their natal and marital villages; to its willingness to downplay or postpone gender equality in the face of local resistance or in deference to other priorities; and to its construction of collectives on the basis of male kin networks.[2]

Most of these accounts have of necessity been based on close examination of the state-run press and other official sources. Even when the authors read such sources with a critical eye, they cannot help but take state policy pronouncements as the main subject. Rural women appear mainly as objects of state attention. As enthusiastic endorsers of particular state interventions (collectivization, the Marriage Law of 1950), they are audible as well, albeit in formulaic and routinized roles. What is far less accessible to the historian is how government policy and local social practice were each understood, implemented, and mutually implicated in the changing gender landscape of the 1950s. What might we learn about the effects of party-state policy, and its permutations and appropriations at the local level, if we placed a doubly marginalized group—rural women—at the center of an inquiry about the 1950s?

Such an inquiry must begin with some very basic questions, the crudeness of which is itself a measure of how little we know about 1950s history. Viewed from the vantage point of a rural community (and recognizing that rural communities varied greatly), how was women's work affected by the state campaigns of the 1950s: land reform, cooperatives, collectivization, and the Great Leap Forward? What sort of work was considered respectable and desirable for women before Liberation, and how did it change during the 1950s? How did change in women's lives come about in rural villages? Who were the main activists, and how prominent were they in local events? What was the role of the Women's Federation? How was local leadership developed? How did changing work roles for women affect the household economy, work in the home, sexuality, marriage, and child rearing? What were the greatest sources of social tension brought about by women's changing roles? How did the way they thought about themselves, their relationship to their family of origin, and their connection to their family of marriage change? How did they compare their lives to those of their mothers and grandmothers? Looking back now on the 1950s, how do they compare the changes in their lives then to the changes that came later? Investigation of these questions requires consultation of the broadest possible range of sources, including regional and local directives for implementing party policy, local records in city and county archives, Women's Federation work reports, and oral history interviews, as well as contemporaneous works of literature, art, and reportage.

The present chapter is a first attempt to address some of these questions, based on documentary research and fieldwork conducted in Xi'an and the rural areas of central Shaanxi (Guanzhong) in the summer of 1996. Guanzhong is the narrow belt of land along the banks of the Wei River that bisects Shaanxi province on a horizontal axis, with the city of Xi'an roughly at its center.[3] Although it abuts the northern part of the province where the Chinese Communist Party made its wartime headquarters, Guanzhong has a very different rural economy from that of northern Shaanxi, and its history in the decades before 1949 was very little affected by revolutionary events in Yan'an (Mao's stronghold after the Long March). Most peasants in Guanzhong learned of the communists only in mid-1949, when the Eighth Route Army (as it was still called locally) marched through their villages. Unlike the mobilization of women under Party direction in Yan'an, change in women's labor in Guanzhong was an event of the 1950s.

This chapter focuses on the story of one woman, Cao Zhuxiang of Wang Family Village,[4] who became a labor model in Weinan district. It confines itself to the early 1950s, up to the time when lower producers' cooperatives *(chuji she)* were formed in the spring of 1953. In addition to interviews with and written material about Cao herself, I draw on the memories of five women villagers who worked closely with her, two women labor models in other townships, four Women's Federation activists at the county level, and four Women's Federation officials who worked at the provincial level but spent significant time in the 1950s countryside.[5]

The creation of women labor models, these sources suggest, was shaped by a confluence of state policy, overlapping but distinct state agencies, and local circumstance. The state did not so much create a new gendered division of labor as valorize, propagate, and remunerate one that already existed among many poor households in rural Shaanxi. In doing so, state authorities at various levels made use of a group of middle-aged women such as Cao Zhuxiang who were old hands at fieldwork and willing to experiment with new agricultural techniques. These women were not, however, experienced public figures, and state intervention in the form of visiting cadres, agricultural technicians, and Women's Federation officials was crucial in their emergence as recognizable revolutionary icons. In the process, some aspects of their gendered experience were emphasized, but others were ignored or deemphasized by state officials and by the women themselves. Finally, the chapter considers generational difference among rural women, asking what features of early socialist transformation were attractive to the labor models and to the younger women who were trained by them.

GENDERED LABOR IN CENTRAL SHAANXI

Unmarried women in Guanzhong villages, as in many areas of rural China, were not supposed to be seen outside the household. Cao Zhuxiang, born in 1917, recalls that in her youth, girls were not allowed out except at dusk, when they sometimes gathered in groups to discuss their dowries. Her memories and those of other women who grew up poor, however, also provide an insistent counterpoint to this norm of female seclusion. Cao Zhuxiang recalls that she was kept in the family courtyard most of the time after she turned five and was taught to spin and weave—proper "inside" work for women (chap. 1); yet she also remembers pushing her brother's delivery cart (he delivered flour to the county seat) and cleaning out his flour sacks in search of traces of flour. She remembers working in the fields breaking up soil until she was 11 or 12, and subsequently being kept in the house; yet she also describes getting her first menstrual period at age 14 while she was out in the fields harvesting opium. Yu Yinhua, 14 years younger than Cao, hoed and picked cotton in her natal family, while Bao Cuifeng worked from the age of 12 ginning cotton in a rural workshop. The social imperative that unmarried girls stay hidden was so strong that women remember themselves as shut away at home, but the details of their stories suggest otherwise.

If the work of married women is considered as well, the blurring of "inside" and "outside" activities is even more pronounced (see chaps. 1 and 3). "Men till, women weave" was the standard adage describing the gendered division of labor, but it did not encompass the full range of women's work. Cao describes how women would cut and tie the grain at harvest time and work together with men at threshing (men drove the donkey around, women separated the wheat from the chaff). When the harvest was completed, the men of the village would move on to work as transient hired laborers *(maike)* in other villages farther east, presumably leaving the women to manage all the remaining fieldwork, including the harvest of corn and millet. Women did weave, using either homespun or purchased thread. Far from being an activity that confined them to the home, however, weaving brought them into frequent contact with periodic markets, where they went to sell the cloth for money to pay local taxes. As a young married woman in the 1930s and 1940s, future national labor model Zhang Qiuxiang took up a permanent post at market, where she sold homemade shoes and bought materials for the next pair.

The circumstances under which they married—including tragedy in natal and marital families—ensured that all of these women would continue to perform a range of tasks that exceeded the normative restrictions. Cao Zhuxiang was betrothed and married at 16, shortly after her father died in the cholera epidemic of 1932. The bride-price was 24 *da yang* dollars. With her father's death her family fortunes had became precarious enough that her meager dowry was paid for entirely with funds she had earned as a young teenager harvesting opium. Her marital family was scarcely more secure: her husband's father was dead, as was his younger brother, and their widows lived with their three unmarried children in a female-headed household with no adult male labor power. Cao's new husband was three years younger than she. Just after her marriage she worked the land with her husband's aunt, assisted by members of her own natal family: her older brother and her nephew. Almost as soon as her husband was old enough to provide adult labor power, he was snatched from the fields by a conscription patrol. After much family intervention he was released and assigned to a job in Weinan for two years, but returned home ill with tuberculosis and a tumor and died in about 1940. His death left Cao a twenty-four-year-old widow with a six-year-old son, a three-year-old daughter, and a sizable medical debt. At that point she decided that she had to learn to farm, and she asked her brother to teach her the complete range of farming skills, including those not usually performed by women: plowing, hoeing, raking, and leveling the land *(li, chu, pa, mo)*.

Cao's widowhood made her family's reliance on her more pronounced than was the case in other households, but her status as a major source of labor power was by no means unique in her village. Wang Baolan, for instance, born in 1928, became a child bride in about 1940. She had a mentally ill mother-in-law who was kept locked in a back room, a father-in-law who gambled compulsively and gave away his own daughter to settle a gambling debt, a sister-in-law who was even younger than Wang herself, and an absent husband who had been paid by a rich peasant to take his place in the army. When she wasn't doing all the housework for this family, Wang provided some of its income by spinning and weaving in the house of Cao Zhuxiang. Bao Cuifeng was another young bride with an absentee husband. She was married in 1948, when her family needed the bride-price money to ransom her father out of the army. Her new family consisted of her husband's disabled uncle, his wife, five of their twelve children, Bao's husband, and three of his younger siblings. Bao's mother-in-law was dead and her father-in-law had been conscripted into the Nationalist *(Guomindang)* army; her new husband left to work in the county seat and later in Xi'an, not returning until 1957. Although the conscripted father-in-law returned home after 1949, this was also a household in which Bao's labor and that of her husband's aunt were crucial in making ends meet.

Normative patterns for women, then—of female seclusion, of limited work in the fields—were frequently contravened in the daily practice of Guanzhong farming households. What is less clear is whether poor women were stigmatized in their own communities for doing fieldwork or appearing regularly at market.[6] After 1949, materials on Cao Zhuxiang as a labor model routinely included statements such as "Her laboring habits were discriminated against in the old society" (*Cao Zhuxiang huzhuzu* 1952; see also *Cao Zhuxiang huzhu lianzu* 1953). This may be merely post-revolutionary puffery. Such sources never specify the concrete form of that discrimination, and the women themselves never mention it directly in retelling their memories of the period before the revolution. It may be that deviation from the female norm was itself normal in Guanzhong—affecting so many poor households that there was no one left to regard it with opprobrium. What women do recall, with great emotion, is the sense that their labor was linked with family disaster, with hardship, instability, and barely getting by. What the revolution did for these women was not so much to remove the stigma of "outside" labor as to change the context and the rewards associated with it.[7]

CAO ZHUXIANG AND THE COOPERATIVE MOVEMENT

Wang Family Village was liberated in May 1949; in June a propaganda team arrived and informed the villagers that they should elect a village head and a women's chair. When someone recommended Cao Zhuxiang, she was so horrified at the prospect that she fled to her natal home; she remembered how the Guomindang had hounded the previous village head about taxes and other matters. Eventually other villagers persuaded her to return to her marital village and take up the job of women's chair.

The events that led to Cao's subsequent recognition as a labor model began in the spring of 1950. When the Party secretary of the district committee asked Cao about problems in her village, she told him that many households were hard-pressed by a spring grain shortage. He asked her what could be done about it, and she proposed organizing women to spin and weave for money, using cotton she had stored in her own house. The secretary offered her an interest-free loan of 80 *yuan* to invest in additional raw materials and promised that the supply and marketing co-op (*gongxiao she*) would buy any cloth the women could produce (Cao Zhuxiang 1996 [see chapter appendix]; for accounts of these events see also *Cao Zhuxiang huzhuzu* 1952; *Cao Zhuxiang mofan* 1957; Weinan diqu 1993, 367).

The next morning Cao Zhuxiang set about organizing seven women into a co-op. Each was from a household in which adult male laborers were either utterly lacking or defective in some way. Each of the women had often gone to the market with Cao before Liberation to buy thread or sell cloth, so she knew them all. Tang Yuying was a widow ten years older than Cao whose son had died some years before. Wang Baolan was the former child bride with the mentally ill mother-in-law who already spent much of each day weaving in Cao's home. Han Airong was Cao's relative by marriage; her husband was in intermittent trouble with the law for petty thievery, card playing, and opium smoking. Du Ailian's husband was conscripted before 1949, and after he returned home he proved not very competent; he later jumped into a well and died. Lanhua (a childhood nickname; Cao Zhuxiang cannot remember her formal name) had a crude and bad-tempered husband who was known for beating his own mother, although he did manage to do the farmwork. Tang Zhuzhen had a shiftless husband who sold the family's land (although he later reformed and became a brigade accountant!). Tang Shulian, whom Cao did not name but who was mentioned by two other interviewees as a co-op member, was the aunt of Bao Cuifeng's husband and the virtual head of household, with a disabled husband and twelve children (Bao Cuifeng 1996 [see chapter appendix]). All these women knew how to spin and weave, and many had done so for the market. It was the crucial state intervention of a loan that enabled them to start co-op production at a time when cash was short.

The seven women went to a periodic market south of the village, purchased some yarn, set up three looms in Cao's house, and began to work (Weinan diqu 1993, 367). Within a few days they had produced and sold several meters of cloth, using some of the money to buy more yarn. The rest of the profits they gave to whichever household was most in need, a procedure facilitated by their long-standing familiarity with each other's household situations. Eventually everyone got equal shares of the money. The co-op not only made enough to support all of its members, but within a month had earned enough money to purchase eight *dou* of wheat (a *dou* was 30–40 *jin*) (*Cao Zhuxiang huzhu lianzu* 1953). As more and more women came to them and asked for advice in setting up cooperatives, Cao returned to the Party secretary and secured additional start-up loans of more than 200 *yuan*.

By the time of the summer harvest, the group of seven had enlarged to twenty-one and transformed itself into an agricultural mutual aid team, taking charge of harvesting the wheat from 89 *mu* of land. This freed up six men to work outside the village as hired harvest hands. It also, says one of the labor model documents, "broke the old habit of believing that women could not do farmwork" (*Cao Zhuxiang huzhu lianzu* 1953), although that belief was already mostly honored in the breach. Having gotten through the spring shortage and the summer busy season, the group disbanded.

The village spent much of the next two years in experiments with mutual aid groups of various types. This was a rocky process of false starts and quarrels. In the spring of 1951, responding to a call from the government (that is, not in a voluntary fashion), many of the villagers organized a labor exchange team, with men in one team and women in another. But the group had no way to reward people differentially according to how hard they worked, and so it broke up before long, with only the core group of seven women continuing to work together. Toward the end of 1951 they tried again, with six small groups of men and six of women. Again there were problems. Some households did not want women working for them, fearing that they would do the job inadequately. When women went to hoe the land, men would also show up to hoe it, and then arguments would break out over who had completed the job and who should get credit for it. Conflicts within families proliferated. In an attempt to overcome these gender wars, Cao reorganized people into eight groups, with households joining as a unit. But labor power and livestock were distributed unevenly among the groups, leading to delays in production. It took until the end of 1952 to put together a stable united mutual aid group of thirty-six households, with Cao as its head (*Cao Zhuxiang huzhu lianzu* 1953; *Cao Zhuxiang huzhuzu* 1952).

In spite of these difficulties, however, the various 1952 experiments yielded impressive results in the production of wheat, cotton, and millet, as well as in collecting fertilizer, digging wells, and caring for livestock (*Cao Zhuxiang huzhuzu* 1952). It was also during this period that Cao was first selected as a county-level labor model (Weinan diqu 1993, 367), and in 1952 she became the second Party member in the entire township (Cao Zhuxiang 1996 [see chapter appendix]). By 1953, the mutual aid group had an elaborate governing structure and was divided into subgroups, each with a head and vice-head and regular procedures for meetings, production planning, labor contests, work point distribution, collective newspaper reading, and criticism/self-criticism. It also made and sold bean curd, in spite of attempts at sabotage by one Du Jingjie who, jealous of the group's superior product, put salt in his own bean curd and sold it as theirs in order to ruin their reputation (*Cao Zhuxiang huzhu lianzu* 1953; Cao Zhuxiang 1996 [see chapter appendix]).

THE PRODUCTION OF LABOR HEROINES

Labor models are made, not born, and in the paper trail their careers leave behind we can discern the process of their creation. As with every historical subject, our understanding of labor models is also profoundly limited by the written materials that survive about them, as well as the vagaries of memory and reinterpretation that shape oral history accounts. In official accounts, Cao Zhuxiang's initial reluctance to become the women's chair disappears. Instead, we are told,

> her hardworking and upstanding style was discovered by the people's government; she became head of the village women; she was politically transformed (*fanshen*), was deeply moved, enthusiastic and active about every kind of work; she protected every policy of the Party and government, respected the laws of the government, and took the lead in responding to every government call. (*Cao Zhuxiang mofan* 1957)

But by her own account, it was not easy for Cao to learn to be a public figure. In 1951, when she was already a veteran mutual-aid team organizer but had not yet joined the Party or achieved model status, she went to her first meeting outside the village, a gathering at the county seat to discuss land reform. She had a difficult time talking to the other conferees, most of whom were men; at mealtimes she would grab a piece of steamed bread and go to her room. Rebuked for her shyness by the male cadre who had first recruited her as a women's chair, she gradually learned to talk to others, particularly after she was chosen as a district labor model and began attending meetings in Xi'an and other places (Cao Zhuxiang 1996 [see chapter appendix]).

Her difficulty in learning to speak in public was not unique. Zhang Qiuxiang, a national labor model from a nearby township, was at first virtually incapable of explaining how she produced her bumper cotton crops in the mid-1950s. Cadres from the Women's Federation spent hours patiently interviewing her and transforming what she said into maxims, then teaching her to recite them until she became a fluent speaker. They were responsible

for composing her most famous jingle, which sounds felicitous in Chinese
if not in English:

Use dialectics
look at the sky, look at the ground
grow the cotton.

Yunyong bianzheng fa
kantian kandi
wu mianhua.

In this anecdote and others like it we can see glimpses of the arduous
process by which labor heroines were produced. (Zhang Quixiang 1996;
Women's Federation officials 1996 [see chapter appendix].) It was a process determined not only by the state propaganda apparatus, but by their
own efforts to learn new skills and overcome personal terrors, as well as by
the painstaking daily work of Women's Federation and other government
cadres.

But because of the conventions of public record keeping about labor
models, we know the most about the aspects of their daily lives that touched
upon national policy. A labor model, the records tell us, was one who consistently made connections between the local production process and the
national political situation, whether that meant preparing care packages for
the soldiers in Korea or taking the lead in selling cotton to the state (*Cao
Zhuxiang mofan* 1957; *Cao Zhuxiang huzhuzu* 1952; Weinan xian minzhu
1952; *Weinan xian* 1962). A labor model worked to develop Party and Youth
League members in her organization, to mediate disputes, to take the lead
in agricultural experiments with new seeds and techniques, to become literate herself, and to communicate what she read about Party policy to those
around her (*Cao Zhuxiang huzhuzu* 1952; Weinan xian minzhu 1952; *Cao
Zhuxiang huzhu lianzu* 1953; Liu and Luo 1953; *Cao Zhuxiang mofan* 1957;
Weinan xian 1962). A labor model showed determination in the face of local reluctance to collectivize.[8] The actions of labor models that were selected for publicity were those that supported current state priorities: to
convince suspicious peasants that joining a mutual aid group was in their
economic interest and that they should try new agricultural techniques.

Typically, the narratives about labor models began by describing the establishment of a production group under the leadership of an unusual individual like Cao Zhuxiang, the overcoming of successive waves of difficulties, and the final success, which the narrative would label as an inspiration
for others to emulate the actions of the model and her group. This narrative formula was employed even if a happy ending, or even stability, had not
(yet) been achieved; overwhelming difficulties were relegated to a section

on "remaining problems" near the end of the piece. One 1953 essay, for instance, gave a very detailed account of organizational problems and then concluded that the members of Cao's united mutual aid group were in debt to the co-op and still extremely poor. One member commented plaintively, "I know that the co-op has a future and many benefits. I also hear what Chairman Mao has to say. It is just that when I go home there is nothing to eat" (*Cao Zhuxiang huzhu lianzu* 1953). This devastating comment barely interrupted the optimistic tone of the piece as a whole, which went on blithely to assert that the government was helping people to develop sideline industries so that they could make more money. The audience for stories about district labor models appears to have been primarily local and rural. Cao Zhuxiang, for instance, was praised in a heavily illustrated 1953 publication that was aimed at village women (Liu and Luo 1953). National labor models such as Zhang Qiuxiang, in contrast, were meant to appeal as well to an audience of urban youth (Gao Xiaoxian 1996 [see chapter appendix]).

It is important to note that female labor models were models precisely because of their pioneering labor, not because they were social pioneers in challenging local standards of virtuous behavior. In fact, many of the women who became labor heroines made deliberate and conscious decisions to conform to normative roles for women. Fu Guifeng, who was recruited as a women's activist and village official near Xianyang in 1949, encountered opposition from her husband, a former hired laborer, when she tried to go out to meetings. Ten years older than his wife, he was convinced by local gossip that she would run off with one of the male cadres who were training her as a local leader. One night in 1950 he became violent:

> Once during the land reform, when we were taking and confiscating land (*zhengshou moshou*), I mobilized women to do a lot of hard work. My husband thought, she isn't home, and he got angry. I was working so hard, and when I got home at night I would stay up spinning on the brick bed (*kang*). I acted just as always in front of him. He lost his temper. He said, you run around all day and at night you waste lamp oil spinning. He cursed me and wanted to take me to the township head. I wouldn't go. He pulled me hard, and bumped my head against the door threshold. My face swelled up.

But when cadres from the Women's Federation and other government organizations wanted to criticize her husband, Fu Guifeng made a canny political assessment of how this would affect her work:

> I wouldn't let them. The old people around him wouldn't accept it. I ran around all day, and he had to watch the children and do the housework. It would hurt the work [if they criticized him]. I explained to them over and over, until the upper-level cadres all got angry with me. They said, if your husband beats you to death we won't do a thing about it. [But] I had to set an example, and a bit of inconvenience didn't matter. I got along well with my

mother-in-law and father-in-law, and I had no intention of divorcing my husband (Fu Guifeng 1996 [see chapter appendix]).

Instead, she chose to explain over and over to her husband that she would not divorce him, that she and he were "bitter melons on the same vine" (yitiao kuman shang de kugua).[9]

Cao Zhuxiang's widowhood contributed to her status as a labor model in interesting and contradictory ways. By her own account, when her husband died in about 1940, her brother persuaded her not to remarry because she had two young children and a mother-in-law to care for. In particular, he said, she had to raise her son no matter what—and, he added, her husband's lineage would not push her out precisely because she had a son. Bringing in a new husband ("calling in a son-in-law") seemed to her impossible; she had watched another family in the village try to do so, and they had faced considerable social embarrassment and opposition. Nor was her decision merely a function of family and village opinion: she felt strongly that she wanted to watch out for her own children and that she didn't want people gossiping about her. Convinced that it was her fate to "eat bitterness" alone, she refused to remarry, even after 1949 when several cadres tried to persuade her otherwise. As a former Women's Federation official shrewdly observes, Cao's honesty, ability to eat bitterness, and desire to raise a son for her husband's patriline were themselves feudal virtues (Women's Federation officials 1996 [see chapter appendix]).

And yet these were precisely the characteristics that raised her prestige among the villagers and enabled her to assume a leadership role. In fact, draft material written in the early 1950s by the village leadership to document the exemplary nature of Cao's activities reworks the widowhood story in the following way: her husband dies, his death brings her terrible economic and spiritual hardships, her natal family pressures her to remarry (something that simply didn't happen), she heroically refuses on the grounds that the family needs her, she regards herself as a determined person who can labor with her own two hands, and why should she depend upon a man? (Cao Zhuxiang mofan 1957). Perhaps it is significant that this odd amalgam of praise for widow chastity and female independence was crossed out in the draft essay. One can also speculate that marriage had not offered much to Cao Zhuxiang: a husband who had not yet reached puberty when she married, who was away from home for the few years in which he was a healthy adult, and who returned home to die at the age of 21, leaving her with dependents of several generations. Almost a decade later, at Liberation, Cao was 32, a mature woman and an experienced farmer. Her mother-in-law had died, and her children were no longer toddlers and could help with farmwork. Reluctance to begin another marriage at that stage in her life is certainly understandable from many standpoints, especially because notions that might encourage remarriage—such as the expectation that marriage would be a source of sexual or emotional companionship—were nowhere operative in her home village. Nevertheless, the salient point here is that her widowhood and her conventional response to it, far from being questioned, were incorporated seamlessly into her emergence as a labor model—not by a faraway anonymous state apparatus, but by the fellow villagers who wrote up her life as a model for outside consumption.

THE GENDERED ATTRACTIONS OF SOCIALISM

The list of virtues ascribed to men and women chosen as labor models was a long one, but it usually did not make more than passing reference to the gender of the model. Cao Zhuxiang, the accounts tell us, was a woman forced by widowhood to learn fieldwork skills before Liberation, and was thus favorably positioned (as were many men) to become a labor model in agricultural production. She was also a widow who steadfastly refused to remarry so that she could bring up her son properly in her husband's patriline. Her relentlessly proper conduct ensured that no gossip swirled about her door and that no subsequent marriage infringed on her loyalties or her time. In short, the particularities of her history as a woman set up the conditions under which she could become a model; they cleared the ground for modelhood.

But in the official accounts, even those generated at the local level by villagers who knew her well, very seldom is her gender cited in reference to her achievements as a model. She was not a model because she did an exceptional job of juggling child care and fieldwork, or because she explicitly addressed the problems of drawing women into production outside the domestic space. She neither articulated nor overcame the gendered differences in daily responsibilities and social expectations that stubbornly inhered beneath the Party's proclamations of equality between men and women. Or if she did so, it is not the job of labor model stories to tell us about it. Their purpose was to publicize local successes in cotton production, group organization, and (increasingly as the 1950s wore on) political fealty. Even as the move of women into collective production fundamentally altered the position of women within a particular social division of labor, the labor heroine literature—and quite possibly, the labor heroine subject position itself—underplayed that massive change.

When labor heroines of the 1950s recall those days now, one difficulty they mention is the problem of caring for children while meeting the demands of modelhood. After many years of marriage Fu Guifeng, a Women's Federation activist, provincial labor model, and co-op cadre, gave birth to a son in about 1954. The child suffered from meningitis and its aftereffects; she blames his illness on having sent him out to a wet nurse with inferior milk. (This was a common practice among emergent labor models and Women's Federation cadres alike. Fu's daughter, born in 1956, was given to a wet nurse after six days and stayed with her until she was in middle school.) In 1958, Fu went to Beijing for three months of meetings, and two weeks after her departure the son's illness flared up and he died. She was not told of his death. When she returned to the province she went first to Xi'an, where she was hospitalized with a stomach inflammation. At the time she was pregnant and wanted an abortion, and was mystified by the refusal of the hospital authorities to give her one. When she learned that her son had died, she returned to her home village, where she pushed through a waiting crowd of sympathetic villagers, went directly to her house, covered her head with a quilt, and cried for a long time. When she gave birth to another daughter several months later, her husband, still almost deranged with grief, reproached her: "A daughter doesn't support the mother's house; you can't use ashes to build a wall. Ten daughters in flowered clothes are not worth one crippled son. You were such an activist that you snuffed out [literally, 'cut short'] the incense on my grave" (Fu Guifeng 1996 [see chapter appendix]).

Cao Zhuxiang's child care needs were less acute than those of women with younger children. Her daughter was about eleven and her son was about eight in 1949. By the age of nine her daughter could already cook and tend the livestock, and the children took care of themselves while Cao attended co-op meetings in the evenings. Cao took comfort in the fact that her daughter was able to go to school at age 11, an opportunity Cao had never had. Yet she immediately interrupts her account of her daughter's better life with a tale of her own maternal neglect: "I didn't have time to take care of my daughter when she was in school. Her legs froze one winter when she was crossing the Wei River to get to school" (Cao Zhuxiang 1996 [see chapter appendix]). When her daughter married in 1958, Cao did not attend the simple ceremony because she was away at a meeting in the county seat. On the second day, when local practice required that she send a meal to the newlyweds, she was still attending the meeting. On the third day, when the daughter returned to her natal home for the customary visit, she was still at the meeting; at that point relatives called her back so that she could present her new son-in-law with a piece of steamed bread and a few eggs.

The serious, even heartbreaking, family dilemmas of labor heroines punctuate their recollections in the late 1990s; their frequency underscores the utter silence on this subject in the official labor heroine literature. Works published in the 1950s discuss how to organize child care facilities for the busy agricultural season, but no labor heroine is ever described as in need of such assistance in order to perform her historical role. Without subscribing to an essentialist notion of a sacred mother-child bond, or assuming an ahistorical norm of concern about child care, a North American feminist writing almost half a century later is tempted to see that silence as a failure by the state, even a cynical attempt to promote women as models without ever acknowledging the material and emotional costs of their modelhood. The silence could be read, in short, as one step in the Long March of bad faith by which the state touted women as equal to men, and as equally available for heroic labor, by simply pretending that their circumstances were the same as those of men.[10]

But such condemnation, no matter how briefly satisfying, is politically foolish and historically untenable. It ignores the zeal with which labor heroines took on (and still recall without apparent ambivalence) their model status and the honors it brought them, as well as the daily work it entailed. Although after four decades these women confuse details from some of the movements in which they played such leading roles, they are unswerving in their eloquence on this score. Fu Guifeng, the labor model who lost her son, is particularly passionate, albeit in official political language, about the way in which the Party literally brought her into being:

> Although my parents gave birth to me, it was the Party that brought me up: Mao and the Women's Federation. . . . In July 1949, the district (quxiang) sent a cadre to my house. I was at the loom weaving. He pulled me off the loom to go to a meeting. They wanted to select someone who had suffered, who was capable. At the time I had no formal name (guanming); my childhood name was Rongrong. My name, Fu Guifeng, was given to me that day. . . . From that time, every level of the Women's Federation came looking for me. . . . Every level of the Party and government consciously trained and educated (peiyang) me. They spent more on me than what it costs to train a university student. (Fu Guifeng 1996 [see chapter appendix])

Cao Zhuxiang is less eloquent but just as clear on what she gained in the early years of collectivization. The new society gave her a way to excel by doing what she had always done—farm work—no longer as a marginal producer, but as a central figure in the village. It made her labor glorious and rewarded her publicly for it, and it gave her an arena in which to develop substantial political skills. She took pride in her growing experience and confidence as a leader. The growth of co-ops also removed the constant threat of economic disaster, which was endured by many peasants but perhaps felt most acutely by female-headed households. In early 1953, when her lower producers' cooperative was founded, Cao felt for the first time the relief of no longer being solely responsible for her own land and livelihood. The Party may have done nothing to acknowledge or relieve women's responsibilities for maintaining and reproducing the household. It did, however, reduce the chance that such households would be obliterated—a possibility that been an unquestioned feature of life prior to the revolution. The revolution succeeded in capturing the loyalty and hard work of its labor heroines because it provided them with basic conditions of existence, as well as possibilities for recognition and glory.

For the younger married women of the village, the rewards of the revolution were less public and more closely entwined with their status as young brides. The changes of the 1950s offered new resources for coping with their liminal status in their husbands' households. Yu Yinhua, who married into Wang Family Village in 1950 at the age of 19, had a childhood and adolescence full of unhappy domestic situations: her mother's death when she was ten, her father's nervous breakdown and suicide five years later, after bandits repeatedly made off with the family's livestock and grain. When she was 18, she was married off by her grandfather, partly because he was afraid that in the social chaos of the late 1940s, an unmarried woman would not be safe in a household unprotected by able-bodied men. A month later her new husband died of heart disease. Nor did her subsequent marriage into Wang Family Village provide her with stability.

What changed Yu's life was Chen Shengmin, a cadre from the Shaanbei revolutionary base area who was living in her marital home. Chen recommended Yu as a mutual aid group leader in 1951, and soon she was elected head of the women's team (*xiaodui funü duizhang*). Her main duties were organizing women in labor exchange groups for the wheat harvest, establishing a day-care center, and mobilizing women to attend school at night and in the slack season. She threw herself into the task of becoming literate, working through three elementary school textbooks, learning to write the name of everyone in the village so that she could record their work points, pasting copies of the *Xibei funü huabao* (Northwest women's pictorial) up all over the walls of her house. She joined the Party in 1955, and describes herself as happiest at that time, comfortable with her growing responsibilities as a cadre, sure that she could do anything.

The new social order in the village brought Yu Yinhua another benefit as well, one that she does not recount in her oral history. Village records from 1953 credit Cao Zhuxiang with a successful mediation in Yu's household, holding a meeting to smooth the fractious relations between Yu and her husband's aunt. This intervention reportedly resolved all tensions, leading the husband's uncle to comment happily of Cao, "No wonder she is a labor model. She mediated in my household so well, everyone is peacefully producing" (*Cao Zhuxiang huzhu lianzu* 1953). One does not have to believe literally in this utterance to note that it was her status as a labor model that enabled Cao to act, that cracked open the authority structure in Yu's new household and enabled a non-kin widow to ease the control of a younger woman by an older one.

For Yu Yinhua and other young brides in the village, the requirement that women labor collectively gave them a sanctioned occasion to see one another. Yu and Bao Cuifeng, who is the same age, remember the early years of the People's Republic as a time of hard work but also easy talk and laughter among young women, who ten years earlier would have been isolated in the homes of their in-laws. Wang Baolan and Li Qingcui, women several years older than the other two, liked the numerous meetings of the co-op period because they provided an opportunity to see other young people, even though the women themselves never spoke publicly in such a meeting. For all of these women, collective labor provided an alternative social universe, a community of peers, that helped them negotiate these difficult early years in their marital village. It is in the unwritten web of relationships formed during that time and now accessible only through memory, as much as in the official documents commemorating women labor models, that the local meanings of gender and work were developed in the 1950s.

APPENDIX

Bao Cuifeng [pseud.]. 1996. Interview by Gao Xiaoxian and Gail Hershatter. Hongxing cun, Weinan xian, Shaanxi, 6 August.
Cao Zhuxiang. 1996. Interview by Gao Xiaoxian and Gail Hershatter. Hongxing cun, Weinan xian, Shaanxi, 2–4 August.
Fu Guifeng [pseud.]. 1996. Interview by Gail Hershatter with Ning Huanxia present. Xianyang, Shaanxi, 15 August.
Gao Xiaoxian. 1996. Personal communication. August.
Li Qingcui [pseud.]. 1996. Interview by Gao Xiaoxian and Gail Hershatter. Hongxing cun, Weinan xian, Shaanxi, 5 August.
Wang Baolan [pseud.]. 1996. Interview by Gao Xiaoxian and Gail Hershatter. Hongxing cun, Weinan xian, Shaanxi, 6 August.
Wang Jican, Wang Mingzhe, Huang Shimin, Wang Shuntian, Huang Meiying. 1996. Village briefing, Hongxing cun, Weinan xian, Shaanxi, 6 August.
Women's Federation officials formerly active in Weinan. 1996. Interview by Gao Xiaoxian and Gail Hershatter. Weinan city, Weinan xian, Shaanxi, 9 August.
Yu Yinhua [pseud.]. 1996. Interview by Gao Xiaoxian and Gail Hershatter. Hongxing cun, Weinan xian, Shaanxi. 4 August.
Zhang Qiuxiang. 1996. Interview by Gao Xiaoxian and Gail Hershatter. Balidian cun, Weinan xian, Shaanxi, 7 August.

NOTES

Virtually all the research for this chapter was conducted in collaboration with Gao Xiaoxian, Research Director of the Shaanxi Provincial Women's Federation, as part of an ongoing exploration of gender and work in the 1950s. Parts of the analysis were developed in long discussions with Gao Xiaoxian, but the views presented here are my own. The research was funded by grants from the Pacific Rim Research Program of the University of California and by the Luce Foundation. I am grateful to Emily Honig, Lisa Rofel, and Wang Zheng, as well as participants in the October 1996 conference on "Gender, Households, and the Boundaries of Work in Contemporary China," for comments on an earlier draft.

1. Many scholars eschew the term "Liberation" because it assumes just this kind of thoroughgoing positive transformation. I use it here because it remains part of the language in which Chinese villagers recall and interpret their own past.

2. Space does not permit a thorough and nuanced exposition of these arguments. Some of the most important English-language sources that discuss the 1950s in rural areas are Andors (1983); Croll (1980); Davin (1979); Diamond (1975); K. Johnson (1983); and Stacey (1983). For an assessment of the entire period of collective agriculture with respect to gender equality, see M. Wolf (1985).

3. The most comprehensive treatment of Guanzhong's regional economy in English is Vermeer (1988).

4. Wang Family Village, now part of Red Star Village, was located in what is now Baiyang township, in the western suburbs of Weinan city, at the southwest corner of Weinan District. Weinan city is about 60 kilometers northeast of Xi'an. Wang Family Village was one of nine "natural villages" *(ziran cun)* that became part of the Red Star Agricultural Producer's Cooperative. The co-op encompassed different villages at different times, making it difficult to estimate the size of the constituent villages. In 1955, the Red Star Advanced Producers' Cooperative (including all nine villages) comprised 224 households according to one source (Weinan diqu 1993, 368) and 294 according to another (*Cao Zhuxiang mofan* 1957). In 1959 or 1960 Wang Family Village split into north and south villages, and the south village, where Cao Zhuxiang lived, became the second production team *(erdui)* under the Red Star Production Brigade of the Baiyang Commune (Wang Jican et al. 1996 [see chapter appendix]). Judging from the size of early mutual aid teams centered in the village (see later in chapter), it appears in the 1950s to have consisted of fewer than 40 households.

5. This chapter walks the precarious methodological border between history and anthropology, posing various ethical and practical dilemmas for the author. Historians aim to reveal their sources and establish the unique circumstances of their subjects by fixing them in time and place. Many historians feel a particular obligation to restore the erasure of non-elite women from the historical record, although here again the question of who "gives voice" to whom is a complicated one (see Hershatter 1997, 24–27). Anthropologists, in contrast, protect the anonymity of their sources and establish the unique circumstances and the shared cultural assumptions of their subjects through ethnographic description rather than straightforward naming. And to this difference in disciplinary practices one must add the uncertainties of conducting fieldwork in rural China, where official approval at one moment (or by one level of authorities) can be succeeded by jittery accusations at the next.

Except where otherwise noted, information presented in this essay is drawn from interviews. Everyone interviewed spoke with the knowledge and approval of local officials. Nevertheless, I have changed the names of everyone mentioned here with the exception of two of the labor models, Cao Zhuxiang and Zhang Qiuxiang. Cao was regionally famous and Zhang was nationally known; numerous published and archival documents, some cited in this essay, attest to their fame, and their interviews supplement and enrich the written record in ways that should not prove problematic for them or their communities. I have given a pseudonym to the third labor model, "Fu Guifeng," because the family matters she discussed with me are not, to my knowledge, matters of public record, and further discussions with her are necessary if I am to publish her name.

6. In considering this question of stigma, I do not mean to suggest that women who worked in the fields had nothing to fear. Several women mentioned in their interviews that the social disorder of the 1940s meant that any woman venturing outside the home was in danger of being raped in the fields by local bandits *(tufei)* or roving soldiers. And women who assumed non-normative work roles before 1949 and in the 1950s did have to guard their reputations as respectable women. As a widow and a fieldworker, Cao Zhuxiang was particularly concerned that no suggestion of sexual impropriety be leveled at her; see later in chapter. The same was also true of some married women who took on prominent roles after 1949, and who did not want their work undermined by suggestions that they were engaged in improper conduct with men (Fu Guifeng 1996). When Bao Cuifeng assumed responsibility for a work group within her mutual aid team in the early 1950s, one of her husband's aunts cursed her and suggested that her children were not her husband's (Bao Cuifeng 1996 [see chapter appendix]). Outside activity, then, did pose various dangers for women, including the danger of a sullied reputation. But it seems by no means automatic that a woman who worked in the fields before 1949 was assumed to be "bad."

7. Lisa Rofel (1999) argues in her study of Hangzhou silk workers that the normative gendered division of labor in prerevolutionary Hangzhou was figured spatially as "inside" versus "outside" labor, and that women who worked other than in household workshops were stigmatized for having gone "outside" (see also chap. 10). She points out that what was stigmatized here was not the fact of female labor itself, but the place in which it was performed, and that the revolution removed this stigma by reconfiguring the spatial arrangements of labor. For observations about stigmatized woman cotton mill workers in Shanghai and Tianjin, see Honig (1986) and Hershatter (1986) respectively. By suggesting that stigma worked differently in Guanzhong, I am not intending to contravene any of these earlier arguments, but merely to argue that there may be more variations on the "liberatory" process than can be subsumed in a single narrative.

8. This last virtue may well have been an artifact of the model-making process.

9. This little homily should not be mistaken for a happy ending. Fu had a continually stormy relationship with her husband. One Women's Federation official who spent a great deal of time in Fu's home recalls Fu chasing her husband around the *kang* with a stick, threatening to beat him. Another remembers that Fu's husband accompanied her on most of her visits to labor model meetings, fearing that she would divorce him if he let her out of his sight. For an account of his reproaches after the death of their son in 1958, see later in chapter.

10. For a discussion of this assumption of equality in a later, urban context see Honig and Hershatter (1988, 13–31).

SIX

Iron Girls Revisited

Gender and the Politics of Work in the Cultural Revolution, 1966–76

Emily Honig

The Iron Girls—strong, robust women capable of performing jobs more commonly done by men, such as repairing high-voltage electric wires—symbolized the Maoist slogan that "whatever men comrades can accomplish, women comrades can too." Celebrated during the Cultural Revolution as the emblem of gender equality, the Iron Girls became the subject of merciless mockery during the 1980s. In the context of the post-Mao economic reforms, the Iron Girls embodied a belief that the Cultural Revolution represented a time of inappropriate equality in the workforce that was detrimental to economic development. Mockery and repudiation of the Iron Girls was part of an argument for a gendered division of labor in which women's work was more closely tied to beliefs about their innate biologically and physiologically determined abilities (Honig and Hershatter 1988, 23–25).

The assumption that the Cultural Revolution represented a time of relative gender equality, particularly in the context of work, not only is central to post-Mao Chinese political discourse, but also informs Western analyses of the impact of economic reforms on women. The increased "biologization," as Margaret Woo calls it, of women in the reform era, the explicit preference of factory managers to employ men while encouraging women workers to leave their jobs, and the concentration of women in special economic zones and private enterprises are regarded as a retreat from a period when women may well have been measured by a male yardstick, but during which they were presumably not the victims of such overt gender discrimination (Honig and Hershatter, 1988; Woo 1994).

This "progressive" read of Cultural Revolution gender relations is perplexing, given that issues of gender were conspicuously absent from the Cultural Revolution agenda. It was in fact the first major political campaign

97

sponsored by the Chinese Communist Party (CCP) that did *not* address gender issues. Class was its main concern. If gender issues were raised at all, it was primarily to denounce their relevance: feminism was declared "bourgeois," the Women's Federation disbanded, and the "sameness" of men and women asserted.

Assumptions about Cultural Revolution gender relations are also puzzling because, political propaganda and rhetoric aside, so little is actually known about the gendered dimensions of work in the period preceding the economic reforms. Popular conceptions of appropriate work for women, the kinds of work women actually did, how they were remunerated, and the extent to which this represented a departure from the 1950's and early 1960's remain obscure. Although a wealth of literature describes the experience of sent-down youth (young urban students sent to the countryside for "reeducation" by peasants), little is known about their experience with work: the specific jobs men and women were assigned, how their presence may have affected rural attitudes toward appropriate women's work, and their perceptions of rural women's work.

This chapter is a preliminary attempt to explore issues of gender and work during the Cultural Revolution—preliminary because it is based primarily on secondary sources, personal testimonies, and memoirs. Ultimately, archival research and oral history interviews will be necessary to develop a more nuanced analysis. Yet even personal testimonies and memoirs reveal that the gendered dimensions of work were far more complex than previously recognized. In almost every arena, from state propaganda to the assignment of work points in agricultural brigades, gender relations were continually contested. In spite of the Cultural Revolution's apparently exclusive emphasis on class, work was central to the broader reconfiguration of gender that was at the very heart of this political movement. Moreover, the gap between women's work experience during the Cultural Revolution and during the 1980s may prove to be far narrower than has been previously imagined (see also chap. 7).

STATE PROPAGANDA AND THE POLITICS OF WORK

In spite of the declaration of class as the priority, the Cultural Revolution was a period of intense propagation of images of women who defied conventional notions of biological weakness and physiological limitations. The media glorified women's public roles as proletarian fighters and as "Iron Girls." Newspapers and magazines, punctuated with the slogan that "women hold up half the sky," valorized the examples of women who joined fishing teams, drilling teams, oil teams, well-sinking teams, those who became policewomen, tractor, truck, and diesel locomotive drivers, turbine generator operators, electricians, and navigators (*Survey of the China Mainland Press*

[*SCMP*] 1970, 1971b, 1972c, 1973b; *Survey of People's Republic of China Press* [*SPRCP*] 1975a).

The Iron Girl model may at first glance suggest that the Cultural Revolution was actually about a state-sponsored contestation of gender roles. On the one hand, the model did hold out to women the possibility of challenging gender norms, and, as we shall see later, some women invoked this model for their own ends. On the other hand, the Iron Girl message was quite limited: women could aspire to become like men. (Nowhere was it suggested that men could hope to become like women.) Moreover, the Iron Girl model made it seem that the issue of gender equality was settled: so long as women could become Iron Girls, no other aspect of gender roles in the workplace need be addressed. Meanwhile, propagation of the Iron Girl model did little, in and of itself, to alter those roles. The Iron Girls represented only a very tiny percentage of the female population and left unaltered (and uncontested) the status of the vast majority of women.

Cultural Revolution state propaganda needs to be contextualized in several other ways. First, it would be misleading to suggest that the Iron Girls, women who boldly crossed traditional gender boundaries in the division of labor, represented the predominant theme of state propaganda about women. It was far more common for the media to emphasize the mere fact of women's participation in the paid labor force, to stress their ever-increasing numbers, to honor the achievements of a woman worker in an occupation (such as textiles) long dominated by women, or to extol an individual woman's creative application of Mao Zedong thought for revolutionizing production (*SCMP* 1971a, 1972a, b, 1973a).

Second, as Kay Ann Johnson points out, save for the Campaign to Criticize Lin Biao and Confucius (1972–74), women's responsibility for housework and child care was conspicuously unquestioned during the Cultural Revolution. In fact, the well-known 1964 attack on the editor of *Women of China*, which represented a prelude to the disbandment of the Women's Federation in 1966, stressed that women should be responsible for both housework and work outside the home (Johnson 1983, 180–81). Even while the Cultural Revolution media honored women's role in the workforce, it took for granted their status as housewives and responsibility for managing their homes, featuring articles with titles such as "Housewives Start Factory from Scratch in Central China Province," "Housewives' Co-op in Shanghai Makes Tele-Communication Equipment," or "More Peking Housewives Join Productive Labor" (*SCMP* 1972c, 1972d, 1976). Even inspirational stories of women who entered professions previously dominated by men unwittingly reinscribed women's responsibility for the domestic sphere. One such story, for example, featured the accomplishments of a model woman metallurgical field surveyor who defied all obstacles—including marriage and childbearing—to succeed. The report notes that she sent her first child to live with her mother so she could continue working unfettered; her second child was entrusted to the care of an older woman neighbor. The report, in other words, documents and leaves unquestioned women's responsibility for child rearing, while highlighting a single woman's success in becoming a field surveyor (Tung 1974, 44–45; see chap. 5 for delineation of this issue in the early 1950s.)

Third, a cursory survey of the media in the 1950s and 1960s suggests there was little that was actually new in the Cultural Revolution message about women's role in the workforce. Throughout the earlier period, one finds similar articles celebrating the success stories of women who became tractor and bus drivers, train engineers, tin miners, policewomen, factory technicians, lathe turners, all the while applauding the ever-increasing number of women to join the paid workforce (*SCMP* 1951a, 1951b, 1953, 1962; Xiang Hong 1965, 14). This is not meant to imply that an identical message was propagated, or that there was a single, static government attitude toward women's work outside the home. During the economic slough of the mid-1950s, for instance, the government clearly emphasized women's potential role as "socialist housewives" to encourage them to withdraw from the industrial workforce, while during the Great Leap Forward (1958–1961), far more emphasis was placed on women's capacity to contribute to socialist production by working outside the home. In spite of a popular association of the Cultural Revolution with women defying physiological limitations, it is not clear that there was anything new or different about what was propagated during this time. The only exception may have been that the Iron Girls, who made their first appearance in the early 1960s, became emblematic of the Cultural Revolution woman.

In fact, scattered evidence suggests that the Cultural Revolution may well have marked a time of greater official ambivalence about these images. For example, the film *Li Shuang-shuang,* based on a story written in 1959, portrayed a young peasant woman's struggle with her feudal-minded husband over the unequal distribution of household chores and showed the inferior status of women in the village workforce during the Great Leap Forward. When the film appeared in 1962, it not only enjoyed a popular audience but then received an award for "best picture" in a contest sponsored by Popular Cinema in 1963. During the Cultural Revolution, however, it was criticized and banned for its attention to "petty bourgeois" personal matters, presumably those related to housework and gender equality (Johnson 1983, 269; Li Shuang-shuang 1963; Leyda 1972, 310–11; Loh 1984, 175).

That Cultural Revolution messages about women's roles were characterized by more ambivalence than previously recognized is suggested as well by the "model" operatic ballet *Red Detachment of Women.* Although it is not about women's role in the workforce per se, the ballet has often been treated as a symbol of state propaganda in which women boasted strength, ferocity, and leadership abilities equal to those of men. Based on real, historical events, the *Red Detachment* takes place on Hainan Island and centers on the heroic efforts of a young slave girl, Wu Qinghua, to resist a wicked landlord. She does break free, "wreaking violence upon male guards along her escape route." Eventually she joins the CCP's Women's Detachment, a group of heroic female guerrillas, who successfully destroy the power of the local landlords. The story concludes with Wu's vow to abide by Mao's motto "Political power grows out of the barrel of a gun" (Witke 1977, 426–29).

Although the *Red Detachment of Women* was primarily a tale that glorified female militancy, its performance reveals some ambivalence about women's unconventional roles. Historical records show that in the actual events on Hainan Island in the 1920s, women taught themselves to use rifles and were organized by a particularly militant female commissar. In the ballet version, however, women are taught by men to use rifles, they are led by a dashing male commissar, and when they are not fighting, they busy themselves mending soldiers' uniforms. When an American visitor to China in 1972 asked about the change, "the ballet troupe explained that the commissar was changed to a male for 'artistic reasons,' because there weren't enough male leads" (J. Barrett 1973, 188–89). This shift in male/female roles may have gone unnoticed by Chinese audiences, for whom the *Red Detachment* remained a story that celebrated female militancy. Nevertheless, though it was popularly understood as advocating gender equality and the liberation of women, the story actually reinscribed certain forms of female subordination, and reveals the qualified meaning of Cultural Revolution slogans such as "Women can do anything men can do," and "The times have changed, men and women are the same." Furthermore, these slogans may well obscure the ways in which the Cultural Revolution, from the perspective of state propaganda, represented a retreat from the preceding period.

ACROSS THE GENDER DIVIDE

State propaganda is, of course, only a small part (albeit the most accessible) of what needs to be understood about the gendered dimensions of work during the Cultural Revolution. Ultimately we need to know how women themselves understood and responded to official messages about their appropriate roles, how the sexual division of labor in both rural and urban areas changed, and what kinds of conflicts about women's roles in the workforce emerged during this period.

Unfortunately, a number of factors obstruct the collection of data about women's work during the Cultural Revolution. First, rigid state control of data collection during the Maoist years, compounded by the practice in many rural and urban production units of inflating statistics in order to fulfill state-legislated quotas, limits the utility of data collected and published during the Cultural Revolution itself. Second, social survey research by both Chinese and Western scholars, which has produced such rich data about issues of gender and work during the economic reforms (e.g., chaps. 7, 8, and 15), was not possible during the Cultural Revolution. Indeed, the field of sociology was abolished and not revived until the late 1970s. The 1980s and 1990s have witnessed an explosion in the publication of nationwide, provincial, and city-specific labor statistics that claim to cover the entire post-1949 era. However, in almost every case, data on the 1965–1977 period are missing (Zhongguo quanguo funü lianhehui yanjiu suo 1991). The Cultural Revolution, in other words, remains a statistical blank.

At this point, besides contemporary media reports, the only set of sources that shed light on issues of gender and work during the Cultural Revolution are personal memoirs. Almost all are written by intellectuals and do not focus on work. Rather, they emphasize tales of suffering, political persecution, violence, and unrequited love. Testimonials of urban workers, not to mention rural women, are all but nonexistent. Even in the recollections of sent-down youth (the collection of which has become something of a cottage industry in its own right, with each province assembling its own volumes), work is a minor theme compared to tales of leaving home, living conditions in the countryside, romance and marriage, problems returning to the city, and rape of young urban women by local officials. Given that work occupied so much of their time in the countryside, the lack of attention to this issue in the memoirs of sent-down youth is perplexing. Perhaps the particulars of their rural labor had little effect on their future careers, and therefore seemed uncompelling.

Nevertheless, these accounts by sent-down youth do offer scattered descriptions of women's work—the experiences of female sent-down youth themselves, and their perceptions of rural women's work lives and responsibilities. They by no means represent a random sample of sent-down youth, but they do suggest how issues concerning gender and work were framed during the Cultural Revolution.

The media accounts of educated youth published during the Cultural Revolution emphasized almost exclusively the positive aspects of the experience for both the urban youth themselves and their rural counterparts. The "scar literature" (or "literature of the wounded") that emerged after the death of Mao and the fall of the Gang of Four in 1976 replaced these upbeat accounts with tales of suffering and wasted youth. In the early 1990s yet another genre appeared, one in which the Cultural Revolution is neither applauded nor condemned, but recalled with a sense of nostalgia. For women, the nostalgia is for a time of opportunity to cross the gender divide.

One woman who spent nearly a decade on a state farm on Hainan Island told me that were it not for the Cultural Revolution her life would have been entirely predictable. She would have graduated from a prestigious all-girls middle school in Beijing, entered a university, married, and had children (interestingly, work did not figure into her notion of pre–Cultural Revolution conventions). Because of the Cultural Revolution, though, she saw parts of China she never would have seen and engaged in work she never could have imagined doing. And—insisting, as she spoke, on single-handedly hauling two large overstuffed suitcases through an American airport—she declared that she had once been an Iron Girl, capable of carrying nearly 200 pounds on shoulder poles in the rubber plantation where she worked.

Perhaps the most unqualifiedly nostalgic account of a female sent-down youth's experience in the countryside appears in the beautifully written memoir by Rae Yang. Recalling her adolescent self—a "peasant woman on a pig farm"—nearly 20 years later, she writes:

> Her face was dark brown and weather-beaten. Her hair was as dry and brittle as straw in late fall. She had strong muscles and a loud voice. She loved to eat dog meat with raw garlic. Her face did not change color after she gulped down several cups of Chinese liquor. . . . Although her clothes and boots carried a lot of stinking mud, the work she did was neat and she took great pride in it. (R. Yang 1997, 8–9)

She looks back on her time in the Great Northern Wilderness as crucial to the development of her subsequent sense of self-confidence and fearlessness about trying to support herself in the United States, where she now lives.

> I don't mean that I have much use for the skills I learned on the farm: castrating piglets, building a good kang or a fire wall, winnowing grains with a wooden spade, cutting soybean with a small sickle. . . . But knowing that I did all these and did them well somehow gives me a safe feeling at the bottom of my heart. I do not lose sleep over my tenure evaluation, for example, because I know that I am not just a professor. I was a peasant and a worker. Today if I cannot make a living with my brain and my pen, I will support myself and my son with my muscles and bones. (R. Yang 1997, 174).

Even more striking than Rae Yang's positive assessment of the future value of her labor in the countryside is her adamant conviction that men and women there enjoyed full equality. They received the same pay for the same work, in her view. Women did all the jobs that men did, and invariably did them better. It was always the Iron Girls, for instance, who collected by far the largest soybean harvest—the most physically demanding job on the farm, by her account. So formidable were these young women that the men, who had initially tried to compete, "gave it up and pretended that they did not care" (R. Yang 1997, 178). It is not entirely clear in her account if she is referring only to sent-down youth or to local peasants as well, a distinction that is central to almost all other accounts.

Most urban women who later reported on their experience in the countryside not only highlighted the differences between themselves and their rural counterparts in general terms, but were particularly insistent that they enjoyed total equality while rural women suffered unimaginable forms of inequality, particularly in the context of work. "We educated youth were not like the herdsmen's families," observed a young woman sent to live in Inner Mongolia. Unlike those families, in which the men were responsible for outside affairs (herding and slaughtering sheep, covering the horses) and women for domestic affairs (fetching water, collecting manure), "we would rotate herding the animals and taking care of the house: we would be women one day and men the next *(zuo yitian nüren zai zuo yitian nanren)*" (Yuan 1991, 412). Her account unwittingly reinscribes the sexual division of labor she seeks to critique: rather than questioning local understandings of "men's work" and "women's work," she instead speaks in terms of switching roles, so that she and her friends essentially assumed a male identity to perform the tasks usually done by men. Another woman sent to Inner Mongolia described a similar arrangement among the male and female sent-down youth, who did "inner" and "outer" work regardless of their sex, such that her Mongolian "mother" pitied this "fake boy" (Nuo 1995, 64). A third young woman relocated from Beijing to Inner Mongolia recalls that since peasant girls were "half-laborers," she and her classmates insisted on the status of "full laborers" by doing "men's work." In the spring, for instance, when the girls would plant seeds, she and other sent-down youth joined the "robust laborers" in steering the ox-plow. At the well, peasant women would only pull the rope, while "we did the heavy jobs at the bottom of the well. . . . We refused to display any weakness: we forged iron, constructed buildings, and carried 200-*jin* gunnysacks. We became true laborers" (Y. Zhang 1995, 219–20).

Many sent-down youth had to confront not only the unexpected reality of rural women's subordination, but their first experiences of gender inequality as well. Zhai Zhenhua, for example, reports her dismay at the discovery that women in the rural area near Yan'an where she had been sent "weren't a major force in production." To prepare meals they worked far fewer hours than men, and it appeared to Zhai that during the winter women did not work outside the home at all. The real surprise for Zhai, though, was finding that when women did work the same hours as men, they earned less. Such was also the case in the assignment of work points to the sent-down youth. For Zhai's group, girls could earn a maximum of seven points for a day's work, while boys could earn nine. "I had always taken for granted the equality of men and women," she confessed. "But now I saw it

fail in reality. We female students did the same work and had the same working hours as men but scored two points less." She did not complain, though,
because she realized that when women did the same work as men, such as
carrying stones, they could not match men's ability. But she did feel dis-
turbed: "Women in the city weren't discriminated against so overtly. All university graduates earned the same salary, as far as I knew. To make a living
in the countryside brains didn't really matter. What mattered was strength
and sex" (Zhai 1992, 170–71).

It is not clear in her account how often women and men actually did exactly the same jobs. Instead, when she describes the project of building cave
dwellings for sent-down youth, she highlights the division of labor between
local peasants and themselves. "The former did the actual laying of stones
for the caves while we were *xiaogong* (little laborers), or those who engaged
in subordinate work." Among the "little laborers," however, was an even
more precise division of labor. "Male students carried stones on their back
to the spot; female students made mud with husks, soil, and water" (Zhai
1992, 198–99). It is difficult to determine whether this division of labor was
prescribed by the local brigade leaders, was consciously developed by the
students, or simply reflected their own "naturalized" beliefs about appropriate work for men and women.

If sent-down youth were shocked by the persistence of gender inequality in the countryside, many saw themselves as crusaders for change and
proudly chronicle their battles against objectionable divisions of labor. One
account describes a girl, Xiao Sun, sent down to the countryside from
Chengdu. She was first assigned to be a health worker in a rural chemical
factory—a job envied by those with much more arduous work. She was not
content, however, and demanded the more challenging "battle assignment"
of working in the mines. When the leader informed her of the regulation
prohibiting women from the mines, she replied, "But the times have
changed. Men and women are the same! Why can't women comrades do the
same things men comrades can do?" The local cadre found it difficult to
oppose her, as the newspapers had propagated so many stories of Iron Girls,
and female heroines such as Hua Mulan and Tie Guiying. Xiao Sun was
therefore permitted to work in the mines during the day and prepare med-
icines at night. Her example was eventually used to persuade reluctant or
unwilling male workers to go down the mines as well: "If female comrades
can work in the mines, is it possible that you are not as capable as they?"
Having crossed the gender divide and worked in a uranium mine for seven
years, Xiao Sun eventually developed lung cancer and died at the age of 30
(Deng 1992, 83–84).

Few accounts of women's battles to do the same jobs as rural men have
such dramatic and unfortunate endings. One woman who was sent to Inner
Mongolia reported that "of all the things we [female sent-down youths] did,

what was most unforgettable to people was our driving the carts." She describes one year at planting time when the team leader became frustrated with the two lazy village men responsible for driving carts to move heaps of dung and dirt. He wanted to replace them, but all the strong male workers had gone to repair a reservoir, and the only villagers left were old, weak, or those with "political problems." The young urban women seized the moment. Seeing the quandary of the team leader, they stood up and in unison declared, "Today men and women are the same! Anything men can do women can do too, and we can do it even better!" From then on, she proudly reports, women were allowed to drive the carts. She does mention that women were designated "assistant drivers," a minor point that apparently did not detract from her conviction that she and her friends had brought some modicum of women's liberation to Inner Mongolia (Hui 1991, 477–78).

Another woman sent to Inner Mongolia boasted of her team's accomplishments in winning access for women to work in the threshing ground. It was harvest time when she first arrived, and she and her friends excitedly anticipated joining in the work of gathering crops. When the morning whistle blew for work they rushed to the commune room, where they found only robust young men waiting to be assigned jobs. "At first we thought this was strange," she recalls, "but as we thought about it figured that maybe they had given women time off to take care of housework, since it was such a busy autumn. . . . We never imagined that the team leader would only permit male laborers to enter the threshing ground."

They were even more perplexed when the team leader assigned an older male peasant to lead the girls to collect cotton stalks that they could use as kindling. Although they still hoped to work in the threshing ground, they realized that they would need the kindling for winter and therefore had no grounds to oppose the assignment. They worked as hard as they could, finishing within half a day, with the hope that they could then go do "real" work. Instead, however, the team leader instructed them to use the afternoon to rest and do laundry. The next day they rushed off to the team gathering even earlier, only to find themselves once again assigned to go off with the older man, this time to trample down a manure heap. "We came to be educated by the peasants," they told themselves in an attempt to quell their frustration. Given how large the harvest was, they could not comprehend why their labor would not be desired, and so finally questioned the team leader directly. "At first he hemmed and hawed, but then finally told us it was because we were female . . . and that threshing grain was men's work." When pressed, he could offer no explanation other than "tradition." "People believed that if women entered the threshing ground it would bring disaster." "Hearing this we were enraged and stunned," she recalls. "This was too backwards! After so many years, how could there still be so much superstition?" She listed the "strange customs" of the village: "women cannot sit on windowsills," "women cannot touch the hats of men they don't know;" "women's clothes may not be dried on the roadside." Finally, there was the belief that to destroy these beliefs would bring disaster to the men and to the village. "These attitudes were an obstacle to our right to work. We Beijing girls, unafraid of the earth or heavens, were determined to destroy these old customs. Some older people didn't want us to enter the threshing ground, but they couldn't stop us."

She and her teammates then confronted the team leader, accusing him of being an "old feudal" *(lao fengjian)* and reactionary for looking down on women. When the Party secretary was summoned, they yelled, "Do Communists still believe in superstitions? Do we still tolerate discrimination against women? We hold up half the sky!" Eventually the Beijing girls were permitted to help harvest grain—work that proved to be far more taxing than they had anticipated, but which they then felt obliged to endure. More important, they had established a precedent. After this, families lacking male labor used their example to persuade the team leader to permit women to harvest grain (Sheng 1991, 381–83).

Several features of these accounts are striking. Whatever ambiguity or ambivalence might have characterized Cultural Revolution state propaganda about appropriate women's roles, these adolescent urban-educated girls clearly took slogans such as "women can do whatever men can do" or models such as the Iron Girls at face value, invoking language provided by the state to contest actual social practice. Too young to have had work experience themselves, they assumed that urban women were indeed liberated and enjoyed full equality in the workforce. These young women adopted a missionary-like attitude in bringing liberation to their rural counterparts. While their intentions were clear, their assessment of rural women's labor may have been flawed, perhaps mistaking beliefs about women's ideal roles for social practice (see also chap. 5).

What led these female sent-down youth to champion the issue of gender equality? What produced "Iron Girlism" among them remains unclear. One can only speculate whether earlier Cultural Revolution experiences, such as participation in the Red Guard movement, had an impact on their self-image as women in the countryside. One wonders as well whether they learned of or ever encountered local labor heroines—those of the 1950s described by Gail Hershatter (chap. 5) as well as subsequent rural female models of the early and mid-1960s. No mention of these models appears in any of these memoirs. Finally, as all the accounts of the sent-down youth experience are written by the urban women themselves, it is impossible to know how rural women perceived the urban women's efforts to champion women's "right" to work. Did they find these young girls naive and foolish or, conversely, did they admire and appreciate their efforts?

In all the accounts described above it is the sent-down youth themselves who took the initiative to challenge rural beliefs about women's roles. Yet on some occasions it may have been local cadres, not women themselves, who instigated these challenges. At least one woman recalls that she and her female classmates, upon their arrival in a rural Shanxi village, were assigned to do jobs never before done by local women, including making bricks, loading them in the kiln, firing the kiln, and then hauling them to construction sites. When asked why female sent-down youth were assigned these jobs, she surmised it was because no local male workers were available; these jobs had previously been done by hired labor, and now the sent-down youth appeared as a readily available source. In some areas local cadres actually "toured" groups of urban women to demonstrate to their village counterparts that women *could* in fact work for remuneration. In these cases, urban women were used as a kind of dog-and-pony show that performed at the behest of local male cadres. How widespread a phenomenon this was, what the cadres' agenda was in staging these performances, and how they were experienced by both the sent-down youth and rural women are questions that remain to be explored.

It is difficult to determine the impact of the presence, battles, and "performances" of the sent-down youth on rural women's work. According to one Chinese analyst, in spite of all the efforts of female sent-down youth to achieve equality for rural women, little changed. Throughout the Cultural Revolution, she observes, the practice of men and women receiving different pay for the same work was so common as to be the rule. Women earned, at best, five to eight work points for every ten made by men (Huang 1990). More than remuneration was at stake, however. One sent-down youth, after proudly recalling her successful efforts to organize an Iron Girl Brigade among the young women in the village, confessed that once she left and the brigade leader married, the Iron Girl team dissolved.

It is important to point out that not all female sent-down youth saw themselves as either inspirational models for rural women or as zealous crusaders fighting local opponents to women's equal status in the workforce. The initial glamour and glory of engaging in hard physical labor was sometimes replaced by a desperation to escape work altogether. For instance, one memoir describes a young woman named Zhang, who had been the author's classmate in Inner Mongolia. "Two years ago," the author recalls, "Zhang had been a very devoted worker who was determined to turn the heavens and earth upside down. She was unafraid of hardship or exhaustion, and quickly became a women's team leader." At that time Zhang complained that the other three female educated youth in her group, unable to bear the hardship of work, had married. They had betrayed the revolution, according to Zhang, and she was unwilling to compromise her determination. Over the next year, though, Zhang found it increasingly difficult to support herself, and eventually found herself a local husband. Although she was not completely satisfied with the idea of marriage, she too had become ex- hausted by work and figured that with marriage she could at least give up hard labor (Xu Huiying 1991, 426–48).

What we see then is that the very phenomenon that some educated youth found so appalling and unbelievable—that once married, rural women (at least in some regions) did not work in the fields—was something that other women could use to their advantage. Marrying into a peasant family be- came a strategy to avoid work altogether—or so it may have seemed, until women like Zhang realized the myriad household tasks for which married women were responsible. (These included, as described in one account "hauling water from the pond, washing vegetables for pig and human food, feeding the fire with brushwood, cooking, scrubbing clothing, repairing the grass roof when it leaked, spinning thread from cotton for mending, and cleaning the kitchen so that not even a fly could feed itself in it") (Liang Heng and Shapiro 1983, 192).

CONCLUSION

The picture of rural women's work that can be gleaned from the memoirs of sent-down educated youth is not altogether surprising and is consistent with the findings of previous studies (A. Chan, Madsen, and Unger 1984, 92–93; Johnson 1983; Parish and Whyte 1978, 235–47): Throughout the Cultural Revolution the value accorded labor in the countryside was based primarily on the physical strength required to perform a particular job. Women could never hope to earn the same number of work points as men and were re- sponsible for the domestic sphere as well. However, these accounts are highly instructive about the ways in which young urban women, most of whom had grown up in the 1950s and early 1960s, perceived their rural counterparts, *their* surprise at what they observed and experienced, and the ways in which they assumed the identity of crusaders to challenge women's unequal status in the rural workforce, wielding official rhetoric to do so.

These accounts remind us of the inseparability of issues of urban and rural women's work during the Cultural Revolution. Although the implica- tions of widespread labor migration in China are most commonly studied in the context of the post-Mao economic reforms (e.g., part 3 of this vol- ume), the Cultural Revolution, too, involved a massive labor migration, al- beit the movement of urban people to the countryside rather than of peas- ants to the city. Any analysis of the gendered dimensions of work, whether an exploration of changing beliefs about women's and men's work or an examination of the sexual division of labor, must take into account the im- pact of their mutual perceptions and interaction. This is not simply a story of naive urban youth who took pride in their attempts to dismantle the barriers between men's and women's work. It also involved the sober realization that the household chores of a peasant wife could be preferable to the arduous physical labor of peasant men.

Issues of women's work during the Cultural Revolution cannot be collapsed into a simple Iron Girl model. The Iron Girls never represented the totality of state propaganda, and certainly never represented cultural norms about appropriate work for women. Far more significant than the model itself is how it was understood and manipulated by local officials, and by urban and rural women. The rhetoric of the economic reforms has effectively reduced the Cultural Revolution history of women's work to the Iron Girls, and in so doing has obscured not only the lives and experiences of most women, but also the terms in and through which issues of women's work were negotiated.

SEVEN

Wage and Job Inequalities in the Working Lives of Men and Women in Tianjin

Yanjie Bian, John R. Logan, and Xiaoling Shu

In this chapter we confront a paradox in the evolution of China's stratification system. On the one hand, income inequality has newly emerged as the most important dimension of inequality in people's life chances. As recently as the mid-1980s, bureaucratic allocation of commodities such as housing and health care seemed to have more importance than income (Henderson 1990; Walder 1986). By the 1990s, however, real incomes of urban residents doubled and income inequality rose by 50 percent (Bian and Logan 1996). In fact, a substantial literature has appeared, asking how these changes are linked to the transformation of China's economic institutions since 1978 under market reform (most recently, Bian and Logan 1996; Nee 1996; Parish and Michelson 1996; Szelényi and Kostello 1996; Walder 1996; Xie Yu and Hannum 1996).

On the other hand, gender disparities in wages seem to have continued untouched. Our previous multivariate analyses of wages in Tianjin have shown that the net effect of gender on wages, controlling for background factors and job characteristics, was essentially unchanged: a 15.2 percent male advantage in 1978 and an 18.3 percent male advantage in 1993 (Bian and Logan 1996, table 4). Further review of the Tianjin data reveals that the gross gender disparity, i.e., the effect of gender with no controls for background factors and job characteristics, was even more stable: a 26.1 percent male advantage in 1978, compared to 26.0 percent in 1993.[1]

How can one account for such stability in gender inequality during a period of rapid change in the economy and class structure as a whole? Researchers have almost universally expected market reform to change the standing of Chinese women workers, although they have not agreed on the direction of change. Let us review their arguments.

One view points to the equalizing effect of market forces as these are introduced into a formerly planned economy. In the planned economy, income inequality is derived from bureaucratic power (Szelényi 1978). However,

> as power—control over resources—shifts progressively from political disposition to market institutions, there will be a change in the distribution of rewards favoring those who hold market rather than redistributive power. Opportunities are more broadly based and diverse when markets replace and augment the opportunity structure controlled by the state. (Nee 1996, 910–11)

This market-as-equalizer argument implies that, because women generally had less political power and therefore lower wages than men before reforms, market reform will tend to equalize labor market opportunities of men and women, and the gender wage gap will therefore decline (Whyte 1984; for Eastern Europe, see Einhorn 1993, 116–26; Sørensen and Trappe 1995). During the transition to a more market-oriented economy, wage differentials would come to depend more upon education and work experience—domains in which men have had smaller advantages over women. Hence Nee and Matthews specifically predict that "the more extensive the shift to markets and the higher the rate of economic growth, . . . [the greater tendency that] the gender wage gap [will] decline" (1996, 428–29).

Exactly the opposite position could be taken by those who credit the Chinese state with having equalized opportunities for women. This state-as-equalizer view is based on the Communist Party's ideological goals of liberating Chinese women after 1949 (Croll 1983; Stacey 1983). The Cultural Revolution of 1966–76 has been seen as an extreme case where the party-state forcefully pushed its equalization programs, including those for women's equalization with men, even at the expense of its economic interests (Parish 1981, 1984a; Whyte and Parish 1984). In the economic sphere, women's relative improvements in work participation, job security, and wages are seen as the coproducts of a strong, ideology-driven, and centralized party-state that achieved these goals through central planning and job assignments (K. Johnson 1976). From this perspective it might be expected that the delegation of authority to work unit managers under market reform would jeopardize women's position in the workplace.

Indeed there is some evidence that this has occurred. Social historians Honig and Hershatter (1988) have observed that work unit managers in the reform era, like employers in a capitalist economy, see women workers as less reliable (married women with children have the potential to interrupt work schedules in order to fulfill child care responsibilities), less effi-

cient (married women are less amenable than men to overtime assignments), and more expensive (work units must provide maternity leave with
full pay and child care services to married women with children) than men
workers. These perceptions of women workers are not new, but in the reform era managers have greater incentives to reduce labor costs and more
authority to adjust their hiring, job assignments, and wage assignments to
their views of women (Ran 1988; Wu 1995) At one point even "reform-
minded" scholars regarded laying off women workers as a means to achieve
economic efficiency and protect men's jobs (Stockman 1994), but this pro-
posal was rejected by the still-influential All China Women's Federation.
Nevertheless, in the 1990s more and more women have been asked by their
work units to "stay home" (an alternative to a formal layoff) and receive a
small percentage of their base salaries (Wu 1995).

Managers in public enterprises are not the only possible source of discrimination against women. Lee (1995) observes that profit-driven managers in the private sector and international joint ventures discriminate
against their female employees. Discrimination also comes from the family
(Davis 1995; Davis-Friedmann 1991). For example, in a multiprovince study,
Entwisle et al. (1995) found that although rural women predominated in
sideline family businesses before reforms, these women are surprisingly underrepresented now that household businesses have become a main source
of family income during the reforms.

The persistent gender wage gap in Tianjin supports neither the "market
as equalizer" nor the "state as equalizer" argument. Chapters 5 and 6 in this
volume have indicated that the Chinese state never equalized labor market
opportunities between men and women. Further, Deng Xiaoping's market
reforms were not designed to equalize gender differences. To be sure, Tianjin does not yet have a completely market economy, nor is it among the most
reformed regions of China. As the third largest Chinese city with a population of 10 million, next to Shanghai (13 million) and Beijing (11 million),
Tianjin is under the jurisdiction of and strongly influenced by the central
government. The general wisdom is that reforms in Guangdong, Fujian,
and Hainan provinces, all in the far south, were implemented earlier and
more completely. Nevertheless, Tianjin belongs to the next category of
coastal regions in east China, where reforms have been more aggressive
than in inland regions of the northwest and southwest. What would account
for the stability of the gender gap in such a place?

THE ORIGINS OF THE GENDER GAP: A COHORT APPROACH

In this study we apply to this question a conclusion recently argued by Walder
(1996) for stratification in general: that the market per se has no inherent

implications for disparities between men and women in the labor force. Under certain assumptions (e.g., that productivity is the main determinant of wages), the market may be an equalizer. This is Nee and Matthews' (1996) assumption. Because women are no less productive than men with similar skills and experience, a free labor market should pay women and men equally. Under other assumptions, the market is not an equalizer. For example, if Chinese families favor employment of men even at the cost of forced retirement for women, the potentially large layoffs that market reform may eventually provoke in deficit-ridden work units will place women at a disadvantage. In the same way, under certain assumptions (e.g., that state policy enforces formal equality of men and women), the state is an equalizer. Under others (e.g., if the ruling Communist Party favors membership by men, whose political authority is then translatable into higher wages), it is not. These issues cannot be resolved at the level of abstract principles. In fact, all the assumptions stated above may be at least partly correct, which means that the market—and the state too—could be both an equalizer *and* a source of inequality.

Therefore we proceed more cautiously to specify the sources of inequality and to see how these have affected successive cohorts of men and women as they entered the labor force and developed their work careers over the last half-century. To this end we make use of the same 1993 Tianjin survey previously analyzed by Bian and Logan (1996), dividing the sample into cohorts of men and women based on when they entered the labor force. Gender inequality potentially begins with differential preparation of young men and women (in terms of education, for example), placement in their first job, and initial wage offers for people in similar jobs. It evolves over people's careers as men and women experience different possibilities of job mobility (or pressures for retirement) and as their wages grow at different rates. All of these processes together yield the particular level of gender wage inequality that we measure at a single point in time. And they are all susceptible to change.

Respondents in the 1993 Tianjin survey entered the civilian urban labor force from 1923 to 1993. Based on this information, we have constructed five labor cohorts whose job placements and wages were influenced by the significant events and policies of the periods of their career entry and of subsequent periods: (1) pre-1949 cohort, whose job histories began prior to Communist rule; (2) 1949–57 cohort, who started their career in a socialist mixed economy of multiple property forms; (3) 1958–65 cohort, who entered the labor force when Mao's government gained total control of the urban economy through the Socialist Transformation (1956–58) and when the Great Leap Forward (1958–61) mobilized women and especially housewives to work outside home; (4) 1966–77 cohort, who acquired their first jobs during the Cultural Revolution, a political and economic crisis in which economic egalitarianism was believed to reach its zenith; and (5) 1978–93 cohort, who started their work career during the new era of market-oriented reforms under Deng Xiaoping.

People in these cohorts differ greatly in how they obtained their first jobs and in the conditions under which they have worked. The pre-1949 Tianjin economy was dominated by foreign investments, especially by Japan during its occupation of the city from 1937 to 1945. Many members of this cohort were migrants from nearby rural areas and their children. This rural-to-urban migration was restricted after January 1949, when Tianjin was liberated from the Nationalist government. However, searching for jobs was an individual action for most members of the 1949–57 cohort, because the new government did not have the capacity to implement full-scale job assignment programs until the Socialist Transformation (1956–58).

Members of the 1958–65 cohort were almost exclusively assigned jobs by the government in the state and collective sectors, but there was a small proportion (about 1–2%) who chose to work as independent laborers (e.g., shoe repairers, ice pop vendors). Many housewives were mobilized during the early years of this period to work for pay, but they were mainly assigned jobs in small collective enterprises managed by subdistrict governments. The next cohort, 1966–77, entered the labor force during the Cultural Revolution. From 1966 to 1969, graduates from all but technical schools were "sent down" to the countryside; only a small fraction could stay in the city for health or family reasons. However, the city was able to assign jobs to all youths who graduated from schools in 1970. Starting in 1971, being "sent down" resumed, but more and more youths began to be assigned jobs in the city. Finally, the 1978–93 cohort entered the economy in a period of market reform. The reform period has evolved considerably in these last 15 years: after 1986 most new workers signed temporary labor contracts (for 3–5 years) with the work units to which they were assigned, and after 1991, job assignments were abolished and replaced by emerging labor markets in Tianjin (Bian 1998). Most relevant to our concerns, work units achieved considerable autonomy in personnel and wage policies in the reform period.

If there have been changes in the extent and sources of gender inequality, these may emerge as differences among these cohorts of workers in any of the following characteristics:

1. The backgrounds of young men and women as they enter their first job, and their achievements up to the time of their current (1993) job or retirement. Within each cohort, we will consider whether men and women entered the labor force at the same age, with similar education,

or similar levels of Communist Party membership, and whether they subsequently had similar opportunities to improve their education or enter the Party, and similar likelihood of retirement at a given age. In a society where the consistent pressure of the state for greater equality was maintained, we might expect strong gender differences in earlier cohorts but a tendency for them to diminish among more recent cohorts.

2. The kinds of jobs that men and women were able to enter, and their job mobility up to their present position. Several job characteristics have been found to affect wages independently of gender and other background factors. These include occupational category as well as the institutional sector and bureaucratic rank of one's work unit. Again, comparisons across cohorts provide a longitudinal perspective on the "gender-typing" of occupations and work units.

3. The direct effects of gender on wages (after controlling for other characteristics), as well as indirect effects (through gender differences in other predictors and in the payoffs from those predictors). Cohort differences in the gender gap in initial wage can be tied directly to state policies and market conditions that prevailed at the time of job entry simply because they coincided in time. Cohort differences in the current (1993) gender gap are more complex. They depend on men's and women's starting points. (Therefore we will control for initial wage as a way of holding constant this factor.) But more important, the current wage of an older worker depends to some degree on what happened during his or her whole work career. Advantages or disadvantages incurred at any point could affect present standing. The current wage—hence, the current gender gap—for workers who entered in the most recent cohort reflects only the conditions of the reform period. Still it will be instructive to examine cohort differences in the direct and indirect effects of gender on current wage.

Details of our 1993 Tianjin sample (N = 1042) can be found in Bian and Logan (1996). Briefly, the sample was based on a multistage probability sampling procedure, including all of the city's 124 subdistricts (the lowest level of government administration in the city residential management structure). Registered households were randomly selected from each sampled subdistrict and neighborhood. The respondent was either the head of household, if available, or an adult person of 18 years or older from the household. Because heads of households are mostly male, two-thirds of the resulting sample is male. The response rate was close to 100 percent, which is typical in Chinese surveys with official authorization (P. Blau and Ruan 1990; Lin and Bian 1991). Definitions of key variables are provided below, as we report the average values for men and women in various cohorts.

BACKGROUND CHARACTERISTICS RELEVANT TO JOBS

Information on background characteristics (age, education, and Party membership) is presented by gender and cohort in table 7.1. Men and women of the pre-1949 cohort entered the labor force at a younger age than did post-1949 cohorts. Little gender variation in age at career entry is observed for all but the 1958–65 cohort. For this cohort, women's average age at career entry is 2.6 years older than men, which suggests that some women not in the workforce in the early 1950s were mobilized to work after 1958.

More consistent gender differences are found in education, at job entry, and at the time of the survey. There is a clear trend of increasing proportions with a high school or vocational education across cohorts, from 15–20 percent in the pre-1949 cohort to over 50 percent in the most recent cohort. Gender differences are erratic: women appear somewhat favored in the two earliest cohorts, at a disadvantage in the next two, and equal in the last one. The male advantage appears, rather, in college education. At job entry there is a 2–8 percent gap between the percentage of men and women with a college education, and the gap widens after that. For some people, attainment of higher education occurs after they enter the labor force. This educational upgrading is more prevalent for men than for women in all but the 1949–57 cohort. We believe this is due to a work unit bias in favor of men. Employees must obtain permission from their work unit to temporarily or periodically leave their jobs in order to attend school. These employees continue to be paid their regular salaries, and they receive additional financial aid from their work units to cover their tuition and related costs in school. These data suggest a work unit bias in favor of investing in men rather than women.

The third background characteristic in table 7.1 is Communist Party membership. Party membership is more common among men than women in every cohort at the time of their first job, and the percentage point difference in the party membership of men and women increases from the first to the current job. Except for the most recent cohort, for whom we hesitate to give much weight because of the strong positive association between Party membership and age, this pattern is the same for every cohort—a surprising finding especially for the Cultural Revolution cohort of 1966–77, when the Party was thought to be at the peak of its promotion of gender equality.

OCCUPATIONS, WORK UNITS, RETIREMENT, AND WAGES

Up to this point we have identified gender disparities in education and Party membership, disparities that increased during the working career of

TABLE 7.1 Respondents' Background Characteristics by Gender and Cohort, Tianjin, 1993

| | Labor Cohort (Time Entering the Labor Force) and Gender | | | | | | | | | |
| | Pre-1949 | | 1949-57 | | 1958-65 | | 1966-77 | | 1978-93 | |
	Men	Women	Men	Women	Men	Women	Men	Women	Men	Women
Number of cases	69	18	161	39	111	75	206	106	154	98
Mean age										
First job	17.1	16.6	22.2	21.8	19.7	22.3	20.1	20.8	21.7	22.9
Current job	66.5	62.9	63.3	62.9	52.7	56.0	41.8	42.6	34.4	35.0
High/tech school (%)										
First job	14.4	22.2	17.3	23.0	36.0	22.6	28.1	25.4	57.7	57.1
Current job	17.3	27.7	21.1	20.5	32.4	18.6	29.1	29.2	50.6	56.1
College and higher (%)										
First job	7.2	5.5	10.5	3.5	15.3	8.0	8.2	2.8	7.7	3.1
Current job	13.0	5.5	15.5	12.8	25.2	16.0	17.4	10.3	18.8	9.1
Chinese Communist Party members (%)										
First job	18.8	5.5	10.5	2.7	7.2	4.0	6.3	2.8	5.1	1.0
Current job	37.6	16.6	37.2	28.2	37.8	17.3	26.2	17.9	12.3	5.1

SOURCE: 1993 Tianjin Household Survey.

our respondents but did not change consistently across cohorts. We turn now to their actual jobs and wages. Table 7.2 provides average values on four dimensions of people's jobs: occupation, work unit sector, work unit rank, and wage.

Occupation

Occupation is coded into five categories, based on an initial three-category classification developed by Bian and Logan (1996) to indicate the worker's participation in decision making or connections to market activity. This classification is intended to be sensitive to the postulate of market transition that rewards in a redistributive system go to those with decision-making power, while rewards in a market system go to those who participate more directly in the market. Two categories of workers participate in decision making: "administrative" (people with the formal authority to make decisions for the organization) and "clerical" (people whose main duty is to assist administrators but who are strategically placed to control information and routine processing of decisions). There are also two categories of market involvement: "market activity" (occupations directly involved in marketing, such as purchasing agents and sales persons) and "market potential" (occupations involving direct contact with customers, such as medical workers and drivers, or whose function is to develop or improve technologies that suit the changing market environment, such as engineers and technicians). We use the term "other" for occupations that fit none of these categories, mostly factory workers who are not in direct contact with customers. Bian and Logan (1996) find that jobs with redistributive power (the first two categories combined) had higher wages than "other" jobs from 1978 to 1993, net of job holders' education, experience, Party membership, and work unit placements. Jobs with market connection (the second two categories combined) had substantially higher wages than "other" jobs only in 1993, when comprehensive reforms had been introduced in Tianjin's economy.

Table 7.2 shows that for the first three cohorts, women's initial job placements were more likely than men's to be in occupations with no market involvement or decision-making power, but this potential disadvantage was reversed for the two more recent cohorts. Have women therefore improved their occupational status? Taking into account changes during their work careers, we find considerable room for doubt. By the time of their current job, there is a general tendency among men and women to leave low-level occupations, but such mobility is greater for men.

The top decision-making occupations—administrators—have tended to be predominantly male for every cohort, both at job entry (by a smaller margin) and at current job (by a larger margin, especially for cohorts with

TABLE 7.2 Job-Related Variables by Gender and Cohort, Tianjin, 1993

| | Labor Cohort (Time Entering the Labor Force) and Gender | | | | | | | | | |
| | Pre-1949 | | 1949-57 | | 1958-65 | | 1966-77 | | 1978-93 | |
	Men	Women	Men	Women	Men	Women	Men	Women	Men	Women
Occupation										
Administrative occupation (%)										
First job	5.8	0.0	2.5	2.6	6.3	1.3	2.9	0.9	2.6	2.0
Current job	17.4	0.0	13.1	7.7	17.1	2.6	10.2	4.7	4.6	3.1
Clerical occupation (%)										
First job	8.7	11.1	12.4	15.4	8.1	5.3	8.3	17.0	8.4	13.3
Current job	8.7	11.1	13.0	12.8	15.3	10.7	16.0	17.9	10.4	18.4
Market activity occupation (%)										
First job	13.0	5.6	11.1	2.6	4.5	6.7	8.3	11.3	6.5	14.3
Current job	10.1	5.6	13.7	5.1	5.4	6.7	10.7	18.9	11.0	14.3
Market potential occupation (%)										
First job	20.3	22.2	29.2	20.5	31.5	28.0	30.1	24.5	35.1	27.6
Current job	21.7	27.8	30.0	23.1	31.5	21.3	32.0	17.9	37.0	26.5
Other occupation (%)										
First job	44.9	50.0	41.6	53.9	48.7	58.7	50.0	46.2	46.1	42.9
Current job	40.6	55.6	32.3	48.7	30.6	58.7	31.1	40.6	36.4	37.8

TABLE 7.2 (continued)

Labor Cohort (Time Entering the Labor Force) and Gender

	Pre–1949		1949–57		1958–65		1966–77		1978–93	
	Men	Women	Men	Women	Men	Women	Men	Women	Men	Women
Institutional Sector										
State sector (%)										
First job	n.a.	n.a.	86.3	82.0	90.0	82.6	85.9	71.7	81.9	64.2
Current job	79.7	77.7	88.2	87.1	88.2	74.6	83.9	71.7	82.4	65.4
Collective sector (%)										
First job	n.a.	n.a.	5.6	10.2	8.1	17.3	13.1	26.4	14.2	31.6
Current job	13.0	16.6	5.6	7.6	9.0	13.3	11.6	25.4	11.6	29.5
New sector (%)										
First job	n.a.	n.a.	8.0	7.6	1.8	0.0	0.9	1.8	3.9	4.0
Current job	7.2	5.5	6.2	5.1	2.7	12.0	4.3	2.8	5.8	5.1
Work Unit Rank										
Work Units with *chu* or higher rank (%)										
First job	n.a.	n.a.	44.1	33.3	50.4	28.0	40.0	26.4	40.2	38.7
Current job	37.6	50.0	49.0	43.5	50.4	37.3	48.0	30.1	42.2	40.8
Retirees (%)	62.3	77.7	44.1	76.9	9.9	50.6	0.0	8.4	1.3	2.0
Wage										
Average monthly wage (in *yuan*)										
First job	60.0	42.4	53.7	41.7	46.4	37.8	60.8	47.3	75.9	80.3
Current job	288.9	229.0	278.7	227.9	290.6	226.6	287.7	222.9	259.9	218.8

SOURCE: 1993 Tianjin Household Survey.

more years of experience). The pattern across cohorts does not conform to any simple hypothesis about the effects of ideology or markets. One of the greatest discrepancies between men and women at first job and in mobility to current job is in the 1958–65 "socialist transition" cohort, and a clear gender gap is found even in the 1966–77 "Cultural Revolution" cohort. Thus it is hard to find any support for the view that state policy specifically favored women's chances of achieving administrative positions during those periods. A better case can be made for greater gender equality in the most recent cohort (as we also found in the distribution of "other" jobs). Women in this cohort remain almost as likely as men to be administrators in their current jobs, although here again we caution that much hinges on the process of future career mobility, which may already be favoring men in this cohort.

It is in the clerical occupations that women have a clearer and continuing (perhaps increasing) edge over men. It is important to note that these are not low-paid and low-prestige occupations. Our analysis of wages below shows that they are paid better than "other" occupations, and they are often perceived as desirable white-collar positions for men and women (note that they are positions that men often move into during their work careers). The most relevant shift across cohorts is what seems to be a greater predominance of women in this category in the two more recent cohorts, and a tendency in the 1978–93 cohort for women to move into this category (from their entry position) at a greater rate than men.

In the two market-connected categories, there seems to have been a shift over time toward female predominance in occupations with direct market activity (sales and purchasing). But occupations with "market potential" have remained predominantly male. As we shall see below, both of these market sectors have higher-than-average wages. Thus the channeling of men into one and women toward the other is neutral in its effects on gender wage disparities.

To summarize this detailed review of occupational differences, the key male advantage seems to be in administrative occupations and occupations with market potential. Women have an advantage in clerical occupations and those with market activity. In the most "political" of these categories, administration, there is little evidence that egalitarian ideology became a more potent factor in the more intensely "socialist" years of 1958–77. There is some indication of female gains in the market reform period, shown as smaller proportions of women in "other" jobs, somewhat greater access to administrative jobs, and a stronger grip on clerical and market activity jobs. But in two of these comparisons (looking at "other" and administrative jobs) there is also evidence of a male edge in mobility from first to current job, which in previous cohorts eventually resulted in clear male advantages. This consideration makes us hesitate to emphasize what would otherwise seem to be a positive result of market reform for women.

Work Units

Work unit rank is a dichotomous variable, comparing ranks of *chu* or higher (i.e., division, bureau, ministry) with lower ranks (i.e., department, section, or no rank). Previous studies have shown that the higher the rank, the higher the wages for workers (Bian 1994b, 167–170; Bian and Logan 1996; Walder 1992b). Work unit sector is a categorical variable, having three broad categories: (1) state sector, (2) collective sector, and (3) new sector. The new sector consists of private and semi-private forms of economic organization, including individual laborers, household business, domestic private companies, foreign firms, international joint ventures, and organizations based on mixed property arrangements. Decomposing the new sector category into subcategories is not possible because of small numbers of respondents in each subcategory. These measures apply only to the post-1949 Chinese economy; therefore we exclude the pre-1949 cohort from our analysis of sectoral placement at career entry.

Overall, at career entry and current job, women are more likely than men to be found in the collective sector and to be underrepresented in the state sector. This disparity is stronger in younger cohorts than in older cohorts, and it is a great disadvantage for women—it is a greater disparity and has more impact on the gender wage gap than the differences in occupation discussed above.

Surprisingly, although women also are generally in work units of lower rank than men, there is no gender difference in rank in the 1978–93 cohort. This indicates that although women in this cohort tend to be assigned jobs in collective enterprises, it is the collective enterprises at higher bureaucratic levels (managed by industrial bureaus or district governments) that have recruited new workers after 1978.

Little gender difference is observed in percentages of men and women working in the new sector of private and semi-private economic organizations. Given the mixed economy of multiple ownership forms in the early 1950s, the 1949–57 cohort had 8.0 percent of men and 7.6 percent of women who started their career in the private or semi-private sectors, but the next two cohorts had only 1–2 percent of men or women having their first jobs in these sectors because of tightening state control over the urban economy during the 1960s and 1970s. The 1978–93 cohort entered the labor force during a new era of reforms, but in Tianjin only about 4 percent of men and women have started jobs in the private or semi-private sectors. As of 1993, each cohort had increased its rate of participation in private or semi-private sectors, with men and women moving equally into these activities.

Retirement

Another indicator of labor force activity shown in table 7.2 is retirement. Here, as with sectoral differences above, we find sharp gender differences. The official age of compulsory retirement is 50 for women workers, 60 for men. Cadres and professionals at high levels are allowed to continue to work until age 55 for women and age 65 for men. These policies enhance opportunities for younger people in an urban economy that might otherwise have a high rate of unemployment for young adults. It is not surprising, therefore, that in the first three cohorts (all of whom include people in their 50s and older), women are more likely than men to be retired. This difference is particularly large for the 1958–65 cohort, in which half the women but only a tenth of the men are retired. But it also appears in the younger 1966–77 cohort, where 8.4 percent of women, but no men, are retired. These latter cohorts have been affected by a new practice of *dingti,* or children inheriting their parents' jobs. When urban youths sent to the countryside during the Cultural Revolution flooded back to the cities during 1978 and 1979, mothers rather than fathers usually took the option to retire early in order for children to work. Although this practice was interrupted during the 1980s (Bian 1994b; Davis 1990), we learned from our field interviews in Tianjin that work units in the state and collective sectors have begun using this practice again in order to relieve unemployment among their employees' children. Women may be pressed into early retirement at reduced pay as a byproduct of market reform.

Wages

We turn finally to wages. Our measure is the total monthly wages including base salary, bonuses, and other nonsalary payments from work. There are likely to be recall errors in first-job wages—more so for members of older cohorts. However, there is little reason to believe that there would be a gender bias in recall errors, so we can focus our attention on wage differentials between men and women within each cohort. Gender differences in monthly wage are observed for first job and current job in almost all cohorts. The exception is entry wages in the 1978–93 cohort, in which women earned more than men. At career entry, women's wage as a percentage of men's increased from 71 percent for the pre-1949 cohort to 81 percent for the 1958–65 cohort, and after a slight decline in the 1966–77 cohort (78%) it reached 106 percent in 1993. So, compared to men, women's wages have steadily improved at career entry. Nevertheless, gender inequality in current wage remains about the same from older cohorts to younger ones, with women earning around 80 percent of what men earn. Comparing first job to current job, it is surprising that women in the most recent cohort already have fallen behind men, reversing what otherwise might have appeared as an achievement of the market reform period.

WAGE DETERMINATION

Tables 7.1 and 7.2 have shown persistent disadvantages for women in college education (despite an equalization of high school education rates), Communist Party membership, access to administrative jobs and jobs in state sector enterprises, high-ranking work units (except for the most recent cohort), and retirement. These disadvantages in themselves could account for the lower wages of women (except for initial wage for the most recent cohort). We wish to look more closely at the wage determination process to answer the following questions: (1) Is there a direct effect of gender on wages net of background factors and job characteristics? (2) Does this gender effect vary among cohorts, either at first wage (where it is clearly linked to a particular historical period) or in current wage? (3) To what degree is the gender wage gap attributable to gender differences in average values on other predictors, and to what degree is it due to different returns to those other factors? Because there is a relatively small sample size in each cohort, our discussion will emphasize not specific coefficients, but sets of predictors taken together.

First Wage

We begin with wage at job entry. We first regress initial wage on gender only. This is the "gross" effect—no other variables are controlled. Then, we add age, education, and Party membership, and the occupation, employment sector, and unit rank of the first job to the equation. The effect of gender controlling for these other variables is the "net" effect.[2] Results are presented in the first section of table 7.3.[3] Gender is coded women = 1, men = 0. Negative coefficients in the table show the monthly deficit for women, in *yuan;* positive coefficients show a wage advantage.

At career entry, women's wages are lower than men's in all but the most recent cohort, but for the most part, these differences are small and not statistically significant.[4] Taking into account gender differences in men's and women's background characteristics and in jobs and work units (hereafter "gender differences in levels") makes little difference in gender wage gaps.

Current Wage

A different pattern is revealed for gender differences in current wages, in the second section of table 7.3. We first regress current wages on gender

TABLE 7.3   Gender Effects on Monthly Wages (in *yuan*)
for First and Current Jobs

	Total	Pre–1949	1949–57	1958–65	1966–77	1978–93
First job						
Gender effect with no controls	−6	−18	−12	−9	−14*	5
Gender effect net of controls[a]	−5	−8	−9	−4	−15*	5
Current job						
Gender effect with no controls	−57*	−60	−51*	−64*	−65*	−41*
Gender effect with first wage controlled	−54*	−62	−49*	−50*	−58*	−43*
Gender effect with all controls but retirement	−37*	−17	−37*	−39*	−36*	−32*
Gender effect net of all controls[b]	−28*	−21	−20	−22	−31*	−32*

SOURCE: 1993 Tianjin Household Survey.

*$p < .05$ (two-tailed test).

[a]Net gender effect is obtained by regressing wages in the first job on gender, age, education (high school, college), Party membership, occupation (job with redistributive power, job with market connection), work unit rank (*chu* rank or higher), and sector (state, new).

[b]Net gender effect is obtained by regressing current wages on gender, first wage, seniority, education (high school, college), Party membership, occupation (job with redistributive power, job with market connection), work unit rank (*chu* rank or higher), sector (state, new), and retirement.

with no controls. Second, we add wage of the first job as a control variable. This means that we are estimating the gender effect on change from first to current wage. Third, we add background variables (education, Party membership, seniority—years worked), and characteristics of the current job (occupation, work unit, rank). Fourth, we add retirement. We considered as predictors marital status, whether respondents have children, and whether respondents had been sent to the countryside or military prior to their first civilian urban job. None of these variables has an independent effect on current wages and therefore we removed them from the final equations.

Women's current wages are significantly less than men's for all cohorts except the earliest. This is not due to women's lower wage at career entry, but due mainly to slower wage growth. After first wage is taken into account, the gender gap in current wage remains statistically significant and is almost as large as that found when first wage is not controlled for. But, the wage gap substantially narrows when gender differences in background factors and job characteristics are taken into account. For the 1978–93 cohort, despite the fact that at career entry women on average make slightly more than men, in current wage, women make 32 *yuan* (or 12%) less than comparable men per month. Given the relatively short period from first to current job for most members of this cohort, women's relative wage reduction to men is rather a significant change during the reform era. Women's disadvantage in wage growth in this and other cohorts is mainly because of their lower levels of college education and Party membership, and their underrepresentation in jobs and sectors with wage advantages. An additional disadvantage comes from the significantly lower returns for women than men working in the new sector of private and semi-private organizations. Finally, after retirement is taken into account, gender wage gaps in the three older cohorts, to which retirement is most applicable, become statistically insignificant. Gender differences in retirement are thus a most important source of the gender gap in current wage.

Predicted Gender Wage Gaps

Table 7.4 presents predicted average monthly wages at current jobs for men and women by cohort, taking into account average levels of the predictor variables. Men's wages are predicted by applying the coefficient estimates for men to the mean levels of the predicted variables for men (tables 7.1 and 7.2). Women's wages are predicted analogously. The gender wage gaps approximate those seen in the actual means in table 7.2, as they should, given the procedure we have followed. Overall, men average 280 *yuan* per month, compared to an ave̶̶ ̶̶ ̶̶e of 223 *yuan* for women (80% of men's).

How much of the wage ga̶
of men and women, and to
answer this question, we pe̶
artificially give women the ̶
retired at ages equivalent ̶
capital, were placed in th̶
men, and had men's occup̶
yuan (still only 90% of me̶
ferential returns (e.g., t̶
Party membership)? Aga̶
taining women's actual b̶
the returns that men e̶
human and political ca̶
be 10 percent less than̶
der differences in the ̶

TABLE 7.4   Predicted Monthly Wage (in *yuan*) for Current Jobs

	Total	Pre–1949	1949–57	1958–65	1966–77	1978–93
Predicted Wage						
Men	280	289	279	291	288	260
Women	223	230	228	227	223	219
Women, assuming men's characteristics and jobs	252	348	255	265	241	231
Women, assuming men's rates of return	253	251	245	255	260	253

SOURCE: 1993 Tianjin Household Survey.

GENDER INEQUALITIES IN JOB MOBILITY OPPORTUNITY

One mechanism whereby men and women can improve their wage levels is job mobility. In discussing table 7.2 we have already described some of the differences in career advancement between men and women. We return to them more explicitly here (see table 7.5). Career advancement was not a common reason given for wanting to change jobs before the reforms (Davis 1990), but it has become a driving force for job mobility during the post-1978 period. In this section, we analyze gender differences in occupational change and work unit change from first job to current job.

Of the 1037 respondents, 41 percent have never changed either occupation or work unit after entry into the labor force. But women were 10 percentage points more likely than men to continue to work in their initial occupations and work units. Women, therefore, have less mobility. Of those who ever changed jobs (58%), most (three-quarters) did so after 1978, rather than before (this is most true of the younger cohorts, of course). This should be interpreted as a consequence of the loosening up of labor control by the government and by work units. However, this policy shift did not have an equal effect on men and women: 46 percent of men changed their jobs 1978 compared to 37 percent of women—a significant difference.

all, slightly more than 60 percent of men and slightly more than of women have ever changed jobs. Gender differences are con- ong those who changed both occupations and work units: n, compared to 25 percent of women, are in this group. generally less mobile than men, but they are less able nd work units simultaneously. These findings are rate analysis (not presented in table 7.5). Con- membership, job type, work unit rank, and en whose mobility rate is set to be 100, rate of 64, but their rate of moving be-

TABLE 7.5   Job Mobility, Tianjin, 1993

	Total	Men	Women
Number of cases	1037	701	336
Never changed jobs (%)	41.5	38.1	48.5*
Ever changed jobs (%)	58.5	61.9	51.5*
When changed			
Before 1978	15.4	15.8	14.6*
After 1978	43.0	46.1	36.9*
What Changed			
Occupation only	22.9	23.8	21.1*
Work unit only	4.5	4.1	5.4
Both occupation and work unit	31.0	34.0	25.0*
Average number of occupations ever worked in	2.2	2.3	1.9*
Average number of work units ever worked in	1.6	1.7	1.4*

SOURCE: 1993 Tianjin Household Survey.

* Gender difference significant at the .05 level (two-tailed test).

tween work units with or without occupational change is only 55. The average number of occupations that people ever worked in is 2.3 for men and 1.9 for women, and the average number of work units that people ever worked in is 1.7 for men and 1.4 for women. Both gender differences are statistically significant.

What are the outcomes of occupational and work unit change? Table 7.6 shows that when men change occupation, work unit, or both, they have the clear advantage of ending up in administrative, market activity, and market potential jobs rather than other jobs. In contrast, while women in any job change category have an advantage of moving into clerical jobs, they have no opportunity to move into administrative jobs, and their chances of moving into jobs with market involvement are less than their chances of moving into jobs with no market involvement or decision making. As shown in the last row of results in table 7.6, men in any job-change category enjoy a 14–18 percent wage gain; for women, however, wage gains only follow changes involving both occupation and work unit, a move they are less likely to make than men.[5]

SUMMARY AND CONCLUSION

Perhaps we should not be surprised that gender inequality has changed so little in China over the last 15 years. In Russia, another "post-socialist" country,

TABLE 7.6   Effects of Job Mobility on Current Occupation and Wage among Those Changing Jobs since Job Entry, by Gender, Tianjin, 1993

Dependent Variables	Changed Occupation Only	Changed Work Unit Only	Changed both Occupation and Work Unit	Model Chi Square	N
Current Occupation:					
Clerical vs. other job					
Men	5.33*	10.21*	5.62*	183.06*	319
Women	1.17	16.12*	5.08*	116.90*	200
Administrative vs. other job					
Men	2.19*	5.94*	4.19*	209.36*	305
Women	0	0	0	85.55*	162
Market Activity vs. other job					
Men	5.27*	9.89*	8.38*	189.26*	298
Women	0.32	1.72	2.45	123.40*	191
Market Potential vs. other job					
Men	1.39	4.64*	3.72*	325.69*	441
Women	0.11	0.27	0.28	210.38*	220
Current Wage:					
Men	1.14*	1.18*	1.14*	$R^2=.05$	690
Women	0.95	1.03	1.22*	$R^2=.03$	333

SOURCE: 1993 Tianjin Household Survey.

$p < .05$ (two-tailed test).

NOTE: The top part of the table reports odds ratios of the effect of occupational change only, work unit change only, and a combined work unit and occupational change on occupation at the time of the survey.

For the dependent variables, the contrast category consists of occupation with no market involvement or decision-making power. Control variables include: seniority, seniority squared, high school, college, Party membership, the 4 job dummies, and the 2 sector dummies. The job and sector dummies are measured at the time prior to job changes.

The bottom part of the table shows the effects of job mobility on the natural logarithm of current monthly wage. The only control variable is natural logarithm of first wage.

Gerber and Hout (1998) show that women's average wage was 63 percent of men's in 1991, fell to 53 percent in 1994, but recovered to 65 percent in 1995. In fact, this last figure is the same as that reported for 1970 (Whyte 1984, table 2). Trends in gender inequality in wages hinge on changes in a wide range of institutions and policies, from those that give women less education and political standing, to those that pressure them to leave the workforce, to those that place them in different kinds of jobs, and finally to those that grant them different wages for the same job. Furthermore, there is a great deal of inertia built into the occupational structure because overall wage differences between men and women at any time are strongly affected by the background, job assignments, and career mobility of cohorts of workers who entered the labor force decades before.

In this context, we believe that the competing views about the impact of economic reforms on Chinese women's economic status relative to men's, reviewed at the beginning of this chapter, are too general and abstract. The Chinese state was never able to deliver equal opportunities to men and women with respect to higher education, Party membership, administrative and market jobs, and wages, even before 1978. Chinese women in the post-1978 reform era also fall short in terms of human capital and their working careers. If we try to squeeze our results into these theoretical boxes, we draw the following conclusions:

The market-as-equalizer argument suggests that the gender wage gap is narrowing because in a more market-driven economy women may enjoy market opportunities not available to them in the previous redistributive system. However, the Tianjin surveys support neither the predicted outcome nor the hypothesized causal process that would lead to a declining gender inequality in pay. First, gender wage gaps persist from 1978 to 1993. They also persist across the five labor cohorts who entered the urban labor force from 1923 to 1993. Second, job assignments after 1956 clearly disfavored women, but post-1978 reforms also did not give advantages to women in job mobility. On the contrary, men are more able than women to move into jobs with power, jobs with market connections, and jobs in the state or new sectors, consequently obtaining higher wages. Although younger persons in the 1978–93 cohort were no longer assigned jobs by the government in the early 1990s, the improved job placements and higher first wages of women in this cohort—comforting from a market transition perspective—must be reconciled with the negative results for women's job mobility occurring mostly after 1978.

Stability in wage inequality challenges the state-as-equalizer model just as it challenges the market-as-equalizer model. The state-as-equalizer model implies that gender inequality in wages should be widening over time, but this does not occur. Even at the entry level, gender gaps are quite persistent from the 1949–57 cohort to the 1966–77 cohort: on average, women's first wages are 21–25 percent less than men's. This is primarily because women are assigned to jobs with no market involvement or decision-making power—the residual category in our occupational classification—and placed in the collective sector or work units with lower rank. As Honig and Hershatter (1988) observed, work units continued to discriminate against women in job assignment in the 1980s, as they had in previous decades. There is evidence that differential job mobility worsens women's placement in occupational and work unit structures, but we found no evidence that before 1978, when job mobility was highly controlled by government bureaucrats and work unit managers, there was any different pattern. There seems to have been persistent gender inequality in job mobility in Tianjin before and after reforms.

What accounts for the unexpected persistence in gender inequalities? First, China's policy continues to require working women to retire ten years earlier than working men. Seniority has a consistent linear effect on base salary over time, and women are largely excluded from salary increases beyond age 50. Second, women continue to have less access to higher education and Party membership—important determinants in the distribution of base salaries and other wages before and after reforms. Third, women are underrepresented in administrative jobs and market potential jobs. Fourth, women are more likely than men to be placed in collective enterprises rather than state work units. Finally, women change occupations and work units less than men, and when they do change, it helps them less. Their wages increase at a lower rate than men's, given these changes.

It appears that neither the state nor the market alone can explain the gender wage gap. Rather, the state and market are structural contexts for the power relations between women and men. These power relations are not necessarily, or automatically, evolving with the economic reforms.

NOTES

Revision of this chapter has benefited greatly from the comments of the participants at the conference "Gender, Households, and the Boundaries of Work in Contemporary China" in October 1996, especially Barbara Entwisle, Gail Henderson, and Martin Whyte. We are also grateful to Peggy Marini and Bill Parish for their helpful comments on an earlier draft and to the Tianjin Academy of Social Sciences for its collaboration on the 1993 Tianjin survey. Funding for various stages of this research has come from a National Science Foundation grant (SES-9209214) and grants-in-aid from the University of Minnesota Graduate School.

1. This is surprisingly close to the report by Hare (1995) that men's average wage is 25 percent higher than women's in Chinese village factories. It is beyond the scope of this chapter to analyze why China has had a persistently smaller gender wage gap than the United States or other Western countries. We do note, however, that it seems to be closer to that found in other East Asian economies (Lau et al. 1994). For a comparative analysis of gender inequalities in market capitalist and state socialist systems, consult Whyte (1984).

2. We did not include any variables of parental status as predictors because too many respondents (50%) provided no data. In a preliminary analysis (not presented) of the respondents who reported their parents' education, occupation, work unit sector, and cadre status, we found no gender difference in the effects of

these variables on respondents' first wages. In a 1985 Tianjin sample, Lin and Bian (1991) show that the father's work unit sector has a significant effect on son's first work unit sector, but not on daughter's. This differential parental influence is partially and indirectly taken into account in our regression analysis of first wages as we include respondents' first work unit sector as well as other first-job indicators in our wage equations. Full results from the regression analyses are available from the authors.

3. In this table, "gross gender effect" is the gender wage gap on the margin; the coefficient presented is obtained from a regression equation in which gender is the only predictor considered. In contrast, "net gender effect" is the gender wage gap between men and women with comparable characteristics measured by the predictors considered in the equations; so the coefficient for gender is obtained from regressing first wage on gender as well as all other control variables. Although first wages vary from cohort to cohort because of inflation effects, which are greatest in the youngest cohort, we still decided to use untransformed wage as the dependent variable because regressions using log form wages underestimate gender wage gaps (see Portes and Zhou 1996 for discussion on estimated effects of self-employment on wages from regressions using original and log form earnings).

4. There is a significant gender effect for the 1966–77 cohort, gross and net. This is surprising, given a widespread belief that economic egalitarianism reached its momentum during the Cultural Revolution (Parish 1984a). Parish's theme originally points to destratification in the post-1966 period by class, education, and occupation, and indeed receives support from the 1993 Tianjin survey: education and occupation dummies have weakening effects on initial wages from the 1958–65 to the 1966–77 cohort (results available from authors). Although the net gender effect on first wage is puzzling, a 1988 study of Tianjin reports the same result (Bian 1994b). Further analysis (not shown) indicates that the net gender wage difference can mostly be traced to persons in the category of "other" jobs (50% of men and 46% of women). Among occupations in this category, men were more likely than women to be assigned jobs in heavy industry in which starting salaries were higher than in other industries.

5. However, there is little gender difference in mobility into state and new sectors, as compared to moving into the collective sector, a result not presented in table 7.6.

EIGHT

Gender Differentials in Economic Success

Rural China in 1991

Ethan Michelson and William L. Parish

This chapter examines three interrelated propositions about the sources of men's and women's educational and economic success in the countryside. The first proposition is that *patriarchy matters*. Because sons provide current income and future old age security, parents continue to invest more in their sons' than their daughters' future. Believing that married women will devote more time to their family than men do, employers continue to favor men over women. The second proposition is that *economic development weakens patriarchy*. Once parents have more money to share among children (and fewer children competing for the same resources), they divide family resources more evenly between sons and daughters. And when economic development causes labor shortages, some employers begin to ignore gender. The third proposition is that *family connections count*. Having parents in favorable occupational situations increases one's chances of getting a good education and a good job. This proposition is more true for sons than for daughters, and it is more true for parents in administrative positions than for parents who have a good white-collar job.

SCHOLARLY DEBATES

Patriarchy

While there is ample debate around each of our propositions, the patriarchy proposition is perhaps the least debated, even though in the existing literature there is uncertainty about the extent to which patriarchal tendencies were strengthened in China after 1978. Even under collective farming, current income and old age support depended primarily on sons (e.g., K. Johnson 1983; Potter and Potter 1990; Parish and Whyte 1978; M. Wolf

1985). This promoted a favoritism toward sons that could only be strengthened by the return to family farming in the early 1980s. There is also ample anecdotal evidence that local employers, newly freed from state labor bureau control (in state enterprises) and never under tight control in the rapidly growing private enterprise sector, exercised their new autonomy to favor men over women (Jacka 1990; B. Liu 1995). One result was an apparent tendency for agriculture to become feminized as men left the village for more lucrative off-farm jobs (Croll 1994; Gao 1994; Judd 1994; chap. 11 of this volume).

Development

The second proposition, that economic development weakens the effects of patriarchy, is highly controversial. There is a large literature suggesting that market development, particularly development spurred by exposure to the world capitalist system, exacerbates the situation of women relative to men. Boserup's (1970) classic statement on these tendencies in Africa has been reinforced many times over by ethnographic evidence from all parts of the world (Benería and Feldman 1992; Lee 1995; Nash and Kelley 1983; Papanek 1990; Tinker 1990; Ward 1990b). Even when young, unmarried women benefit because of the demand for nimble young fingers to make the clothing, toys, and electronic goods desired in the international market, married women are often excluded from the more lucrative parts of the labor market.

These tendencies may be more severe in East Asia than elsewhere. Based on research in contemporary Japan, Brinton (1993) suggests that women are greatly disadvantaged by a human capital development system dominated by parents. Assuming that few good jobs are open to women and that a woman's future is more highly shaped by whom she marries than by where she works, parents steer their daughters into types of education and types of jobs that provide little career potential. Educators and employers complete the formation of a system that makes it unlikely that women will succeed economically. With poignant data from Taiwan, Greenhalgh (1985) suggests that similar problems exist in Chinese cultural contexts. Desiring to get a quick return on an investment in daughters, parents have their daughters quit school early so that the daughter can work to support the son's further education. While sons get a chance to experiment in jobs that provide valuable training for long-term career mobility, daughters are relegated to dead-end jobs that provide good current income but few career prospects. In a series of wonderful personal vignettes, Salaff (1981) documents similar tendencies in the 1970s in Hong Kong, while Kung (1983) illustrates some of the same issues in factory work in Taiwan. With data on pre-World

War II world-market silk production, Bell (1994) reports similar negative consequences for rural women in the Yangzi Delta Region of China.

While the many ethnographic and other accounts are compelling, there is ample evidence that things do not always develop in a simple linear fashion. Lim (1990) argues that many of the negative consequences of production for the world market are short-lived. Others note that even though the conditions in factories are frequently appalling by developed country standards, women often report the work and personal income to be liberating (e.g., Stichter 1990; D. Wolf 1992). In silk-producing regions near Guangzhou, before World War II, Topley (1975) and Stockard (1989) found that work in silk factories gave women more autonomy in marriage arrangements. Examining Chinese rural data for around 1930, M. Johnson, Parish, and Lin (1987) argue that world market production improved the situation of rural women.[1]

One possible inference from these diverse findings is that one needs to pay more attention to variation by time and space. Examining Taiwan patterns at a later date, Parish and Willis (1993) report that many of the negative consequences reported by Greenhalgh, Kung, and others were short-lived. Once development provided more income, parents began to invest more equally in sons' and daughters' education and work. Similarly, comparing women's work in Taiwan and South Korea, Brinton, Lee, and Parish (1995) suggest that the outcomes for women depend greatly on how work is organized. Where work is organized in large, capital-intensive firms, men are greatly favored. Where work is organized in small, labor-intensive firms, high levels of labor demand and flexible production schedules tend to draw married as well as unmarried women into the labor market. The result of these tendencies is that married women in Taiwan remained in the formal labor market and received greater income advantages than women in South Korea.

These observations suggest the need for a more differentiated set of propositions about the consequences of economic development and world market production. In the initial stages of development, lingering patriarchal norms may well slant opportunities toward men. At later stages—assuming that production is organized in small, competitive firms emphasizing labor-intensive light industry—married and unmarried women may gain many of the same advantages as men. Parents may be able to spend more on their daughters' education. Employers, finding few men available in local labor pools, may begin to hire more married as well as unmarried women. It takes a period of time for these processes to work out. Unmarried women would enter the best jobs first and then be forced to leave these jobs by de facto marriage bars. But, in time, the stage would be set for a more extensive reworking of the labor market for married and unmarried women.[2]

Social Capital

Our third proposition is that social capital matters in a gender-differenti-ated manner. Social capital here consists of family background and family connections. It is commonplace to note that parents' education and occu-pation are closely related to children's education and occupation. This pat-tern is common not only in market societies but also in socialist societies. Despite the mighty strives to weaken parentally induced advantage in past decades, these advantages are still strong in China (e.g., Bian 1994; Whyte and Parish 1984). What is less commonplace in the scholarly literature is to note whether males are particularly advantaged by family connections and whether parents in administrative jobs are uniquely positioned to help their family members.

With data from Tianjin, China's third largest city, Lin and Bian (1991) find that sons are greatly advantaged by having a father who worked in a high status work unit. To use an American expression, a son can be born with a "silver spoon in his mouth." Daughters do not share in this "silver spoon" syndrome. They have to earn their education and occupation ad-vantages the "old-fashioned way," excelling in school or through other kinds of personal effort. This kind of differential advantage, of course, is consistent with a lingering patriarchal emphasis, where even urban parents use their social capital more for their sons than for their daughters (see chap. 16). This chapter examines whether these tendencies to use social capital to advantage sons more than daughters also exist in the countryside.

Both sons and daughters might be uniquely advantaged by having kin in administrative positions. Examining this issue has been somewhat of a growth industry in American studies of China. Victor Nee (1989, 1991, 1992, 1996) leads the optimists in claiming that market forces are erasing the advantages of administrative leaders—if not in the country as a whole, at least in the more marketized coastal regions, and particularly in compari-son to the rising star that is the new rural entrepreneurial class. Others are more skeptical. With systematic data from the late 1980s, Parish and Mi-chelson (1996) find that much of the administrator advantage has contin-ued, even in the more marketized regions. There is also ample anecdotal evidence of a continuing (some say, intensifying) tendency for people to use gifts, favors, banquets, and other special connections to get the best jobs and to guarantee success in business (P. C. C. Huang 1990, 294; Yan 1995, 1996; M. M. Yang 1994).

The debate may be partially solved by noting that there are not only ma-jor variations between more and less marketized regions but also marked variations over time. Szelényi and Kostello (1996) suggest that some of the futile debates over marketization and administrator rewards in China and

Eastern Europe can be resolved by paying attention to the rapid changes from year to year. Most of the debates about the consequences of marketization in China have been based on 1980s data. By the early 1990s, the pace of marketization had begun to accelerate. The 1991 dataset used in this chapter allows us to begin to note some of the changes that have occurred more recently, when market forces finally may have begun to significantly weaken administrator privileges. Besides noting the role of administrator privileges in general, we pay special attention to how the social capital provided by administrators in one's family helps males versus females.

DATA AND METHODS

We analyze data from the second wave of the China Health and Nutrition Survey (CHNS), fielded in 1991 in eight provinces: Liaoning, Jiangsu, Shandong, Henan, Hubei, Hunan, Guangxi, and Guizhou. Data were collected at community, household, and individual levels, providing us with information on 14,811 individuals in 3,629 households in 189 communities. Of the 189 communities, we are interested in the 127 villages, including regular and suburban villages that are closer to cities.[3] The individual, household, and community level material in the data set constitute the three types of explanatory variables that will be used in our analysis. The following paragraphs set forth our expectations regarding the effects of these variables.

Individual Effects

People come to the education and job world with a particular set of individual characteristics that favor or impede success. In education, they include the values and knowledge learned from educated parents. In jobs, they include prior education, age, gender, and marital status.

Household Effects

At the household level, a person has connections to parents and other family members with different occupational traits. Depending on the specific analysis, we will use these traits in three ways. First, in the school enrollment analysis we compare children with fathers of different occupations. Second, in our analysis of the determinants of occupational sector, connections are not limited to fathers; they include any other household member. Here we have two dummy variables for cadre (administrator) connection: village cadre and nonvillage cadre (more than likely township-level or higher). In case any significant effects from the cadre variables are caused by the effects of white-collar or professional/technical connections, we also control for any noncadre white-collar worker connection. Third, in the household income analysis, cadre connections are measured as the total number of cadres in the household. Two variables are used, one for village and one for nonvillage cadres.[4]

Community Effects

Rich data on community characteristics available in the CHNS allow us to describe and assess economic context. We can compare the results of living in regular as opposed to suburban villages, which have more subcontracting work as well as providing relatively easy access to city jobs. The proportion of villagers in nonfarm work provides information about the nature of local labor demand. Average income in the community measures the amount of revenue available to governments and families. We also have information on whether the local economy is largely privatized or in the hands of local governments. We construct a three-way index of communities that distinguishes those that are (1) largely privatized, (2) largely corporatized (enterprises and services provided by local governments), and (3) largely agricultural, with few nonfarm employment opportunities. We construct this index by using community information on the number of private enterprises, the number of collective enterprises, the proportion of all enterprises that are collectively owned, and the number of community/welfare services that are provided by local government and funded by revenues from local collective enterprises, and by combining these indicators with aggregated individual-level information on the proportion of community labor working as entrepreneurs. For our school enrollment analysis we also use information on the distance between each community and the nearest lower-middle school.[5]

In short, in our analysis we emphasize how a combination of community, individual, and household traits shape one's life chances. In all of this analysis we will emphasize how this shaping is gender-differentiated, with women expected to benefit more from favorable background characteristics. We begin with an analysis of education and then proceed to examine jobs and income. This order is dictated by the belief that many of the advantages that a well-connected parent can provide are not directly, through access to better sources of current income, but indirectly, through providing a child with more education and better access to an initial job.

EDUCATION

Educational achievement is likely to be influenced by supply and demand factors. The supply side includes the number of nearby schools with ample teaching staff. Distant schools, particularly at the lower- and upper-middle school levels, may particularly disadvantage daughters. The demand side includes whether parents and teenagers believe that education is of any use in the labor market; whether parents need their children to help at home; and whether many children are competing for scarce family resources, or only a few.

In the mid-1980s, village education suffered. As education funds were withdrawn from the countryside and shifted back to cities, fewer rural schools and teachers could be funded. The result was a massive retrenchment, with much consolidation of lower- and upper-middle school districts and decertification and early retirement of teachers who had been hastily recruited in the 1966–76 Cultural Revolution decade. Students had to walk longer distances to attend school and most likely also had to pay higher tuition and book fees than in the past (People's Republic of China 1995, 585 ff; Pepper 1990; Taylor 1988; Thøgersen 1990; N. Zhang 1992). On the demand side, the scholarly and anecdotal literature suggests that parents came to think that education was virtually worthless. With well-educated teachers, clerical workers, and others in the countryside making less than semi-literate private entrepreneurs, construction, and transport workers, parents and their children concluded that continuing in school was of little utility.[6]

Because of this combination of supply and demand factors, enrollment rates declined sharply from 1976 to 1985. Counter-intuitively, the falloff may have been sharper for sons than daughters. Sons had more income-earning possibilities outside of school, and therefore they and their parents were likely to count the opportunity costs of continued schooling as too high (Parish and Zhe 1995; Tang and Parish In press). The ironic result is that educational achievement levels for sons and daughters probably converged during the initial years of market reform.

Since 1985, though school consolidation has continued, the Ministry of Education has made a greater effort to prop up school enrollment rates. And, with the growth of more nonfarm jobs where at least a lower-middle education is a requirement, parents and children may once again see the utility of getting an education. Because of these forces, by the early 1990s when our current data set was collected, enrollment rates had returned to 1970s levels.

This analysis examines the kinds of forces that shape educational opportunity for sons and daughters. To provide a sense of the nature of rural education in 1991, we begin with a few descriptive details. First, enrollment is highly related to age. Though there are a few latecomers, most children enter school by age six or seven. Well over 90 percent of all children are in school through the primary school years. After the primary school years, enrollment begins to decline rapidly—down to about two-thirds for the lower-middle school ages and to about one-third for the upper-middle school years.[7] Through primary school, male and female enrollment is very similar. Starting with lower-middle school, a gap of about five percentage points emerges. Though this gap is more modest than in some developing countries, it is likely a result of the influence of patriarchy in rural China.

In addition to age, school enrollment is also sensitive to level of community development. Youth aged 12–17 are on the cutting edge of declining school enrollment. Looking at this age group, in the least-developed communities with few people in nonfarm work, less than 60 percent of the youth are in school. In the most developed communities, in contrast, almost 80 percent are in school. This pattern varies by gender. In the least-developed communities, where nonagricultural employment is less than 10 percent, female enrollment lags male enrollment by about 10 percentage points. In the most developed communities, where nonagricultural employment is 60 percent or more, the situation is reversed, with female enrollment exceeding male enrollment by a few percentage points. It may be that female enrollment catches up with male enrollment in the most developed regions because high labor demand attracts young men into the labor force at an early age. Regardless of the exact cause, the pattern suggests that development helps young women more than young men.

Finally, school enrollment responds to school availability. Though distance to the nearest school has little effect on male enrollment, female enrollment is sensitive to that distance. When the nearest school is more than a kilometer away, female enrollment begins to decline. This is consistent with a story of increasing school consolidation (and hence greater distances) inhibiting female school enrollment after the start of the 1980s.

We attempt to put all these influences together in a single analysis of school enrollment among youth (table 8.1).[8] Because we are particularly interested in male/female differences, we explore gender interactions throughout. In the table, the coefficients for "female" show the additional impact, positive or negative, of being female as opposed to male. When "female" is interacted with other determinants of enrollment, carets (ˆ) show the joint significance of main and interactive effects.

What do the results show? First, community characteristics matter more for young women than young men. Young women who live in the suburban villages and in villages with more nonfarm employment are more likely to remain in school than those in rural villages and villages with fewer nonfarm opportunities.[9] Young women who must travel longer distances to school are less likely to remain in school. More schools and more off-farm jobs have significant effects on women's life chances. They are largely irrelevant to men's. This fits the hypothesis that level of development matters more for females than for males.

Second, family background matters.[10] When parental education alone is examined, sons and daughters benefit from father's education. Daughters, but not sons, benefit from mother's education (Model 1). When parental

TABLE 8.1 Determinants of Rural School Enrollment,
Population Age 12–17

	Model 1		Model 2	
	Coefficient	Adjusted t	Coefficient	Adjusted t
Community characteristics				
Nonfarm labor force (10s)	0.04	(1.5)	0.02	(0.7)
× female	0.05^^	(1.5)	0.07*^^	(1.9)
Distance to middle-school, km (log)	−0.01	(−0.2)	0.00	(0.0)
× female	−0.12*^	(−1.9)	−0.14**^^	(−2.2)
Suburb	0.04	(0.2)	−0.05	(−0.3)
× female	0.49	(1.4)	0.60*	(1.7)
Individual characteristics				
Male	0.83***	(3.5)	0.80***	(3.2)
Years of education, father	0.04*	(1.7)	0.02	(0.8)
× female	0.01^^	(0.4)	0.02	(0.7)
Years of education, mother	0.00	(0.2)	0.00	(0.2)
× female	0.07^^	(1.6)	0.06^	(1.5)
Occupation, father				
village cadre			0.63**	(2.4)
other white-collar			0.77***	(2.6)
manual/service			0.40**	(2.1)
entrepreneur			0.25	(1.0)
farmer (comparison group)			—	
× female				
village cadre			−0.84**^^	(−2.4)
other white-collar			−0.19^^	(−0.5)
manual/service			−0.37	(−1.3)
entrepreneur			−0.06	(−0.2)
farmer (comparison group)			—	

SOURCE: China Health and Nutrition Survey, 1991.

*$p < .10$ **$p < .05$ ***$p < .01$ (two-tailed tests).

NOTES: Two variance-corrected probit models for sample-survey data (STATA) specifying the community as the primary sampling unit. Sample consists of youth age 12–17 with parent in household. The equations also include unshown indicator variables for ages 12–16 (comparison group age = 17) as well as dummy variables for living in a community with pronounced privatization, living in a community with pronounced corporatism, father with missing educational information, and father with missing occupational information.

The joint significance of standard and female interaction is indicated by the caret (^) next to the female interaction coefficients: ^$p < .10$, ^^$p < .05$ (two-tailed tests).

Cases = 1,152.

occupation is included (Model 2), the results are a bit more complex. Sons benefit from fathers having higher status occupations. Compared to the sons of other white-collar workers, the sons of village cadres are not uniquely advantaged. They are, nevertheless, distinctly advantaged when compared to the sons of ordinary farmers. The sons of entrepreneurs, who might well be pulled out of school to help in the family business, are only slightly advantaged, if at all. Thus, for sons, enrollment follows the status order, with sons of higher-status fathers being more likely to remain in school. Adding father's occupation attenuates the effects of father's education on the enrollment of sons. Daughters continue to be helped by their mother's education, but not by their father's education or occupational advantage. Daughters of other white-collar workers are somewhat more likely to remain enrolled, but still not so likely as the sons of other white-collar workers. Daughters of village cadres are actually disadvantaged in this sample.[11] Thus, the transmission of father's social capital to daughters is weaker than we expected.

JOBS

Our next question is: To what extent do community, individual, and family characteristics make a difference in the types of jobs that men and women secure? Of particular interest is the distinction between agricultural and nonagricultural work, and with respect to the latter, distinctions between state, collective, and private employment.

Again, we begin with some descriptive patterns. First, in rural China, virtually all able-bodied females are at work. Unlike in Japan or South Korea, there is no sharp decline in work once women get married and have children, nor any late-30s/early-40s return to informal sector work once their children mature. To the extent that there is a decline in these years, when women are in their late 20s and early 30s, the decline is slight. The prototypical M-shaped curve of labor force participation is here replaced by an inverted U. The downside of the U begins only in women's late 40s as their sons marry, bringing in daughters-in-law. When this happens, women begin to retire to help with grandchildren and family chores (see Judd 1994). But before this time, the vast majority of women, like the vast majority of men, are at work.

To be sure, much of this work is in agriculture. Fewer women than men share in prized nonfarm work opportunities. Unmarried women aged 16–23 participate in nonfarm work just about as much as men. But after this time, married women return home to raise children and take care of their new family. Because most rural women move from their home to their husband's village, they lose many of their initial job contacts when they marry (Parish, Shen, and Chang 1997). The result is that after marriage many fewer women are in nonfarm employment. This is particularly true of the oldest women (and men), who came of age at a time when fewer nonfarm jobs were available. All of this illustrates not only the late spread of non-farm jobs but also how married women fail to get the best jobs available to villagers.

In an era when most jobs remain highly localized, local employment environment has a great deal of influence on whether one is able to leave farming. Nonfarm employment opportunities for individuals rise steadily with the level of nonfarm employment in the larger community, though in a gender-differentiated manner. The effect of marriage on the chances of securing nonfarm work is also gender-specific. Married men are more likely than single men to work off the farm. In contrast, for women marriage dramatically reduces nonfarm employment in most places. Through modest levels of development (50% of community in nonfarm employment), married women participate very little in industrialization of the countryside. However, at much higher levels of development (60% or more of labor force in nonfarm work), even the married women begin to be pulled into nonfarm work opportunities. This staged development of labor force opportunities has been noted elsewhere around the world (Lim 1990).

Finally, despite many anecdotal accounts about the low value of education in the countryside, education does help in obtaining nonfarm jobs. Again, given their lower educational status, the boost provided by education is greater for women than for men. At the highest levels of education, women are about as likely as men to leave farming for nonfarm work.

Nonfarm jobs can be in work units owned by the state, collective, or private sector. State-owned work units run the gamut from factories to schools, hospitals, and administrative bureaus. Collectively owned units encompass a similar range, though there is a concentration in township and village-owned factories. In 1991, most of the privately owned endeavors were of a self-employed or family-business nature *(geti)* with most in family-run restaurants, stores, and workshops.

In the 1991 rural data, among prime working-age people, aged 20–59, work was distributed as shown in table 8.2. This fits the anecdotal accounts of a feminization of agriculture. Women are about 20 percentage points more likely to remain in farming while their brothers and husbands leave for nonfarming jobs. When women do leave farming jobs, they are more likely to go to nearby rural collective firms and less likely to make long commutes to state jobs or take up work in the private, largely self-employed sector (although see chap. 11).

A multivariate analysis helps summarize these simple descriptive results (table 8.3). In this analysis we are concerned with the type of nonfarm job secured. Because we are interested in the primary working ages—after a person has left school and before most people have retired—we restrict the analysis to people aged 20–59. The coefficients in the analysis are relative

TABLE 8.2   Percentage Rural Occupational Sector
by Gender, Population Age 20–59

Ownership	Males	Females	Total
State	11.9	6.4	9.2
Collective	13.5	10.0	11.8
Private	19.3	6.8	13.2
Farming	55.3	76.9	65.8

SOURCE: China Health and Nutrition Survey, 1991.

risk ratios, showing how much one's chances of leaving farming are increased or decreased by a given background condition. A coefficient of 2.00 means one's chances are doubled, a coefficient of 1.00 means that one's chances are unchanged, and a coefficient of 0.50 means that one's chances are cut in half by a given background condition. We show gender interactions for each background condition, with carets to show when the main and interactive effects are jointly statistically significant.

Much as in the simple descriptive analysis, community characteristics are important. Generally speaking, with rising nonfarm employment, suburban location, and higher average incomes, nonfarm opportunities increase sharply. Community-level nonfarm employment is modeled with a quadratic term to test our hypothesis that female nonfarm employment rates rise more rapidly only after most men have already been employed off the farm. Though there are exceptions, this tendency is typically stronger for women than for men. Thus, location is very important, particularly for women.[12]

The importance of location can be seen with greater clarity in table 8.4. This table, derived from table 8.3, shows relative risks of employment in the state, collective, and private sectors by gender and level of nonfarm employment in the community and supports our hypothesis that nonfarm employment will benefit women more than men. That is, it appears a critical mass of nonfarm employment is necessary before women get pulled off the farm in significant numbers. However, since in 1991 it was relatively rare for rural areas in China to have nonfarm employment levels greater than 50 percent, we highlight the suggestive nature of these results.

Findings reported in table 8.4 also reflect a labor queue process: men move into the best locally available jobs first, and women follow only after vacancies emerge as the local demand for labor increases—for example, when men move into even more lucrative positions. The results show that in communities with a privatized character, men are the first to move into private-sector jobs as nonfarm employment rises. When employment outside agriculture reaches the 20 percent level, men are 37 percent more likely to be in the private-sector than on the farm, while women remain

TABLE 8.3 Determinants of Rural Occupational Sector
(Relative Risk Ratios [RRR] from Multinomial Logit Analysis)

	State		Collective		Private	
	RRR	Adjusted z	RRR	Adjusted z	RRR	Adjusted z
Individual characteristics						
Female	0.11	(−0.9)	2.13	(0.3)	0.25	(−0.8)
Single	0.60*	(−1.9)	0.59**	(−2.3)	0.41***	(−4.8)
× female	8.69***^	(5.3)	5.73***^	(4.9)	4.06***^	(4.3)
Age	1.03***	(3.5)	1.00	(−0.0)	0.98***	(−3.4)
× female	0.95***	(−2.8)	0.98	(−1.0)	1.01^	(0.6)
Years of education	1.26***	(8.5)	1.16***	(6.0)	1.12***	(6.0)
× female	1.09*^	(1.7)	1.08*^	(2.0)	1.02^	(0.6)
Family connections						
Nonvillage cadre	9.04*	(1.9)	4.66	(1.3)	1.20	(0.1)
× female	0.41^	(−0.7)	0.67^	(−0.3)	0.60	(−0.3)
Village cadre	4.26***	(3.3)	3.12**	(2.6)	1.06	(0.1)
× female	0.32*^	(−1.8)	0.81^	(−0.4)	0.98	(−0.0)
Other white-collar	4.09***	(4.2)	2.69***	(2.9)	1.35	(0.8)
× female	1.56^	(1.0)	1.42^	(0.8)	1.35	(0.6)
Community Characteristics						
Mean income (log)	2.19***	(4.8)	6.49***	(10.8)	3.12***	(9.3)
× female	1.21^	(0.6)	0.77^	(−0.9)	0.95^	(−0.2)
% labor nonfarm (10s)	0.91	(−1.0)	0.95	(−0.6)	1.13*	(1.7)
× female	0.90	(−0.7)	0.86	(−1.1)	0.72**^	(−2.5)
(% labor nonfarm)²	1.04***	(3.9)	1.04***	(3.8)	1.00	(−0.2)
× female	1.02^	(1.3)	1.03*^	(1.7)	1.04**^	(2.5)
Suburb	3.01***	(6.3)	1.02	(0.1)	0.93	(−0.5)
× female	1.76*^	(1.8)	1.69*^	(1.9)	1.06	(0.2)
Privatized	0.98	(−0.1)	1.19	(0.9)	1.08	(0.5)
× female	1.02	(0.0)	0.92	(−0.3)	1.19	(0.7)
Corporatist	1.05	(0.2)	1.37	(1.5)	0.88	(−0.8)
× female	0.56	(−1.6)	0.71	(−1.0)	1.70*	(1.8)
Pseudo R^2			0.26			
Cases			5,129			

SOURCE: CHINA HEALTH AND NUTRITION SURVEY, 1991.

*$p < .10$ **$p < .05$ ***$p < .01$ (two-tailed tests).

NOTE: The coefficients are relative risk ratios from a single multinomial logit analysis. They show the relative risk of working in the state, collective, and private sectors compared to working in the agricultural sector. For example, roughly speaking, if one has a family member who works as a nonvillage cadre, one's chances of working in the state sector are nine times greater than one who lacks this connection.

The joint significance of standard and female interaction is indicated by the caret (^) next to the female interaction coefficients: $p < .10$ ^^$p < .05$. The sample is age 20−59.

TABLE 8.4   Relative Probabilities of Occupational Sector by Gender and Level of Nonfarm Employment in Community (Relative Risk Ratios)

	Males			Females		
	State	Collective	Private	State	Collective	Private
Privatized communities						
5% nonfarm employment	0.95	1.17	1.15	0.92	1.00	1.16
10% nonfarm employment	0.93	1.17	1.22	0.87	0.95	1.08
20% nonfarm employment	0.96	1.25	1.37*	0.86	0.94	0.98
40% nonfarm employment	1.29	1.78*	1.72*	1.22	1.34	1.00
60% nonfarm employment	2.38*	3.43*	2.12*	2.82*	3.22*	1.35
80% nonfarm employment	6.05*	8.97*	6.05*	10.70*	12.94*	10.70*
Corporatist communities						
5% nonfarm employment	1.02	1.35	0.94	0.54*	0.89	1.36
10% nonfarm employment	0.99	1.35	1.00	0.52*	0.84	1.26
20% nonfarm employment	1.03	1.44	1.12	0.51	0.83	1.15
40% nonfarm employment	1.38	2.05*	1.40	0.72	1.19	1.17
60% nonfarm employment	2.56*	3.95*	1.73*	1.67	2.86*	1.58
80% nonfarm employment	6.49*	10.34*	2.09*	6.34*	11.49*	2.87*

SOURCE: China Health and Nutrition Survey, 1991.

*$p < .05$ (two-tailed test).

NOTE: The above relative risk ratios are point estimates calculated as linear combinations of main effects and interaction effects presented in table 8.3.

equally likely to work on the farm. Only at the upper extremes of nonfarm employment, when men shift first into the collective sector and then into the state sector, do women move out of agriculture. Likewise, in corporatist communities characterized by a strong collective sector, proceeds from which are invested by the local state into infrastructural development and other forms of local subsidy, men are the first to benefit from collective-sector jobs. These findings are consistent with our staged development hypothesis.

Returning to table 8.3, we see that individual characteristics are also important.[13] Consistent with our descriptive results, single women are greatly advantaged in nonfarm work relative to women who are or have been married. One thing that is new, however, is that the marriage handicap not only applies in the small collective and private sectors, where employers might be expected to use their discretion in hiring, but applies even more strongly in the state sector. For whatever reason—longer travel times, increased employer discretion over the most valuable jobs—even the state sector, once thought to be the bastion of equal opportunity for women, turns out to be just as unfavorable to married women as any other sector. For men, the situation is just the reverse. Marriage enhances men's chances of working off the farm; or, men marry after securing off-farm jobs. As in the descriptive analysis, education increases one's chances of nonfarm work in all sectors, more so for women than for men. Thus, marriage and education matter, though in different ways for men and women.

Family connections also matter—though, again, in somewhat different ways for men and women. We begin with the coefficients in table 8.3, showing the effect of having other white-collar workers in the household. The presence of other white-collar workers increases one's chances of having a state or collective job. The increased chances are particularly pronounced for state enterprises, and considerable for collective firms as well. Several mechanisms may be at work, ranging from the benign (family members share similar interests, employers prefer to hire through family introductions, husband and wife met at work) to the not so benign (outright nepotism). Distinguishing the exact mechanism is difficult with these data.

However, we can note that administrative cadres, who should be in a position to influence appointments, are not particularly advantaged in doing so. Though larger in magnitude, the coefficients for a nonvillage cadre in the household are based on so few examples that they are statistically no different from the other white-collar coefficients. Even in the rural collective sector, where local officials should be able to wield more influence over appointments, local officials do no better than others in securing good jobs for their family members.[14] If there is a family connection advantage, it tends to be the standard white-collar advantage common almost everywhere in the world. Social capital through household connections appears to count for something, but the mechanisms of this advantage have little to do with characteristics specific to administered economies.

To the extent that there is any difference between administrators and other white-collar workers in the use of family connections, the data suggest it is in how those advantages are used on behalf of male and female family members. The differences are modest and largely insignificant in statistical terms. Nevertheless, to the extent that there is a pattern, it roughly parallels that found for education. Administrator social capital is expended more for males than for females. Other more average white-collar workers expend social capital for male and female kin. These tendencies are so modest and so unstable (given the small sample sizes) that we are reluctant to push inferences any further. They do present an interesting pattern, however, with administrators typically favoring sons over daughters.

INCOME

Finally, we move to the analysis of income. For the determinants of individual income we have a detailed set of results that we will summarize without showing the statistics that lie behind these generalizations. We have found that in individual income returns, education is very important for getting the best jobs. However, once in the better jobs, education is of only modest importance in determining who gets higher and lower incomes. It is this modest return to education within any one job that is often noted in accounts about the extremely low return to education in China. Thus, the significance of education for parents and teenagers is that education provides access to a better job, not that it determines one's success once in that job.

Our primary analysis is not of individual income in jobs but of total household income (table 8.5). We constructed total household income by

TABLE 8.5   Determinants of Rural Household Income
(OLS Regression Coefficients)

	Males		*Females*		*Male/ Female Differences*
Household labor characteristics					
Mean years of education	0.02*	(2.0)	0.00	(0.4)	
Sum labor by occupation					
white-collar	0.41**	(5.8)	0.55**	(7.0)	
blue-collar	0.56**	(9.4)	0.32**	(7.5)	^
entrepreneur	0.72**	(11.7)	0.38**	(5.1)	^
farmer	0.02	(0.5)	0.16**	(3.2)	
Cadre members					
Nonvillage			0.43**	(3.8)	
Village			0.36**	(4.5)	
Community characteristics					
Mean income (log)			0.79**	(19.0)	
Constant			−0.07	(−0.1)	
R^2			0.45		
Cases			1,969		

SOURCE: China Health and Nutrition Survey, 1991.

*$p < .05$ **$p < .01$ (two-tailed tests).

NOTE: Coefficients and t-statistics are from a single variance-corrected linear regression model for sample-survey data (STATA) where the community is specified as the primary sampling unit. The model also includes unshown coefficients for age and age squared of laborers, none of which is significant.

The following coefficients are statistically different from the nonvillage cadre coefficient at $p < .05$: male entrepreneurs, female white-collar workers, and farmers. The following are statistically different from the village cadre coefficient: male blue-collar workers, male entrepreneurs, and farmers. Whether any difference between male labor and female labor for a given occupation with respect to the contribution made to household income is statistically significant is indicated by a caret: $^p < .05$.

aggregating individual income components and adding them to household income components in the original questionnaire. Our computed median income of 2,249 *yuan* per household is similar to the median in larger State Statistical Bureau surveys for the same year, which suggests that we are close to the right figure for households (People's Republic of China 1992, 306). Within the household, we counted the mean (average) age and education level of everyone in the labor force. We also counted the number of male and female laborers by occupation—being careful not to double-count cadres, who were counted separately.[15]

The results suggest three observations. First, we show that nonfarm jobs are far more economically rewarding than farm jobs. Second, males generate more income than females—though much more so in blue-collar work and entrepreneurial activities than elsewhere. What lies behind these differential income returns is probably different experience levels. Many female blue-collar workers are in the labor force for only short periods of time. Once a woman marries, she leaves the nonfarm labor force, losing the additional income that might come from working many years in the same job. On average, in these data male blue-collar workers are five years older than their female counterparts. The result, of course, is to further convince parents that their sons are more valuable to them than their daughters or daughters-in-law. The third observation is that families with cadres have few, if any, advantages over households with nonfarm labor. Indeed, families get more income from having a male entrepreneur or male blue-collar worker than from having a cadre in the household.[16] Thus, in this 1991 data set, we find that cadre advantages have faded relative to several other nonfarm occupations.[17]

DISCUSSION AND CONCLUSION

Let us return to the three propositions with which we began. Not surprisingly, much of the first proposition that *patriarchy matters* was sustained. Though the educational difference has shrunk, leaving only about a five percentage point difference in enrollment through the middle teenage years, the gender gap still favors males. In occupations, the gender gap is particularly large for married women. Most married women retreat from nonfarm work and return to tend the house and work in the nearby farm fields. In total, including single and married women, women are 20 percentage points more likely to remain in agriculture, where they contribute much less to total family income. Under these conditions, family members may devalue women's labor, concluding, among other things, that women do not need the same level of education as men.

The other patriarchal pattern involves the use of social capital, particularly by administrators. When it comes to staying in school and to finding a good job, scarce social capital is more often expended for men than for women. Patrilocal residence patterns explain part of this. A woman's initial social capital is not that of her husband's parents but that of her own parents. In the labor force analysis, however, the kin that we know about are not her own parents and siblings, but those of her husband, into whose home she has married. This fact alone could lower the apparent influence of household social capital. This is not all that is occurring, however. For when it comes to the daughter's education, we find no advantage gained from having a cadre father, whereas the benefit is clear for sons. Further, with regard to occupation, most unmarried daughters continue to live with their fathers, who could thus have some influence over their daughters' early careers. Moreover, the differential use of social capital applies much more to administrative cadres than to other white-collar workers. All this suggests that there is something about administrator use of social capital that is gender-differentiated in a patriarchal manner. In short, there are clear patriarchal patterns that exist to this day. This part of our first proposition about lingering patriarchal patterns is confirmed.

Our second proposition was that, whether for the international market or domestic markets, *economic development* sharply improves the position of women. Again, this proposition has been supported. Women who live in more developed communities (as indexed by more nonfarm work, suburban location, higher community income, more schools) appear to enjoy distinct advantages. The same is true of women whose parents were more educated. Under these conditions, women appear to make greater advances than men. Usually, they do not surpass men in education or work, but from a lower starting position in poorer communities and poorer families, they begin to catch up with men in education and work. Women's chances of lucrative nonfarm work take off only after total nonfarm employment has reached a critical threshold. This contrast between high and low nonfarm labor demands repeats a contrast found between Taiwan and South Korea. In the labor-intensive, low-unemployment economy of Taiwan, women have more opportunities than in the capital-intensive, high-unemployment economy of South Korea. The way in which work is organized also makes a difference. When industry remains largely in collective hands, men have an advantage in getting the better collectively owned jobs. The larger conclusion is that women are advantaged by more open economies where men have fewer opportunities to influence hiring decisions.

In the average locale, as development increases, women gain much more education. This gain is not only because there are more schools nearby, but also, it would seem, because of increased demand for educated labor in off-farm jobs. Under these conditions, teenage daughters remain in school.

Once educated, women are advantaged in the labor market. Indeed, at the highest education levels, they equal men in getting nonfarm jobs. At modest levels of development, most of the initial gains are captured by single women, who get nonfarm jobs just as often as single men. Unfortunately, at modest levels of development, most women still leave the labor force when they marry. This fits a staged pattern, where initial development does little to help married women. This is the early stage of development that caused so much concern in writings about Taiwan in the 1970s (e.g., Diamond 1975; Greenhalgh 1985; Kung 1983), and has caused similar consternation elsewhere in the world.

In contrast, at high levels of development, when nonfarm work in a community reaches 60 percent or more, even married women enter the nonfarm labor market. This is similar to what happened in Taiwan in the 1980s. In a more open labor market based on small enterprises and considerable self-employment, labor demand rises to such a level that employers cannot help but turn to married women for assistance. Thus, work has a queuing character. Men are first in the queue, followed by single women (Goldin 1990; Oppenheimer 1970; Reskin and Roos 1990). But at higher levels of development, employers turn to married women. This in turn leads parents and daughters to rethink their options.

Of course, conditions in these new work places are often substandard. Lee's (1995) report of conditions for female workers in a Hong Kong-owned enterprise in China's Shenzhen special economic zone can be repeated many times over. Nevertheless, for women (and men) with few economic alternatives, these types of work opportunities can still be appealing.

Our third proposition was that *social capital matters* for one's life chances. This proposition had two parts. The first was that social capital matters not only in the more commonplace advantages that one gains by growing up with parents who are more educated and in white-collar occupations, but also when one comes from a family with administrative connections. The second part of the proposition was that social capital advantages men more than women.

We were not able to confirm administrator-driven advantage. Men from administrator households are advantaged in education and in jobs, but this advantage is no greater than that secured by men from households with professional employees, clerical workers, and other types of white-collar occupations. What little administrator advantage is present seems to be more of the "garden variety" white-collar advantage common to most societies. We found little of the advantage expected if redistributive authority and the role of special connections remain partially intact. Moreover, the household income of administrators—local, village administrators and slightly higher-level administrators—failed to keep pace with that of either male blue-collar workers or with new private entrepreneurs. The lag in relation to entrepreneurs was particularly severe.

What is one to make of these findings from the 1991 CHNS data set, which are so at variance with our findings from 1988 rural data (Parish and Michelson 1996)? Can three years have made such a striking difference in the fates of rural residents? One explanation is that the methods of analysis are not comparable. That is certainly true in part. In 1988, we were able to examine the more narrowly circumscribed 1.7 percent of the labor force who served as top local administrators, who clearly wielded authority in the countryside, and who therefore were in a better position to use connections to advantage their own family members. In the 1991 data set, we are forced to use a broader definition of local administrators (4.1% of the labor force). The 1991 results could be picking up more ordinary clerical workers who have little authority to wield on behalf of their family. This would depress the apparent value of administrative connections in the 1991 data relative to the 1988 data.

Conversely, we might argue that the 1991 results are more valid because they provide a more accurate estimate of entrepreneurial income. The 1988 data set is weak in this dimension. Additional sources of data will be needed to settle the issue.

Taken at face value, the apparent weakening of administrator influence between 1988 and 1991 is consistent with the Szelényi and Kostello (1996) emphasis on timing. In 1988, *siying qiye* (privately owned enterprises with eight or more employees) were officially sanctioned. By late 1990, small enterprises were beginning to recover from the 1989 recession. Though still at an early stage, the development of the private sector was beginning to accelerate by 1991. Perhaps by then the countryside was moving into a more marketized phase, with blue-collar and entrepreneurial jobs becoming far more attractive than administrative work for villages, townships, and other types of local government.

Wank (1995) argues that this evolving political economy creates a system of increasing dual dependency, with entrepreneurs depending on administrators for favors, and administrators depending on entrepreneurs for income. It is unclear in Wank's account whether the administrators are pocketing the money that comes from entrepreneurs or whether they are simply relying on entrepreneurs for government revenue through regular taxes. Taxation dependency certainly did increase in the early 1990s. Counties could not pay their bills without the increasing flow of income from self-employed *(geti)* and private *(siying)* enterprises. If administrators were also dipping their own bucket into this new revenue stream, that "dip" is not reported in the figures here. Otherwise, administrators would not be receiving such modest incomes compared to other nonfarm workers.

Though our conclusion must be tentative, given the many "ifs" and "buts" about the data, we are ready to conclude that by the early 1990s rural China was moving in a more marketized direction, with most local administrators losing their past advantages to other types of white-collar workers. Moreover, though administrators still kept up with other white-collar workers, they were falling behind entrepreneurs. Their income was more secure than that of entrepreneurs, and above the village level, administrators continued to enjoy subsidized housing, health insurance, pensions, and other long-term benefits poorly recorded in our data. But with regard to take-home income, an administrative position was no longer the way to exceptional economic success. Thus, our conclusion concurs with Walder's (1995b) generalization that administrative authority is no longer what it used to be. These findings also call into question the easy assumption that the only way to get ahead is through connections (Yan 1995, 1996; M. M. Yang 1994; Wank 1995).

Regarding the issue of male and female benefit from social connections, though the findings are not entirely consistent and are often only modestly significant, they tend to support Lin and Bian's (1991) conclusion that social capital is differentially expended. Particularly among administrators, when it comes to helping household members stay in school or get a better job, males are helped in preference to females.

To conclude, we wish to emphasize that one must pay attention to place and timing. As with many developing countries, and particularly other reforming and post-socialist societies, conditions in rural China are changing rapidly. Generalizations true yesterday may not be true tomorrow. Women in the most developed communities are finally acquiring more education and job advantages. In the most developed communities these advantages are even expanding to benefit married women. Similarly, as marketization advances, administrators are losing many of their advantages to other types of white-collar workers and to entrepreneurs in the private sector. Generalizations that fail to pay attention to these rapid changes may quickly become out of date.

NOTES

Ethan Michelson's work on this project was assisted by an International Predissertation Fellowship from the Social Science Research Council and the American Council of Learned Societies with funds provided by the Ford Foundation. For their critical comments and suggestions, we express our gratitude to Barbara Entwisle and the anonymous reviewers. We retain responsibility for all flaws that remain.

1. See Bell (1994) for a critique of all of the last three cited works.
2. For an elegant exploration of the historical staging of these trends in the

United States, see Goldin (1990). Also note Oppenheimer (1970). For evidence on the possible beginnings of some of these trends in rural China, see Judd (1994) and Parish, Zhe, and Li (1995).

3. We have used not the rural/urban code in the original data set but instead our own recoding (available on request) based on observed community and individual characteristics.

4. In constructing the cadre connection variables, care was taken to avoid double-counting. That is, in the occupational sector analysis, a person who is a cadre is not considered to have a cadre connection unless another member of the family is also a cadre. In the household income analysis, cadres are not double-counted as white-collar workers.

5. The variable for distance to lower-middle school is adjusted to correct for possible recording errors by replacing it with distance to upper-middle school if the upper-middle school is recorded as closer. The distance to upper-middle school is adjusted in the same way if greater than the distance to the nearest vocational (technical) upper-middle school.

6. For systematic studies of the extremely modest income returns to education, see Griffin and Zhao (1993), Peng Yusheng (1992), Parish and Zhe (1995).

7. In World Bank estimates, about half of secondary (lower- and upper-middle) school age youth were enrolled in school in 1991—which is close to the figure in these data (World Bank 1994, 216).

8. The analysis is based on bivariate probit models using STATA's variance-corrected multivariate estimation procedures for sample-survey data.

9. In this analysis, 134 girls and 131 boys belong to villages with at least 60 percent nonfarm employment.

10. One aspect of family background that should matter is the number of siblings competing for the same family resources (see Parish and Willis 1993). When introduced in a separate analysis, more siblings at home did reduce school enrollment. However, because this reduction was statistically nonsignificant, it was not included in our final equation.

11. The daughters of other fathers are little different from the daughters of farmers—once one subtracts the negative daughter coefficient from the initial positive coefficient one is mostly left with zero coefficients, suggesting that father's occupational advantage is neutral for daughters. For daughters, the net effect and significance of each father's occupation is as follows: village cadre −.15^^, other white collar .13^^, manual or service worker −.01, and entrepreneur .06, where ^^ indicates that coefficients of this size would occur less than 5 times in a 100 by chance alone.

12. In this analysis, 645 women and 691 men belong to villages with at least 60 percent nonfarm employment.

13. Because here the gender coefficient serves largely as an anchor point for the many female interaction terms in the equation, we will not attempt to give the gender coefficient any substantive interpretation.

14. P. C. C. Huang (1990, 294) provides details on how local connections are more important for work in collectively run enterprises.

15. The numbers of people in different occupations is, of course, highly skewed

to the right, with only a small number of families having three or more people in each occupation. Nevertheless, truncating the number of people per occupation and rerunning the equation leads to similar results, which suggests that the potential problems of outliers distorting the results does not occur.

16. There are too few female cadres to treat them as a separate category.

17. One might argue that the fading of cadre advantage should have been more rapid in more developed and more privatized regions. We examined these kinds of interaction effects and found few stable patterns. This may be in part because of insufficient sample size and in part because of the increasing prosperity of most nonfarm work in comparison to cadre administrative work by the early 1990s.

NINE

The Perils of Assessing Trends in Gender Inequality in China

Martin King Whyte

Those who study China have an understandable desire to reach conclusions about the overall extent of gender equality and inequality in that society, and whether things have gotten better or worse over time, particularly as a result of China's reforms. All of the chapters in this section, and to some extent most of the other chapters in the volume, wrestle with these questions. I want to stress how difficult it is to reach such summary judgments. Very little of what I have to say will be new, and in fact many of the same comments have been made about stratification in general and in any society, not just regarding gender inequality in China. Many of the points I make will seem quite obvious. However, given the frequency with which analysts ignore these complexities and problems while pursuing summary evaluations, I think these points are worth reiterating.

REALMS, INDICATORS, MEASURES, AND DATA

The first obvious point to stress is that if we want to assess the extent of gender inequality at one point in time, or judge the trend in such inequality over time, we need to decide what realms, dimensions, and indicators to consider. Obviously, there are multiple realms in which gender equality and inequality can be observed. One approach is to consider women's relative position in economics, politics, religion, cultural images, family life, and so forth. Even if we restrict our attention more narrowly, as in the present volume on gender and work experience, there are still multiple indicators and measures. At the outset we need to note that there are both objective and subjective dimensions of the relative position of women in the world of work. The subjective feelings women (and men) have about their jobs, their relations with colleagues and superiors, their chances for advancement, and the influence of such things on their social standing are the focus particularly of Hershatter's chapter 5, and also to some extent of Honig's chapter 6. While less often systematically studied than objective dimensions, these subjective dimensions are important socially and politically. Individuals and groups are moved to feelings of satisfaction or resentment not by trends in objective indicators of status, but in response to these subjective factors. But by their very nature these are quite difficult to systematically measure.

Consider the images of women conveyed in the Hershatter and Honig chapters. The young urban women described by Honig who were sent to the countryside in the wake of the Cultural Revolution saw themselves as achieving rough equality with their sent-down male peers, and perhaps even with village men. However, they viewed village women as locked into a subservient status. The boldness and pride of the rural female labor models of the 1950s portrayed in the Hershatter chapter is missing from this picture of subservient rural women. Obviously, the differences between the times and places dealt with in these two chapters and among the types of individuals who provided the information upon which they are based may help explain this contrast. But just as obviously, it is difficult to use such subjective accounts to construct a summary evaluation of the relative situation of women and whether it has improved or deteriorated.

Difficulties such as these lead most social scientists and informed observers to rely on objective statistics rather than subjective accounts. However, even if we focus on objective indicators of trends in women's relative standing in the world of work, we face a complex terrain. We can try to measure, for example, women's rates of labor force participation relative to men's, their relative income (or even relative share of various kinds of income—wages, bonuses, subsidies, and so on), relative representation in various occupations or industries, relative representation in different kinds of work units, relative access to various advantaged positions (e.g., work unit leadership positions, promotions in rank and pay, voluntary job changes, enrollment in specialized training, model worker status) and relative vulnerability to various disadvantages (e.g., being laid off, demoted, fired, involuntarily transferred, forced to work overtime). We can even spread our net more broadly and consider such things as relative autonomy in daily work, exposure to hazardous work conditions, difficulty of commuting to work, relative likelihood of being assigned housing, extensiveness of *guanxi* networks, and other realms. The list of possible indicators becomes longer if we consider, as do the chapters by Bian, Logan, and Shu (chap. 7) and by Michelson and Parish (chap. 8), that we also need to consider women's relative access to education and Party membership as well as divergent retirement ages, since these realms have clear influence on men and women's work status and opportunities.

Given such complexities, even if we are only concerned with assessing overall gender inequality at one point in time, we are likely to see a confusing and apparently contradictory picture. To start with, we rarely have access to the kinds of data that permit a confident assessment of the overall situation. For any single indicator, furthermore, we need some sort of comprehensive or representative statistics of the situation of women relative to men. However, we often have only fragmentary statistics from possibly atypical work organizations or localities or anecdotal information, and these refer only to the situation of women, rather than to that of women compared to men. Even when we can find systematic statistics of women's situation relative to men we may not be on safe ground, since we need to consider how accurate and meaningful those statistics are. In the case of statistics derived from Chinese publications, we may have little idea of how the data were collected and whether there are systematic biases built into them.

Even if we were able to assemble a range of representative statistics on the relative situation of women compared to men in various work domains, we could not expect these to reveal a clear or consistent picture. Instead we would find, for example, that women are fairly close to parity with men in labor force participation rates, at least between the ages of 20 and 50 (for rural China, see chap. 8); however they are much further away from equality in realms such as university attendance and Party membership (see chap. 7, table 7.1). The fact that we may get different pictures from alternative indicators leads to another cautionary note. Given such disparities, there is no single indicator that can be taken as the "best" or even a "good" summary measure of the relative status of women in China. This is not, I stress again, a situation distinctive to China, but rather a reflection of the complexities of gender stratification around the world (Whyte 1978). Therefore, in order to assess the relative situation of women we need to assemble as many meaningful indicators as possible.

The "one point in time" assessment is also made complex by the question "Compared to what?" and by its logical cousin, "Is the glass of water half-full or half-empty?" In every country in the world, gender inequalities are visible, and such inequalities were certainly sharp in China's past. By what standard can we judge whether the gender gap revealed by any particular Chinese indicator is large or small? In some cases the comparative verdict may be quite clear. For example, female labor force participation rates in China, at over 90 percent and close to parity with males, are among the highest in the world. In terms of wages the common finding in Chinese urban surveys—that women earn about 75–80 percent as much as men—also looks pretty good in international comparison (see chap. 7 and the comparative statistics cited there). However, in other cases what we should conclude is not so clear. Is the fact that women constituted only about 13 percent of all members of the Communist Party in the early 1980s bad

or good, given the very considerable underrepresentation of women in political leadership in every society around the world? Even if we were able to
assemble internationally comparable data on the indicators we are using for
China, the picture is likely to be mixed, with Chinese women faring better
than women in comparison societies according to some indicators and
worse according to others. Which other societies are most suitable for such
comparisons is also a matter of some debate. China is often compared to advanced industrial societies and particularly to the United States, perhaps
primarily because those doing these comparisons come from such societies
and are most familiar with the situations in their home countries. Arguably,
comparisons with other East Asian societies, other developing societies, or
Soviet bloc countries (pre-1989) would be more appropriate, but comparable statistics from such places may be hard to locate.

The problems of reaching summary judgments are compounded when
we want to answer the question of whether gender inequality is increasing
or decreasing over time. In addition to all of the complexities already noted,
one needs comparable data from different time points for any single indicator in order to talk about trends. Unfortunately, analysts quite commonly
find current data indicating something good or bad about women's relative
situation and conclude that things have changed for the better or worse,
without examining the situation at an earlier point in time.

Obviously, in order to make assessments about changes over time we
need comparable baseline data for the earlier period in our comparison.
Once again it may be difficult to locate such information for many of the indicators of interest. Few systematic statistics on the relative position of
women in work and other realms were published in the pre-reform period.
There was also little in the way of survey research using scientific methods
carried out in China prior to the 1980s. In some cases, such as school en-
rollments at various levels, figures were reported and collected but not
openly published during the Maoist period. In the more open atmosphere
of the reform era such statistical series have been openly published, making
baseline figures available for some indicators (e.g., Research Institute of All
China Women's Federation 1991). Of course, with little information provided in most cases about how the data were reported and tabulated over
the years, one may question how accurate these recently published statistical series are. In other cases estimates for earlier periods can be derived
from retrospective data provided in current surveys or from cohort comparisons within such surveys, although such indirect estimation methods
are far more problematic than would be data that had been collected at the
earlier time.[1] However, for some indicators of interest it is very difficult or
impossible to locate or construct baseline estimates for earlier periods. For
example, it would be very difficult to get accurate retrospective figures from
the Maoist era on indicators such as male versus female pay levels, overtime

work stints, or personal *guanxi* networks. Carrying out the sort of regression analysis presented by Bian, Logan, and Shu (chap. 7) and by Michelson and Parish (chap. 8) to see the *net* effect of gender on work status, controlling for background factors, requires access to data on individuals, and access to any such data collected in China prior to the 1980s is rare. For a variety of reasons, then, we may hope that data collected in recent years will be analyzed and archived to provide baselines against which to compare the future situation of Chinese women. But the availability of only fragmentary baseline data on the past means that systematic examinations of the impact of the reforms on gender relations remain problematic at present.

A further obvious point is that to make meaningful statements about changes over time we need data not only on the situation of women but also on their situation relative to men in two or more time periods. Figures on changing numbers of female college graduates, administrative cadres, engineers, or other relevant categories may be affected by general trends in China, and without comparable data for men, we cannot tell from such figures how any increase or decrease compares with what is happening to men.[2]

THE PERILS OF DRAWING CONCLUSIONS

The perils of drawing conclusions from current phenomena are perhaps especially great in China, where official history has been rewritten repeatedly. In addition, the reform era has seen a rise in "proto-feminism" within the official Women's Federation and elsewhere in Chinese society, with one manifestation of this trend being a sharp increase in exposés of the mistreatment and disadvantages suffered by women. We face a classic case of what social psychologists call a "labeling problem"—has mistreatment of women increased, or was it simply ignored and covered up in the past and is being highlighted now? Given this situation, presuming what the past situation was like is very risky. Obtaining accurate information about the past in order to make judgments about changes over time is quite difficult, as noted above. Given this cautionary note, however, I still applaud efforts such as those by Hershatter and Honig (chaps. 5 and 6) to use oral history interviews, contemporary documents, and memoirs in a cautious and critical manner to get us beyond prevailing stereotypes about the lot of Chinese women in the 1950s and 1960s.

Let me elaborate on the difficulties posed by the "labeling problem." Conventional wisdom says that women have lost some ground relative to men during the reform period. Explanations for this deterioration are somewhat different as applied to urban versus rural China. For urban areas it is argued that market reforms and the profit motive lead decision-makers to prefer men and discriminate against women more than was the case during the

Maoist era. In rural areas any harmful influence of market forces is com-pounded by weakened state control over peasants and the revival of tradi-tional beliefs and customs, which encourage discrimination against women. For evidence of these alleged trends conventional wisdom cites figures on scant hiring and excessive layoffs of women by urban firms and of abduction and sale of women and female infanticide in rural areas.

There are at least two problems with using apparently "hard" statistics on such phenomena to conclude that women face increasing discrimination in the reform era: (1) we lack comparable data for earlier periods, and (2) we may have reason to doubt the objectivity of the sources of such figures. As already noted, a very healthy trend in the reform era is that muckraking journalism and critical social science have focused attention on the many disadvantages faced by women. At the same time, since there were no such critical voices raised during the Maoist period, it is hard to know whether the phenomena described have become worse, have existed all along but are only now being criticized, or perhaps have even improved as a result of the critical attention. We can try to examine some specific claims more closely and see whether we can find supportive or disconfirming evidence. In regard to claims about discrimination in hiring and excessive layoffs of women by urban work organizations, there are several reasons to be skepti-cal. First, we know from earlier research that at certain times during the Maoist era there were similar claims that women were disproportionately pushed out of jobs, leading to some doubt about whether the reform era re-ally initiated a new trend (e.g., L.J. Huang 1963). More to the point, such systematic data as we have for urban China in recent years indicate either stability or improvement in the employment situation of women, rather than deterioration.[3] Finally, we need to keep in mind the observation in Michelson and Parish's chapter 8 that some of the difficulties affecting women in the early years of the reform may be transitory. In particular, any propensity to resist hiring women or to disproportionately select female employees for layoffs because of the supposed negative impact of women employees on productivity and profits is likely to disappear in the face of evidence of the dynamism and success of other firms employing substantial numbers of women workers.[4] In sum, a variety of evidence leads to consid-erable doubt about a consistent trend toward increased discrimination against women in urban employment during the reform era.

What about the claims that in rural areas the reform era has seen an in-crease in the abduction and sale of women? Accounts tell us that recent years have seen more and more cases in which thugs deceive and kidnap women and sell them as brides to men in other villages. These men are of-ten portrayed as beating and raping the women in order to keep them from escaping. In some instances organized gangs are said to engage in this sor-did trade (e.g., Sun 1992; Tefft 1994). Yet even in regard to such disturbing claims there are grounds for skepticism. Once again we are presented with anecdotal evidence and fragmentary statistics only for recent years,[5] but no comparable evidence on any earlier period. Might not these reports indicate a continuing phenomenon, rather than a genuine increase over time? We also know that Chinese authorities have made efforts to denounce trafficking in women and to arrest and imprison those engaged in the trade (e.g., Huang Wei 1991). One added consideration is the comment in Honig's chapter that urban observers during the Cultural Revolution (the sent-down "Iron Girls") were startled at how traditional and down-trodden the village women were. Given these observations, how can we be sure whether the number of abductions and sales of rural women have increased, or whether critics and authorities (most of them of urban origin) have simply been drawing more attention to an existing phenomenon that has not increased?[6]

Further, many of the behaviors noted sound not too different from the features of Chinese arranged marriages over the centuries: a rural family, in exchange for a substantial payment (bride wealth), sends their young and often terrified daughter off into a strange and perhaps distant village to be married to a man she has never met. Her husband is expected to use force if necessary to initiate sexual relations and to prompt his unwilling bride to show proper respect for his family, and she cannot expect other villagers or even her own natal family to come to her assistance. Arranging such marriages becomes a lucrative business for some individuals (marriage go-betweens). We know that this kind of totally arranged marriage became substantially less common in rural China during the Maoist period but did not disappear entirely (Parish and Whyte 1978, 169–80). While not condoning such practices, we need to ask: when does an arranged marriage become a case of abduction and rape? If there is something new here, it may be that some of these unwilling brides are educated and able to utilize the provisions of China's marriage laws (of 1950 and 1980) and sympathetic urban allies to escape from such arrangements and bring down sanctions against those responsible for them. If this interpretation rather than the conventional "rise of abductions of women" is correct, perhaps we should regard these cases as a sign of progress, rather than as evidence of deterioration in the treatment of women.

The third claim I want to examine is the purported rise in female infanticide in the reform era. Here one has some of the same reasons for doubt as in the two cases just discussed. Evidence about distorted sex ratios and anecdotal information about female infanticide provided a crucial opening for Women's Federation cadres and others to make better treatment of women part of China's political agenda. Precisely for this reason one might wonder how typical or new the described phenomena are. In this case we have a basis for checking these claims against systematic evidence regarding the past. This is possible because demography leaves indelible traces in the characteristics of the living. Even though data on female infanticide and sex ratios at birth were not published during the Maoist era, with proper estimation procedures one can use information on the gender, birth order, and other characteristics of Chinese cohorts born over the years to determine what the trends in excess female infant mortality have been. The results reveal a very significant decline in excessive deaths of infant females beginning before 1949 and continuing into the 1950s, a significantly lower but still nonzero level maintained during the 1960s, and the beginnings of a new rise in excess female infant mortality in the 1970s, which escalated in the early 1980s (Coale and Banister 1994; K. Johnson 1996). Based on this evidence, we can have confidence that the rise in excess deaths of infant females in China in recent years is not simply the result of selective data and "labeling" processes, but represents a genuine deterioration in the treatment of Chinese women.

That said, it should also be noted that this trend is a product not so much of economic reforms, but of China's draconian birth planning policy. The latter corresponds roughly in time to the economic reforms, but its spirit and implications are quite different. Conventional wisdom says that in the reform era decentralization has weakened the power of the state to carry out "affirmative action" policies that benefit women, allowing traditional patriarchal (and new capitalist) practices to emerge that harm women. In the case of the resurgence of female infanticide, however, this is not what has happened. Instead we see here a still surprisingly strong state successfully enforcing policies on the population that directly endanger women.[7]

I have discussed quite briefly three specific claims about trends in the treatment of women, and my verdict is mixed. I am quite dubious about the claims of increased job discrimination against urban women during the reform era, troubled but still not persuaded by claims about a rise in abduction and sale of rural women, but quite convinced by the evidence of a new rise in female infanticide.

A MIXED PICTURE

To attempt an overall assessment of whether women have gained or lost ground relative to men during the reform era, a systematic analysis is necessary of a much larger number of indicators of gender status carried out in a less cursory way than I have done here for these three indicators. I presume that such a comprehensive analysis would again lead to a mixed picture. In some realms, such as the relative educational attainment of young women in urban (Bauer et al. 1992) and rural areas (chap. 8), female Party membership,[8] and particularly the rise of what I have called "proto-feminism," we see clear signs of improvement for Chinese women; in others, such as urban relative income (as discussed in chapter 7), perhaps our verdict would be one of little change; while in still other realms, such as the survival chances of infants, we would conclude that women have been harmed by recent changes. In regard to still other indicators, as Michelson and Parish suggest (chap. 8), we would not find any clear or linear trend. This is the case, for example, in regard to female access to university-level education. During most of the pre–Cultural Revolution period (before 1966), female students constituted only 23–26 percent of all university students; when universities reopened after the Cultural Revolution, this figure rose to 32–33 percent; during the initial phases of the post-Mao reforms of university enrollment, the percentage fell back to 24–27 percent; but by the late 1980s it had risen again to 33–34 percent.[9] Clearly, in such a case no simple conclusion about the impact of the reforms captures the actual trend over time.

As a further cautionary note, the part of China's population to which any statements about trends apply and how broadly any conclusions can be generalized are also important considerations. As the chapters in this volume and my earlier comments imply, there are major differences between the social worlds of rural and urban China that affect the lot of women. Quite possibly, women's lot in urban areas as measured by a particular indicator will have improved over time, while in rural areas their lot will have deteriorated. Important regional and local variations, age cohort differences, class and status differences, subethnic variations, and so forth are also likely in regard to gender relations. Because most of the data we use come from particular locales or types of work organizations, it is important to carefully consider the extent to which any trends observed could be atypical.

A final cautionary point concerns the difficulty of attributing causation for any trends we do observe. In regard to the "impact of reforms" question in particular, the post-1978 period has seen not only the launching of a market-based transformation of the economy, but also rising incomes, urban expansion, growing contacts with the outside world, the collapse of the Soviet bloc, increasingly harsh enforcement of birth control, and a number of other trends. In this situation it is risky to attribute any particular change in gender inequality to market reforms unless one can rule out some of the other social forces operating during the same period as possible causes.

My conclusions should now be fairly clear. Appropriate evidence is not currently available to make any sort of overall assessment of the relative situation of Chinese women and how it has changed over time. If more systematic evidence can be assembled, I think it is very unlikely that such evidence would lead to a simple answer about whether women's situation relative to men has improved or deteriorated in the reform era and as a result of those reforms. By presenting my laundry list of cautions and complexities here, my intention is not to persuade analysts to throw up their hands and stop their research on gender inequality in China. All really important subjects for social investigation are fraught with similar complexity and difficulty. My purpose is simply to point out that the search for an overall conclusion to the question of the impact of reforms on Chinese women can easily lead to biases and oversimplifications. The quest for sexual equality, in China or in any other society, is a battle in which progress or retrogression occurs in many domains and subpopulations, and only by documenting and explaining the outcomes of these many separate skirmishes will we gain a sense of how the overall battle is going.

NOTES

1. Retrospective reports may be biased; the use of older cohorts to estimate earlier experiences ignores period and aging effects; differential mortality and migration make the current population sampled different from those who would have been found in the same place if an earlier survey had been carried out; and so forth.

2. Obviously there are some indicators for which no meaningful comparative indicators for men exist, such as the frequency of abortions or cases of women being sold into prostitution.

3. Chapter 7 by Bian, Logan, and Shu and also an earlier article by Bian and Logan (1996) support claims of stability in the treatment of women in work in Tianjin over the course of the reform era. In a related analysis by Tang and Parish (2000), urban Chinese survey data reveal that younger women are generally faring better in terms of employment and income than did older women when they started work, suggesting an improvement in working conditions for women, rather than a deterioration. For similar results based on the urban portion of the 1988 national income survey, see Rublee (n.d.).

4. The claims made during the 1980s that Chinese employers were loath to hire women primarily involved the contention that managers believed the family burdens disproportionately shouldered by women and the paid maternity and sick leave provided by the work unit would make a woman more costly and less "efficient" than a man. However, other stereotypes—that women are more diligent, less likely to engage in behavior that interferes with work (alcohol abuse, violence), and willing to work for lower wages—point in the other direction and might lead managers to prefer to hire women. Research in the United States provides no support for the view that family burdens mean that employing a woman entails a cost for the firm compared to hiring a man. See Bielby and Bielby (1988).

5. The Tefft article quotes the Chinese newspaper *Legal Daily* as claiming that in 1991 and 1992 there were 50,000 cases of abduction of women in China.

6. Not all accounts of abductions of rural females claim that the phenomenon has increased during the reform period. Some of the proto-feminist voices argue simply that this is a social evil that has been ignored rather than attacked (with the question of prevalence during the Maoist era left ambiguous). It may be impossible to assemble accurate information on how common such abductions were in earlier periods, thus preventing any confident assessment of trends over time.

7. To be sure, rural Chinese families would not selectively abort female fetuses and abandon infant daughters if they didn't hold traditional attitudes favoring sons. However, the analysis of Coale and Banister (1994) indicates that those traditional attitudes did not produce much excess infant female mortality when rural families had three or more children; they only had such repercussions once the state tried to enforce a limit of two children or fewer.

8. In 1983 it was reported that women constituted only 13 percent of all members of the Chinese Communist Party (see *People's Daily,* 11 December 1983, p. 5). By 1997, the figure had risen to 20.1 percent (from Xinhua News Agency report, Beijing, 7 July 1997, translated in *Summary of World Broadcasts, Asia-Pacific,* July 9, 1997, FE 2966, p. G/3.)

9. See the figures presented in Research Institute of All China Women's Federation (1991, 168). In 1992 the figure was 33.7 percent. See *Beijing Review* Staff (1995, 9).

PART THREE

Gender and Migration

TEN

The Interplay of Gender, Space, and Work in China's Floating Population

Li Zhang

China's recent economic reform has stimulated large-scale de facto rural-to-urban labor migration in the past ten years. From countryside to cities, from farming to commodity-based production and wage work, from living in a stable locale to floating in a transient market-oriented world—how have family and gender relations among rural migrants been transformed in this profound economic, spatial, and social reordering? This chapter explores the interconnections between gender relations, social space, and the value of work in the context of this mass migration. Based on my year-long anthropological study of the largest migrant settlement in Beijing (from June 1995 to September 1996), I offer an ethnographic account of the ways gender relations in various kinds of migrant households are reshaped. To demonstrate how gender politics is shaped by the interplay of socioeconomic and cultural practices, my analysis highlights the dialectical relationship between power and the construction of gendered spaces, linking it with the transformation of migrant households and value of work in the floating population.

Western studies of China's floating population have focused largely on its macrolevel economic, demographic, and political effects (Banister 1992; S. Goldstein and A. Goldstein 1985; Solinger 1993, 1995a, 1995c; for an exception, see Lee 1994). In contrast, this chapter looks at the interplay of gender, space, and work in a Chinese migrant settlement in Beijing by focusing on migrants' everyday experiences, while, at the same time, situating the local analysis in the broad context of China's rapid marketization and commodification. In China, most existing research and popular discourse tends to view migrant women as a monolithic underclass (Chen and Feng 1996) and regards the experience of working in the cities as a uniformly positive one for all migrant women, enhancing their social and domestic status. This modernist discourse presumes that women's participation in urban economic activities and urban culture through migration will lead inevitably to the emancipation of rural women from poverty and patriarchal domination (see chap. 8). My ethnographic research among the floating population suggests that the diverse lived experiences of migrant women cannot fit neatly into this linear-progressive model. More recently, as part of the trend of female scholars investigating the lived experiences of women, a group of feminist-inspired Chinese scholars (Chinese Academy of Social Sciences 1996) have begun to focus on the lives of Chinese migrant working "sisters" *(dagongmei)*. This project aims to highlight in a descriptive manner the unique situations and problems facing various kinds of migrant women. It does not, however, provide an analytical framework for rethinking gender, power, and social reproduction in a changing socioeconomic context.

This chapter attempts to fill this gap by making two main arguments. First, the floating population is a highly stratified and diversely situated social group, and accordingly, migrant women occupy various social positions and encounter changes in gender relations in very different ways. To substantiate this claim, I describe and analyze the various ways gender relations among rural Chinese migrants change under differentiated household situations. The major body of the chapter is devoted to an ethnographic account of gender and power in three kinds of household situations within the Zhejiang migrant settlement: wealthy migrant households; middle/lower-income migrant households; and the circumstances of young female wage-workers living in these households. Second, I argue that the increase of migrant women's participation in economic activities does not necessarily go hand in hand with their empowerment. Gender inequality cannot be probed solely from a perspective of economic determinism. Instead, a fuller understanding requires an account of how gender relations are reshaped by mutually constitutive social, cultural, and economic factors in the total process of social production. Thus, the analysis of migrant gender politics needs to be situated also in another closely related arena—the construction of and control over social spaces, from which power is partially derived. More specifically, I show that changing gender relations among Chinese rural migrants are closely linked with the reorganizations of their household and production space in the urban settlements. By focusing on space, I by no means suggest that spatial control is the causal factor in the formation of gender domination. Rather, my point is that the asymmetric control over social spaces by migrant men and women is both an effect of the structure of social domination and a condition for producing gender exploitation.

SOCIAL CONTEXT AND ETHNOGRAPHIC SETTING

I begin by providing a sketch of the social context and the ethnographic setting—the Zhejiang migrant settlement in Beijing. Beijing, as China's political and economic center, has been one of the major magnets for migration during the reform years. The burgeoning urban economy—in particular, construction projects and the service sector—requires an enormous amount of labor to perform work in low-paid, dirty, and risky jobs. At the same time, the breakdown of what Solinger (1995a) calls "the urban public goods regime" allows rural migrants access to housing, grain, and other basic foodstuffs and services in the urban market economy. According to the census conducted by the Beijing Municipal Government on 10 November 1994 (B. Liu 1995), the city contained 3.295 million unofficial residents *(waidiren)*, making up the floating population *(liudong renkou)*.[1] This equals one-third of the total registered Beijing official population. Most of this floating population (82.7%) is concentrated in Beijing's near suburbs—the "urban-rural transitional zone."

Zhejiang Village (Zhejiangcun), with over 100,000 rural migrants from several provinces,[2] is the largest spontaneous migrant settlement in Beijing. The majority of its residents come from the rural Wenzhou region of Zhejiang province, after which this migrant settlement was named. (For a description of the reasons for interprovincial migration from Zhejiang province, see chap. 11). The remainder are wage-earning migrant workers and small business owners from Hubei, Anhui, Sichuan, Henan, Shandong, Hebei, and other provinces. Originally coined by local Beijing residents, the term *Zhejiangcun* has been gradually adopted by Wenzhou migrants themselves to construct their own community based on their common place of origin.

The development of Zhejiangcun took its course over ten years with the gradual opening-up of state economic policies and the Beijing commercial reform (S. J. Wang 1995; Xiang Biao 1993). The influx of migrants into this area began with spontaneous, small migrant groups, and then evolved into long-term, large-scale chain migrations based on kinship and native-place networks. In late 1995, however, the social and economic life in Zhejiangcun was seriously set back by a political campaign initiated by the central state and the Beijing municipal government. During the event, 48 privately owned large migrant residential compounds were demolished because the growing localized power and social autonomy in this enclave were viewed as a potential danger to the socialist state. But three months later, the majority of Wenzhou migrants who had been forced out of Beijing returned to this area to rebuild their community and businesses.

Given the Chinese residential registration system *(hukou)* and the history of the structural separation between urban and rural socioeconomic life, Wenzhou migrants can be regarded as sojourners or de facto temporary migrants[3] because regardless of how long they have been in the receiving area, they normally can not obtain a permanent Beijing *hukou,* and hence, "should" ultimately return to their rural homes in the future. Wenzhou migrants in Zhejiangcun are different from other Chinese rural migrants in at least three ways. First, they tend to migrate with a significant amount of initial capital to develop their own family-based garment production and market networks. A complex social stratification based on economic status, occupation, and fame has formed within the community. Second, their household-based garment businesses have developed to such a degree that they can afford to hire wage workers (from provinces other than Zhejiang in most cases). Hence, a new class distinction between Wenzhou private business owners and other wage workers has emerged along the line of native places. Third, most Wenzhou migrants moved with family members and are concentrated in a common place for living, commercial production, and trading in the city. These three features all have significant influences on how gender relations are reshaped in this migrant settlement.

HOUSEHOLD AS A SOCIAL FIELD

In conceiving of different forms of gender dynamics in the floating population, I choose household *(hu)* as a basic social site for analysis while simultaneously looking at how other social spaces are constructed and made meaningful in relation to the household. I treat household not as a bounded coresidence with prefixed social functions, but as a multiforced, microsocial space in which agents are situated (cf. Bourdieu 1977; Giddens 1979). Its dimensions include not only socioeconomic aspects but also cultural and symbolic aspects. Particularly because the majority of Wenzhou migrants' economic activities take place in and around private households rather than collective communes or state units, an individual's status is generally identified by his/her household's socioeconomic position.

Far from being a natural, uniformly defined entity, the household is a particular kind of social space whose boundaries shift and whose meanings are contested and transform over time and across places. In post-Mao China, during rapid economic, social, and spatial changes, it has become even less meaningful to talk about "the Chinese family" or "the Chinese household" in an undifferentiated way. What constitutes a household in China and what its relationship is to other social spaces need to be reexamined and reimagined in specific social and historical contexts (see chap. 1). In Chinese semantics, the two native terms *jia* and *hu*—often translated in English as two juxtaposed concepts: family and household—contain very similar meanings. Both can simultaneously refer to family, household, abode, and home. Their specific meanings are contingent upon the context of speech and referential background. The very distinction between household as a coresidential group and family as kin group, as summarized by Rapp (1979, 176) in her critique of family history in Western discourse, is simply a Western theoretical construct that is not quite applicable to the Chinese case. In this chapter, I use "household," not to juxtapose it with "family" as Davis does in chapter 14, but to stress the undetermined, flexible nature of what is called the domestic realm, whose members, boundaries, and meanings are contingent upon specific contexts.

In comparison with the majority of existing forms of Chinese households, three distinct features in the Wenzhou migrant households are worth noting. First, the majority of Wenzhou migrant households, in which three generations used to coreside prior to migration, are now not necessarily located at a single geographic place. Instead, they are bilocal or even trilocal across the geographic space between their rural villages and the urban settlements. Members at the two or three locations frequently come back and forth and fulfill kin obligations at more than one site. These multiple locations are not viewed by my informants as separate households. They constitute the same household, but dispersed at different places. When I asked Wenzhou migrants where their *jia* (family) is, they often replied: "Do you mean the part in Beijing or the part in my hometown?" I answered: "The one that you consider as your *jia.*" They usually told me that the two *jia* located in Wenzhou and Beijing are both their *jia,* but the one in Wenzhou is a permanent one even if no one or only grandparents live at home, while the one in Beijing is temporary even if that is where the majority of the family members reside. Although the meanings and weights of these two *jia* are different, they are all considered inseparable parts of a large dispersed household. In demographic surveys by local governments at their rural origins, household members who migrated out are also considered as members of the rural household (see chap. 11).

Second, Wenzhou migrant households are not solely a place of residence and consumption, but also the primary site for economic production. The two conceptually separated realms—household and work place—are now combined in a shared physical space.[4] For clothing traders, their small trading stalls and counters in a public marketplace, although physically separate from the living space, are also conceived of as an extension of the household. The traditional boundaries between workplace, market, and home have been blurred in the process of rapid economic changes. The domestic realm now assumes new business functions, while other public spaces, like privately owned clothing stalls, are domesticated.

Third, hired young workers who are non-kin but share the same domestic space can practically be counted as household members, while grandparents, parents, and children, who are normally considered as the core members of a rural Wenzhou household, no longer necessarily live under the same roof as a result of migration. The relationship between wage workers and the Wenzhou migrant households for whom they work is particularly ambiguous because workers have no blood or conjugal ties with the boss's kin group; but at the same time they work, eat, and sleep with the owner's family members, in the same space. They are regarded as family members of that household in everyday rhetoric and for government demographic survey purposes.

In sum, although I still employ the term "household" and take it as a primary social field in my analysis, it conveys different meanings: it is a flexible, power-laden, conflict-charged space whose meaning and boundary are to be drawn and re-drawn by social groups in specific contexts. As a dual work/living space, the household among Wenzhou migrants is a primary social field in which gender relations are reshaped and negotiated. In the following sections, I discuss gender inequality in relation to the reorganization of work and space in very wealthy households (*dahu*), in middle/lower-income households (*zhong-xiao hu*), and among wage-earning young workers in Wenzhou migrant households.[5] Based on ethnographic description, I explore how such changes occur under the multiple, interrelated social forces across different spaces, and what household means to different migrants.

WOMEN IN *DAHU*

The very wealthy households in Zhejiangcun are called *dahu* (big households). The head of this kind of household, known as "big boss" (*da laoban*), is normally a male figure. "Big" here does not refer to the size of the household but to its economic and social status. "Big households" were not big at the beginning but have evolved over time to arrive at their current positions. Members of *dahu* generally migrated to Beijing in the early 1980s, about ten years earlier than many other Wenzhou migrants. This timing is crucial for capital accumulation and the consolidation of economic power because economic competition was less intense then. Many started their businesses from small-scale cottage production and clothing retail sales, and later developed into real-estate-oriented multi-businesses. In the early stages of life in Beijing, *dahu* women were the primary producers in the family economy. They not only operated the sewing machines themselves and supervised production by hired workers, but also went out with their husbands to sell the products on the street. As Mei, a wife of a "big boss," recalled, "We produced clothes all night long and then went out to sell them in the morning. We did not have money to take taxis, so we rode the bus with a big bag of clothing products—very embarrassing." Those days were difficult and tiring, but working wives felt closer to their husbands. Their family-based production took place virtually in the same space as sleeping and eating. Hence, a household at that time included two inseparable parts —production site and residence.

With growing economic and social status, some important changes regarding the space of *jia* took place. Many now-nouveau-riche Wenzhou migrants gradually dropped labor-intensive garment production by turning to the development of clothing market facilities and migrant housing in Zhejiangcun. Formerly combined production and domestic spaces began to separate. Women in *dahu* were gradually pushed out of what is perceived as the productive realm and confined to activities defined as domestic and nonproductive. Capital accumulated through their previous hard work was transferred to the control of the husband. Meanwhile, because wealthy Wenzhou migrant men usually do not set up a separate office space from their family-based industry, business-related activities generally occur at two kinds of places. First, the household began to serve as a place for "talking business" *(tan shengyi),* from which women are generally excluded. This private domestic space, once occupied both by male and female family members, was gradually turned into "inside" and "outside," "feminine" and "masculine," "proper" and "improper" zones for men and women as a result of their new economic practices in the city (see chap. 1).

Consider the spatial division of Lin's home, for example. Lin's husband was a widely recognized de facto community leader whose home I visited frequently. There were six rooms in the house, including a living room, two bedrooms, a dining room, a children's piano room, and a kitchen/bathroom. Every time I visited Lin's family, the husband and his wealthy migrant entrepreneur friends, dressed up in Western suits and ties, were gathered in the living room to smoke and chat. The living room is regarded as an "outside" space for business matters; therefore it is not a proper place for women. Male guests normally did not bring their wives. If they did, or if female visitors came, the women tended to gather in the dining room or the kitchen. When women did stay in the living room, they took a seat in the corner, keeping quiet all through the male-dominated conversations. Only when there was no men's gathering would women occupy the living room to chat. In this way, wealthy migrant women's space inside a household recedes to the back rooms when men are present.

Second, a new kind of consuming place—karaoke bars, restaurants, and hotels—began to assume a salient function in the lives of wealthy Wenzhou entrepreneurs. These places, traditionally viewed as for entertainment and consumption only, now serve as popular sites for business negotiation and the consumption of sex. I call this phenomenon the "bar culture of doing business." Wealthy migrant entrepreneurs spend less and less time at home, simply telling their wives "I have business to take care of outside." This "outside" is primarily singing and dancing bars. It is true that business negotiations among Wenzhou migrants are often reached at these sites, but the nature of their activities, often involving sex traffic, is ambiguous and troubling to their wives. In Zhejiangcun, newly emergent urban spaces like bars and hotels bear a double meaning: they represent modernity, social status, and economic power of the male consumers, but they are also associated with hedonism, prostitution, and other "ills of capitalism." In local culture, bars and hotels are marked as a space exclusively for men. If women are present in those places, especially if alone, they are immediately condemned as "bad women." Wives of *dahu* can go out only to domestic consumption sites: food markets, department stores, and homes of kin and close friends. It is very unlikely that intimate interactions with male strangers can occur at these places. This form of control over women's spatial mobility is both a function of sexual control and a way of limiting women's engagements in social activities.

The relative shrinkage of social spaces for women and the expansion of men's activities into other wider spaces have a direct influence on the configuration of gender relations. Women are becoming more and more dependent on their husbands financially and socially, leaving them little leverage to make claims and demands in the household. More importantly, diminishing access to public spaces makes it even harder for women to develop their own business and social skills, or to obtain potential social support from a wide range of social networks. One wealthy "big boss" told me that he just cannot bring his wife out with him to business-related banquets and ceremonies because "she does not know how to act and what to say." Other people confirmed this attitude by relating an episode that occurred at the opening ceremony of a rich man's "entertainment city." He and his brother both showed up in their red Mercedes-Benz not with their wives, but with two pretty Beijing girls. One of them was a college student, majoring in music, whose karaoke singing won an abundance of applause and thus a great deal of "face" *(mianzi)* for him. Thus, wives' failure to keep up with their husbands' social expectations (if true)—which is a consequence of excluding them from socially constructed public spaces in the first place—now is used as a seemingly sensible excuse to further keep them out of these areas.

Although the power balance in *dahu* is becoming more and more tilted toward men, women are not passive. As social agents, they make pragmatic choices and employ diverse strategies to achieve different ends given their specific social circumstances. By focusing on gender strategies, we can better understand that the so-called social norms and rules are in fact unstable and are constantly reinterpreted and contested in practice (see Moore 1978). In the remaining part of this section on *dahu,* I present different strategies commonly adopted by *dahu* women and discuss the effectiveness and costs of such actions.

"Control the Throat of Fate"

"Control the throat of fate" *(zhuazhu mingyun de yanhou)* is a Chinese expression for taking initiative to control one's own life path instead of being a passive victim. This expression describes a strategy employed by some *dahu* women: engaging in relatively open and direct struggles for power to control their own lives and personal development. This form of resistance to gender oppression is more likely to occur among women with cultural capital—higher education levels, better rhetoric skills, and richer business experiences. These women, dissatisfied with being housewives, try to participate in the male-dominated business and political sphere. If they cannot hold a formal, independent position in business, they frequently express their opinions in informal business negotiations at home and provide suggestions to their husbands privately.

The responses from their husbands are contradictory. On one hand, because of their strong social skills and perceptiveness, which greatly help business negotiations through the "back door," these women have largely influenced the formation of the household's economic direction, although the final decision is usually made by men. Over a period of time, the husbands have also become accustomed to, if not dependent on, their wives' semi-formal participation. But in public, when a good deal is made, it is the husband who is credited, never the wife, even if she has played a significant role. A *dahu* wife told me: "Without me, he would not be able to make any money. He always loses money in his deals. Other people do not know this and think he is so capable. But I am actually in charge of all the counters and transactions and make most of the money in our family. But outside, people only give credit to him just because he is a man and I am a woman." Despite the unfair ascription of value and renown, some strong-willed *dahu* women take every opportunity to gain more control over the household economy and push their way into a male-dominated business world.

This strategy is well illustrated by Lin's case. Lin and her husband Zhen came to Beijing together in 1985. She graduated from high school, but he barely finished elementary school. When they first arrived in Beijing, they did not have much money. Borrowing cash from relatives, they rented four small counters to sell clothing in Wangfujing, Beijing's busiest commercial district. At that time, renting counters from Beijing state stores was highly competitive and needed not only the right kind of personal connections *(guanxi)*, which this migrant couple lacked in the city, but also a "honey tongue" to persuade the managers to allocate the counter space to them. Zhen could not speak proper Mandarin then and was afraid to socialize with Beijingers. In contrast, Lin already spoke good Mandarin and had better social skills. Thus, she played a major role in all matters related to negotiations with non-Wenzhou people. As she recalls, "Every time we went to visit a manager, he [her husband] always asked me to please go with him because he was afraid that Beijingers would laugh at his heavy local accent and ruin the business." Zhen was not opposed to her participation in business activities, but rather depended on her support. A few years later, with more capital accumulated from clothing retail, they opened their own household-based production of leather jackets. Lin was in charge of the production process, including handling quality control, learning sewing skills, and maintaining ten employees, while Zhen took care of purchasing raw materials and finding wholesale buyers. Their business soon became prosperous and a large amount of capital was rapidly accumulated. In those years, Lin had wide access to different social settings and had more say in major decision making in the household.

Later, the situation changed. Having accumulated more economic capital and social skills, Zhen decided to quit clothing production and turn to real estate development because it was potentially more profitable. Lin disagreed with him, pointing out the extremely high risk of housing development because they were outsiders without official Beijing residency and the state's attitude toward Zhejiang migrant enclaves was particularly negative. She argued that it was safer and equally lucrative to stick to leather production; or if he insisted on developing real estate, they should engage in other community-based business at the same time to reduce the risk by diversification. Zhen and his followers instead plunged into housing development. He sold their house back in Zhejiang for 200,000 *yuan*, gathered a total of 50 million *yuan* from some 20 share holders (mainly kinsmen and close friends), and built the largest residential compound in Zhejiangcun in 1995. This "big yard" *(dayuan),* which hosted more than 1,500 Wenzhou migrant households, however, was summarily bulldozed by the Beijing government after only five months. The official reason given by the Beijing government for dismantling the migrant compounds was that they were all illegal constructions without approval from the appropriate government office. But the underlying reason was to disperse highly concentrated Zhejiang migrants, whose enclave was regarded as a dangerous zone for the development of autonomous social power outside direct state control.

This political incident was beyond Zhen's personal control and prediction. It caused a huge loss to his family as well as other desperate shareholders. It also had significant influences on the use of social space and gender dynamics for migrant families in exile. In the preceding two years, Lin had persuaded her husband to let her open a shop selling leather clothes in Zhejiangcun. The business was successful and made 500,000 *yuan* in the first year, part of which was invested in building the "big yard." But Zhen was not happy. He was feeling insecure because he thought Lin had too much interaction with other men and that this was bad for her reputation (and consequently for his authority). Eventually, after several serious fights, she was forced to close down this remarkably profitable shop. Lin did not completely give up, but she had to change her strategy to meet the same goal. "I know I am better and I can make a lot of money. I am not that type of woman who can just stay at home." She then opened a large day care center, supervising several teachers, cooks, and workers. Because this space was viewed as domestic and less challenging to the existing gender boundaries, her husband did not interfere with it. This center turned out to be an important backup for the survival of the family after the "big yard" was torn down.

Negotiations over spatial mobility and business participation, illustrated by Lin's case, give women room to pursue their goals and power to control their own lives. But in a male-dominated world women's resistance sometimes can result in domestic violence, particularly when gender is linked with politics. During the government's campaign of tearing down all the "big yards" built by Wenzhou migrants in Zhejiangcun, district and local officials put constant pressure on Zhen by visiting his house almost every day. To avoid direct confrontation, Zhen often left home purposely while Lin stayed at home to meet the officials. The logic was that since she was a woman, the officials could not do much about her. Lin tried to take advantage of these opportunities by talking to the work team with her "honey tongue," hoping to gain sympathy from the local officials to win more negotiation time. One police officer, a member of the leadership of the campaign, was friendly to her and showed sympathy for their situation. At this time, the son of Lin's good friend was arrested by the police for drug use. The youngster's mother begged Lin for help, and Lin approached the most appropriate person for solving the problem, the same police officer. Zhen soon found out, and became enraged and then violent. This officer not only presented a potential sexual threat in Zhen's mind; he was also the primary local Beijing official assigned by the government to dismantle Zhejiang migrants' housing. Zhen justified his violent behavior as follows: "This so and so [the police officer], he tore down my big yard. We are enemies. How could she go to beg him for help?" His argument glossed over his sexual jealousy with political concerns by invoking the collective cleavage between "us" and "them," victim and violent authority. Wife-beating was transformed into beating a traitor from the community on a symbolic level. Hence, public opinion would lean toward him even if he was the one who exercised violence.

The account of Lin's case indicates that women are not simply locked in their structural positions. Instead, they constantly negotiate their positions through everyday practices. Women's agency can create room for maneuvering under seemingly unchangeable rules and norms. But this everyday form of resistance has not developed to such an extent that it

fundamentally challenges the social structure. At times, women's direct contestation can also lead to great emotional and physical costs, and thus it
should not be romanticized (Abu-Lughod 1990; Greenhalgh 1994).

The Use of "Virtue"

In contrast with the *dahu* women who choose relatively open ways of resistance and negotiation, *dahu* women with little educational background and
few social skills tend to choose indirect ways of gaining leverage in domestic politics. The main reason why they do not engage in open conflict is the
fear of losing property, young children, and "face" in the event of divorce.
According to local practice, the amount of money a wife can receive in a divorce depends on the mercy of her husband, since women normally do not
have enough money to hire a lawyer or enough legal knowledge to fight for
their own rights. In most circumstances, the custody of children is given to
men because it is assumed that women have no means of supporting themselves, let alone children; and it is extremely difficult for divorced women
with children to remarry in the cultural milieu of rural Wenzhou.

From these women's point of view, direct confrontation causes more
problems than it solves and it pushes their husbands further away from
them. As one woman told me, "If your husband goes out to play with other
women, it's no use to know about it. Once you find out, the result is quar-
reling. The more you quarrel, the worse it gets. You see, when he thinks you
do not know, he has to be cautious about what he does, so he might not do
something too extreme. But if you tear his 'face' away, what else does he
care about?" Another woman puts it this way: "If he has other women outside, that means he is already tired of you. If you complain and argue with
him all the time, he will get more sick of you and never come back. Maybe
that is exactly what they want, and you just fall into the trap."

Mei is one of the women who share these feelings. Her husband, a rich
man in the community, is seldom at home, but spends most of the time having fun outside. Mei knows clearly what is going on with her husband, but
does not like to talk about it. In most people's eyes, she represents the ideal
image of a virtuous wife who is pretty, quiet, and more importantly rarely
complains or interferes with whatever her husband does. She takes care of
all the housework and arranges the children's education well (a son in a
very expensive private school, two daughters in a fairly good Beijing elementary school). But deep inside, "I feel lonely, helpless, and even angry,"
Mei told me.

Maintaining the image of a virtuous wife is not simply a gesture of sur-
render, however. "Virtuousness" *(xianhui)* can be used by women as an effective weapon to win sympathy and support from kin members and friends,
forming strong social pressure for their husbands not to go too far in extra-

marital affairs. The logic is that if the wife is so virtuous and perfect, the husband has no excuse to abandon her or treat her badly, although moderate affairs are still tolerated. Further, virtuous women in wealthy households also expand their social space and power by maneuvering in the domestically marked sphere. Since wealthy women like Mei are restricted from male-dominated social spaces, they begin to extend their activities into other spaces generally viewed as domestic and feminine. For example, they make more frequent visits to women in the extended circle of kin members and friends, drawing emotional and pragmatic support from chatting (viewed as trivial by men), sharing tactics of coping and resistance. Talking, therefore, has become a powerful way for them to relieve their frustration, make sense of their situation, and gather social support to deal with the endangered marital relations.

Two images are drawn most frequently in the conversations to explain and critique the currently deteriorating changes in domestic relations: "excessive money" and "bad women." It is important to note that what money can bring to men and women is quite different. While wealthy Wenzhou migrant men are still in the craze for more and more money, a new discourse is widely shared by their wives, who condemn money as an alienating devil who is eating away at men's hearts and morality. These women feel the irony of their situation and also a sense of betrayal because they migrated with the hope of making more money in order to live a better life, yet have lost control of their own lives just when they began to enjoy their long anticipated prosperity. "Now we might have more money to spend. We do not need to stand in the cold winter snow to sell ten *yuan* per pair of pants, and we can buy an imported dress for 1,000 *yuan* without hesitation, but we do not feel happier or more respected." This is not to say that money simply does not do any good for wealthy women. Indeed, while rich women have lost some power in certain important realms, they have gained a lot of consuming power. But the scope of their consumption is limited to clothes, food, and jewelry; men can use money to expand the business, to increase fame, to buy sex, and to explore the urban jungles of pleasure.

Another image, "bad women," is constantly invoked by *dahu* women. This anxiety about prostitution and the threat to conjugal bonds is directly linked to a nation-wide social insecurity and uncertainty felt in the transition to a market economy. In the economic reform era, prostitution has become a prevalent social problem in China. Despite the state's several attempts to combat prostitution, its anti-prostitution policy has been ineffective. Migrant women in Zhejiangcun view the rampant prostitution in Beijing as an inevitable result of the national "opening up" *(kaifang)* policy. They feel that, like money, prostitution is also something beyond their personal control. It is important to note that such moral critiques are no longer limited to the personal realm, but extend to problems brought by the larger structural transformation. One woman puts it this way: "Aren't we all in the era of 'opening up'? That means everything can become 'open.' You see, men can date and sleep with girls and then drop them. There are more and more divorces nowadays, but that was not the case before." Such interpretations of state policy and cultural change by women reflect that all men and all women do not benefit from the economic reform and modernization project in an equal way. The liberal economic practices of the market are not automatically liberating for women and can turn out to be further oppressing for some women in certain circumstances.

In sum, the preceding analysis of changes in gender relations in very wealthy households and the different strategies employed by women suggests two things: First, with the diminishing of women's access to social spaces they once enjoyed, gender equality has decreased in most wealthy migrant households, demonstrating that migrant women's economic status does not go hand in hand with their empowerment (Whyte, in chapter 9, makes a similar point about the multifaceted nature of gender equality). Second, despite this circumstance, it is possible for *dahu* women to actively adopt strategies to improve their immediate conditions, while challenging the patriarchal order.

WOMEN IN *ZHONG-XIAO HU*

In this section, I turn to middle/lower-income Wenzhou migrant households *(zhong-xiao hu)*, in which the majority of women in Zhejiangcun live. In comparison with the very wealthy households, women in these households enjoy a more egalitarian gender relationship. This is manifested in a more democratic family decision-making process, freer access to social spaces, and higher satisfaction with their marriages. But even if these women are highly active in the "productive" work realm, the value of their work is still largely underestimated. Thus, it is not work per se but the value of what is perceived as work that defines gender equality in the Chinese context. The question we need to explore further is: How does the value of women's work become transformed in this local context? I argue that the transformation of actual work into socially recognized values is closely related to the cultural conception of the space in which work is performed. This transformation, operating through the patriarchal ideology, serves as a critical means by which gender exploitation is made possible.

Most middle/lower-income households in Zhejiangcun have specialized in garment production and trade. These economic activities often take place in individual households. Both women and men in middle/lower-income households participate in production and trade in order to reduce internal costs of their businesses. But there is a clear gender division of labor in this production process. Cottage clothing production involves at least four integrated parts: (1) purchasing and preparing raw materials (such as leather, cloth, buttons); (2) gathering information on the most popular designs and patterns; (3) actual production (tailoring and sewing); (4) bringing the products to the market to sell. Women are the primary producers in the third stage, which is central to the whole clothing production. Although the husband in a household is considered the *laoban* (boss), the wife *(laobanniang)* is the one who actually takes care of all the details of production and coordination of members of the household. Because the amount of work to be done depends on rapidly changing market demands, the work rhythm is sometimes irregular and intense. *Laobanniang* and young female workers often have to spend more than 12 hours per day in a production cycle that extends from noon to four or five o'clock in the morning so that finished products can be brought to the market in the very early morning.

The male household head is mainly responsible for obtaining raw materials and arranging the products to be sold. Not anchored at a single work site, these men enjoy the freedom of going out to chat with friends or wandering in garment markets. I was told that the action of moving through various social spaces itself is valued as one of the most important ways of collecting market information, which is central to the success of the business. Sometimes men also help with production at the peak of the business season. But under almost no circumstances do women go out to purchase raw materials if the supply site is outside Beijing. Such gendered spatial boundaries show that division of labor among Wenzhou migrants still falls along the normative "inside/outside" dichotomy: men take up work performed outside the home, while women take up work inside the home.

Although women play a key role in the essential parts of economic activity—garment production, marketing, and the reproduction of labor and social relations necessary for the continuation of production—their work tends to be seen as less productive and secondary. I once questioned a Chinese colleague of mine who has done extensive research on Wenzhou migrants, "Why are 90 percent of your informants men?" His answer shocked me: "I am not interested in gender issues. I think the development of Zhejiangcun is based on men's activities, not those of women." His answer represents a widely shared way of thinking, which reduces women's essential work simply to a separate gender issue, inconsequential to the development of Zhejiangcun and its economy.

To probe how the work performed by men and women is assigned unequal value and symbolic meaning, I look at how social spaces are used and conceived by these Wenzhou migrants. In Zhejiangcun the demand for housing by Wenzhou migrants is far greater than the local supply. Migrants without the Beijing *hukou* can only rent rooms from local Beijing households. In the early 1990s, after negotiating land use with local rural production teams, Wenzhou migrant groups began to build their own residential compounds, or "big yards" *(dayuan)* in several preexisting suburban villages to accommodate several thousand families.

Because of tight living space, the Wenzhou garment production households commonly serve as a combined site for production and residence. Hence, for them "household" is a realm whose primary function is for economic production. In an average Wenzhou production household, space is efficiently used for multiple purposes. What is most interesting is that, in a one-room apartment, physical space is divided into two vertical sections by adding an overhead wood platform as an extra sleeping area, which takes up almost half of the upper level of space in the room. The production area takes up nearly 80 percent of the lower level of space, with a large board for cutting cloth or leather and several semi-automatic sewing machines. The almost concealed, dark space underneath this cutting board is also used for sleeping. Cooking is mainly done outside at the corner near the door, and an eating area is provided temporarily by a folding table set up in the middle of the production space. Other slight variations of household spatial organization are all based on this pattern. The majority of middle-income households consist of a young or middle-aged married couple, their children, and a few hired young working girls. This multifunctional space is shared by men and women, bosses and employees. Young workers, although having no kinship relationship with the boss's family, are also considered part of the household for reasons I will discuss later.

Because the boundary between work and domestic space is not clearly demarcated in middle/lower-income households, there is a tendency toward what I call the "domestication of production" side by side with the new gender division of labor. But because of the overlapping feature of production and domestic site, the labor-intensive work performed by women at home is less visible and coded as feminine, private, and thus natural work for women. Women's work is also less valued because it can be easily conceived of as an extension of domestic chores, which are traditionally regarded as less productive than publicly visible work (see chap. 1).

In fact, among Wenzhou migrants, neither domestic work nor private economic activities are called work *(gongzuo)* (see chap. 2). *Gongzuo* is a term reserved for formalized urban job appointments associated with state work units *(danwei)*. Domestic work, which does not usually generate direct cash income and takes place primarily at home, is called *jiawu huo* (similar to "chores" in English). All other forms of economic activity among Wenzhou private entrepreneurs are specifically called *zuo shengyi* (doing business), presumably involving profit-making through production and trade of commodities. This semantic distinction is not simply a description of different kinds of activities, but assigns values to actions and renders asymmetric power to social agents. Performed in the household and often mixed with domestic chores, clothing production—a traditional female occupation—

is feminized, privatized, and therefore devalued despite its high labor intensity. In men's narratives of labor division and productivity, the roles of their wives and daughters as the primary producers and supervisors of production often fade away in the domestic background. A Wenzhou migrant man once explained to me the division of labor in their households like this: "It is our custom for men to do business outside home, while women just cook and take care of kids and chores at home." When I pressed him further by asking who is in charge of the workers and production in his house if he often goes out to purchase materials, he answered without even thinking: "my wife." But then he added: "Her chores (*huo*) are simple. She just stays at home helping out and looking after things when needed." What he was telling me first was the normative ideology of what men and women are supposed to do. But what they actually do in the new socioeconomic context significantly differs from that seemingly unchanging custom. My point is not that the patriarchal ideology in which this man lives is simply a false reflection of the changing reality, but rather that this ideology itself helps shape his conception of what the reality is.

Another related process is the social transformation of space previously conceived as "outside" into "inside" space. For households specializing in garment sales, marketplaces with their numerous clothing counters and stalls are the most important social site on which their daily activities take place. Wenzhou private entrepreneurs invest a tremendous amount of time at their counters and stalls, which mean life and death to their business careers. Although physically separated from migrants' urban abodes, these trading sites in the public space are regarded as an extended part of the domestic realm because they are stable, bounded, and privately owned. It is wives and daughters of Wenzhou migrant households who are most likely to work at these counters and stalls. Better-off households hire other young female migrants to do the actual selling, sending senior family members only to oversee the transactions. In the domestication of privately owned trading sites, women's work performed in such space is coded as informal and less productive. (See chap. 5 for discussion of rural women engaged in marketing outside the home.)

In contrast, men's work is highly valued mainly because it is performed in a space far from home (for example other cities and provinces) and requires frequent spatial mobility. Since staying outside the home overnight is constructed as a taboo for women, work that has to be performed in distant areas from home becomes a privileged thing that only men are entitled to do. A man explained to me: "Women are more cowardly. Further, it is not good for them to stay in hotels. But for me, there is no problem. If I cannot go back home that night, I just phone her. That is it. But women cannot act like this." Another woman echoed this view: "You know nowadays there are so many bad guys. If we women also go on a trip to buy materials and stay

outside, they would think we are 'bad women' and come to harass us because women are not supposed to go to that kind of place." Thus, work re-
quiring staying overnight is regarded as a masculine activity that women are
unable to accomplish. This impossibility for women is grounded more in a
cultural construct than in physical factors. But such culturally formed constraints on women's outside activities are then transformed into a natural,
biologically based inferiority of women.

I would like to elaborate on another important but often neglected role
of middle-class Wenzhou women in the reproduction of social relations
necessary to production. Marxist analysis reminds us that to insure the continuation of the capitalist production, besides the supply of labor power,
capital, and technology, the relations of production also have to be constantly renewed (Engels 1891, Sangren 1996). This part of work, mostly
done by women in this case, is productive in that it provides the necessary
conditions for material production. In Zhejiangcun there are some 40,000
wage-earning rural migrants, mostly young girls, from other provinces
working as cheap labor for Wenzhou households. Although they interact
with the employer's kin all the time in a shared space, there is an insur-
mountable class tension between wage workers and their employers. Because explicit class differentiation is still somewhat alien to most Chinese
people after over 30 years of socialist collective ownership,[6] the hiring of
laborers by private entrepreneurs is politically sensitive and easily subject
to social criticism. Public imagination tends to liken Wenzhou migrants'
household-based production to early capitalist cottage industry. Aware of
this danger, Wenzhou migrants are cautious about how to present their relationship to their wage-workers. The female head of the household (usually the wife) plays a key role in creating a familial atmosphere through the
kinds of food she cooks for workers and the way she interacts with them.
"Being like a family" is important not only because it can shade class exploitation, but also because it helps improve proficiency and productivity
when working girls develop feelings of loyalty to the boss's family (see
Kondo 1990). Two girls from Henan told me that they were very unhappy
about their boss's arrogant attitude, and if it were not for the wife of the
boss, they would have left. "We have been here for more than a month, but
the *laoban* never cares to ask for our names and treats us very coldly. We feel
depressed and just want to drag in the work. It is true that we came to work
for them. But if we sleep and eat together, they should treat us more kindly.
Then we would be willing to work hard and sacrifice for them. The *laobanniang* is better. She cooks for us and talks to us in a warmer way, not looking
down upon us." In most households, the *laoban* does not interact with his
workers. When workers have problems or hope to obtain a small amount of
advance pay, they like to go to see the *laobanniang*. Because it is often their

first time away from their rural homes, young female workers become home-sick and frightened about possible sexual harassment in this new place where they are isolated and without social and legal protection. Emotional bonds that keep workers loyal to their bosses thus ensure the continuity of economic production.

Finally, let us look at the different ways in which Wenzhou men and women in middle-income households perceive the new social spaces for consumption—bars. Working wives are generally very critical about men going to those places, arguing that this form of consumption is time consuming and money wasting. Moreover, they are deeply concerned about the potential crisis in conjugal bonds that may result from extra-marital sexual relations. Men's attitudes toward karaoke bars and hotels are different and ambiguous. Although middle-class men have little time for activities beyond markets and production sites, they admire wealthy men who can spend time and money lavishly in these places. They wish to show off and win social status, but they also fear becoming financially drained. Seeking prostitutes on a long business trip to other provinces, however, is not uncommon among middle-class merchants. They justify their behavior as a "natural" male tendency and argue that it is not immoral if one keeps it within a certain limit. Such is a common attitude: "As long as it does not interfere with my family life proper and I do not abandon my wife, I do not think it is a problem. It is natural." Such sexual practice is expected, if not required, as a demonstration of one's economic power and manhood in the Wenzhou merchant culture. Even if wives detect the potential danger, they feel that they can do little to stop it. Frustrated, they attribute men's extramarital practices to "bad women" and the alienating influence of money. Many women told me that they do not want their families to become too wealthy because "all men will turn bad as soon as they get rich; they think they can do everything and will not care about you any more."

In sum, women of the middle/lower-income Wenzhou migrant households play the primary role not only in overseeing the quantity and quality of material production, but also in ensuring the reproduction of labor power and social relations for the continuity of production. But their essential productivity is still inadequately articulated or is downplayed by the local gender ideology in the Wenzhou migrant community. Thus, although middle-class working wives enjoy a more egalitarian relationship with their husbands than before and in comparison with wealthy *dahu* women, their productive work, which is performed and coded in domesticated spaces and in an overarching patriarchal system, is not sufficiently translated into socially recognized value and power. To improve this situation is not simply to make women's work "outside" or "public," but requires a new way of thinking about work and productivity in terms that transcend this spatial dichotomy.

WAGE-EARNING WORKERS IN COTTAGE INDUSTRY

The last social group I discuss are those on the lowest economic and social stratum in Zhejiangcun: female wage-earning workers in Wenzhou migrant households. The majority of these wage workers are young unmarried women, 15 to 20 years old, from poor rural areas in provinces like Guangxi, Anhui, Hubei, Henan, Sichuan, or Hunan. Migrating with friends, not family members, they usually arrive in Beijing through informal native-place networks *(laoxiang guanxi)*. Lacking any initial capital and means of production, these young working women can only sell their labor in exchange for limited cash income. In this section, I discuss gender and class exploitation and some troubling changes facing these young women as they move into Wenzhou entrepreneurs' cottage industries.

First among these changes is the shrinking access to social spaces and the increasing vulnerability for young workers in social isolation. Working girls in Zhejiangcun are usually restricted to the workshop, where they spend nearly 24 hours a day. Many of them told me that they have not been outside the community in which they live since their day of arrival. I have charted the places where their daily activities occur and found that they are roughly within a diameter of one kilometer from their domiciles: home/ workshop, public bathroom, vegetable market, grocery stores, and clinic (in case of illness). A number of factors have led to the shrinking of accessible social spaces for these migrant workers. To begin with, their wages are very low and things in Beijing are expensive. As one working girl stated, "If you go out to do something, you have to pay a lot of money for transportation, food, drink, and high park entrance fees if you go sightseeing. We cannot afford it." Many of them told me how difficult it is to make money in the city, and that it is almost a sin to spend this *xuehanqian* (money exchanged for blood and sweat). In addition, Beijing is enormous and baffling to young girls who once lived in small villages where social relationship are face-to-face. They find it difficult to travel in the city and often become lost in the forest of street signs and commercial advertisements. Further, working girls have little control of their own time and spatial mobility. For every minute they leave the boss's house approval must first be obtained from the *laoban* or *laobanniang*. During busy seasons they are usually not allowed to leave the sewing machine except for going to the bathroom. Public bathrooms often become a resting place where working girls try to prolong time, chatting and stretching out. Given their isolation, these young women are extremely vulnerable to potential violence from the boss's family. The social isolation among working girls is more an effect of their economic position than of the cultural construction of "proper" and "improper" spaces, which is more the case for wealthy women.

The second change is a shift in the primary form of gender oppression from kin-based patriarchal relations to class-based production relations. In the studies of Malay factory women and Mexican *maquiladora* women, Ong (1987) and Fernández-Kelly (1983) argue that the employment status of working women might have loosened them from the traditional kind of male domination (father-brother) at home, but at the same time, it exposes them to modern, institutionalized male domination at the work place. This shift of social control holds in my study too, but with an interesting twist: the transformation of gender oppression from home to workplace is blurred by a reinvented family ideology that attempts to conceal gender and class exploitation.

Working in the Wenzhou cottage industry, migrant girls are subject to strict discipline. Like other forms of primitive capital accumulation in world history (Mintz 1985), the unbelievably rapid capital growth in Wenzhou migrants' garment production is built on maximizing the extraction of surplus value from labor. This is achieved through hiring young women who will work long hours at wages that are as low as possible. It is widely acknowledged that Wenzhou bosses prefer to hire young unmarried women not only because they are docile *(tinghua)* and cheap (they eat less than men), but also because as women they are viewed as more adept at sewing, and more patient in long-term, repetitive manual work.[7] Young working women have little freedom to arrange their own lives in terms of either time or space. Even when they get up and when they go to bed is decided by the *laoban* or *laobanniang*. There is no break except for meals, carefully calculated for 15 minutes at a time, throughout a long work day of 10 to 12 hours. Then they must rush back to the sewing machine. Any delay will cause criticism and even curses by the boss's kin. Many workers told me that their backs hurt from hours of sitting in front of the sewing machine. Some said that at night they can hardly open their eyes and almost fall asleep at their machines. "It is not free at all. We cannot go anywhere. If you do something the boss does not like, you have to see his *lianse* (unhappy expression) and may be fired later, if not immediately." Migrant girls may have left the direct parental control of their rural homes, but they immediately became subject to another kind of gender oppression in the capitalist-oriented production system, one which is colored by the traditional form of family discipline. This form of discipline by a patriarchal figure (not necessarily a male) is justified by the notion that young working girls are considered part of the employer's household *(yijiaren),* and thus their activities should be directed and scrutinized by the head of the household.

Young workers may be rhetorically treated as family members of the household they work for, but their position and physical mobility are shaped and controlled by deference to the employer's kin. In the name of protecting young girls' interests, the boss pays workers' salaries only in one lump sum, at the end of a year. A *laobanniang* explained to me, "This is because they [working girls] are too young and do not know how to keep money well. If we pay them once a month, they will spend it all. This way [once a year] they can take all the salary back home before the Spring Festival." But, from the workers' point of view, a monthly salary would be preferred. How the salary is paid is directly related to power and autonomy. "If we are unfairly treated or want to leave the boss before the end of the year for some reason, we are very likely to lose all the unpaid salary. But if we do not leave, we must tolerate the unfairness." In the worst situations, a boss can expand his control over the workers by holding their identification cards and clothes, making it impossible for them to leave. If some households lose business or make little profit, working girls might not receive their wages at all despite their year's hard work. Isolated in small social spaces, they have no one to ask for legal help because "we are *waidiren,* the major target of governmental regulation; if we go out to seek help from them, they will simply deport us."

Yet, this newly invented family ideology that places working girls under a patriarchal umbrella is a double-edged sword. It allows bosses to exercise domination over working girls' time and activities by claiming parental authority, but it can also can be used by workers as a weapon to criticize and limit unreasonable treatment by bosses. For example, many young workers routinely demand a small prepayment of their salaries (around 15 to 20 %) each month in the name of purchasing clothes and daily-use items as a common strategy to reduce the degree of possible loss if their bosses refuse to pay them at the end of the year. They told me that except for buying a few things like toothpaste and socks, they usually save the prepayment. The negotiation with employers is not easy. When workers' demands are turned down, they complain to the employers and to others that if they are not treated like family members, they cannot be expected to work so hard and remain loyal to their employers. This discourse plays into the image of "being one family," but aims for different ends that may benefit the workers themselves.

Finally, I turn to the changing cultural conceptions of gender relations and the dilemma of returning home. The majority of migrant "sisters" *(dagongmei)* come to work in the city for two goals: to make money to improve their family's economic status and their dowry, and to see the outside world *(jian shimian)* before marriage. At home, they are under the direct control of parents or senior siblings. They believe that after marrying and having children they will have no chance to work as a migrant wage-laborer (see chapter 8 for confirmation of this). Hence, they view this period of migration as their only opportunity to experience personal freedom, even if their income is frequently appropriated by their parents. Most working girls bring their annual salaries back to their parents at the end of the year and hope that if they contribute more to their families' economies now, their parents will offer more money for their dowries later. Many girls left their home villages with such dreams, thinking they would return permanently after a few years. But things do not often work out as expected. Their dream of a free, independent working life ends almost the moment they begin to work for a Wenzhou boss.

At the same time, after working in the city for a period of time, working girls begin to feel that the future spouses arranged for them in the village no longer fit their image of an ideal husband. They begin to pay attention to how urbanites and Wenzhou migrants act and dress in comparison with their fellow villagers. In their eyes, Wenzhou migrants are modern, rich, and fashionable, more so than local Beijingers. Young working women are exposed to all sorts of images identified as "urban," "modern," and "civilized." These attractive, romanticized modern images regarding marriage and love, provided by the mass media or their own experiences, are often juxtaposed with undesirable rural practices. Under these new cultural influences, after staying in the city for a year or two, young working women begin to spend money on clothes, shoes, and make-up, rather than saving every penny as they had planned in the beginning of migration. Some girls end up marrying Wenzhou men or finding boyfriends, causing a huge turmoil at home when previously arranged wedding engagements are called off. Many informants told me that canceling the engagement *(tuiqing)*, a social taboo, is accepted by more and more young rural migrants. Most girls, however, are not willing to go so far, but at the same time do not want to "just get married to anyone." Thus, a common strategy is to delay marriage by working in the city, hoping for something better. The physical distance between migrant girls and their kin in the village makes this form of resistance, which would otherwise be crushed by direct social pressure at home, possible.

CONCLUSION

The preceding analysis makes two main points. First, changes in gender relations among the floating population do not follow a single path; rather, they vary greatly in accordance with specific household situations. To demonstrate this point in a concrete way, I provided a detailed discussion of the reworking of gender relations and women's coping and resistance strategies for three different social groups in Zhejiangcun. For wealthy migrant households, gender equality actually has decreased with the family's economic gain. Being gradually pushed out of what is culturally defined as the productive sphere and other social spaces, women in *dahu* are trapped at home and have less control over their own lives than before. In middle/lower-income households, wives are the primary producers in the cottage industry, sharing a more egalitarian relationship with men than prior to migration. But their essential work tends to be devalued because it is performed at home and is subsequently assigned less productive value. Finally, young female workers have little freedom of spatial mobility and are subject to exploitation in social isolation.

The second point that runs through all the sections is the dialectical relationship between work, power, and gendered space. My analysis suggests that linking gender relations to control over social spaces and means of production can illuminate how socioeconomic and cultural factors intersect in reshaping the lives of Chinese migrant women. The preexisting asymmetric power relations between migrant men and women set the conditions to reconfigure and recode new social spaces to advance men's superior position; at the same time, the socially formed spatial boundaries and meanings of these spaces can in turn reshape the power relations in gender politics. Women's participation in and contribution to economic production and trade are of course important for them to gain power and enhance their social status, as Boserup (1970) has forcefully argued. But, it is certainly not the only determinant factor. More recent anthropological accounts (Judd 1994; Munn 1986; Sangren 1996) have also rightly pointed out that women's economic activities are not automatically translated into socially recognized value. In the case of Zhejiangcun, I suggest that gender domination and the value of women's work are closely linked to the reconfiguration of gendered spaces (household, workshop, trading area, bar and hotel, business sphere, and so on) and to the cultural interpretation of these places in terms of proper and improper, domestic and wild, pure and dangerous, productive and unproductive.

Although in this chapter I have tackled different forms of gender inequality and male domination in China's floating population, I by no means suggest that current rural-to-urban migration is a uniformly negative experience for rural Chinese women. Quite to the contrary, I believe that the grand flows of labor, capital, wealth, and skills in the post-Mao China between rural and urban areas (detailed in chapters 11 and 12) deserve celebration. But at the same time, we should not become blind to gender-specific problems. If post-Mao labor migration marks a significant step for economic liberalization, it is not automatically liberating for all migrant women. Positive changes in gender equality are contingent upon not only women's economic participation but also a transformation of societal values and beliefs. That is to revalorize work performed by men and women and envisage more flexible social spaces that migrant women in diverse social positions can freely embrace. By solely stressing how poor rural households can achieve prosperity through migration—as the popular discourse goes in China—we might fail to discern that some women might be further disempowered during the process of getting rich.

NOTES

This chapter is part of a larger study of the floating population in Beijing based on 15 months of anthropological fieldwork (1995–96) in China. Field research was supported by a Fulbright-Hays Doctoral Dissertation Research Abroad Fellowship and a grant from the Committee of Scholarly Communication with China. The Wenner-Gren Foundation and President's Council of Cornell Women also provided supplementary grants for this research. Cornell's East Asia Program, Center for International Studies, and Peace Studies Program provided travel grants for the preliminary stages of this research. I would also like to thank the following colleagues and friends for their valuable comments on this essay: Dorothy Solinger, Steve Sangren, John Borneman, Gail Henderson, Barbara Entwisle, Wang Feng, Mark Miller, participants of the conference on "Gender, Households, and the Boundaries of Work in Contemporary China" at Chapel Hill, and members of the dissertation writing seminars at the Departments of Anthropology at Cornell University and the University of California at Berkeley.

1. Throughout the chapter, I use the term "floating population" as a socially constructed category. For detailed discussion of the formation of this category and its deep-seated social ramifications, see my doctoral dissertation (L. Zhang 1998).

2. Because of their frequent spatial mobility, no accurate census of migrants in this area has been completed. "A Report on Constructing the North Zhejiang Commercial City" by a joint committee of Wenzhou government and private organizations quotes 110,000. Xiang Biao (1996) provides a figure of 96,000.

3. In anthropology and sociology, "sojourner" and "migrant" are defined as two different categories (cf. Chavez 1988, Skinner 1976), primarily based on whether the person intends to return to his/her home origin. Considering the *hukou* practice in the People's Republic of China, S. Goldstein, Liang, and A. Goldstein (chap. 12) and Yang (chap. 11) propose to differentiate "permanent migration" from "temporary migration" or "de facto migration" on the basis of whether one can obtain official resident status at the arrival point. In this chapter I use the term "migrant" purposely to deconstruct the theoretically drawn boundaries between these terms and to denaturalize the often taken-for-granted "intention," which, I argue, is indeed shaped by the larger structural factors (the *hukou* system) in China.

4. Elsewhere, Davis and Sensenbrenner (1997:24–26) also observed this merging of work and family lives, production and consumption in a single expanded private realm of family in China, particularly among self-employed private entrepreneurs.

5. The annual income of what I call "very wealthy households," which make up less than 10 percent of all Zhejiang migrant households, is usually above 800,000 *yuan*. The majority of households in Zhejiangcun are what I call "middle/lower-income households," whose annual incomes range from 100,000 to 500,000 *yuan*. Although the middle/lower-income households are also considered rich in comparison with average urban Chinese households, it is important to differentiate them from very wealthy households to understand Zhejiangcun's social stratification. A young worker in a Zhejiang migrant household makes 3,000 to 10,000 *yuan* a year with a few exceptions.

6. Whether private individual business owners *(getihu)* should be granted permission to hire helpers was a highly debated issue in the beginning of the economic reform. Over a long period of time, government policies shifted carefully from defining a private employer-employee relationship as an exploitative, capitalist class relation to allowing a limited number of helpers. For details of this change, see the Chinese State Administration and Regulation Bureau of Independent Economy (1987).

7. Compare the use of such gender ideology based on the construction of female docility and manual dexterity with the employment strategy of multinational industry elsewhere (Fernández-Kelly 1983; Lim 1983; Ong 1987).

ELEVEN

Interconnections among Gender, Work, and Migration

Evidence from Zhejiang Province

Xiushi Yang

Recent economic growth in China has been accompanied by increasing rural-urban migration, which has provided not only a timely outlet for rural surplus labor but also the opportunity for many peasants to move away from subsistence farming and to achieve upward mobility. Being highly selective, rural-urban migration in turn exerts an impact on the labor force profiles in places of rural origin. While a considerable literature has emerged in recent years dealing with internal migration in China (e.g., A. Goldstein and S. Goldstein 1996; S. Goldstein and A. Goldstein 1985, 1991; Zai Liang and White 1996; Q. Yang and Guo 1996; X. Yang 1993, 1994), little research has specifically addressed the role of gender in migration and economic growth. Do men and women participate equally in migration? Do men and women migrate for the same reasons and experience similar changes in their economic activities? Does rural out-migration lead to feminization of agricultural production, as has been recently portrayed in the media? This chapter addresses these questions, with a particular focus on de facto or unofficial migration, defined as migration that involves no change in migrants' official household registration *(hukou),* but nonetheless lasts more than one year in duration. The migrant households described in chapter 10 by Zhang fit this description, for example. Using Zhejiang province as a case study, this analysis seeks to examine specifically: (1) gender differences in migration propensity, (2) differences in characteristics of male and female migrants as compared to their nonmigrant counterparts, and (3) the connection between rural out-migration and female participation in agricultural production. Throughout the analysis, comparison will also be made to de jure or official migration, defined as migration accompanied by a change in official household registration.

BACKGROUND

Until recently, the Chinese government controlled not only macrolevel production and exchange but also microlevel consumption, employment, and residence. Despite large differences in standard of living between rural and urban areas, rural-urban official migration was effectively controlled through the household registration *(hukou)* system and other administrative measures (Banister 1987; Christiansen 1992; S. Goldstein and A. Goldstein 1985, 1990; X. Yang 1993). In China, everyone is born with one of two types of official household registration: agricultural or nonagricultural. The type of household registration determines one's eligibility for and access to government provision of social services and benefits. For either type of household registration, one must be officially registered as a resident to receive these services and benefits.

Changes in official residence across administrative boundaries have been strictly controlled by local governments. This does not mean, however, that people could not move. In fact, one could move anywhere one wished. But without government approval, migrants could not register at the new location; and without this official local registration, they could not find a job, buy food and other daily necessities, or have access to most social services in the new place of residence. Thus, while people could move freely, with no market alternatives for obtaining employment and social services it was very difficult for them to survive economically and socially unless their move was approved by the local government. By attaching employment and social services to local residence registration, the government successfully controlled official migration through approval or denial of a change in household registration.

The significance of the household registration and its role in regulating migration have been reduced considerably, however, by changes in labor force dynamics and market conditions associated with the economic reforms, and by recent changes in employment and residence policies. Since 1978, when the economic reforms were first initiated, more relaxed employment practices have resulted in an increasingly differentiated employment structure, which places more of the labor force outside the direct control of the government (Walder 1984; Wilson 1990). This increasing employment in small-scale collective units and other informal sectors is, however, often characterized by little job security, few employment benefits, and poor working conditions. Even state firms have increasingly turned to temporary workers, offering no job security and very limited employment benefits, as they attempt to cut costs (Solinger 1995b). Like employment in small collective units and informal sectors, temporary jobs in state firms are largely rejected by urban youth, forcing many firms to look for migrant workers to fill their vacancies.

Concurrently, reforms in rural areas have dismantled a considerable portion of government control over agricultural production and substituted individual incentives and decision making. Under the "household responsibility" system, land is allocated to and cultivated by individual households under contract; nonagricultural activities, including cottage industries, are promoted; and peasants are allowed to keep the sideline products as well as the balance of basic agricultural production under the contract. These policy changes have offered rural peasants a greater incentive to maximize their production. More efficient household-based organization of agriculture and sideline production has resulted in hundreds of millions of rural surplus laborers looking for nonagricultural alternatives (Taylor 1988; Xie Shusen and Bing Chen 1990; L. Yang 1992).

Thus the combination of demand for workers in some urban sectors and available rural surplus labor has led many work units to hire migrant workers from rural areas (Solinger 1995b). In addition, a pent-up demand for services of all kinds in urban areas provides countless self-employment opportunities in retail trade, restaurant, and other personal services. It is probably not a coincidence, therefore, that a series of government regulations now sanction the hiring of temporary workers based on employers' needs and workers' qualifications rather than on whether they have an urban household registration (Wilson 1990). Similar policies have also been implemented to allow rural peasants to enter commercial channels and work in urban places through individual or collective contracts, or simply self-employment. Furthermore, the government started relaxing its control over urban residence in the late 1980s, allowing rural peasants with no official urban residence registration to live in urban places as temporary residents, provided they meet their own employment, housing, and other service needs. Zhejiangcun, described in chapter 10 by Zhang, is one such community.

Meanwhile, the burgeoning urban free markets, together with reforms and relaxation of government control over education and other social services, have enabled people to buy virtually all daily consumer goods and to obtain education and most social services. This has provided a timely market alternative to government provision of services, thereby allowing migrants to live outside the government's ration system tied to official residence registration (X. Yang 1993). For the first time in decades, the legal and market barriers to living in cities without an official household registration have been considerably reduced. Not surprisingly, rural-urban migration that involves no change in migrants' official residence registration has increased rapidly.

While both men and women could participate in the process and reap the benefits, recent development in China has shown mixed impact on women's participation in labor force and internal migration. On the one hand, the market transition has weakened the institutional support for gender equality in the workplace. Increasingly governed by market forces and driven by cost-saving and profit-making calculations, many private enterprises as well as state-owned firms have shown a reluctance in hiring women. Measures are being taken to further reduce female employees' job tenure by granting long maternity leaves and by encouraging their early retirement (Wilson 1990). On the other hand, the rapid expansion of retail trade and service sectors may provide a unique opportunity for increasing female participation in rural-urban migration and off-farm employment. As an integral part of development, migration is not only a means for realizing the potential of female contribution to economic development, but it can also act as a mechanism for changing the social and cultural norms and values that define women's roles and activities (Bilsborrow and United Nations Secretariat 1993). Therefore, the participation of women in rural-urban migration and the changes—positive or negative—that women migrants experience after migration play a critical role for future socioeconomic development in China. Equally important are changes at the place of origin and the issue of feminization of agricultural production as a result of male-dominated rural out-migration. Unfortunately, as in many other developing countries (e.g., Bilsborrow 1993; Pedraza 1991), the role of women in migration has been largely neglected in China. The analysis that follows attempts to fill the gap by using census data from one province.

RESEARCH SETTING AND DATA

Zhejiang province lies along China's east coast, bordering Shanghai to the south. Because of the lack of major government investment, Zhejiang's economic performance fell behind the national average during the pre-reform era. Between 1949 and 1978, the gross domestic product (GDP) increased 9.7 percent annually nationwide, but it grew only 7.6 percent annually in Zhejiang. By 1978, the per capita GDP averaged 375 *yuan* nationwide, but it was only 331 *yuan* in Zhejiang (State Statistical Bureau 1993; Zhejiang Provincial Statistical Bureau 1993). Since 1978, thanks to the new economic policies associated with economic reforms, Zhejiang's economic growth has greatly exceeded the national average. Between 1978 and 1992, while the GDP grew 14.6 percent annually for the country as a whole, it expanded 17.8 percent annually in Zhejiang. By 1992, the per capita GDP reached 2,850 *yuan* in Zhejiang compared to the national average of 2,051 *yuan* (State Statistical Bureau 1993; Zhejiang Provincial Statistical Bureau 1993). During the same period, the rural economy grew at a phenomenal rate of 23.9 percent and 34.5 percent annually for rural total and rural industrial output in Zhejiang, compared to 19.7 percent and 28.1 percent, respectively, for the nation as a whole. By 1992, the per capita net income of Zhejiang's rural population reached 1,359 *yuan,* the third highest in the country, next only to the two municipalities of Shanghai (2,225 *yuan*) and Beijing (1,572 *yuan*).

Despite its above-average economic growth since 1978, Zhejiang is characterized by a high population density, scarce natural resources, and insufficient capital investment (Wang Sijun 1994). This, together with the lack of a strong urban economy, has made it difficult to absorb rural surplus labor within the province, forcing many peasants to search for economic opportunities in other provinces. Furthermore, the patterns of rural economic development in Zhejiang province promote interprovincial migration (X. Yang 1996). Since 1978 the rapid growth of small rural industries and individual businesses in commerce, handicrafts, and other services has been the driving force of the rural economy and the main source of rural nonagricultural employment. Although some rural industries are under contract by larger industries within the planned economy, most of them operate outside the government economic plan. Consequently, they depend upon markets to acquire all their raw materials and energy inputs. Given Zhejiang's poor energy supply, this has led to a great number of workers engaged in searching for, acquiring, and transporting coal and other raw materials from resource abundant provinces (Zhou and Gu 1994). It is not surprising that, other than the five provinces that are adjacent to Zhejiang, coal-rich Shanxi province ranked number one in 1990 in receiving de facto out-migrants from Zhejiang province.

For individual businesses in retail trade and commerce, survival depends on their success in taking advantage of regional differentials in production and consumption. Given the greater disparities between provinces than within them, these entrepreneurs naturally relocate to major urban centers in other provinces, where they can take full advantage of price differences through trade. Individual craftsmen, too, find the demand for their services mainly in other, remote provinces, where handicrafts are not a tradition. As a result, the development of individual businesses in retail trade/commerce and the revival of traditional handicrafts have led to a high frequency of unofficial migration between provinces. This has been particularly pronounced in Wenzhou region in southeastern Zhejiang, where commerce and handicrafts constitute a strong tradition and where in 1990 interprovincial de facto out-migrants (301,429) outnumbered their intraprovincial counterparts (106,855) by a margin of almost three to one (X. Yang 1996).

Because of its rapid economic growth and spatial differentials in opportunities, Zhejiang provides an ideal setting to examine the interaction between gender, work, and migration. The main data used in this analysis come from the 1990 census of Zhejiang province. Zhejiang was the only province in 1990 that attached a questionnaire to the national census to collect additional information on the unofficial migrant population.[1] The data are unique in at least two aspects. First they allow the analyst to compare de facto out-migrants with the nonmigrants at their places of origin, which is the best way to assess the consequences of migration for migrants (Bilsborrow and United Nations Secretariat 1993). This linkage to place of origin also permits direct comparison of the magnitude of rural out-migration to the degree of women's involvement in agricultural production. Second, the data provide a better measurement of unofficial migration than the standard census approach, which identified only those who were living in established households at the time of the census.

But, like any migration data collected in places of origin, the data have their own limitations. Chief among them is that they fail to include those unofficial migrants whose whole family had moved. The result is a potential downward bias in the magnitude of out-migration. To the extent that women are more likely than men to migrate as part of their families, the bias may be greater for female than for male migrants. Where possible, this data shortcoming will be addressed by attention to information on de facto in-migration contained in the standard census questionnaire. Also excluded are temporary migrants who have spent less than a year at the place of destination.

In addition to the census data, information at the county level from statistical yearbooks and other sources is used to examine the community-level causes and consequences of rural out-migration.

PREVALENCE OF FEMALE MIGRATION IN ZHEJIANG

In 1990, 579,434 Zhejiang women had left and spent over one year away from their home county/city, although retaining their official household registration there. These women constituted 40.7 percent of the de facto, or unofficial, out-migrants in Zhejiang province. On average, women had a lower out-migration rate than men: 28.9 and 39.5 per 1000 population, respectively. But the difference came mainly from interprovincial migration, of which the rates were 14.2 for women and 23.0 for men per 1000 population. For intraprovincial migration, women had a much more comparable rate to men—14.6 and 16.4 per 1000, respectively. Although intraprovincial de facto in-migrants are not exactly the same as intraprovincial de facto out-migrants,[2] they provide a useful check for the possible under-reporting of out-migration noted earlier. The intraprovincial unofficial in-migration rates, being 16.7 and 17.6 per 1000 population for women and men, respectively, indicate some under-reporting of female migrants, but the difference is small.

In contrast to the strictly regulated official migration, de facto migration is largely free of government control and thus is directly responsive to market forces and spatial differences in opportunities. The very nature of the opportunities to which unofficial migrants respond and the long-distance travel involved very likely affect the predominance of men in interprovincial movement. Supply/sales *(gongxiao)* jobs have been and still are mainly occupied by men. This is true regardless of the type of ownership and the size of the enterprises. In 1990, for example, men outnumbered women in supply/sales occupations by a margin of 8.3 to 1. Furthermore, the greater familial responsibility of women as well as social and cultural norms make it more difficult for women to participate in economic activities far from home (see chap. 10 for further discussion of the gendered construction of space). Close to one third of the interprovincial de facto migrants from Zhejiang ended up in frontier provinces such as Heilongjiang, Jilin, Gansu, Xinjiang, Shaanxi, Inner Mongolia, Yunnan, and Guizhou. Women's participation in de facto migration may also be reduced by their lack of access to apprenticeships in traditional handicrafts.

In comparison to the figures for unofficial migrants, there were only about 236,312 Zhejiang women who migrated officially in 1990—less than half the number of de facto woman migrants. In general, although these women were less mobile than the men, their rates of interprovincial and intraprovincial official migration were more similar: 4.1 and 7.8 per 1000 population respectively for women, and 5.5 and 10.1 per 1000 population for men. An interesting contrast between official and unofficial migration is that while intraprovincial movement predominates in the former, interprovincial moves are more common for unofficial migrants.

Women are less mobile than men with respect to both official and unofficial migration. It should be pointed out, however, that both the standard census and the additional questionnaire attached to it in Zhejiang province defined migrants as people who crossed county/city boundaries. As a result, those who moved within counties and cities were excluded from the migration statistics. To the extent that women move shorter distances than men, their lower mobility could partly result from the definition of migration used. Had a smaller spatial unit been used, e.g., a township instead of a county, women might have had mobility rates more comparable to men's.

WHY DO WOMEN MIGRATE?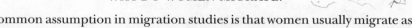

A common assumption in migration studies is that women usually migrate as "associational migrants," accompanying family members, joining husbands who migrated earlier, or creating families through marriage. Data on unofficial migrants from Zhejiang indicate that while a considerably higher percentage of women than men migrated for noneconomic reasons, namely, to accompany other family members (15.2%) and to marry (10.9%), economic motives predominated for female as well as male migrants. Close to two-thirds of migrant women and over 90 percent of migrant men migrated for direct economic reasons. Given that some women "accompanying family members/relatives" may have actually moved to join the family business, the predominance of economic motives among migrant women may be even more significant. In any case, in Zhejiang, female de facto out-migrants are hardly "associational migrants." Most of them actively participated in the migration process to search for economic opportunities.

Economic reasons play a far more important role in unofficial than official migration. Whereas economic motives predominated among unofficial migrants, fewer than half of the official migrants between 1985 and 1990—24.2 percent for women and 48.2 percent for men—moved because of job transfers, graduate assignments, and other economic activities. Among women, almost half (47.5%) of the official migrants moved because of marriage, another 7.9 percent to accompany family members. Only a small fraction of the official migration among males occurred for these reasons (1.5% and 2.4%, respectively). Study and training (22.1%), retirement (4.2%), and other noneconomic reasons (20.6%) account for official migration among males. Although these other reasons also explain some of the official migration of females, they do so to a lesser extent (14.5%, 1.1%, and 3.2%, respectively).

WHICH WOMEN MIGRATE?

Migration is a selective process. In general, migrants are younger and better educated than nonmigrants at the place of origin. Do women who are unofficial migrants also fit this general picture? I address the question by comparing patterns of migrant selectivity in terms of age and educational attainment.

Age

The most consistent pattern of migrant selectivity everywhere is with respect to age. Migrants are heavily concentrated in the early adulthood ages. Unofficial migrants in China are no exception. Compared to nonmigrants, male and female de facto migrants are heavily concentrated in the 15–29 years age range. The Index of Dissimilarity (ID)[3] is 13.65 for men and 10.05 for women. These values suggest that the male and female de facto migrant populations have a similar degree of departure in the age distribution relative to their respective nonmigrant populations. This is in sharp contrast to the age patterns of official migrants, where age concentration is more pronounced among female migrants, who are disproportionately clustered in ages between 15 and 24. For them, the category is dominated by marriage migrants in the nubile ages. The Index of Dissimilarity comparing official migrants to the nonmigrant population is 14.3 for men and 20.4 for women.

In terms of migration propensity, men have higher rates of unofficial migration than women throughout the working ages. The difference is particularly pronounced in the 20–24 age interval, when, for each 1000 population, 81 men out-migrated as compared to only 56 women. This age group also has the highest rate of unofficial migration for both men and women. For official migration, peak mobility for men occurs at age 20 to 24, but for women, this peak falls during their later teens, when they have a considerably higher rate than men. Official migration is also characterized by less of a gender difference in migration rates than de facto migration.

That the highest mobility rates generally occur in the 20–24 years age range is no surprise to those familiar with the literature on migration. This is the critical life stage when young adults enter the labor force and get married. These years are also the most rebellious and adventurous ones, where young adults may be easily dissatisfied with the status quo and eagerly search for something new. While young men and young women experience the same life course transition, the different role expectations that society and families usually hold for young men and young women can affect their likelihood of migration differently. Young men must establish themselves and assume responsibility for the social and economic well-being of their families. In rural areas especially, a combination of poor employment prospects and the image of a bright urban life puts young men under increasing pressure to search for opportunities elsewhere to better themselves and their newly established families. Young women become wives and mothers during their twenties. Zhang (chap. 10) describes the experiences of rural women who migrate prior to marriage. Later on, when they are married, these women would be accompanied by young children if they migrated. Unless the entire family moves, women's ability to move away from home can be greatly restrained by their familial roles. In addition, if their wives were to migrate alone, husbands might consider it an indication of failure on their part to provide adequate support and protection for their families.

When it comes to official migration, however, the control exercised by the government through its migration policies diminishes the impact of gendered role expectations on mobility. This is reflected in weaker gender differences in official as compared to unofficial migration. Moreover, in rural areas, the migration of one marriage partner to join the other upon marriage is automatically justified by policy. Brides rather than grooms generally make the relocation. This is why female official migrants are particularly concentrated in their late teens. Different role expectations in combination with government migration policy explain the differences in the migration behavior of men and women during their early adulthood years.

TABLE 11.1   Migration Status and Migration Rates, by Highest Level of School Attended by Nonstudent Population and by Gender, Zhejiang Province, 1990

| | Migration Status | | | | | |
| | Nonmigrants (%) | | Unofficial Migrants (%) | | Official Migrants (%) | |
Educational Attainment	Male	Female	Male	Female	Male	Female
College	1.8	0.7	0.8	0.4	16.6	7.0
Vocational school	1.6	1.1	0.6	0.6	10.3	7.4
Senior high school	7.7	5.3	8.1	5.6	17.3	10.3
Junior high school	31.5	22.5	39.7	30.8	31.4	33.1
Elementary	42.2	36.1	43.3	44.6	20.4	32.2
Illiterate	15.3	34.4	7.3	17.9	3.9	9.9
Index of dissimilarity [a]	n.a.	n.a.	9.85	17.2	33.2	28.3
	Migration Rates (per 1000 population)					
College			20.7	22.1	140.3	129.6
Vocational school			19.5	17.3	103.4	88.6
Senior high school			50.1	35.6	35.2	24.7
Junior high school			59.9	45.9	15.7	18.7
Elementary			48.7	41.4	7.6	11.4
Illiterate			22.8	17.4	4.0	3.7

SOURCE: 1990 Census of Zhejiang Province.

[a] See note 3 for details.

Educational Attainment

Table 11.1 shows the educational profiles of migrant and nonmigrant populations. Among unofficial migrants, when compared to nonmigrants, men and women with a junior high school education are considerably overrepresented, while those who have received either no formal education or more than a high school education are considerably underrepresented. For women, also significantly overrepresented among unofficial migrants are those with an elementary school education. Among official migrants, by contrast, both men and women with more than a junior high school education are overrepresented, while women who have a junior high school education are also overrepresented. On average, official migrants are much better educated than unofficial migrants, who in turn are better educated than nonmigrants. Gender differences in educational selectivity are greater in unofficial than official migration, as suggested by the Index of Dissimilarity. This is the same as what we saw for age selectivity, where gender differences were greater for unofficial than official migration.

The education-specific migration rates in table 11.1 further show that unofficial migration rates are higher for men than women at every educational level except college, where women actually have a higher rate than men do (22.1 per 1000 population for women, as compared to 20.7 for men). For official migration, by contrast, gender differences are less uniform. Women with either a junior high school or elementary school education are actually more mobile than men. The patterns suggest that lower levels of education among women than among men explain to some extent the lower overall rate of official migration for women. The gender difference in education is unlikely to be the main cause of the gender difference in the rates of unofficial migration, however. In fact, the largest difference in de facto migration rates occurs for those with a high-school education — a level of schooling reached by no more than 25 percent of the rural population. The inverse U-shaped relationship between level of education and de facto migration rate also stands in sharp contrast to the relationship for official migration, where rates increase monotonically with one's educational level.

Several factors account for the educational pattern of unofficial migration. First, the market transition has increasingly diversified employment structure, opening the job market to a greater segment of the population with different educational backgrounds. In particular, jobs in the informal sector are usually less demanding in terms of formal education. Nonetheless, some minimum education is still important for working in urban areas. Given the great diversity in local dialects across geographic locations in China, the ability to speak Mandarin (putonghua), often acquired through formal education, becomes critical in peasants' ability to respond to and survive in urban labor markets, especially those far away. (See chap. 10 for an anecdote about the value of Mandarin for Zhejiang migrants in Beijing.)

Second, college and vocational school graduates are avoiding temporary jobs — to which most unofficial migrants respond — because these graduates can obtain better, permanent jobs and thereby move officially. This in turn reduces the share of college and vocational school graduates in the de facto migration flow.

Third, the market transition has weakened the institutional guarantee for gender equality in the workplace. Cost considerations have made many enterprises reluctant to hire women regardless of type of ownership (i.e., state, collective, private). A typical practice is to set a higher minimum score for hiring women than men in job entrance tests. Such discriminatory practices probably have little impact on women without much formal education because their main source of employment is in the informal sector, where education is not a prerequisite and where jobs are often shared within the family or close kin network. It also probably has little impact on women at the top of the educational distribution because they will be looking mainly for permanent professional or administrative positions in the formal sectors, where hiring is still supposed to be subject to government regulations, including the principle of gender equality.

Particularly affected, then, is the hiring of temporary or contract workers in urban industries, which is increasingly open to migrant workers. To the extent that most temporary jobs in urban industries require some high school education, women with a high school education may experience disproportionately the negative impact of discriminatory practices in hiring, which in turn severely limits their ability to migrate as compared to men with similar education. The likelihood of unofficial out-migration among women with a high school education may be further reduced by their greater ability to secure alternative employment in rural industries. Data at the provincial level suggest that the probability of a woman having a job in rural industries more than doubles if she has an elementary school education and almost doubles again if she has a junior or senior high school education. As a result, the difference in rates of de facto migration between men and women is particularly pronounced for persons with some high school education.

WHAT DO MIGRANT WOMEN DO?

Table 11.2 presents the sectoral distribution of employment of the migrant and nonmigrant populations. Given the substantial difference in employment structure between rural and urban areas, the table presents the nonmigrant populations separately for urban and rural areas. Since 85 percent of unofficial out-migrants originated in rural areas and most ended up in urban places, the nonmigrant population in rural areas represents reasonably well the population at the place of origin, while that of urban areas the population at the place of destination. The one exception consists of rural women who move to another rural location upon marriage, an important component of the official migration stream for women.

Compared to the rural nonmigrant population, unofficial migrants had higher percentages employed in almost every nonagricultural sector. For both men and women, very few unofficial migrants remained in agriculture after migration; the proportion of unofficial migrants engaged in agricultural activities was much lower than that of the urban population. Compared to the urban population, unofficial migrants had considerably higher proportions working in construction, commerce, and service sectors, but lower proportions employed in industry, transportation and communication, and the "other" category. By contrast, a considerable percentage (44.5 %) of female official migrants, and a lesser but still significant proportion of male official migrants (20.0%), remained in agriculture after migration. Official migrants are also less likely than unofficial migrants to be employed in construction, commerce, and service sectors, but are much more likely to be in

TABLE 11.2   Sectoral Distribution of Employment among the
Nonmigrant and Migrant Populations, 15 Years of Age or Older,
by Gender, Zhejiang Province, 1990

Industries	Rural Non-migrants (%)		Urban Non-migrants (%)		Unofficial Migrants (%)		Official Migrants (%)	
	Male	Female	Male	Female	Male	Female	Male	Female
Agriculture	76.4	75.0	30.8	26.9	7.4	8.1	20.0	44.5
Industry	13.5	19.6	33.4	43.4	23.2	25.5	29.6	26.2
Construction	2.3	0.1	5.2	1.1	25.2	5.7	11.2	3.7
Transportation	2.3	0.2	6.1	1.9	2.2	0.6	5.3	1.1
Commerce	2.4	2.6	10.0	13.3	15.8	22.6	6.1	7.3
Service	0.7	0.6	2.8	3.3	17.3	29.0	2.2	2.0
Other*a*	2.4	1.9	11.6	10.1	8.9	8.5	25.5	15.1
Total (000)	9967	6926	4393	3289	653	305	214	166

SOURCE: 1990 Census of Zhejiang Province.

a"Other" includes surveying, mining, and quarrying; health, sports, and social welfare; education, arts and culture, and media; research and technical services; finance and insurance; government office and social organization.

the "other" category. Note that the "other" category includes many white-collar workers (see note to table 11.2). The pattern suggests that while post-migration employment represents a clear shift away from agricultural activities for unofficial and official migrants, unofficial migrants experienced greater difficulties than their official counterparts in gaining access to white-collar occupations and were more heavily concentrated in the construction, commerce, and service sectors. This should not be surprising, since white-collar employment is still favored by urban residents over jobs in construction, commerce, and the service sectors, and is less open to unofficial migrants, who have no local urban household registration. Even if some white-collar jobs are open to unofficial migrant workers, their higher educational requirements make it difficult for de facto migrants to compete with urban residents.

Among unofficial migrants, the sectoral distributions of postmigration employment further suggest that male and female migrants respond to different job opportunities and do different jobs at their urban destinations. For male unofficial migrants, the most frequent postmigration employment was in construction (25%) closely followed by industry (23%); for female de facto migrants, it was the service sector (29%), again followed by industry (26%). The female Zhejiang migrants described by Zhang (chap. 10) fall into these two categories.

Unofficial migrants—men or women—are doing quite different jobs than the urban natives. Further, most jobs in the construction, commerce, and service sectors lack job security and stability, and are characterized by poor working conditions, low pay, and few benefits. These jobs are often rejected by native urban youths entering the labor force. Because of this, migrant workers present neither a real challenge to urban residents nor a burden to the urban economy as far as employment is concerned.

UNOFFICIAL MIGRATION AND COMMUNITIES OF ORIGIN

Individual migrants seldom act alone in their migration decisions; nor is the impact of migration limited to migrants themselves. Socioeconomic factors in communities of rural origin can affect the degree of migration pressure and influence who will migrate. Being selective, rural out-migration can in turn alter labor force profiles at places of origin. In particular, gender-differentiated migration streams have been blamed for the increasing feminization (*nühua*) of agricultural production in rural China (R. Barrett et al. 1991; Christiansen 1992; Taylor 1988). The analysis that follows briefly examines the county-level causes of unofficial out-migration and focuses on whether rural out-migration is related to women's involvement in agricultural production. Counties in China are mainly rural, although they include urban towns as well as rural villages. Because close to 90 percent of the population in all counties in Zhejiang province is engaged in agricultural production, migration from counties can be reasonably considered to be migration from rural areas.

Table 11.3 presents zero-order correlation coefficients between rates of unofficial out-migration and selected socioeconomic indicators at the county level in Zhejiang province. For men and women, the rate of de facto out-migration correlates negatively with income level and land/labor ratio, while the rate of de facto in-migration correlates positively with these two indicators. De facto migration apparently follows a typical push-pull model: migrants are leaving counties with fewer opportunities and moving to counties with more opportunities.

With respect to the connection between the out-migration of men and the increasing participation of women in agricultural production, at the county level, the correlation coefficient of −.200 indicates that the out-migration of men is related to a decrease in the involvement of women in agricultural production, but the correlation is not significant. A closer look, however, reveals that there may be some kind of substitution of women for men in agricultural production. First, the almost perfect positive correlation between the overall female employment rate (FEMEMP) and the proportion of agricultural labor force composed of women (FEMAG) indicates that the employment of women in rural areas is overwhelmingly tied to agricultural activities. Second, the positive correlation between FEMAG and the proportion of the rural labor force engaged in rural industries (RURIND)

TABLE 11.3   Correlation Coefficients between Rates of Unofficial
Migration and Selected Socioeconomic Indicators among Counties
in Zhejiang Province, 1990 (*N* = 78 counties)

	FOUT	*IN*	*FEMAG*	*RURIND*	*INCOME*	*RATIO*	*FEMEMP*	*MALEMP*
MOUT	.936*	−.307*	−.200	−.262*	−.414*	−.465*	−.264*	−.146
FOUT		−.210	−.286*	−.256*	−.375*	−.430*	−.319*	−.162
IN			−.063	.176	.316*	.403*	.037	−.137
FEMAG				.414*	.165	.355*	.923*	.500*
RURIND					.578*	.310*	.485*	.146
INCOME						.326*	.241*	−.092
RATIO							.413*	.304*
FEMEMP							-	.630*

SOURCE: 1990 Census of Zhejiang province and Zhejiang Provincial Statistical Yearbook, 1991.
*p = 0.05 (two-tailed test).
NOTE:
MOUT Rate of male unofficial out-migration.
FOUT Rate of female unofficial out-migration.
IN Rate of unofficial in-migration.
FEMAG Proportion of agricultural labor force that is female.
RURIND Proportion of rural labor force employed in township and village industries.
INCOME Per capita income among rural population.
RATIO Land/labor ratio.
FEMEMP Overall rate of female employment.
MALEMP Overall rate of male employment.

suggests that employment in rural industries is associated with greater involvement of women in agricultural production. Men's involvement in agricultural production decreases as jobs in rural industries increase. Finally,
the correlation between the overall employment rate for men (MALEMP)
and RURIND is not significant, while that between MALEMP and the land/
labor ratio (RATIO) is significant and, moreover, positive. The overall level
of employment among men seems to be unrelated to the availability of jobs
in rural industries but rather tied to agricultural opportunities captured by
the land/labor ratio.

The results suggest that the overall level of employment among women
in rural areas is largely determined by the demand for their labor in agricultural production, and women's participation in agricultural production
in turn serves as either a supplement to or a substitution for men in agricultural production. When there is more land than men can handle, women
are called upon to supplement male labor. When jobs in rural industries
become available, it is the men who benefit from them first and who switch
employment from farming to rural industry (in chap. 8 Michelson and

Parish report similar findings in eight provinces). Women are then called upon to fill the vacancies and substitute for men in agricultural production.

In sum, while there is some evidence of female substitution for male labor in agricultural production, this is not so much a result of increasing outmigration of men as it is a function of overall rural industrialization. This does not affect the overall level of employment among men but offers them the opportunity for upward mobility. As men move away from agriculture in response to jobs in rural industries or industries in nearby urban places, women will move in to substitute for men in agricultural production.

IMPLICATIONS

Increasing rural-urban migration during the last decade provides an opportunity to examine the interaction between gender roles and migration in the context of swift social and structural transitions. Using Zhejiang province as a case study, my analysis suggests that women have a lower rate of unofficial migration than men. In this chapter, unofficial or de facto migration refers to migration to and residence in a new location for more than a year, but with no change in household registration. While a considerably higher proportion of migrant women than men moved for noneconomic reasons, almost two-thirds of migrant women moved for economic reasons. Their migration can hardly be characterized as "associational." Nevertheless, other than definitional flaws that may have led to underreporting of the migration of women, the greater familial roles women usually play, reinforced by the gendered role expectations from society, has no doubt restrained their participation in activities like migration, which involve a physical separation from family. This is particularly pronounced during women's early adulthood years.

While lack of formal education among women can also limit the opportunities available to them, improvement in education is no guarantee of equal participation in labor migration. The transition toward a market economy in China has weakened the institutional support for gender equality in the workplace, which may have a particularly adverse impact on women from the middle of the educational distribution as they compete for jobs in urban industries and other formal sectors with urban residents and male migrants. Structural changes and changes in labor force dynamics have made more and more urban jobs available to migrant workers, yet migrant women's options are still limited to jobs in the traditionally female-type retail trade and service sectors. Their access to other economic sectors tends to be restricted, perhaps by the often negative social norms or perceptions about women, which have been heightened by the increasing cost-saving and profit-making calculations in management. Consequently, women's participation in labor migration may be circumscribed in comparison to men's.

The county-level analysis points to some evidence of female substitution for male labor in agricultural production. But the main cause of women's increasing involvement in agricultural production is not the out-migration of men; it is more likely the structural and social factors that have limited the nonagricultural opportunities available to women. In order to realize the full potential of women's contribution to development via their participation in labor migration, it will be necessary to enforce the principle of gender equality, to eliminate discrimination against women in the workplace, and to make every option available to women who are otherwise fully qualified.

NOTES

1. The standard census questionnaire also collects information on de facto migration, which can be separated from official migration by migrants' type of household registration. But the information obtained refers only to migrants joining established households and provides no information on places of origin, except for a simple classification distinguishing between origin inside and outside the province of enumeration.

2. Theoretically, these two numbers should match. But the cumulative de facto in-migrant statistics can only be inferred from the standard census question on individuals' official household registration; it is not possible to separate intraprovincial from interprovincial migrants in the cumulative statistics. It is possible, however, to obtain the number of five-year de facto in-migrants by intraprovincial and interprovincial movement. The number of intraprovincial in-migrants used here was, therefore, derived from subtracting the five-year interprovincial in-migrants from the total cumulative de facto permanent in-migrants.

3. The Index of Dissimilarity is calculated as half of the sum of the absolute difference in each age category between the corresponding migrant and nonmigrant populations. It indicates the average cumulative difference in percentages across all age categories between migrant and nonmigrant populations. If there is no difference between the two percentage distributions (the two populations having the same percentage for all categories), the index will be zero. The higher the index, the greater the discrepancy between the two distributions under comparison.

TWELVE

Migration, Gender, and Labor Force in Hubei Province, 1985–1990

Sidney Goldstein, Zai Liang, and Alice Goldstein

Although China has a policy of gender equality inscribed in its constitution (People's Republic of China, *Quanguo Renmin Daibiao Dahui* 1983, 27), in reality women's roles often continue to be circumscribed by traditional patriarchal norms (Emerson 1982; Parish 1984b). This situation is reinforced if women move under strict family auspices (e.g., marriage migration to join a husband's family) or if their movement is in connection with job assignments that perpetuate gender differences in the workplace (see Tinker 1990). On the other hand, migration may provide a vehicle for change that allows women to break out of traditional family controls and achieve some economic independence (Rodenburg 1993, 282–83). This may be especially true for women who, as short-term and unofficial migrants, are separated from families and enter into situations of relative autonomy (see also chap. 10).

While increased spatial mobility for women and men has thus become an important aspect of the transition from a socialist to a market economy in China, limited opportunities have been available to assess who moves, what kind of mobility is chosen, and what the impact is on origin and destination. Particularly important is the question of how men and women differ in their participation in official, permanent migration[1] and unofficial, temporary movement with respect to volume of mobility and sociodemographic and economic characteristics. The situation for China is not unlike that for many other developing countries, especially as it relates to the study of female migration (Bilsborrow 1993; Pedraza 1991).

Our analyses attempt to gain insights into these relations. Data from China's 1990 census and from a migration survey conducted in Hubei province in 1988 are used in complementary fashion to assess the interrelations among migrations, gender, and labor force patterns in the period of transition from a command to a market economy. The census analysis begins with an overview of how men and women differ in their rates and direction of migration between rural and urban places, with major emphasis on how these patterns differ between men and women who move as official migrants and those who move unofficially (defined later). The reasons for movement associated with the two types of migration are also explored. The gender/migration status groups are further compared in terms of their socioeconomic differentials, including age, labor force status, and occupation, and by rural-urban migration streams. The Hubei survey is also used to gain fuller understanding of the differing adjustments of official and temporary movers (defined later) at their destination and the possible factors involved in their attitudes.

SOURCES OF DATA

The 1990 census was the first to include questions on migration. For all persons living in a given location for more than one year, and for those who lived there less than one year and had officially changed their registration, the census ascertained whether they lived in a different county or city five years earlier. Among those identified as migrants in this way, distinction is possible between those who have changed their official registration to current residence (official migrants) and those who have not made such a change, but who have been away from their official place of residence for at least a year (unofficial migrants). Much of our analysis focuses on these unofficial migrants. The 1990 census does not include at their current place of residence persons who have been away from their place of registration for less than one year, unless they have officially changed their registration. Such short-term migrants are counted as residents where they are registered. Thus, census data provide an incomplete picture of the overall "temporary" migrant population, which includes all migrants living in a location who are not registered there.

Surveys in several cities of China have indicated that a high proportion of temporary migrants have been resident there for less than a year. In Shanghai, for example, in 1984, only half of the temporary migrants had lived in the municipality for a year or more; of those who came specifically to seek work, some 71 percent had been there for less than a year (unpublished tabulations of the Shanghai Temporary Migration Survey, Brown University 1986). The Beijing Survey of Temporary Migrants of 1985 showed similar patterns: Of the temporary migrants who came to Beijing to work or live, only 40 percent had been living there for a year or more (unpublished tabulations, Brown University 1986).

The volume of temporary migrants identified by the census is therefore an undercount, making it impossible to obtain a full profile of the socio-economic characteristics of temporary migrants with census data. Within the constraints of the census definitions, our analysis distinguishes among nonmigrants, official migrants, and unofficial migrants. We focus mainly on those aged 15–59, the age range largely encompassing those still in or eligible to participate in the labor force, reflecting the fact that in China women retire in their 50s and men in their 60s. To fully distinguish types of migrants and their characteristics, survey data are necessary. The 1988 Survey of Migration, Fertility, and Economic Change in Hubei Province provides some of the needed information.[2] It encompassed 4,070 households containing 18,178 individuals living in cities (including the provincial capital), towns, and villages in three regions of the province. Its temporal proximity to the 1990 census facilitates integrated use with the census data. Located in central China, Hubei's population size and level of development place it among the top third of all provinces; its considerable mix of industrial and agricultural production make developments there sensitive to those occurring in the country as a whole as part of the transition to a market economy (see chap.2, table 2.1).

Like the census, the survey identified as an official migrant anyone who had changed the location of the household registration. Unlike the census, however, the survey identified as temporary migrants anyone who was living away from place of registration, *regardless of the length of time since the move or whether a county boundary had been crossed.* Anyone changing village, town, or city of residence was identified as a migrant. To clarify this important difference between the census and the survey, and to facilitate comparisons with patterns in other provinces (e.g., chap. 11), we will distinguish between census counts of "unofficial migrants," who have lived in the destination for more than a year or been away from place of registration for at least that long, and survey data on "temporary migrants," who have lived in the destination for short as well as long periods of time.

Better coverage of short-term and short-distance migration is provided by the survey. Coverage is not complete, however. The survey did not sample persons living in group quarters. Those official migrants who moved to enroll in higher education programs and live in dormitories are therefore not included, nor are the relatively small number of people living in group quarters provided by state enterprises.

One other limitation of the survey should be noted. Since the survey used purposive sampling to ensure adequate numbers of official and temporary migrants, it does not provide weights to allow the relative approximation of each migration status category in the province. The survey therefore does not lend itself to estimation of the relative size of the various migrant categories within the total population.

TABLE 12.1   Migration Status by Gender
(Population Aged 15–59), Hubei Province 1990

	Resident Status (%)			Percentage Female in Category
	Total	Males	Females	
Non-Migrants	95.9	95.5	96.3	48.6
Official migrants	2.6	2.8	2.4	44.3
Unofficial migrants	1.5	1.7	1.3	42.9
Total				48.4

SOURCE: State Statistical Bureau. 1993. "Tabulations of the 1990 China Population Census." 4 vols. Beijing: China Statistical Publishing House.

MIGRATION IN HUBEI

As shown in table 12.1, the 1990 census indicates that of the total Hubei population aged 15–59, 2.6 percent had moved there since 1985 as official migrants and 1.5 percent as unofficial migrants. This pattern held for both men and women, although slightly more men than women were migrants. Women constituted 48 percent of the province's entire population age 15–59, but they made up fewer of both migrant groups—44 percent of the official migrants and 43 percent of the unofficial movers. In Hubei's adult population as a whole, women engaged in unofficial movement to about the same extent as in officially sanctioned migration, although in both cases they did so somewhat less than men. The two types of migration together approximate the kind of movement that would be expected in a situation of uncontrolled mobility, although, as mentioned, census data exclude short-term migrants.

Provincial and Regional Migration Streams

Of the official and unofficial migrants living in Hubei in 1990, most had moved within the province, indicating the importance of short-distance migration. This was especially true for women (data not shown). Some 70 percent of male official migrants and 55 percent of male unofficial migrants had moved intraprovincially, compared to 74 percent of the female official migrants and 80 percent of the female unofficial migrants. The higher proportion of women moving shorter distances stems in part from the greater constraints on women's activities and in part from the greater importance of marriage in female migration.

Rural-Urban Migration Streams

The heavy movement to Hubei's cities and towns by men and women is evidenced by comparison of the 1990 type of residence of the two migrant

TABLE 12.2   Distribution of Official and Unofficial Migrants
by Rural-Urban Origin, Destination, Gender, Hubei Province 1990

| 1985 Residence | 1990 Residence | | | | | |
| | Official Migrants | | | Unofficial Migrants | | |
	City	Town	Village	City	Town	Village
	Males (%)					
City	66.3	25.1	8.6	52.3	31.2	16.5
Town	73.1	20.6	6.3	60.9	26.7	12.4
Village	72.5	11.5	16.0	64.6	21.8	13.6
Total	70.8	18.4	10.8	63.3	23.1	13.6
	Females (%)					
City	80.3	16.4	3.3	62.5	35.6	1.9
Town	70.7	21.3	8.0	71.0	23.0	6.0
Village	37.5	10.6	51.9	70.3	21.2	8.5
Total	56.5	15.1	28.4	70.1	22.1	7.8

SOURCE: State Statistical Bureau (SSB). 1993. "Tabulations of the 1990 China Population Census." 4 vols. Beijing: China Statistical Publishing House.

groups with their residence in 1985 (table 12.2). The census data show sharp differences between men and women who are official migrants. Whereas a majority of male and female official migrants resided in cities, almost 71 percent of the men did so compared to 57 percent of the women. A reverse pattern of gender differentials characterizes the unofficial migrants. While a majority of men and women in this migration status group are found in cities, this is especially true of women. These gender differentials suggest that temporary migration serves as a complement to official migration, and that individuals turn to one form of movement when the other is not possible.

This pattern especially characterizes migrants originating in rural areas. Among males, a higher percentage of official than unofficial rural-origin migrants moved to cities, but among females twice as high a proportion of rural-origin unofficial migrants as official migrants went to cities. The relative differences were as sharp for those going from villages to towns. By contrast, only 9 percent of female unofficial migrants from villages moved to other villages, compared to 52 percent of the official migrants. Marriage migration is a key explanatory factor: whereas it can lead to a change in permanent residence status for rural-to-rural migrants, it does not provide a legal basis for change to permanent residence in cities for those leaving rural

TABLE 12.3   Unofficial Migrants as a Percentage of All
In-Migrants by Rural-Urban Origin, Destination, Gender,
Hubei Province 1990

1985 Residence	1990 Residence			
	City	Town	Village	Total
Males				
City	8.0	12.0	17.4	9.9
Town	19.1	26.8	35.9	22.0
Village	51.6	69.4	50.3	54.4
Total	34.5	42.5	42.5	37.0
Females				
City	8.6	20.8	6.7	10.8
Town	25.4	26.8	20.3	25.3
Village	62.3	63.7	12.7	46.9
Total	40.9	45.0	13.3	35.8

SOURCE: State Statistical Bureau. 1993. "Tabulations of the 1990 China Population Census." 4 vols. Beijing: China Statistical Publishing House.

areas. Marriage to an official resident does not automatically qualify the spouse for permanent registration. Temporary migration is a way to join a spouse. Further, to the extent that female migrants engage more often in occupations outside state employment, such as domestic and other service work and market sales, they qualify less frequently for permanent registration.

The data suggest that unofficial migration complements and substitutes for official migration. This interpretation is supported by the evidence on migration streams (table 12.3). As mentioned, a majority of men and women moving from villages to cities and towns are temporary migrants. The importance of this migration stream is underscored when compared with the much smaller proportion of male and female intraurban migrants who are temporary movers. Migrants between urban locations have less need to rely on temporary movement because persons with urban registration can move more easily to another urban location. The desirability of urban locations also explains why such a high percentage of men moving to villages from cities and towns are temporary movers. Women are not characterized by the same pattern (very few are temporary migrants going from cities to villages) because they are much less likely than men to be assigned jobs in villages in connection with rural development (cf. S. Goldstein and A. Goldstein 1991).

Census Compared to Survey

As we have pointed out, the census definitions of official and unofficial migration are circumscribed temporally and spatially. Some insights into the impact of definition is provided by data from the Hubei survey (data not in table). For men and women, it shows (1) a higher percentage of temporary movement between cities and (2) a much higher proportion of movement between towns and from villages to towns among permanent and temporary migrants of both genders. However, the gender differentials identified by the census data are consistent with the differentials apparent from the survey.

In examining patterns of official migration, for example, according to the survey, 57 percent of city-origin male official migrants went to other cities, whereas this was true of 66 percent according to the census. For females, the comparable percentages are 70 and 80. Even greater discrepancies characterize movement from towns and villages to cities, showing the impact that enrollment in programs of higher education has on official migration rates to cities. In sharp contrast, the survey data show movement to towns to be substantially higher among city-origin official migrants.

When temporary migration is considered, the survey shows much higher percentages than the census for moving between cities for both men and women. Many of these persons may have moved for less than a year in connection with a business venture or to visit relatives. The survey also shows that half of the movement from towns is to other towns among both men and women, whereas the census identified much higher levels of town-city movement. Again, much of the temporary movement captured in the survey may be intracounty and of relatively short duration and therefore not identified by the census.

Finally, the survey showed much higher rates of rural-rural temporary migration than the census. Whereas the census levels for men were 14 percent and for women only 9 percent, the survey found that among temporary migrants about 40 percent each of the men and women moved between rural places. Many men participated in rural industrialization efforts, bringing skills with them that were unavailable at their destination. Women were more likely to move in connection with marriage and simply not change their registration at the time. In both cases, moves were likely to have been within the same county and thus measured in the survey but not defined as migration by the census.

REASONS FOR MIGRATION

The reasons for migration recorded by the census vary between official and unofficial migrants as well as between men and women in Hubei. Among males, one-third of the official migrants but only a small percentage (4%) of the unofficial movers changed location because of job relocation or assignment. An official residence change was even more common in conjunction with schooling or training (46%), but exceedingly rare among male unofficial migrants (<1%). Among male unofficial migrants, by far the largest number (79%) moved because of business, which for most probably meant trying to take advantage of the new economic opportunities in sales and service work outside government-owned enterprises. Only 3 percent of official migrants gave business as a reason for their move. Marriage or other family reasons accounted for 12 percent of the moves made by male official migrants, 9 percent of male unofficial migrants.

Many fewer female than male official migrants moved in conjunction with job relocation or assignment—only 11 percent. Only 2 percent of female unofficial migrants moved for this reason. Women apparently are selected less often than men for official relocation in conjunction with work. In large part, this pattern reflects China's policy of moving children with their mother and the consequent reluctance to relocate women who are likely to bring children along and thereby add to urban growth and demands on urban infrastructure.[3] Far more female official migrants (28%) moved in connection with schooling than for economic reasons, but their proportion was well below that of men (46%). Hardly any female unofficial movers gave education as a reason for migration, which was also true for male temporary migration. Like men, female unofficial migrants most frequently cited business as their reason for moving, although the 54 percent who did so was well below the 79 percent for men. Female unofficial migrants were much more likely than males to cite marriage and other family reasons for migration. Because legal restrictions often preclude family reasons as a justification for official change in registration, many women may rely on temporary movement as a way of maintaining or achieving family residential unity. Results of the Hubei survey strongly corroborate the census findings.

DIFFERENTIAL CHARACTERISTICS BY MIGRATION STATUS

The impact of migration on origin and destination varies not only by number of migrants but also by the degree of selectivity selected on demographic and socioeconomic characteristics. Such selectivity may operate differently for official and unofficial migrants. The analysis below uses census data to focus on gender, age, labor force status, and occupation differentials in Hubei.

Age Differentials

Male and female migrants are younger than nonmigrants. Official migrants are disproportionately concentrated in the youngest age group (15–24).

Many are students or just initiating their careers through government assignments. Women in this age group migrate in connection with marriage as well. The age distributions are quite similar for males and females who are official migrants. Among unofficial migrants, however, women are more concentrated than the men in the youngest group, possibly because this movement is more likely to occur before marriage. These young women may take up activities like child care and housekeeping for pay, or even jobs in the industrial sector (e.g., textiles or electronics) as a way to enhance the skills that make them more marriageable, allow them to send remittances to their family, or help them save money for a dowry (chap. 10). Married and older women are more tied to their place of residence by family duties, and by additional economic responsibilities when their husbands have moved away temporarily. As temporary migrants, married women are more likely to engage in market or other activities that allow regular return to place of origin; they would thus be less likely to be identified as migrants under the census definitions.

Differences in Labor Force Status and Occupation

The labor force status of persons age 15–59 differs considerably by migration status, official or not, again reflecting in part the legal restrictions on permanent changes in registration in China. More than nine in ten male nonmigrants and almost as many female nonmigrants are employed. Male unofficial movers are even more concentrated in the labor force because so much of their movement is economically motivated. A much lower proportion of the female unofficial migrants are labor force participants. Marriage and accompanying a spouse explain the considerable number engaged as homemakers, although it may be that this work is just not visible (see chaps. 2 and 10). Official migrants provide a strikingly different profile. Just half of the men and four in ten of the women are in the labor force.

Among men, regardless of migration status, all but a small number of those not in the labor force are students in technical schools or universities. Nevertheless, the proportion of students among official migrants is sharply higher than among nonmigrants and unofficial migrants. Enrolling in higher education is clearly a major mechanism for obtaining a change in registration. For women, too, students account for almost all of those not in the labor force. The small proportion who are homemakers indicates the high level of labor force participation among women in China and also suggests that official migration for marriage and family factors does not lead to withdrawal from the labor force.

For those in the labor force, legal constraints on changing registration from rural to urban help explain occupational differences among migration types (table 12.4). Large percentages of male government officials and

TABLE 12.4   Occupational Composition by Migration Status and Current Residence and by Gender, Hubei Province 1990

	Nonmigrants			Official Migrants			Unofficial Migrants		
	City	Town	Village	City	Town	Village	City	Town	Village
Males (%)									
Professional/ technical	11.7	18.8	3.6	25.1	37.8	9.0	2.1	4.5	2.5
Cadres	8.3	12.6	1.4	10.9	6.5	2.2	0.9	1.5	0.7
Clerical	8.0	10.9	1.0	16.4	22.2	5.1	2.3	2.5	0.7
Sales	8.2	9.4	1.3	6.0	5.4	4.3	18.6	9.7	3.0
Service	5.1	5.6	1.0	3.2	5.0	1.8	12.1	8.8	3.0
Agriculture	18.2	2.3	85.2	6.7	0.1	63.5	6.7	1.4	32.4
Production/ transport	40.5	40.4	6.5	31.7	23.0	14.1	57.3	71.6	57.7
Females (%)									
Professional/ technical	15.3	21.9	1.5	24.8	31.9	1.6	2.4	4.3	0.6
Cadres	1.6	1.6	0.1	1.0	0.5	—	0.1	0.3	—
Clerical	3.9	4.6	0.1	5.1	7.3	—	0.7	1.3	0.6
Sales	10.2	12.7	1.1	10.4	10.2	1.6	21.0	11.7	2.6
Service	9.6	10.0	0.7	12.3	14.1	0.7	18.0	13.0	5.8
Agriculture	21.8	2.9	94.1	15.4	0.5	93.7	10.1	0.5	67.8
Production/ transport	37.6	46.3	2.4	31.0	35.5	2.4	47.7	68.9	22.6

SOURCE: State Statistical Bureau. 1993. "Tabulations of the 1990 China Population Census." 4 vols. Beijing: China Statistical Publishing House.

employees in urban places are classified as official migrants; they have clearly been transferred to these locations. The same pattern, but to a somewhat lesser degree, is true for women. By contrast, male and female official migrants in rural places are heavily concentrated in agriculture. Among unofficial migrants in urban places, men and women are found predominantly in the sales, service, and especially production/transportation occupational categories.[4] This pattern is consistent with their taking advantage of the economic reforms to enter into collective or private enterprises and to do so without a permanent change of registration. In rural areas, male unofficial migrants are more heavily concentrated among production/ transport workers than are women, although women are also disproportionately represented in this category. Many of these migrants come from other rural places to participate in rural industries that cannot find the appropriate labor force locally; others are on temporary assignment from urban enterprises. Thus, legal restrictions on changes in registration—especially those involving rural-to-urban shifts—as well as the needs of the expanding urban economy and the pressures of surplus labor in rural locations together help explain the differential occupational composition of nonmigrants, official migrants, and unofficial migrants.

The Multiple Determinants of Migration Status

Several multinomial regression models were estimated to evaluate the differential importance of age, gender, education, current residence, and occupation on the likelihood of becoming an official or temporary migrant. We include education in the model, even though it is not discussed in our analysis of characteristics, because previous research has shown sharp educational differences between men and women and among migration categories (A. Goldstein, S. Goldstein, and Gu 1993). We limit the analysis to those aged 18–59 in the labor force to focus on migrants who are economically active. Note that doing so excludes some students, who made up a substantial fraction of these official migrants. Table 12.5 presents the results separately, comparing official migrants with nonmigrants (column 1), unofficial migrants with nonmigrants (column 2), and unofficial with official migrants (column 3).

Age has a strong effect on official and unofficial migration, with younger persons more likely to be migrants than older individuals. In addition, other things being equal, younger people are more likely to be unofficial than official migrants. Education has a positive effect on being an official migrant, but a negative effect on unofficial migration. Those with higher education, especially university education, are more likely to be official than unofficial migrants. These findings document the impact of government policies with respect to the transfer of skilled persons.

Surprisingly, when other variables such as education are controlled, men are less likely than women to be official migrants compared to nonmigrants; men are much more likely to be unofficial migrants than either official ones or nonmigrants. This suggests that gender roles play an important part in determining who becomes an unofficial migrant. The high level of female migration in relation to marriage also helps explain the relatively small gender differences in official migration once sociodemographic variables are controlled. The strong probability of being an unofficial rather than an official migrant in urban places indicates the effectiveness of government policy in controlling official migration to cities and the great attraction of urban places to those who move in response to economic opportunities but without a change in household registration.

Compared to those in agriculture, persons in every occupational category are more likely to be either official or unofficial migrants than non-

TABLE 12.5 Parameter Estimates for Logistic Regression Models of Migration Status, Hubei Province 1990

	Official Migrants vs. Nonmigrants	Unofficial Migrants vs. Nonmigrants	Unofficial Migrants vs. Official Migrants
Age			
18–24	1.5552 (0.064)	1.926 (0.066)	0.374 (0.091)
25–34	0.981 (0.063)	1.247 (0.067)	0.266 (0.091)
35–44	0.464 (0.066)	0.246 (0.070)	-0.217^{ns} (0.095)
Education			
Elementary	-0.129^{ns} (0.073)	-0.611 (0.070)	-0.482 (0.100)
Secondary	-0.186^{ns} (0.075)	-1.447 (0.073)	-1.260 (0.104)
Vocational	-0.004^{ns} (0.084)	-2.382 (0.085)	-2.378 (0.118)
University	0.981 (0.089)	-3.008 (0.143)	-3.990 (0.167)
Gender: Male	-0.104 (0.031)	0.735 (0.033)	0.839 (0.044)
Current Residence			
City	0.942 (0.048)	2.112 (0.058)	1.169 (0.075)
Town	1.113 (0.056)	1.927 (0.065)	0.814 (0.085)
Occupation			
Professional/ Technical	0.534 (0.067)	1.092 (0.112)	0.814 (0.130)
Cadre	0.504 (0.094)	0.844 (0.191)	0.340^{ns} (0.212)
Clerical	0.979 (0.073)	1.051 (0.131)	0.072^{ns} (0.148)
Sales	0.337 (0.076)	2.506 (0.701)	2.170 (0.102)
Service	0.584 (0.078)	2.341 (0.073)	1.757 (0.105)
Production/ Transport	0.149 (0.056)	2.073 (0.062)	1.925 (0.082)

SOURCE: State Statistical Bureau. 1993. "Tabulations of the 1990 China Population Census." 4 vols. Beijing: China Statistical Publishing House.

ns = $p > .01$

NOTE: Data limited to persons in the labor force. Numbers in parentheses are standard errors. Reference groups are: a) age 45–59; b) no education; c) females; d) village; e) agriculture. Number of cases is 303,443.

migrants, although the differentials are not large for official migrants vis-à-vis nonmigrants. Persons who are in sales, service, or production/transport occupations are especially likely to be unofficial migrants, a finding that is consistent with government policy. Since these are the types of jobs that are most often available to women, the finding also suggests that many women can benefit from economic change only by becoming temporary migrants and that their entrée into the nonagricultural sector may be more tenuous than that of men.

Because of the complexity of the interplay between type of move, place of residence, and gender, we also specified a series of models that controlled separately for gender and current residence (available on request from authors). In general, these data confirm the patterns suggested by our analysis presented in table 12.5. Life-cycle or life-stage effects and government policy have a strong impact on women; they are likely to be official migrants in rural locations at those ages associated with marriage, but in urban places also more likely than men to be unofficial as opposed to official migrants. Higher levels of education are directly related to obtaining a change in household registration for men and women in all locations. Therefore, increasing the education of women would clearly enhance their status. As more women obtain higher levels of education, they are more likely to migrate to take advantage of opportunities in urban places.

These logistic regressions using 1990 census data for Hubei present results similar to those obtained from a multinomial logistic model using the Hubei survey (A. Goldstein, S. Goldstein and Gu 1993). The major differences are the higher likelihoods of mobility indicated for temporary migrants who are sales/service/other workers in the Hubei survey. Since this occupational category especially encompasses migrants who have been at their destination for less than one year, the discrepancy in findings can be attributed at least in part to the differential coverage of our two data sources. It underscores the importance of considering short-term migration in any assessment of temporary mobility, since such migration is particularly selective of persons in the tertiary sector.

BEYOND THE CENSUS: ISSUES OF ADJUSTMENT

While the census provides valuable information on levels and streams of movement and on the characteristics of migrants, it does not enable the researcher to obtain any insights on a variety of issues pertaining to migrant adjustment. For such purposes we turn to the 1988 Hubei survey. Several questions in the survey dealt with the networks that the official and temporary migrants used for acquiring information and support at their destination; other questions ascertained migrants' relative satisfaction with their new circumstances. Such areas of inquiry may be especially important in analysis of gender differences among migrants. A brief review of the survey findings follows.[5]

Networks are a central feature of life in China; for persons planning a move they may be especially useful as sources of information about opportunities and as support once the move has been made. For official migrants, formal agencies, including employers, were instrumental in providing information for many (60–80%) of the men and women moving to cities. However, because so many women moving to towns and especially to rural areas did so in connection with marriage, agencies were less important sources of information for these migrants. Friends and relatives were sources of information in a minority of cases, regardless of gender or residence, although ruralward migrants tended to rely on them somewhat more than others.

Men and women migrating temporarily to cities and towns were much more likely to turn to relatives or friends. Many temporary migrants, especially men, simply moved to establish their own business. Strikingly, one in four of the temporary migrant women to cities also moved in connection with their own business. Since temporary migrants moved outside the official channels, it is not surprising that they also did not use formal connections for finding work. Only in towns, where government policy has encouraged temporary movement, did some 30–40 percent of the temporary migrant men and women use agencies. Those moving to rural places used a variety of sources to obtain information.

Because so many official migrants move to urban places under state auspices, only one-quarter had friends or relatives at their destination. The percentage was even lower for women in rural places because so many moved for marriage. The temporary migrants form a sharp contrast to official migrants—those moving to cities had an especially high level (some, 60%) of connections and half or more of these provided help in obtaining jobs and housing. Women were especially likely to receive help with obtaining jobs and housing, perhaps because many became temporary migrants to take positions as household workers in cities. Temporary migrants to towns and rural areas had fewer contacts and received less help. In part this is because they maintain closer ties to their places of origin; this is again partly due to the high percentage of women who move in connection with marriage.

A large majority (70–80%) of official and temporary migrants—both men and women—reported that they experienced some difficulties in adjusting to their new place of residence. In general, men were more likely to indicate economic problems while women were more likely to cite cultural problems. Economic problems were most pronounced among temporary migrants who had gone to cities.

Despite these problems, some 80 percent of the migrants indicated that they were better off in their new place of residence than their origin. Among official migrants, this was most true of men; among unofficial temporary migrants, more women indicated satisfaction with the move. A regression analysis (not shown) taking into account a large variety of factors explored the determinants of levels of satisfaction with the destination. While occupational skills and economic opportunities, as well as level of development at the destination and type of migration, all contributed to whether an individual was satisfied with the change of residence, other important considerations seem to be expectations about living conditions and how the move affected the traditional roles of women. For example, those women who moved as temporary migrants to engage in their own business and who received relatively little help from friends or relatives expressed greater levels of satisfaction than others who had more help or moved in connection with marriage.

Both men and women had their expectations raised by the economic changes of the 1980s and the perceived opportunities for many of them in cities. However, reality often failed to meet their expectations. Moreover, women are still discriminated against in many areas of the job market, and cultural norms continue to restrict their career options. As a result, women's mobility (especially temporary movement) does not result in the kinds of advancement that many of them had anticipated, and their levels of satisfaction are therefore lower than might be expected. Nonetheless, in those areas where women are able to exercise some degree of autonomy (for example, as temporary migrants who come to urban places independently and engage in market activities), satisfaction appears to be higher.

CONCLUSIONS

Economic reforms instituted in China since 1978, first in rural areas and then in urban locations, unleashed massive population flows. But because of the nation's continued policy of strictly limiting migration to cities, much of the mobility of the 1980s was outside the official system. The consequences are both positive and negative. Unofficial migration has allowed development of a much needed tertiary sector, and it has been responsible for a significant shift from agricultural to nonagricultural employment (S. J. Wang 1995). It has also been instrumental in the growth of Special Economic Zones and their joint-venture enterprises (Zai Liang 1996). On the negative side, temporary migration has placed great strains on the infrastructure of many cities. Beijing and Shanghai, for example, were each estimated to have one million temporary migrants in residence in 1988; the numbers have risen substantially since then (*China Daily* 1988b; Roberts and Wei 1996). Temporary migrants are also thought to cause a variety of social problems.

One area of particular concern is the effect of migration on the lives of the migrants, and particularly on the women. Because many women move by themselves, their dislocation from familiar support networks of family and friends, their employment in enterprises and households that provide no benefits, and their vulnerability to exploitation may all have serious detrimental consequences for the migrants (Peng Xizhe 1995). Women's own assessment of their situation may be quite different, however: many believe that migration has enabled them to benefit from the economic changes and that it has provided them with a degree of autonomy that was not possible at their place of origin (see also chap. 10).

Many of these conclusions remain speculative because few data have been available, especially on a large scale, either to provide a sociodemographic profile of the men and women who are temporary migrants in comparison to official migrants or nonmigrants, or to determine their own assessment of their circumstances. The 1990 census was the first in China to include questions on migration, and we have used those data to analyze levels and streams of migration in Hubei province and to delineate some of the characteristics of the various migrant types. Census coverage is, however, not as comprehensive as desirable because intracounty moves and temporary migration of less than a year's duration are not defined as migration. We therefore supplemented the census data with the fuller coverage provided by the 1988 Hubei survey.

Movement in China is clearly and strongly from rural to urban places. Official and unofficial migrants participate in these streams. Women, however, tend to move shorter distances. They apparently continue to have more constraints on their mobility than men, and a substantial fraction move in connection with marriage. Nonetheless, many women are economic migrants, moving from rural to urban areas to take advantage of the economic opportunities available in cities and towns.

Overall, the census and survey data suggest that temporary migration is a way for women to participate in the economic changes taking place in China. That the survey suggests this even more strongly than the census partly reflects the survey's fuller coverage of temporary migrants. For a variety of reasons—many related to government policy, some to culture—women are more tied to their places of origin than are men. The household registration system was a powerful means of perpetuating this situation. With the breakdown of the constraints inherent in the system, however, women have become increasingly mobile, using temporary migration as their vehicle for change. Moreover, those women who were able to take advantage of the new urban opportunities believe that their way of life has improved.

China has continued its rapid development into the 1990s, and despite occasional controls, temporary migrants are generally allowed to move freely. In the process, temporary migration has come to serve as a supplement and complement to official migration. As a result, migration patterns in China are increasingly similar to those of other developing nations. Whether China is able to avoid many of the negative consequences of rapid population redistribution, and especially of the unchecked growth of large cities, remains to be seen. Another open question is what kind of impact the economic and demographic changes that accompany development will have on the status and roles of women. Our data suggest that changes are indeed taking place and that some women are benefiting from them. The trajectory of change in the future deserves careful monitoring.

NOTES

The authors are grateful for the constructive comments of the organizers of the conference "Gender, Households, and the Boundaries of Work in Contemporary China," and of the discussant, Dr. Wang Feng. Funds for undertaking the 1988 Survey of Migration, Fertility, and Economic Change in Hubei Province were provided by a grant from the Rockefeller Foundation to the Population Studies and Training Center of Brown University in collaboration with the Population Institute at Wuhan University. Professors Gu Shengzu, Wu Shinmu, and Zhu Nong were instrumental in the data collection and processing phase of the study. Also gratefully acknowledged is the support for Zai Liang from the National Institute of Health and Human Development (1R55HD/0D34870 and 1R29HD34878) and the Queens College Presidential Research Award.

1. "Official" migration/migrants is often termed "permanent" migration/migrants. As used here, "official" refers only to permanent changes in residence that have received government approval.

2. For a fuller description of the survey and the characteristics of the sample, see A. Goldstein, S. Goldstein, and Gu Shengzu, 1993.

3. This observation is based on our conversations with registration authorities.

4. For occupational codes we use the coding scheme devised by the State Statistical Bureau of China to collapse the over 800 occupation codes detailed in the census into seven broad categories. The production/transport category is a heterogeneous one that includes transportation, skilled, semi-skilled, and unskilled laborers, and extraction and construction workers.

5. The discussion in this section is largely based on material contained in A. Goldstein and S. Goldstein (1996).

THIRTEEN

Gendered Migration and the Migration of Genders in Contemporary China

Wang Feng

Throughout history women in China have always moved as frequently as, if not more than, men. Women moved with their parents or husbands, but more often, they moved by themselves on the occasion of marriage. Indeed for several decades of the recent past, when migration in general was under tight government control, women's movement via marriage was the largest migrating force circulating the blood of the Chinese population. The exogamous nature of Chinese female marriages is a well-established social fact. According to the 1988 Two-per-Thousand Fertility and Birth Control Survey conducted by the State Family Planning Commission of China, marriage migration accounted for 83 percent of all within-province permanent migrations before 1949, 74 percent in the 1950s, 72 percent in the 1960s, and 60 percent in the 1970s. Almost all of these marriage migrants were women (Liang and Chen 1993). Whereas most of these within-province marriage migrations occurred in rural areas, migration to urban areas demonstrates a similar gender pattern. A 1986 survey of people residing in urban households (excluding those residing in institutions and construction sites) in 74 cities and towns found that over 60 percent of permanent female migrants moved for marriage and family related reasons. By contrast, less than 2 percent of men moved for marriage and more than half of all male migrants moved for work-related and demobilization reasons (S. Goldstein and A. Goldstein 1991).

Most of these female migrations, however, moved women downwards on the social ladder. Women, not men, had to leave their familiar natal home and move to the home of a stranger, to live with their husbands and often also with parents-in-law. In the worst cases, women were abducted and sold to far away places (see chap. 9). Female migration in the past was an expression of the patrilineal, virilocal nature of Chinese society.

This gendered pattern of migration continued with little change under the post-1949 socialist rule. For the most part, migration policies of the socialist government, intentionally or unintentionally, benefited men more than women. First, at the same time that rural-to-urban migration became tightly controlled, the government did not attempt any serious alteration in the tradition of patrilocal marriage arrangements. However, the increased regional inequality between communities down to the village level, and increased equality within a village maintained under the collective farming system, may actually have started to change the tradition of female exogamy. Women in poor villages were willing to marry out to better villages, whereas women in rich villages were inclined to marry men in the same village. Whereas increased village endogamy may have created a marriage market problem for men in poor villages, it may have also contributed to greater power for women who remained in their natal villages.

Second, the limited upward migration opportunities from rural to urban areas were almost exclusively reserved for men. Not only were men more likely to be recruited directly for newly created urban employment opportunities, but the two major mobility routes to leave the countryside after 1960—urban job assignments after graduating from universities and after serving in the military—were also almost solely available to men.[1] Thus, whereas women moved in larger numbers and more frequently than men under the collective and planned economy era, their migration was mostly horizontal between rural villages, and they were largely excluded from the opportunities of social and economic mobility. Migration associated with social and economic mobility was largely male-dominated. Perhaps for the same reason, female migration was largely invisible and hardly appeared as a topic of interest in the discussion of migration.[2]

During the present era, in which the Chinese social landscape is being drastically re-drawn by the massive movement of people between different locales especially from rural to urban areas, are gender relations also being redefined by the increased population mobility? In this review chapter, drawing from the three chapters in this section and other recent research, I raise and then explore the following three questions: (1) To what extent have Chinese women participated in economic migration in recent years? (2) Are women moving independently or mostly in association with their husbands and families? (3) To what extent has migration affected women's work and gender relations in China?

WOMEN IN MIGRATION

My first question is this: Is migration mostly an opportunity reserved for and seized by men? More to the point: Is upward mobility, from rural to urban areas, an activity monopolized by men in China? To answer this question we need to separate different kinds of migration streams and examine the gender composition of each of them.

Whereas there is a clear consensus that the overall volume of migration has increased tremendously in China since the late 1970s, there is little agreement about the exact volume and the composition of the migrant streams. What is not clear is how the increase should be measured. The volume of migration, as well as the gender composition of migrants, depends on the definitions used and the kind of migrations considered.[3]

First, there is the difference between permanent and temporary migration. The former is associated with the change of household registration (*hukou*), which S. Goldstein, Liang, and A. Goldstein (chap. 12) and Yang (chap. 11) label as "official migration," while the latter is not. To be able to change one's household registration from rural to urban or from agricultural to nonagricultural was until a few years ago perhaps the most difficult and yet the most valuable change that could affect one's identity and fate (Cheng and Seldon 1994; Solinger 1999; Wang Feng 1996; X. Yang 1993). Second, there is the difference in the direction of migration. Rural to rural migration, especially female marriage migration, does not necessarily improve one's chances of upward social and economic mobility, as compared with rural to urban migration. Most attention has focused on the migration from rural to urban areas, mainly because this type of migration is relatively recent and is more closely related to the broad changes taking place in Chinese society. A meaningful assessment of women's share in the migration streams needs to go beyond the broad description of migration volume or rates by gender.

Males represent a clear majority in the de jure, or official, migration from rural to urban areas. Even though approximately the same proportion of males and females were counted as official migrants between 1985 and 1990, many more men than women moved from rural to urban areas. Nationally, among migrants who originated from the countryside, only 49 percent of females versus 73 percent of male migrants moved to cities and towns. A similar picture is shown for Hubei province, where 71 percent of male official migrants ended up in cities while only 57 percent female official migrants did so (chap. 12, table 12.2). Most female official migrations involved marriage migration, moving from one village to another. In other words, if we exclude marriage migrations, labor migration (the major type outside of marriage migration) associated with change of residence is more frequent for men than women. Even though male and female official migration seems to have maintained a balanced sex ratio, men are much more likely to move to cities permanently.

When we turn to temporary or unofficial migrants—those not acquiring the institutional privilege of changing household registration status from agricultural to nonagricultural—we find that women are much better represented than they are in the case of official migration. In Zhejiang, females constitute 47.1 percent of total migrants moving within the province and staying at their destination for more than a year. The gender gap is much smaller than in the case of official migration (chap. 11). In Hubei, the percentage of unofficial migrants that ended up in cities is found to be higher for women than men (70 versus 63 percent) (chap. 12, table 12.2). Controlling for age, education, and occupational characteristics, S. Goldstein, Liang, and A. Goldstein (chap. 12) found a *higher* propensity for females than males to be temporary migrants. Sociodemographic differences between men and women are important in explaining their different migration propensities.

These comparisons lead to two observations. First, women are well represented in the migration streams. Migration is not a mostly male activity. Men still outnumber women in the absolute number of migrants, but women's share in economic migration is more than substantial. In some cases they make up 40 percent or more of the total migrants. Among young temporary migrants in Shenzhen Special Economic Zone, for instance, females outnumber males by 2.5 to 1 among those aged 15 to 19 and 1.25 to 1 among those aged 20 to 24 (Liang 1996). Second, the existing institutional arrangements are still clearly biased in favor of men, as shown in the case of gender differences in official rural-to-urban migration. A much higher percentage of men than women move from rural to urban areas as permanent migrants. Where institutional barriers pose less of a hurdle, as in the case of temporary migrants, women are at least as able to seize the opportunities of mobility as men. This is seen in the much narrower gap in the gender composition of temporary migrants.

WOMEN DURING MIGRATION

Are women "associational" migrants, meaning that they move with their family and mainly for family-related reasons? The answer is no for the majority of female unofficial migrants. As shown in Yang's study on the province of Zhejiang (chap. 11), the majority of female migrants moved specifically for economic reasons. This is especially so when marriage migration, which is dominated by women and dictated by the patrilocal tradition, is excluded. In Hubei, as shown by S. Goldstein, Liang, and A. Goldstein in chapter 12, close to 80 percent of female temporary migrants were employed in the labor force. Such a high concentration of voluntary, economically motivated migrants among women demonstrates a high degree of female independence. Even for those who reportedly moved for family reasons, their role in economic activities should not be dismissed.

The fact that women migrated largely independently of men is also illustrated by another very interesting demographic phenomenon, namely, the difference in marital composition between female and male rural-to-urban migrants. Among male migrants a higher percentage are married, whereas among female migrants, many more are single. A survey conducted in Sichuan and Anhui provinces in 1995 by the Ministry of Agriculture found that among young migrant laborers, 68 percent of females in Sichuan and 63 percent in Anhui were not married, whereas the numbers for males are only 44 and 49 percent (Rural Economy Research Center 1996). There is, in other words, a coexistence in urban China of unmarried female migrants and married male migrants living apart from their spouses. Because of the nature of male migrants' work (many work in construction) and difficulties in housing, child care, and schooling in their destinations, many wives and children cannot move with their husbands even if they would like to. In Shanghai, for example, even though 64 percent of rural migrants are married, the spouses of only about one-fifth of them are in Shanghai (Wang Feng and Zuo 1996). While many unmarried rural migrants may desire to marry someone in the city, there simply may not be a market for them to realize this goal. In Shenzhen where 2.4 million temporary migrants heavily dominate the city's rapidly growing population (accounting for 72 percent of all residents), sex ratios in the young age groups of 15 to 19 and 20 to 24 are only 39 and 83 respectively (Liang 1996). Moreover, because of female migrants' ambiguous resident status and uncertain employment prospects, most of them are not attractive to urban bachelors. At the same time, many of the female migrants living in the cities start to look down on farmers back home and even spurn unmarried male migrants in cities. This combination of increased expectations and meager living conditions has consequently delayed their marriages, for some perhaps indefinitely.

Partly because of their unmarried status and fewer family obligations, young rural women may find it easier to embark on a journey earlier rather than later in their lives. Among migrants surveyed in Shenzhen and Foshan of Guangdong province, 57 and 67 percent of female migrants reported that they made the decision to move by themselves (versus 81 and 86% among male migrants). In Hubei, based on a 1992 survey, more women than men (39 versus 35%) made the decision to move by themselves (Guo 1996).[4] Many women leave home before marriage with the hope of making a living and saving money for their dowry and perhaps even accumulating some capital to start a small business.

Migrants' types of work also reveal a unique gender pattern. The composition of female temporary migrants' employment is different from that of both male migrants and female permanent residents of cities. For instance, the percentage of female temporary migrants working in sales and service sectors is not only higher than that of male migrants, it is also much higher than nonmigrating female employees (Q. Yang and Guo 1996). Working as a nanny (baomu) is one occupation in which female temporary migrants are prevalent in cities all over China. The 1990 census, which seriously undercounts the large number of unofficial migrants, found that men outnumber women by 2.3 to 1 among rural-to-urban unofficial migrants. In sales and service occupations, the ratios are only 1.7 and 1.1 to 1. In fact, the percentages of women working in these sectors are much higher than men: 1.37 to 1 in sales, and over 2 to 1 in service (Q. Yang and Guo 1996). Among Zhejiang unofficial, or de facto, permanent migrants, women outnumber men 1.43 to 1 in commerce and 1.68 to 1 in service. Among the nonmigrant population, either at the origin or at the destination, no such sharp gender difference in these occupations is observed (Q. Yang and Guo 1996, table 4). In fact, not only do female migrants choose to work in sales and service sectors, they are also more welcome in cities, since they are perceived as safer to bring into urban households and more trustworthy than male migrants.

The massive flow of rural female migrants to urban areas as temporary migrants and the unique employment pattern just described are products of supply and demand factors, some of which are especially conducive to female migration. From the supply side, rural women, especially the large number of young, unmarried women born during the high-fertility decades of the 1960s and early 1970s, find it especially difficult to find employment opportunities in rural areas. The few available farming and rural industry jobs were first given to men (see chap. 8). Unmarried rural women may feel a greater push to go out to make a living before getting married. In the receiving destination for these migrants, however, there are not only jobs in manufacturing and electronics industries, where women are especially welcomed for their presumably finer motor skills, but the prior economic arrangement in urban centers under the planned economy also created a large vacuum in service and sales sectors, to be filled mainly by women.

WOMEN AFTER MIGRATION

What effect does migration have on women's work and on gender equality? In other words, along with the female and male migrating armies, do we also see changes in gender relations, or the migration of genders, in China? This issue should be examined from the perspectives of those who have moved from rural to urban areas as well as those who have stayed in the countryside.

Clearly, migration has increased work opportunities for women. Even though men still outnumber women in most migration streams, the need for labor in the service and sales sectors has made it easier, in some cases, for women than for men to work in urban areas. The benefits of migration are more than economic. Female migrants are more gainfully employed in cities than back in the countryside, and they are establishing economic independence, and even making financial contributions to their families. At the same time, from a social perspective, moving to urban areas has expanded women's—especially young women's—worldviews. Along with the newly gained economic independence, migration has enhanced female migrants' sense of independence and freedom. Indeed, most female migrants enjoy such a change in life.[5]

Female migrants' work, however, seems to be highly concentrated in a few sectors and therefore is segregated from other labor force segments in China. There is a high concentration of young, female, temporary labor migrants (dagongmei) working in plants that produce toys, shoes, garments, and electronics. Women are welcomed here because they are perceived not only as having better motor skills than men, but also as more docile and more easily disciplined (Lee 1995). Making certain industries "female" is clearly viewed as an advantage for capitalists—foreign and domestic alike. There are also a large number of female migrants, perceived as more or less controllable, who work either as boarding labor in family workshops (chap. 10) or as household maids. These women are working in more dispersed and isolated environments than male migrants or urban female workers.

Even when working in the same industries, women migrants are less likely than men to occupy positions of power and high salary. An analysis of the 1990 census data shows that among rural-to-urban temporary migrants, the percentage of men in professional/cadre/clerical positions was twice as high as for women (Q. Yang and Guo 1996). A more recent survey in Shanghai in 1995 found that women constitute only one-fifth of all the migrants in the professional/cadre/clerical occupations. Even though there is a higher proportion of women than men working in the commerce sector, the more powerful and lucrative positions of purchase agents are predominately held by men (6 to 1 ratio). Not only are women underrepresented in the high earning occupations, their income is also generally lower than men's. Female migrants in Shanghai, for example, earned at least 20 percent less than males, even when factors such as age, educational attainment, and occupation were taken into account (Wang Feng and Zuo 1996).

Moreover, in comparison with urban women, female migrants lack any institutional intervention for gender equality. Because the majority of them work outside the formal economic sectors controlled by the state, they are largely on their own. This problem is not exclusively women's, but it is more pronounced for them, as their work is more segregated than that of the male migrants. The state, by refusing to take an active approach to incorporate unofficial migrants into urban society, has by and large perpetuated the dual nature of Chinese society. Unofficial migrants, called the "floating population," have been treated just so—as a floating population. Little effort has been made to provide these people with a permanent home or with resident services in urban areas. Furthermore, migrants have generally been portrayed as a high-risk group of gangs and burglars, people who can be "good laborers during the day time and thieves in the night" (Yuan et al. 1996, 130). Unorganized and unprotected, female migrants are much more likely than their male counterparts to be subject to exploitation and manipulation. In the Special Economic Zone of Shenzhen, for example, single female migrants, who staff over 80 percent of the many processing plants controlled by foreign capital, are socially constructed as "maiden workers," emphasizing their "single status, immaturity, imminent marriage, consequent short-term commitment to factory work in Shenzhen, low job aspirations, and low motivation to learn skills" (Lee 1995, 385). In the absence of state intervention in the form of providing welfare and regulating industrial relations, single migrant workers, who rely on wage employment for their livelihood and whose wages are tied to performance, are highly vulnerable and are subject to what Lee terms a rule of "localistic despotism."

For female migrants working within the mode of household production, Zhang (chap. 10) provides an excellent example of the gender stratification process, analyzing the interplay of class and gender in the migrant Zhejiang Village in Beijing. Female migrants are central to the migrant economy. For those who moved with their husbands, as their economic status improves, some also find themselves increasingly deprived of their personal freedom and under pressure from a more traditional form of patriarchal rule. The husbands of the most successful migrant households, being not subject to any political or social control, enjoy enormous power over their wives, who tend to suffer both emotional and physical battering. At the other extreme of the social ladder, a young migrant woman working in a family shop lives under two sets of social relationships—one as an employee and the other as a fictive junior female member in the household. In both scenarios, the power resides within the same person, the male head of the household. This kind of social experience is drastically different from that of urban women or, for that matter, of migrating men.

Different marital composition among male and female migrants may also suggest to some extent different motivations of migration and imply different long-term prospects for these migrants. Given that most male migrants are married, their move is primarily a family matter, motivated by family economic obligations. Most male migrants report the use of their remittance for household daily expenditure and for savings to build a house. By comparison, unmarried female migrants are not as often subject to such obligations. In cases where they have control over their earnings, they may spend more for themselves, or keep more for themselves, and send home less. In these cases, female migrations appear to be more individually and socially motivated. Many female migrants clearly state that their purpose of migration is to see the outside world before marriage. In the long run, while married male migrants have a home to return to, the strength of this connection is not clear for unmarried female migrants.

Migration, especially migration by men away from rural villages, has led to another much discussed concern in women's work, namely, the feminization of farming (Taylor 1988). It has been argued that as more and more male labor leaves the field for more lucrative nonagricultural activities, farming has increasingly become the job for women, children, and the less mobile elderly. Evidence on this concern is inconclusive. Some scholars have confirmed such a statement (for instance, Entwisle et al. 1995). Others, such as Yang's analysis of the Zhejiang county-level data (chap. 11), find no clear sign of any relationship between the out-migration of men and participation of females in agricultural production. It may indeed be the case that with the abundance of rural surplus labor in China, out-migration by men does not have the same negative effect on women's work in China as in other developing countries (Davin 1996).

CONCLUSION

Few social changes in China in the past decade or so have had as much impact on women's work as has the current phenomenon of migration. The goal of equal pay for equal work *(tonggong tongchou)* in the heyday of the Cultural Revolution was to push more rural women to work in the fields. But the general context of their work was by and large confined within the male-dominated communes and close to their male-dominated home. Opportunities for migration have led to a different kind of work. A large number of women have moved, often independently of men. By migrating away from home, their work has become not only productive but also more easily and clearly definable, as compared with their work in the earlier context of household farming (see chap. 2). Even for those women who have taken over the responsibility of farming in the countryside, not only is their labor more fully used, but their work has also become more recognizable and therefore more appreciated.

Contrary to the belief that men go out to make a living and women stay home to raise children and to take care of the family, women have constituted a large share of the unofficial migrating streams and have seized the opportunity of upward social and economic mobility via the route of migration as much as men. Alongside the many married men who migrate and leave their wives and children behind, there is a very sizable migrating force composed of unmarried women. Women have not only found a niche in industries such as textiles, tailoring, and electronics, they have also filled the need for domestic services and sales in urban areas, left unfilled by men. Increased labor force participation in the extrafamilial context has

empowered a large number of rural women with increased economic resources and expanded social horizons.

Work associated with migration, however, has also generated a number
of dilemmas and uncertainties. At the same time that women escape from
the patriarchal control of their families and kin, many of them plunge into
a sea of migrating workers who are neither protected by the family nor, unlike their urban sisters, by the state. Depending on their rank within the
stratification ladder of migrants, female migrants can be subject to more
overt discrimination and unscrupulous exploitation both in the workplace
and in society at large than they would have experienced back at home.

Such a price might be worth paying if, in the long run, migrants' increased economic standing through hard work can translate into a better
life for them. So far, such a prospect is not at all certain. Within the context
of a sustained urban-rural dual social system, female rural migrants, like
their male counterparts, have not been incorporated into urban society.
They have been largely treated as transient, as there only to serve the un-
met needs of the urban population and urban economic growth (Solinger
1995c, 1999). In other words, they are allowed to "float" but denied the
right to stay. Migrants' housing arrangements are mostly temporary, as
Zhang's story (chap. 10) of the demolition of a huge housing compound
eloquently demonstrates. Family life is at best transitional, and access to basic benefits such as medical care, labor insurance, and old age pensions almost nonexistent. These institutional disincentives, a legacy of China's
long-standing dual economy and dual society, pose hard barriers for rural
migrants to cross.[6]

These institutional barriers seem to be more difficult for female than for
male migrants to overcome. Female migrants may indeed be paying a higher
price for being able to work more and for the current increase in economic
status and personal freedom. Female migrant workers are segregated into
special trades that may lead to being either exploited collectively (in the
case of female-dominant processing factories) or controlled individually (in
the case of household servants and workers). Among rural-to-urban permanent migrants, men still outnumber women by a large margin. Many female
temporary migrants in the cities have postponed their marriages, and it is
not clear whether such a postponement will be temporary. Female migrants
may find it much harder than men to entertain the idea of returning to the
countryside to marry either a farmer or a fellow male migrant, partly because on a daily basis a substantial number of them experience a higher
layer of Chinese urban social life than men do, by working as domestics in
well-to-do urban families. The lifestyle they have witnessed at close range
makes it harder for them to adjust to life back in the countryside.[7] The work
of migrant females, therefore, is defined simultaneously by the institutional
legacy of China's socialism and by the rising tide of capitalism.

NOTES

I would like to thank Dorothy Solinger for her comments and suggestions in revising this essay.

1. The proportion of females among university students stayed at a level of 25 percent for the 1950s and 1960s, and around 30 percent in the late 1970s and early 1980s (Bauer et al. 1992). It is safe to assume, however, that most female university students were from urban families. Also see chapter 12 for the sharp contrast between genders of permanent migrants in association with job assignment and schooling.

2. A notable exception is Lavely (1991).

3. Solinger (1999) gives an excellent account of the definitions and count of migrants. The 1990 Chinese census, for example, gives a total number of migrants for the period from 1985 to 1990 as 33.84 million, which results in a rate of migration of 3.5 percent. By comparison, a 1994 survey conducted by China's Ministry of Agriculture reports the number of rural-to-urban *labor* migrants as 64 million, implying a magnitude of total migrants several times of that of the census only a few years earlier. Other commonly seen numbers give anywhere between 80 million and 100 million migrants at any point of time in the early 1990s. The rate given by the census is extremely low compared with 20 to 23 percent in Japan and Austria and 45 to 48 percent in Canada, New Zealand, and the United States (You 1993). This migration rate from the census is clearly an undercount, since the migration population only included those who changed place of residence between 1985 and 1990, and excluded all those who moved back and forth between locations and returned to the place of residence of 1985 at the time of the 1990 census and those who had moved for less than a year.

The larger numbers of migrants reported in the media, however, may also include temporary visitors who are not necessarily migrants. For example, in the migration survey of 1986, which surveyed 74 cities and towns, over 70 percent of female and over 65 percent of male temporary immigrants listed "visiting" as the reason for being away from home, and roughly another 5 percent listed "hospital care" and "travel" as reasons. In other words, only a very small minority of migrants admitted to migrating for work-related reasons (S. Goldstein and A. Goldstein 1991). This distribution is a result of the definition of migration (who are considered migrants), precoded categories of answers (visiting is a very loose category) and the nature of the sample (only the population residing in households were surveyed). By comparison, a survey of migrants in Hubei province conducted in 1988 found that over 80 percent of male and 55 percent of female temporary migrants reported their movement as job or business related (chap. 12). The 1990 census results, with permanent and temporary migrants combined (but excluding those circular migrants who moved out of their home residence after 1985 but returned before the census in 1990), reveal that over half of all male migrants and close to one-third of all female migrants moved for job and business reasons.

4. All these numbers are in fact predicted probabilities based on multivariate analysis. These predicted percentages are preferable to raw percentages tabulated, as they are controlled for factors such as age, education, marital status, and birth order in the family.

5. S. Goldstein, Liang, and A. Goldstein (chapter 12) report that among temporary migrants in Hubei province, more women indicated satisfaction with their move than men.

6. Such barriers are clearly perceived by most rural migrants in Shanghai. A 1995 survey of migrants in Shanghai found that only about a third of all migrant respondents expressed the intention to stay, *if possible* (Wang Feng and Zuo 1996).

7. I would like to acknowledge Danching Ruan for raising this aspect of some female migrants' experience.

PART FOUR

Households and Work

FOURTEEN

Reconfiguring Shanghai Households

Deborah S. Davis

In cross-national research on how economic development alters household structures and family life, comparisons of size and membership are routinely given pride of place. Thirty years ago when the modernization paradigm dominated, scholars assumed that rapid industrialization and urbanization would produce smaller and less complex households with weaker intergenerational ties, especially between men and their parents (Goode 1963; also see Levy 1949). When sons and daughters left farming for jobs in industry, it was presumed that they would increasingly choose spouses without parental intervention, establish new households independent of the older generation, and have more egalitarian relationships between spouses. With better health care, and higher levels of female education, marital fertility would decline and as a result households would become smaller as well as less complex in terms of generational composition. In short, economic development would promote nuclearization of households and weaken the dominance of patrilateral allegiances.

Subsequent research has challenged the logic and universality of these causal links, documenting an independent effect for cultural norms, inheritance practices, and welfare policies (Anderson and Allen 1984; Angel and Tienda 1982; Davis and Harrell 1993; Elman and Uhlenberg 1995; Hajnal 1982; Kamo and Zhou 1994; Kanjanapan 1989; Loefgren 1984). Longitudinal ethnographic research on household formation in a variety of cultural settings further challenged the causal model of the early modernization paradigm, which had treated households as stable entities with single preferences. Instead, this often explicitly feminist scholarship (Thorne 1982; Yanagisako 1984) demonstrated that individual members of a single household could hold contrary preferences and that therefore households should be approached as the outcomes of negotiations among men and women at

245

different stages of the life course over how to configure (or reconfigure) household membership. When cultural expectations about coresidence were uniform and rigid, or when housing shortages curtailed division or expansion, there could be little variation. But even under conditions of outwardly homogeneous units, these authors urged scholars never to ignore the multivocal reality of household formation. Within this perspective, which is also incorporated into the analysis of this chapter, households are treated as bounded but dynamic entities, ever subject to reconfiguration.

In a society such as contemporary China, where the preexisting economic certainties have been "under siege" for more than a decade, household membership is especially vulnerable to renegotiation, and thus examination of who moves and who stays offers an ideal opportunity to observe how economic reform has altered underlying normative logics. Focused on the household arrangements of 75 Shanghai female retirees and their 157 adult married children, this short chapter cannot possibly address all the normative shifts initiated by the upheavals of the Chinese political economy. However, by illustrating how urbanites at two different stages of the life course changed their housing arrangements in an era when the institutions of state socialism conceded considerable moral legitimacy and material resources to the calculus of market mechanisms, one can specify some of the consequences of market reforms for the norms of urban household formation. In particular, by placing analysis of household formation in the context of the collapse of many public welfare supports and increased privatization of home ownership, the experiences of these women and their adult children illustrate how China's shift away from a planned economy dominated by bureaucratic authority and a socialist redistributive ideology has inadvertently revived pre-Communist norms for division of family property that favor parent-son ties over those with daughters.

CHINESE URBAN HOUSEHOLDS IN THE 1980s AND 1990s

Over the decade of the 1980s, the Chinese government pursued reform policies that systematically affected the environment within which urban residents established and reconfigured their households. Although the one-child policy is most frequently discussed, the demographic changes induced by the one-child quota are only one component. Equally important have been the policies to marketize the "public goods regime" (Solinger 1995a), within which most urban residents established homes and balanced household budgets. Most critical for understanding the norms of household formation is the decision to recommodify housing and encourage private home ownership.

During the 1970s, urban housing stock was treated as a noncommercial welfare item, distributed by city or enterprise bureaucrats to needy and worthy employees and city residents. In this environment, Chinese urban residents confronted severe structural constraints when forming or reconfiguring their households. Chronic shortages in the absence of a housing market made apartments a scarce and highly desired welfare item available only through bureaucratic queues. Intrusive police controls over residential moves and a national system of household registration created other rigidities and minimized the role of individual preference. In addition, Cultural Revolution policies such as relocating 17 million urban high school graduates to the countryside and reducing access to post-secondary education severely curtailed the financial independence and occupational mobility of young adults approaching marriage age. As a result, young urban couples in the 1970s and early 1980s were more dependent on their parents at the time of their weddings than young couples had been during the 1950s. Few had access to housing on the basis of their own work records, and thus many had no alternative but to crowd into an already existing home headed by the parents or grandparents of the bride or groom. By the late 1970s, housing shortages had become so acute, and young couples stood so low on enterprise housing queues, that the percentage of multigeneration households had begun to increase after two decades of decline (Shen and Yang 1995; Tsui 1989; Whyte 1990, 1993). External constraints were no less decisive at later points in the family life cycle. Once adequately sheltered, many urbanites "aged in place" rather than relocating in response to changing economic status. For those already living with members of the older generation, there was no need to merge two separate households to provide care for the older generation because in most cases both generations had already lived for decades in a multigeneration household wih a shared budget (Davis-Friedmann 1991).

Macrolevel constraints on urban households changed with accelerated marketization of the Chinese political economy after 1990. Urban residents approached housing decisions with new resources and expectations. They simultaneously entered uncertain terrain, where individual claims of household membership or family property would be more contested than in the preceding decades, when the morality and logic of a public goods regime prevailed. Without the same level of intervention and censorship by the party-state over personal decisions, individuals would be freer to act on their preferences. They would also be required to be more entrepreneurial and financially astute.

In the years just prior to my Shanghai interviews, housing reform accelerated. Communist orthodoxy, which had denigrated individual property ownership as bourgeois and antisocialist, became increasingly irrelevant, and even official publications encouraged residents to purchase their homes. In 1994 the municipal government began to press hard for Shanghai to follow the Singapore model of real estate provident funds, and by

December of that year one-third of the public housing stock had been sold off to current tenants (*Renmin Ribao* 14 September 1995, p. 1). In 1995, the national government identified 35 cities (including Shanghai) where all new employees would be required to deposit 5 percent of their monthly wage into a housing fund (*Renmin Ribao* 29 April 1995, p. 2; 20 June 1995, p. 2; 10 August 1995, p. 2).

Weakening of the former public goods regime, however, is not equivalent to its immediate demise, and urban China is a case in point. As of 1995, the majority of urban residents still qualified for some type of medical coverage, unemployment insurance programs cushioned the blow of rising unemployment, and most who held official urban household registration lived in heavily subsidized housing (Wang Feng 1997). Overall, Chinese urban residents therefore lived within a more comprehensive social welfare regime than that of the pre-Communist 1940s. But the certainties, as well as the rigidities and shortages, of the collectivist years could no longer be assumed, and urbanites of all ages had entered a new era, where each individual and family would be required to take greater responsibility for short-term and long-term security.

The case materials used in this chapter are drawn primarily from one working-class neighborhood in the city of Shanghai where the author has been interviewing a group of middle-aged and elderly women since 1987. The initial group of 100 respondents was selected randomly from neighborhood women born between 1925 and 1935. In 1995, an additional 19 women born between 1936 and 1945 were interviewed in order to gain insight into a broader range of historical experience.[1] In the first interviews, I focused on a comparison of the work histories of the parents and adult children. Beginning in 1990, I gave equal attention to gathering current and retrospective data on the marital experience and residential moves of the mothers and their adult sons and daughters. Interview materials from one neighborhood in Shanghai cannot resolve the issue of national trends, but they can refine our understanding of how marketization—and especially the privatization of home ownership—has altered the context in which housing decisions are made. In particular, longitudinal family life histories highlight the way in which individual family members strategize to realize personal preferences and how commodification of property has placed questions about membership in a "private family estate" at the heart of decisions about coresidence.

HOUSING ARRANGEMENTS OF SHANGHAI ELDERLY AND THEIR SONS AND DAUGHTERS

For both parents and married sons and daughters in my sample, average household size decreased and membership became less extended between

TABLE 14.1   Percentage Distribution of Household Size among Shanghai Respondents

	1	2	3	4	5	6	7+	Average Size (% with 2 Generations of Married Adults)
				Number of Members				
Mothers								
At Marriage (N = 75)	5	42	7	8	7	0	21	3.88 (47)
1990 (N = 75)	0	11	21	16	35	9	8	4.41 (59)
1995 (N = 75)	0	13	28	19	29	7	3	4.05 (53)
Adult Married Sons								
At Marriage (N = 68)	0	35	4	18	18	13	9	3.96 (62)
1990 (N = 67)	2	16	33	5	30	6	9	4.08 (46)
1995 (N = 75)	3	15	41	8	20	7	7	3.88 (41)
Adult Married Daughters								
At Marriage (N = 67)	6	51	13	19	4	4	1	2.85 (46)
1990 (N = 90)	0	9	41	14	28	1	7	3.97 (47)
1995 (N = 95)	0	8	60	13	16	2	1	3.46 (30)

SOURCE: Author's interviews in 1990 and 1995.

1990 and 1995. For mothers, average size fell from 4.4 to 4.1, and the fraction living with a married child fell from 59 to 53 percent (see table 14.1). For married sons, average size fell from 4.1 to 3.9, and the fraction living with a parent or in-law fell from 46 to 41 percent. For married daughters, average household size declined from 4.0 to 3.5, and the fraction living with a parent or in-law fell from 47 to 30 percent. As in 1990, if married children lived with a parent or in-law, the most common arrangement was parents sharing a home with a married son (see table 14.2).

A further comparison of how members of these families moved among types of households between 1990 and 1995 speaks to the relative stability of each type of household at different stages of the life course. Among mothers, there was a slight increase in the percentage living with a married son (from 43 to 46%) and a slight decrease in the likelihood of living either in a nuclear household without married children (from 35 to 30%) or in multi-generation home with a married daughter (from 13 to 9%) (see table 14.2). For mothers, the most stable as well as most typical arrangement was co-residence with a married son. Of the 32 women living in such households in 1990, 81 percent continued with this form, although not necessarily with the same married son (see table 14.3). Six percent of mothers who shared quarters with a married son in 1990 switched by 1995 to live with a married daughter, and nine percent no longer lived with any married children.

TABLE 14.2   Percentage Distribution of Household Forms
among Shanghai Respondents

| | | Coresidence with Married | | |
	Nuclear	Son	Daughter	Other
Mother ($N = 75$)				
At marriage	45	35	6	14
1990	35	43	13	9
1995	30	46	9	15

| | | Coresidence with Parent(s) | | |
	Nuclear	His	Her	Other
Married Sons ($N = 65$)				
At marriage	38	54	7	1
1990	48	46	5	2
1995	54	37	6	3
Married Daughters ($N = 92$)				
At marriage	34	53	8	1
1990	51	39	9	1
1995	71	25	4	0

SOURCE: Author's interviews June and July 1995.

Between 1990 and 1995 adult sons and daughters shifted toward nuclear households (for sons from 48 to 54%, and for daughters from 51 to 71%) (see table 14.2). The nuclear arrangement was also especially stable (see table 14.3). Among the 31 married sons who had established a nuclear household in 1990, 90 percent remained in such homes. For the 47 married daughters in nuclear households, the fraction was 96 percent.

Most unstable were households of mothers and married daughters. Only 40 percent of such 1990 arrangements among mothers and 38 percent among daughters endured until July 1995. By contrast, between 1990 and 1995, 81 percent of mothers and 77 percent of married sons continued to live in parent-son households (see table 14.3). Although the small sample size does not justify definitive conclusions, I should note that this greater instability of households with married daughters is consonant with previous fieldwork I did in several Chinese cities between 1979 and 1988 (Davis, 1989, 1992, 1993; Davis-Friedmann, 1991). Parents lived with married daughters primarily when they had no sons, or in times of crisis.[2] Additional support for continued preference for residence with married sons is found among the housing arrangements of the Shanghai respondents' children who married after 1989. Among these 21 newlyweds, 12 shared quarters

TABLE 14.3   Changes in Household Forms of Shanghai Respondents and Their Adult Children between 1990 and 1995

1995 Household Form (%)			
	Coresidence with Married		
	Nuclear	*Son*	*Daughter*	*Other*
1990 Household Form				
Mothers (N = 75)				
Nuclear (N = 26)	58	19	4	19
Married son (N = 32)	9	81	6	3
Married daughter (N = 10)	10	300	40	20
Other (N = 7)	43	14	—	43
	Coresidence with Parent(s)		
	Nuclear	*His*	*Hers*	*Other*
Adult married sons (N = 65)				
Nuclear (N = 31)	90	3	0	6
His parent(s) (N = 30)	20	77	1	0
Her parent(s) (N = 3)	0	33	66	0
Other (N = 1)	100	0	0	0
Adult married daughters (N = 92)				
Nuclear (N = 47)	96	2	2	0
His parent(s) (N = 36)	42	58	0	0
Her parent(s) (N = 8)	50	13	38	0
Other (N = 1)	100	0	0	0

SOURCE: Author's Interviews June and July 1995.

with the parents of the husband, and another three moved to apartments set up by the husband's family. Only one new couple moved to the home of the bride, and the extremely unusual circumstances of this family underline the widespread preference for households with married sons in contemporary Shanghai. In this home, the parent was a widow whose only child (a son) had died during the Cultural Revolution. To avoid an old age as a childless widow, the woman adopted a teenage niece from the countryside in the early eighties and sponsored her through technical school. In 1990, when this young woman married a youngest son with two older married brothers, he joined his bride in the apartment of her adopted mother. In 1995, they maintained a four-person household of three generations and were making plans to purchase the apartment in the name of the niece and her husband. Thus, these Shanghai interview materials indicate that urban residents in the mid-nineties established coresidence with a married daughter primarily in situations of crisis, or where either generation had no viable alternative.[3]

HOUSEHOLD RECONFIGURATION UNDER
AN ALTERED PROPERTY REGIME

Analyses of household arrangements in China before 1949, or in Taiwan after 1945, frequently put considerations about the role of joint property ownership among coparcener males at the heart of any explanation of household division or reconfiguration (Cohen 1970, 1976; Greenhalgh 1985; Lavely 1990). Essential to these studies are the assumptions that (1) land and housing are commodities subject to division among all male descendants and (2) savings and investments are the primary means by which family assets are accumulated. However, after 1950 urban family members on the Chinese mainland established their households under a fundamentally different property regime.

For residents of Chinese cities, housing was a welfare good secured by virtue of workplace seniority where "rights of occupancy" had replaced "rights of ownership" (Bian et al. 1996). To improve their housing situation, individuals strategized to make themselves worthy of consideration in the eyes of housing committee bureaucrats. Wealth or high income potential had relatively little impact, and savings accounts, banks, real-estate speculators, or mortgage companies played no role in allocating housing. Instead, in this decommodified and noncommercial housing environment, priority went to those living under the worst conditions of crowding. Those of highest status were often housed in a different category of residences, but within an occupational category, the same criteria of need—as opposed to the ability to pay—were decisive.

At the death of the individual to whom the right of occupancy had been awarded, the surviving spouse and coresident children could continue to occupy the apartment. In some cases (e.g., if a coresident child worked in the same enterprise as the deceased parent), headship was formally transferred to one survivor. In contrast to how family property was treated in pre-1949 China or contemporary Taiwan, however, questions of equal partition of family assets among all children (or all sons) were not central.[4] Legally there was no distinction between coresident daughters and sons. Moreover, nonresident sons had absolutely no claim on the "right of occupancy." Thus without making it an explicit policy goal, the Chinese Communist Party (CCP)'s program to decommodify urban real estate after 1949 had three major consequences for Chinese family life. First, it suppressed rivalry among brothers at the time of a parent's death or a son's marriage. Second, it weakened the role of property considerations in defining relationships between parents and their adult daughters. Third, it strengthened the identification of a household as a conjugal unit where obligations between husband and wife were more decisive than those between parents and son.

Following the Second National Housing Reform conference in October 1991 (*Renmin Ribao* 8 Oct. 1991, 12 Oct. 1991), however, pre-Communist definitions of family property rights again became salient as new rules for ownership and tenancy defined the financial consequences of coresidence. In the short term, commodification bolstered the financial position of parents near or at retirement whose stagnant wages or uncertain pensions had begun to put them in a more dependent financial position vis-à-vis their adult children (Ikels 1996). It also created potentially divisive claims on the parental home among siblings, especially between those residing with parents and those who were not. In addition, the return of private ownership of homes appears to have increased incentives for parents to privilege relationships with sons over daughters.

Nearly half of my Shanghai respondents purchased their homes between 1993 and 1995. Among their children over age 35, a quarter also entered the property market. By contrast, among the recently married children in their twenties and early thirties, only 3 percent of sons and 6 percent of daughters had purchased a home. This could be a life cycle phenomenon, but it also reflects recent changes. Respondents reported that family conversations about the costs and benefits of ownership had generated many hours of heated debate and lengthy consultation with a wide range of relatives and friends. Several cadres as well as respondents told me that in the year prior to the July 1995 interview, they had found it impossible to finish a single meal without at least once deliberating the pros and cons of buying an apartment. Because in 1995 I only interviewed mothers, I have heard only one side of what is a very complex and multivocal debate. Nevertheless, when combined with the data on shifts in household size and composition (shown earlier), the interviews consistently suggest that the economic reforms have directly challenged inheritance norms of the socialist era. In particular, during the initial wave of privatization, it appears that the most immediate impact has been a return of the ideal of a patrilineal "estate" and heightened tensions among brothers and between parents and sons.

As in Taiwan families where each son is a coparcener, a primary tension is *when* a son will take out his share. In Shanghai, conflicts also arise over which son (or sons) will be able to purchase the parents' apartment. It appeared some respondents were postponing buying their apartments precisely to avoid this crisis, although what they actually said was that they were waiting for a higher quality place. However, because the price of these two-room apartments (with bathroom and kitchen) for newly retired workers with forty years of seniority was only 4,500 *yuan* (or less than the cost of one high-quality Japanese air conditioner), I was not convinced that financial calculations alone justified the decision to delay home purchase. Rather, a primary concern was how to achieve equitable division of a family "estate" after two generations had matured and established households during 40 years of collective ownership. Two cases of mothers living in joint households in 1995, whom I reinterviewed in July 1996, suggest how efforts to be equitable to all sons, previously calculated by giving each son a comparable wedding feast and set of home furnishings at marriage, now centered on questions about equitable division of the parental home.

Case 1

This respondent lived with three married sons, their wives, and their children. The family occupied two apartments, maintained a joint budget, and ate together as a household of 11 until January 1995, when the second son and his wife set up a separate kitchen. In fall 1995, the mother of the second son's wife obtained a one-room apartment from her work unit to solve the housing problem of her daughter. The allocation of this new room, however, did not resolve the squabbles over housing. Instead, it exacerbated them.

The plan of the second son and his wife was for his parents—my respondent and her husband—to move to the one-room flat obtained by the wife's mother and allow him to buy the two-room apartment for his wife and son. My respondent was completely in distress. The apartment offered by the daughter-in-law's mother was smaller than what she and her husband currently occupied, and the new place required major renovation to be habitable. But the main conflict was not about the young couple leaving or the expense of setting up a new household. Rather, it was about the son's claim on his parents' home. As the respondent explained, first in measured tones, and then through tears:

> If we move to the little apartment in Pudong, then each son would have his own place. My eldest son has just been promised by his employer that next year when the unit allocates new apartments he will get a new three-room place, which he can first rent and then purchase. When my eldest and his family move out, my third son who now lives with my eldest in the apartment we bought two years ago would have his own place. Then if we move out, our second boy can buy this place we now share.
>
> I want the best for each son; equal shares for each. But to move is really a hardship for me. I will be far from my children. What if I need their help? What if they need our help? Now, for example, during summer vacation I care and feed all the children of my three sons every day. How can I do this in one room in Pudong? Moreover, this new place would belong to my second daughter-in-law's family, not to my husband and me. I don't feel comfortable relying on them for our housing. And finally, it is in a transitional neighborhood, where people live while waiting to be moved to new housing when their old place has been condemned, so the quality of services and amenities is far inferior to what we have here. We estimate that to make it livable would cost

20,000 *yuan*. But my second son and his wife keep pushing me to move. I want to be fair with each son, but I don't want to move to Pudong.

Case 2

This respondent lived with her husband, two married sons, their wives, and their children in a two-room apartment. Two married daughters also lived in Shanghai. The elder daughter maintained a household of four consisting of herself, her father-in-law, husband, and son. The younger lived in a private home owned by her husband and his mother, but maintained a three-person nuclear household with her husband and young son. Neither the respondent nor her sons had purchased their current apartment because of the terrible conflict between the two brothers. Initially sibling conflict was accentuated by the police controls over migration into Shanghai from the nearby suburbs, but now issues of equal rights to family property had also become central to the controversy.

In 1979, the respondent moved to the apartment with her husband and their three youngest children. The eldest daughter was then working in the countryside. In 1980, the eldest girl came back to Shanghai and rejoined her parent's home. In 1983, she married and moved to live with her husband's parents. In 1985, the second daughter married and moved to live with her husband and his mother. Later that year, the youngest son, who had just finished technical high school, was assigned a job outside Shanghai and moved to a factory dorm in a suburban town. In 1987, the eldest son married and brought his wife to live with the respondent and her husband, furnishing one room in the apartment as his conjugal space but maintaining a shared household budget.

In 1990, the younger son married a suburban girl who worked in his factory. They quit their factory jobs and came to Shanghai to try their luck as peddlers. The parents built a small sleeping loft for themselves in the corridor and vacated the second room in order to create a separate conjugal space for the second son and his new wife. In 1995, when I first interviewed them, they maintained an unhappy household of three married couples and two small grandsons. The younger son and his wife had become long-distance traders of duck-down quilts, spending several weeks each month away from Shanghai. Their TV, refrigerator, and other wedding furnishings remained in the respondent's apartment, and they and their son continued to consider it their home. The crowding was intense, and the elder daughter-in-law was especially unhappy, complaining constantly to my respondent that the second daughter-in-law and her child had no right to live in the apartment because neither had a Shanghai city registration.[5] Obviously, she could not make the same argument against her brother-in-law, who was officially registered as a member of this household.

In 1995, when I interviewed this woman, she repeatedly broke down in tears during the interview, and her entire body was covered with an intense rash and welts that resulted from sleeping in a mosquito-infested alley to escape the intense heat of the sleeping loft. The only strategy she was pursuing to resolve the housing crisis was to file an appeal with her husband's former employer requesting a second apartment to which they and the younger son could move on the grounds of extreme hardship. But no one at the husband's old unit would acknowledge their claim of hardship because according to the official household registry, which did not count the younger daughter-in-law and grandson as permanent members of the household, they were a household of two married couples in two separate rooms. They therefore did not meet the criteria for excessive crowding. In May 1996, unable to handle the constant bickering, the family split into three conjugal units by creating three kitchens in the 26-square-meter apartment.

When I reinterviewed this respondent in July 1996, she told me that her younger married daughter was urging her parents to join her household and leave the two brothers to divide the apartment (which presumably the parents would buy and give to the two sons). The respondent's husband absolutely refused because he considered it a terrible loss of face to live with a married daughter and to live in a house owned by his daughter's mother-in-law. The respondent was so distraught that she even considered leaving her husband and joining her daughter. But if she took this option, she worried there would be no one to feed her husband: "We have 'split the stoves' so no one can cook for him except me."

LIMITATIONS OF THE SAMPLE AND
THE SPECIAL CASE OF SHANGHAI

The interview materials cited here cannot represent national trends. Interviewing only women born before 1946, the voices I "heard" were those of women of a particular generation and a specific stage of the life course. Further, although the initial group was drawn randomly and provided equal percentages of households headed by male professionals, routine white-collar workers, and manual workers, by 1995 a disproportionate number of economically successful households had moved out of the neighborhood, and a disproportionate number of the poorest women had died.[6] The 19 new respondents added in 1995 matched the 56 "survivors" in terms of husband's occupation, but were better educated and had on average one less child. They were drawn by convenience rather than randomly and did not include as high a percentage of families in acute financial or psychological distress as in the initial sample. The small size of the sample is also a limitation. Finally, all respondents were drawn from one housing estate built in

1978–79 on the western fringe of the city.[7] These interviews therefore disproportionately represent the post-1949 working class and do not capture the experiences of upper-level cadres, descendants of the pre-1949 middle classes, or the millions who have migrated to Shanghai from rural China since 1980.[8] Also because all respondents lived in a relatively new housing estate, the physical conditions of their homes were above average. As a result, it is possible that these women and their coresident children may have been less likely to reconfigure their household or relocate to a new home than the majority of Shanghai residents.

In addition to these special characteristics of my respondents, I need to note several ways in which Shanghai itself may foster higher than average levels of immobility. Before 1949, Shanghai was China's most modern city in terms of urban infrastructure. Through the mid-1970s Shanghai maintained its premier position. It generated a disproportionate share of industrial output and goods for export, and per capita income and quality of consumer goods were superior to those in other cities. A home in Shanghai was highly desirable. Once settled in the city, very few residents sought to relocate. Thus my respondents and their children may represent an especially "inert" population for whom the new freedom and affluence of the reform era generated rising expectations for comfort but not the incentive to relocate residentially.

There is also a demographic peculiarity of Shanghai that should be noted. While all other metropolitan populations had increased in each decade after 1949, due to a policy of relocating coastal experts to the interior, Shanghai's population actually began to shrink in absolute numbers as early as the mid-sixties and did not regain its 1965 size until 1984. Nevertheless despite this distinctive and unique pattern of negative population growth between 1965 and 1983, the total number of Shanghai households steadily increased over these two decades.[9] These macro-demographic trends suggest that in Shanghai the drive to establish new households and create officially recognized boundaries around small conjugal units may be stronger and more persistent than in other cities of China.

CONCLUSION

The recommodification of residential space has challenged the norms and strategies Shanghai families pursued in forming households during the first four decades after 1949. Between 1956 and 1990, neither parents nor adult children imagined a situation in which the parents' home would become a valuable *financial* asset that could generate income or provide a sizable inheritance. Individual family members strategized about who should live with whom, and access to space controlled by parents could create tension among closely spaced siblings, all of whom were eager to marry and start a new family. To deal with these rival claims on living space (usually controlled by the father's employer), parents attempted to handle each child's housing crisis in turn. If there were no way to secure a new room or second apartment at the time of a son's marriage, married sons would live with the parents (as in cases 1 and 2). Similarly, parents would shelter a daughter and her husband if they had nowhere else to go, but as the statistical frequencies indicate, coresidence with sons was more acceptable and enduring. Over time, urban multigeneration households were knit together by a combination of self-interest and affection. Issues of property ownership were generally irrelevant because legally most parents only retained "rights of occupancy."

After 1991, parents and children confronted a more commodified and monetized environment in calculating the costs and benefits of different household arrangements. Apartments to which employees had secured "rights of occupancy" became available for purchase to current household heads, with the option to lease or sell at market price after five years. Although Shanghai residents had lived in a noncommodified property regime for almost half a century, most quickly grasped the value of assuming ownership. However, the norms for establishing the claims between coresident and non-coresident children, were not immediately clear.

Prior to the sudden commodification of residential real estate, Shanghai residents already strongly favored coresidence of parents and married sons over coresidence of parents and married daughters. However, as housing became increasingly commodified, coresidence could be equated with co-ownership. As a result, the emerging property regime had the potential to resuscitate patrilineal norms of inheritance, a change that may prove as consequential for understanding contemporary norms of household formation as the revival of more general "laws of the market."

Twenty years after the death of Mao Zedong, some elements of the command economy continued to define parameters of household life. In 1994 only one-third of urban homes had been commodified; two-thirds continued to be rental units allocated through workplace politics at prices far below cost. Individuals seeking better accommodation therefore made claims by invoking socialist principles of need; but when these same people dealt with conflicts over commodified real estate, an older vocabulary of patrilineal inheritance and coparcener sons surfaced. By the mid-1990s, macrolevel demographic and economic trends had only partially reshaped the financial and legal environment in which urban Chinese establish their homes, and because the process was extremely dynamic, it is premature to identify long-term consequences. However, in the short term, one trend is evident: in a more marketized urban economy, the norms of patrilineal succession emerge as a salient parameter of coresidence and the normative boundaries of household membership have become more explicitly gender specific.

NOTES

1. In 1990 I returned to the neighborhood for a second two-month visit and reinterviewed 73 of the original 100 respondents; in 1995 I interviewed 56 of them for a third time, as well as 19 new respondents. Interviews in 1987 were conducted primarily in respondents' homes and lasted two hours. In 1990 and 1995 they took place in the office of the residence committee and lasted between 60 and 90 minutes. Interviews were conducted by the author in the presence of a young woman cadre either from the office of the Shanghai Union or the Shanghai Academy of Social Sciences.

2. For example, during the Cultural Revolution, when coresidence with a politically stigmatized parent might have jeopardized the son's livelihood, parents turned to daughters. Coresidence with a daughter was considered more temporary and therefore less worthy of censure. In both the 1970s and 1980s, daughters who were confronting unusual hardship (usually as a result of abuse or desertion) returned to their parents' home. But unless a daughter married a man with extremely poor housing resources, daughters rarely remained in their parents' home after marriage if a married brother was living in the same city.

3. In a 1993 survey in Shanghai that gathered retrospective data on marriages registered between 1950 and 1994, uxorilocal households peaked during the Cultural Revolution decade (1966–76) and steadily declined thereafter (Shen and Yang 1995, 125).

4. In a study of Beijing youth, Riley (1994) argued that for urban families parental *guanxi* (connections) are equivalent to family property in Taiwan for determining young adults' residential situation, but she does not document this claim with comparative material on household formation. Moreover it is impossible to equate the two. Unlike property in Taiwan, *guanxi* in China is not a tangible, fungible resource with universal monetary value. The *guanxi* resource also lacks another essential characteristic of family property in Taiwan: equal right of ownership among all (male) coparceners regardless of what the parents want, how the son behaves, or where the son actually resides. In Taiwan, sons have an irrevocable claim on the parental home, which by virtue of birth is also their estate. In China, such notions of family property and rules for partition no longer defined the underlying dynamics of urban household reconfiguration after the Communist revolution.

5. In China since the establishment of the household registration system in the 1950s, children "inherit" the registration of their mothers, although they routinely take their father's surname. This policy was established to curb migration into cities by the dependents of male migrant workers, but was also applied in city areas.

6. Among the 35 women who had been married to men with managerial professional jobs, 16 had moved and one had died. Among the 35 women whose husbands were routine white-collar workers, seven had moved and six had died. Among the 30 women whose husbands were manual workers, only three had left the neighborhood and three had died.

7. In 1987, there were 3,016 people registered in 814 households; in 1992, there were 2,750 in 875 households; and in 1995, there were 2,745 in 916 households.

8. Forty-seven percent were born in villages, 21 percent in county or market towns. Forty-seven percent received no education as a child. At age thirty, 68 percent had been manual workers and 11 percent low level clerks. Twenty percent were CCP members.

9. After 1985, the number of households grew at twice the rate of the population. Between 1985 and 1995, the officially registered population grew by 37 percent but the number of legally registered households increased 72 percent (*Shanghai Tongji Nianjian 1995*, 1996, 40–41).

FIFTEEN

Household Economies
in Transitional Times

Barbara Entwisle, Susan E. Short,
Zhai Fengying, and Ma Linmao

The shift towards a market economy, the rise of household businesses, and the industrialization of the countryside are all components of economic change currently underway in China. In what ways are households participating in these shifts? Does it depend on the size of the household, or gender composition? The answer is: we know very little. In China, as everywhere, statistics on work are generally reported for individuals, not for households. It is easy to know the fraction of the labor force in agriculture, for example, but more difficult to know the fraction of households exclusively in agriculture, exclusively outside of agriculture, and straddling this important economic divide. Similarly, studies of household labor allocation mostly look at the involvement of individual members in farm and off-farm activities in rural areas (e.g., Benjamin and Brandt 1995; Nee 1996; D. T. Yang 1997), yielding only indirect information about the degree to which households might be involved in both.

The same is true for other key divides in the Chinese economy. Employment statistics show the involvement of individual workers in household businesses *(getihu)* as compared to economic activities organized outside of the household, and the involvement of individual workers in private as compared to state and collective sectors of the economy (e.g., see table 2.1 in chap. 2). However, analyses of which households start up household businesses—whether *getihu* or household-based activities more broadly defined—have considered this outcome independently of other economic activities in which the household and its members might be engaged (e.g., Entwisle et al. 1995; Short and Zhai 1996). The determinants of participation in the state, collective, and private sectors have been investigated for individuals only (e.g., chap. 7). Little is known about the relationship between households and work in the context of economic change (also see Moen and Wethington 1992).

Households are of particular interest now because, in contrast to a waning influence most everywhere else in the world, in China economic reforms renewed and enlarged the role of households as economic units. Rural Chinese households have received particular attention in this respect. Decollectivization transferred land to small holders and returned control over labor power and many aspects of economic production to households (Judd 1994; Walder 1996). For many researchers, rural households are a basic economic unit (e.g., Benjamin and Brandt 1995; Judd 1994; Nee 1996; D .T. Yang 1997). Urban households and their economic activities have not received as much attention, perhaps because they have not been a target of economic policy. Nevertheless, with the weakening of state control over labor allocation and the gradual opening of labor markets in urban areas, household members have more opportunity to coordinate their work choices in urban areas as well. Further, expanding markets for consumer products and services provide a context in which household-based entrepreneurs can succeed. Mann (chap.1) comments that of all historical work structures, the household has been the one most resistant to change.

Many aspects of the relationship between households and work are of potential interest. In this chapter we investigate the degree to which households specialize or diversify their work activities, with particular attention to the consequences of household size and gender composition. Household economic pattern need not reflect an explicit household strategy or deliberate action on the part of household members. It may simply be the aggregation of individual outcomes, independently chosen. But specialization and diversification at the household level could reflect coordination among members, possibly a jointly chosen economic strategy. For example, members may diversify the types of work they do to minimize risk to household income. Alternatively, they may maximize household income by all working in the most lucrative sectors, regardless of risk. Of course, households may also specialize or diversify to meet other, non-income-related goals. Little is known about households' involvement in this type of coordination, or the degree to which households are specialized or diversified. Until now, attempts to measure household economic patterns and to quantify their distribution have addressed small samples or local populations (e.g., Johnson 1993; Judd 1994; Ritchie 1994).

We use China Health and Nutrition Survey (CHNS) data, covering many households in diverse settings, to examine the extent to which households specialize or diversify. We document household economic patterns in three ways, orienting around whether or not households bridge three major dimensions of economic structure and change: occupation and industry (agricultural or not); mode of production (household-based or not); and employment sector (private, or state and collective). We describe urban/rural differences in patterns of specialization and diversification, and consider household size and gender composition as potential determinants of these patterns. Of particular interest is whether household involvement in diversified or specialized economic activities reflects coordinated activity, or even explicit household strategy. Our approach to this question is indirect. Whereas the CHNS has detailed data on income-earning activities of all household members, it has no information on the goals, strategies, and decision making that might lie behind these activities. Instead of examining the question of coordination directly, we simulate what household economic patterns would look like if household members made independent choices and simply obtained the best possible job given their individual circumstances, and then compare the simulated patterns with those observed in the data. If observed patterns follow the simulated patterns, then it would appear that household members are acting independently and that there is little if any collective decision making. If observed patterns depart from the simulated patterns, then the evidence suggests that there might be some coordination in work choices, possibly a jointly chosen strategy. As we will show, the latter is the case in the CHNS data.

HOUSEHOLD ECONOMIC PATTERNS

The context for our analysis is China in 1989. Economic reforms had created a climate characterized by new, diverse, and dynamically changing economic opportunities (Davis and Harrell 1993; Judd 1994). Whereas the collective regime had enforced a uniformity in household activities and arrangements, by 1989 it was possible for households to organize themselves in diverse ways (Croll 1994; Odgaard 1992). Administrative practices binding the rural population to agricultural pursuits and to specific villages and households had loosened (chaps. 11 and 12; Johnson 1993). Households in rural villages could diversify by starting up a small business (e.g., a small restaurant, a cycle repair shop, a clothes shop, a tractor transport business, a noodle-making shop; Judd 1994, 138), having one or more members obtain employment in a local industry, or sending one or more members to some other locale for nonfarm employment (e.g., chap. 10) while continuing to farm the assigned plots. Urban households could diversify by gardening or continuing to farm assigned plots, starting up a household business such as a small shop, or finding employment for one or more household members in a private company or joint venture while continuing to keep at least one member in a state or collective sector job.[1] After rapid economic expansion in the early 1980s, growth had fallen off by 1989 in all sectors of the economy, in both urban and rural areas (Perkins 1994). As it was the year of the Tiananmen Square pro-democracy movement, 1989 was also a politically uncertain year.

Our first goal is to develop a broad description—to use survey data to characterize economic patterns in a large and diverse sample of urban and rural households. We do so with respect to three overlapping dimensions of economic structure and change. The first is occupational mix—involvement in agricultural versus nonagricultural jobs. The second is mode of production—whether work activities are organized by the household, such as household-based farming or household businesses, or organized outside of the household. The third is employment sector—dependence on the state and collective sectors versus the private sector. There is overlap between these three dimensions, of course. Private sector employment, for example, may be agricultural or not, household-based or not. Employment by the state, in contrast, precludes a household-based mode of production, and since the decollectivization of agriculture, has almost always implied nonagricultural work as well.

Our consideration of specialization and diversification with respect to multiple dimensions of economic structure and change is a departure from standard practice. Studies of household economic behavior (in China and elsewhere) have typically looked at the involvement of farm households in nonfarm activities (e.g., Benjamin and Brandt 1995; Besteman 1989; Judd 1994; Quataert 1985; Ritchie 1994; Rosenfeld 1985; Rozelle and Jiang 1994; D. T. Yang 1997). A few have examined diversification with respect to mode of production, particularly in urban areas (e.g., Hareven 1991; Tiefenthaler 1997). None to our knowledge has considered specialization or diversification with respect to employment sector.

There are several reasons for considering households in relation to employment sector in a study of contemporary China. The Chinese economy has a dual structure right now, with redistributive elements coexisting with market elements, and at times the boundaries are unclear (Perkins 1994; Walder 1992a). Workers may labor in the state or collective sectors, the private sector, and even both private and either state or collective (though this last possibility has not been examined much). In parallel fashion, households may derive their income exclusively through jobs held by members in the state and collective sectors or in the private sector; or they may derive their income through jobs held by members in both. If we are to understand household behavior in relation to the changing structure of the larger economy, then, it is important to look at employment sector. Risks and rewards differ across these sectors, with state and collective jobs generally more secure but paying less than private sector jobs. Diversifying across employment sector thus has some potential benefit for households, just as it does for larger economic units (Stark 1996).

Our data come from the 1989 wave of the China Health and Nutrition Survey (CHNS89), a collaborative effort between the Carolina Population Center (University of North Carolina at Chapel Hill) and the Institute of Nutrition and Food Hygiene (Chinese Academy of Preventive Medicine). Data were collected from eight provinces in China—Liaoning, Jiangsu, Shandong, Henan, Hubei, Hunan, Guangxi, and Guizhou. Sampling was based on a stratified multistage cluster design. Two cities in each province were selected for the sample, (usually) the provincial capital and a lower-income city. Within these cities, urban neighborhoods and suburban villages were selected randomly. Also, in each province counties were stratified by income and four counties selected. Villages and town neighborhoods were sampled in each county selected. A sample of 20 households was drawn from the official household registration system *(hukou)* for each village and neighborhood. Household membership, determined at the beginning of the interview, included individuals formally registered with the household (including those working elsewhere at the time of the interview) and others who either lived in the household on a long-term basis or had economic relations with the household, such as dependent students or those who worked out of town and shared their income. Our analyses are based on data for 3792 households—1275 urban and 2517 rural.

Our approach is aggregative. Households are classified based on the work of their members. The survey includes sections with detailed questions on the involvement of each household member in a variety of activities, including wage work, farming, gardening, fishing, livestock raising, and household businesses. The questionnaire is designed to identify multiple work activities, and indeed, many people engage in multiple activities (Entwisle et al. 1995; also see table 15.4 in this chapter). For every individual in the sample we classify every type of work reported as either agricultural or nonagricultural, public or private, and household-based or not. We take account of any income-earning activity, whether formal or informal, even if the income earned is small or some of the product is for home consumption.

To create household-level measures of specialization and diversification, we first classify the economic activities of household members and then characterize households according to the joint pattern of activities.[2] Consider employment sector. For each household member, we determine involvement in the state or collective sector (including township and village enterprises), private sector, both, or neither. Then, aggregating over all household members, we see whether there is employment in the public sector only, the private sector only, both, or neither. A *specialized household* is one in which all household members work in a single sector, whether state, collective, or private.[3] A *diversified household* is one in which some members work in the public sector and others in the private, or one or more members

TABLE 15.1   Household Diversification across Employment Sector, Mode of Production, and Occupation/Industry: Observed Patterns

	Employment Sector	Mode of Production	Occupation/ Industry
Urban Households (N = 1275)			
Specialized household (%)	69.7	82.0	69.6
Diversified household (%)	30.3	18.0	30.4
Not internally specialized	4.7	9.9	7.2
Internally specialized	25.6	8.1	23.2
Rural Households (N = 2517)			
Specialized household (%)	79.0	65.4	61.2
Diversified household (%)	21.0	34.6	38.8
Not internally specialized	11.4	21.6	25.4
Internally specialized	9.6	13.0	13.4

SOURCE: China Health and Nutrition Survey, 1989.

work in both. Among diversified households, we also consider the division of labor within the household and distinguish between those in which at least one member works in the public sector *and* in the private sector *(not internally specialized)*, and those in which each working member works exclusively in either the public or private sector *(internally specialized)*. Measures of specialization and diversification with respect to occupational sector and mode of production are formed analogously.

As shown in table 15.1, significant fractions of households are diversified. Between 21 and 39 percent of the rural households in the CHNS sample are diversified, depending on whether employment sector, mode of production, or occupation/industry is under consideration. Between 18 and 30 percent of urban households are diversified. Through the work patterns of individual members, whether their work is coordinated or not, households are participating in and contributing to major shifts in the economy. Indeed, it may surprise some readers that so many *urban* households in our sample bridge the agrarian and industrial economies. This is because the CHNS sample design disproportionately represents the experience of town households.[4] Nevertheless, it is still noteworthy that so many of these urban households span occupational sectors. As noted, previous studies of household diversification with respect to occupation and industry have focused on rural households exclusively (e.g., Besteman 1989; Quataert 1985; Ritchie 1994; Rosenfeld 1985; Rozelle and Jiang 1994).

The extent of diversification differs between urban and rural areas. Diversification across mode of production shows the most pronounced urban/rural differences in the CHNS sample: 35 percent of rural households obtain income from a combination of household-based and non-household-based activities, compared to 18 percent of urban households. Diversification across occupation and industry follows the same pattern, although the differences are less striking: 39 percent of rural households span agricultural and nonagricultural occupations, compared to 30 percent of urban households. If we had a representative sample of urban households, undoubtedly this difference would be wider and probably would be associated with mode of production also. In contrast, differences with respect to employment sector are reversed: 30 percent of urban households obtain income from private sector and state or collective sector activities, compared to 21 percent of rural households. Patterns of economic activity among households thus reflect the nature of change occurring within the larger economic context in which they are embedded: in rural areas, industrialization; in urban areas, the shift towards a market economy.

There are also marked differences in *how* households diversify across urban and rural areas. When urban households diversify, it is because household members specialize in different types of economic activity. When rural households diversify, it is because the activities of at least one member span a major economic divide. Take occupation, for example. In urban areas, households gaining income from agricultural and nonagricultural activities are three times more likely than not to have a division of labor such that some members specialize in agricultural activities exclusively and other members specialize in nonagricultural ones. In rural areas, such complementarities are only about half as common, relatively speaking. The "part-time peasant" is thus a *rural* phenomenon. Although the pattern is not quite so clear for employment sector and mode of production as it is for occupation, the basic point still holds.

COORDINATED ACTION OR NOT?

Do patterns of economic activity observed at the household level reflect a household strategy, with coordination among household members? When asked "Overall, what do you think is the best job to have? If all the adults in your family had this job, would it be best?" participants in focus group interviews conducted in towns and villages in Hubei province in 1995 gave a variety of responses. Several participants identified a particular type of work, such as state sector work, as best for all family members. Still, many recommended that family members do different types of work. For example, one man commented, "Running an enterprise yourself is very dangerous, so everyone in the family shouldn't be doing this together. Don't put all your eggs in one basket." Despite differing opinions, one thing was clear: On the whole, participants were comfortable responding in terms of what a family or household should do. Only two participants seemed to think in terms of individuals making their own choices. But even of these, one did not neglect to mention the family: "Everyone in my family should do their own thing. That way they can complement each other. It is secure."

Patterns of economic activity observed at the household level may reflect a household strategy, with coordination among household members. Indeed, those who write about rural economic life, in China and elsewhere, commonly assume that households are economic units and theorize about household economic strategies (e.g., Benjamin and Brandt 1995; Chayonov 1966; Hareven 1991; Judd 1994; Nee 1996; Rosenzweig 1980; D. T. Yang 1997). It is not clear how one would go about *proving* the existence of a household strategy, however (Moen and Wethington 1992). Household members may not always be able to describe and explain a household strategy, even if one exists. Further, a claim by household members that they are acting in accord with a household strategy might be nothing more than a post hoc explanation of choices made for other reasons. The focus group respondents who were just quoted seemed perfectly comfortable with the notion of household strategies, but of course without more observation and analysis, we cannot know whether they are reflecting cultural myths or everyday realities. Our approach to the problem of interpretation—is there really coordinated action?—is indirect. As explained in the next several paragraphs, we compare empirical patterns with those predicted assuming coordinated economic activity among household members, and with those predicted assuming that members act independently of one another.

If household members do coordinate their economic activities with respect to jointly held goals and strategies for reaching them, then it should be possible to make some predictions about patterns observed at the household level. We are particularly interested in household response to risk. Risk reduction is a relevant consideration throughout China, and in urban as well as rural areas. Profound economic transitions are underway—a situation that creates an environment of uncertainty for households as well as for larger economic units (Guthrie 1997; Stark 1996). Adding to this economic uncertainty are the political upheavals of the past 50 years, and the fact that certain kinds of economic activity—especially nonagricultural household businesses—have at times had serious negative political consequences for those engaged in them. Nee and Young (1991, 298) describe it this way: "Imagine what peasants must think when they listen to the exhortations of local cadres, who only a short time before preached the virtues of collectivism but now urge peasants to enrich themselves by pursuing private entrepreneurship oriented to the free market. It must surely cross the minds of some that such a reversal could be changed yet again, possibly in the near future." To the extent that households do have strategies, this is an environment that would encourage strategies oriented towards risk reduction.

Diversification is a risk-reducing strategy (Guthrie 1997; Odgaard 1992; Rozelle and Jiang 1994), although not always (Fligstein 1991; Harrell 1993). Even a one-person household can be diversified, but the ability of households to minimize risks by diversifying will depend on their size: larger households are in a better position to diversify their "labor force" than smaller households. Because of the greater risks inherent in agriculture (Judd 1994; Rozelle and Jiang 1994), diversification may be especially appealing for rural households, and particularly with respect to occupation/industry and mode of production. Further increasing the risks to peasants is the fact that they do not own the land assigned to them (Nee and Young 1991; Rozelle and Jiang 1994). In many contexts, migration is a potential element of a diversification strategy (chap. 10; Moen and Wethington 1992). In China, though restrictions have eased and in some cases the volume of migration is quite large (chaps. 11 and 12), migration rates still remain low by international standards. Diversification is more likely to be a strategy implemented in situ.[5]

But suppose there is no household strategy and no coordination among household members: each member simply obtains the best possible job, without regard to the economic activities of other members. If this is so, then the pattern of economic activity observed at the household level is simply an aggregation of individual outcomes. As an economic unit, the household is no more than the sum of its parts. We should be able to reproduce the aggregate patterns by appropriately clustering predictions made for individuals. As we will demonstrate formally, assuming household members make their work choices independently of one another, we would expect diversification to be more common in rural than in urban areas and among larger rather than smaller households. Note that the household strategy argument also predicted these effects. As a consequence, we cannot select between the household strategy hypothesis and the independent action hypothesis based on predicting a positive effect of household size on diversification, or predicting more diversification in rural than urban areas, and simply checking conformity to these predictions. We need to make our predictions more precise.

Our first step is to simulate what the distributions would look like if households were simply aggregations of individuals, with the work activities of each household member independent of the activities of other members. We do this by calculating separately for each of the three dimensions (occupation, mode of production, and employment sector), for urban and rural areas and for each given household size, the probability that a household of that size will be specialized or diversified; and among diversified households, we distinguish between those with and without internal specialization. The probabilities are based on the assumption of independence—that

TABLE 15.2   Simulated Patterns of Household Diversification across Employment Sector, Mode of Production, and Occupation/Industry: Assuming Independence

	Employment Sector	Mode of Production	Occupation/ Industry
Urban Households			
Specialized household (%)	59.2	68.7	58.5
Diversified household (%)	40.8	31.3	41.5
Not internally specialized	6.1	11.8	8.8
Internally specialized	34.7	19.5	32.6
Rural Households			
Specialized household (%)	72.0	51.6	54.7
Diversified household (%)	28.0	48.4	45.3
Not internally specialized	14.3	26.5	26.5
Internally specialized	13.7	21.9	18.9

SOURCE: China Health and Nutrition Survey, 1989, and formulas in chapter appendix.

the type of work done by any member of the household is independent of the type of work done by any other member. In these calculations we assume the likelihood that any individual engages in any particular activity is the sample mean, given place of residence. The chapter appendix presents the formulas that we use.

Table 15.2 presents the distributions of household economic patterns under the assumption of independence. In fact, the general patterns are fairly similar to those observed in the data, shown in table 15.1. But there are some interesting deviations. There is less household diversification and more household specialization observed in the data (table 15.1) than we see in the economic patterns predicted under the assumption of independence (table 15.2). This is true for urban and rural households, but a bit more so in the urban ones. It appears, then, that household members might coordinate their work activities, but to the extent they do, it is to *concentrate effort* in one sector of the economy rather than to diversify. Given the climate of risk in China, we expected to see diversification, not specialization, so this result comes as somewhat of a surprise. To explore these patterns further, we now turn to household size and its effects.

SIZE EFFECTS

Labor supply is central to economic models of labor allocation (Chayonov 1966; Rosenzweig 1980). Correspondingly, household size and structure are central to social and historical studies of households and economic change (e.g., Goode 1963; Hareven 1991; Kriedte, Medick, and Schlumbohm 1981). In many different studies of households in rural China, based on a variety of theoretical approaches and statistical specifications, household size affects the participation of individual members in nonfarm work activities, whether they are based in the household or not (e.g., Benjamin and Brandt 1995; Entwisle et al. 1995; Nee 1996; D. T. Yang 1997). None of these studies has considered that individuals might participate in multiple economic activities, however. Nor has any study modeled household economic pattern directly. Rather, to the extent that attention is given to the interrelated nature of labor allocation decisions, it is treated as a problem of endogeneity in predicting what individuals do (Benjamin and Brandt 1995; D. T. Yang 1997). In other words, in making a decision about work, one household member might be influenced by what another household member is doing, but there is no attempt to consider the household as a whole. Our approach is quite different. We treat the household as a collectivity and attempt to predict specialization and diversification directly.

Table 15.3 reports results from multinomial logistic regressions of household economic pattern (an unordered three-category variable that distinguishes two different ways that households can diversify from household specialization) on household size and type of place of residence. The coefficients reported in the table for "rural" show the effects of rural context on the log-odds of one household economic pattern versus another, controlling for household size. The coefficients reported for size represent the effect of each additional household member aged 15 or older, controlling for type of place of residence. Earlier, we predicted that larger households would be more diversified than smaller households, and the data confirm this prediction. Size has a consistently positive effect on household diversification versus household specialization (comparing diversified households having no internal specialization versus specialized households [column 1], and comparing diversified households having internal specialization versus specialized households [column 2]). Larger households are not only more likely to be diversified, they are also more likely to have all members specializing in one type of economic activity or another (comparing diversified households having internal specialization versus those with no internal specialization [column 3]). This pattern is clear for all three dimensions of economic activity.

The size effects just described are irrespective of whether the household is urban or rural. We wondered whether the effects might differ—whether size might make more of a difference in one context as opposed to another. There is good reason to expect this. For one thing, the degree to which households act as decision-making units may well vary. In urban areas, until recently, individuals and households had little direct influence over their

TABLE 15.3   Multinomial Logistic Regressions of Household Economic
Pattern on Household Size and Place of Residence

	Diversified (no Specialization) vs. Specialized	Diversified (Internal Specialization) vs. Specialized	Diversified (Internal Specialization) vs. Diversified (No Specialization)
Mode of production			
Size	0.13*	0.33*	0.21*
Rural	1.02*	0.74*	−0.29
Constant	−2.52*	−3.41*	−0.89*
χ^2	211.4 with 4 df		
Occupation/industry			
Size	0.15*	0.31*	0.16*
Rural	1.39*	−0.42*	−1.81*
Constant	−2.72*	−2.09*	−0.63*
χ^2	325.9 with 4 df		
Employment sector			
Size	0.14*	0.30*	0.16*
Rural	0.76*	−1.12*	−1.87*
Constant	−3.12*	−1.94*	1.17*
χ^2	272.8 with 4 df		

$p = .05$ (two-tailed test).

work assignments (chap. 7). Work registration bureaus matched individuals and their qualifications to specific jobs and their requirements. Initial job assignments were crucial. Opportunities for household members to coordinate their economic opportunities were thus quite limited (Whyte and Parish 1984), other than using connections *(guanxi)* to obtain the best initial placement, which often meant a job in a state-run work unit *(danwei)*. Rural households, by contrast, have a tradition of coordinated action that even collectivization did not entirely undermine (Judd 1994; Parish and Whyte 1978; Stacey 1983).

A further reason for expecting urban and rural households to behave differently is that in urban areas individuals are more likely to be remunerated for their own work. To the extent that coordinated action on the part of household members is the result of one or two individuals making decisions about economic activities, a coordinated economic action could be more difficult to effect when individual members control significant shares of resources. Whereas in rural areas it is often assumed that the eldest males represent the household and make decisions on behalf of the household, especially concerning economic production, this assumption holds less sway in urban areas. Common budgets and joint decision making are less common in city and town families (Croll 1987; Siu 1993).

If the size effects are because of households acting as economic decision-making units, we might expect the size effects to be stronger for rural than for urban households. The evidence does not support this expectation, however (results not shown). The effects of size on diversification are the same for rural and urban households with respect to mode of production and with respect to occupation. There is some suggestion that size effects differ when it comes to diversification with respect to employment sector. Interestingly, in this instance, size effects are *weaker* in rural areas. The differences are not very pronounced, though, and achieve only marginal statistical significance.

As discussed earlier, interpretation of size effects depends on the proper comparison. Size effects are *expected,* regardless of whether or not household members coordinate their work activities. We need to compare the size effects in our data with those expected when household members act independently and do not coordinate their work choices. When we do so, what we find confirms our earlier results: Household diversification is less common than we would expect under the assumption of independence. With a few exceptions for very small households (one or two members aged 15 and older), the patterns observed earlier for all households also apply to households of every size. Further, differences between what is observed in the data and what is predicted assuming no coordination of economic activity increase with household size. For every dimension of economic structure and change, and for rural and urban households, the effects of size on diversification are *weaker,* not stronger, than predicted based on independent action. This is the reverse of what we expected. We thought that households would prefer to diversify and would be especially likely to do so when they are large. Instead, what we find is that households might prefer to specialize, especially when they are large.

GENDER COMPOSITION

Although we find specialization when we expected to find diversification, the results do suggest that household members might coordinate their income-earning activities. Of course, the latter inference can only be made if we have properly predicted the consequences of independent action on the part of household members. Assessing the validity of the inference requires us to consider the circumstances under which these predictions might be wrong. These predictions treat household members as interchangeable with respect to their participation in various income-earning activities. We know that this assumption is not realistic, and in this section, we give particular attention to gender composition.

In China and elsewhere, men and women often engage in different types of work. Historically, the ideal pattern for peasants was for men to work "outside" in the fields and for women to weave "inside" the house (chap. 1). With respect to the contemporary categories of interest in this chapter, "outside" work translates into nonfarm work, especially outside of the household; "inside" work translates into household-based work, including agricultural fieldwork to an increasing extent. "Outside" includes the state and collective sectors and some but not all of the private sector (e.g., it does not include *getihu*). Corresponding to the general alignment of male with "outside" work, men are more likely than women to hold jobs in the state and collective sectors, to have jobs outside of agriculture, and to work outside of the household. Interestingly, men are also more likely than women to do more than one type of work, bridging major divides in the economy, most notably in rural areas (see table 15.4). This may be for very practical reasons revolving around women's many other responsibilities in the household: cooking, cleaning, doing laundry, taking care of children, and looking after the elderly. Or, it may reflect a greater pressure on women to align their gender and work identities. Or, it may reflect constraints on the range of work opportunities available to women.

Gender composition thus may be very relevant to household economic pattern. If household members plan together, then it should not surprise us that these plans take into account the economic opportunities available to specific members and preferences regarding appropriate work. To the extent that opportunities and preferences are specific to gender, opportunities to specialize or diversify at the household level will depend on gender composition as well as household size. Indeed, studies of labor allocation typically take into account the gender as well as the number of adult workers (e.g., Benjamin and Brandt 1995; Entwisle et al. 1995).

Earlier we found that household size increases the odds of household diversification as opposed to household specialization. If we rerun the analysis, distinguishing the effects of men from women, we find that increases in the number of men largely explain the effect of size on diversification (results not shown). Households with more men are more likely to diversify. However, the way in which households diversify depends on the number of women. Households with more women are more likely to specialize internally.[6]

To illustrate the size and nature of these effects, table 15.5 simulates household economic pattern, based on estimates of the effects of household size and gender composition derived from the empirical data, for households with four adult members, varying the gender makeup. We show results for households composed of one woman and three men, two women and two men, and three women and one man. Altogether, households of this size and these gender compositions comprise 20 percent of all urban

TABLE 15.4   Percentage Participation of Men and Women in Different Types of Economic Activity

	Urban		Rural	
	Men	Women	Men	Women
Employment sector				
State and collective only	24.8	18.7	7.2	4.0
Private only	47.2	40.0	69.0	73.3
Public and private both	1.8	2.0	6.0	3.3
No income-earning activity	26.1	39.3	17.8	19.3
Occupation/Industry				
Agricultural only	19.8	21.5	52.7	66.7
Nonagricultural only	51.0	36.3	14.8	7.9
Agricultural and non-agricultural both	3.1	2.9	14.8	6.1
No income-earning activity	26.1	39.3	17.8	19.3
Mode of production				
Household-based only	7.7	12.2	52.1	65.8
Outside only	61.3	44.8	16.8	9.0
Household and outside both	4.9	3.7	13.3	5.8
No income-earning activity	26.1	39.3	17.8	19.3
N (Members aged 15 and older)	1901	2028	3806	3846

SOURCE: China Health and Nutrition Survey, 1989.

CHNS89 households, and 16 percent of all rural CHNS89 households—a minority, but a considerable one.

Table 15.5 shows that shifting from a household composed of three men and one woman to a household composed of one man and three women does affect overall level of diversification or specialization. In rural areas, although an increase in women relative to men tends not to affect household diversification overall, or even decreases it, it increases household diversification with internal specialization. Consider diversification over mode of production. A significant minority of rural households containing three men and one woman are likely to be diversified (38.1%). Reversing the sex composition to one man and three women has little effect on household diversification (39.1%). The change is more noticeable if we consider forms of diversification. A sex composition favoring men is almost twice as likely to produce diversification without internal specialization as diversification with internal specialization (24.0% vs. 14.1%). A sex composition favoring women is only a little more likely to do so (21.8% vs. 17.4%). Looking at it

TABLE 15.5   Gender Composition and Household Economic Pattern
for Households with Four Adults: Simulations Based on
Multinomial Regression Analysis

	One Man, Three Women	Two Men, Two Women	Three Men, One Woman
Urban households			
Mode of production (%)			
Specialized household	81.8	79.1	75.7
Diversified household	18.2	20.9	24.3
Not internally specialized	8.1	11.0	14.6
Internally specialized	10.0	9.9	9.8
Occupation/Industry (%)			
Specialized household	62.7	63.8	64.9
Diversified household	37.3	36.2	35.1
Not internally specialized	8.1	7.8	7.5
Internally specialized	29.2	28.4	27.6
Employment sector (%)			
Specialized household	66.0	62.8	59.3
Diversified household	34.0	37.2	40.7
Not internally specialized	4.8	5.8	7.1
Internally specialized	29.2	31.4	33.6
Rural households			
Mode of production (%)			
Specialized household	60.9	61.4	61.9
Diversified household	39.1	38.6	38.1
Not internally specialized	21.8	22.9	24.0
Internally specialized	17.4	15.7	14.1
Occupation/Industry (%)			
Specialized household	57.8	57.2	56.3
Diversified household	42.2	42.8	43.7
Not internally specialized	24.7	27.2	29.8
Internally specialized	17.5	15.7	13.9
Employment sector (%)			
Specialized household	77.9	76.7	75.5
Diversified household	22.1	23.3	24.5
Not internally specialized	10.7	12.0	13.3
Internally specialized	11.4	11.3	11.2

SOURCE: China Health and Nutrition Survey, 1989, and estimates from a multinomial logistic regression analysis similar to that in Table 15.3 but distinguishing numbers of men and women.

another way, shifting the sex composition from one that favors men to one that favors women decreases diversification with no internal specialization (24.0% vs. 21.8%), and increases diversification with internal specialization (14.1% vs 17.4%).

In urban areas, there tends to be a tradeoff between specialization at the household level and specialization within diversified households. A shift in the gender composition of the household tends to affect these two patterns in opposite ways. For example, again consider household economic pattern with respect to mode of production. Urban households containing three men and one woman are likely to be specialized (75.7%). Reversing the sex composition increases household specialization by six percentage points (to 81.8%). The same positive effect is observed for household specialization with respect to employment sector, although this is counterbalanced to some extent by a negative effect on diversification with internal specialization (from 33.6% to 29.2%). The patterns are opposite for occupation/ industry, with increasing representation of women in the household decreasing overall specialization but increasing diversification with specialization. For urban households, then, a sex composition favoring women also tends to favor some type of specialization.

As noted before, an empirical relation between gender composition and household economic pattern does not by itself constitute evidence of a household strategy or of coordination between household members. This is because some relationship might be expected even if households are no more than aggregations of their members. Earlier we used observed participation rates for individuals to predict the amount of diversification at the household level that we would expect if household members behaved independently of one another. We do this again, now taking gender as well as size into account. We use observed participation rates for each gender to predict household economic pattern, assuming independence. Just as we found earlier that the effect of household size was weaker than expected based on the assumption of independent action, the effect of gender composition is also *weaker* than expected.

To demonstrate and illustrate this result, table 15.6 shows economic patterns for households containing four adults predicted under the assumption of independence. It can be compared to table 15.5, the patterns derived from the empirical data. In rural areas, shifts in gender composition lead to greater changes in household economic pattern under the assumption of independence than we find in the data. A change in gender composition from three men and one woman to one man and three women should increase the relative number of specialized households by 8 to 14 percentage points in rural areas (looking at all three dimensions of economic structure and change). The actual effects of gender composition, as summarized in table 15.5, fall short of this (1 to 4 percentage points). In

TABLE 15.6 Gender Composition and Household Economic Pattern for Households with Four Adults: Simulations Based on a Model of Independence

	One Man, Three Women	Two Men, Two Women	Three Men, One Woman
Urban households			
Mode of production (%)			
Specialized household	55.0	56.0	57.4
Diversified household	45.0	44.0	42.6
Not internally specialized	15.1	16.1	17.2
Internally specialized	29.9	27.9	25.4
Occupation/Industry (%)			
Specialized household	42.0	40.7	39.8
Diversified household	58.0	59.3	60.2
Not internally specialized	11.3	11.5	11.7
Internally specialized	46.7	47.8	48.5
Employment sector (%)			
Specialized household	44.9	41.5	38.2
Diversified household	55.1	58.5	61.8
Not internally specialized	7.6	7.4	7.2
Internally specialized	47.5	51.2	54.6
Rural households			
Mode of production (%)			
Specialized household	43.7	36.1	30.0
Diversified household	56.3	63.9	70.0
Not internally specialized	27.5	33.3	38.6
Internally specialized	28.8	30.5	31.2
Occupation/Industry (%)			
Specialized household	45.3	37.3	30.0
Diversified household	54.7	62.7	69.2
Not internally specialized	29.5	36.0	41.9
Internally specialized	25.2	26.7	27.2
Employment sector (%)			
Specialized household	69.0	64.7	60.6
Diversified household	31.0	35.3	39.4
Not internally specialized	15.0	17.4	19.7
Internally specialized	16.0	17.9	19.7

SOURCE: China Health and Nutrition Survey, 1989, and formulas in chapter appendix.

urban areas, differences between the effects of gender composition assuming independence and the effects observed in the data are quite small. Taking gender into account thus clarifies the results found earlier. Although the number of adult men and women has similar implications for household economic pattern in urban and rural areas, these effects differ more from those expected under the assumption of independence for rural areas than for urban areas. This result confirms the initial hypothesis that household size and gender composition would matter more in rural areas.

The particular way in which the observed data depart from what we would expect under the assumption of independence is also quite interesting. In both rural and urban areas the income-earning activities of household members are more likely to be in the same broad occupational category, in the same employment sector, and in the same relation to the household than we would otherwise expect based on household size, gender composition, and gender- and place-specific participation rates. In both rural and urban areas the effect of increasing household size in moving households into the diversified household categories is less than we would expect. In rural areas the effect of increasing the number of men relative to women in moving households into diversified categories is also less than we would expect. There is some interdependence among household members that works against the diversifying effects of increasing numbers of men in rural areas. We speculate about the nature of this interdependence in the concluding section of the chapter.

IMPLICATIONS

Transitional economic times are often characterized by more potential and more risk. If one goal of household economic activity is to maximize income while limiting risk to acceptable levels, one means of accomplishing this goal is to diversify across activities. This chapter has documented patterns of household diversification with data from the 1989 wave of the China Health and Nutrition Survey. Significant fractions of CHNS89 households are diversified: 20 to almost 40 percent, depending on the particular dimension of economic structure that is of interest. Indeed, there is ample reason to expect Chinese households to diversify. The reform period has brought a more diversified economy—industrialization and major shifts in mode of production in the countryside and a growing private sector in towns and cities. Furthermore, the uniformity in household strategies enforced by the collective regime has been lifted. Even if diversification were not an explicit strategy, diversified households nevertheless would benefit from the reduced risks it implies.

Economic transitions have proceeded differently in urban and rural areas, and we expected patterns of diversification to differ as well. We expected to see more diversification according to occupation/industry and mode of production in rural areas, where industrialization is key. We expected to see more diversification according to employment sector in urban areas, where shifts towards a market economy are key. These expectations were borne out to some extent, although the differences were not as sharp as anticipated. In China, at least, household diversification is pervasive throughout the economy.

Household economic involvement in diversified or specialized economic activities may reflect coordinated economic activity, or even explicit household strategy. Or it may not. It is difficult to infer from an outcome the social processes that give rise to it. To address the issue of coordination among household members, we simulated economic patterns assuming that the type of work performed by each household member is independent of every other household member and compared the results to what was found in the data. We expected household size to have a positive effect on household diversification. It did, but the effect was weaker than we expected. We expected that economic pattern would reflect gender composition as well as household size. It did, but again, the effect was weaker than expected. Rather than diversifying, households specialize. Perhaps it was the very instability of economic change in the late 1980s that encouraged a short-run strategy focused on gain (Judd 1994).

But there are other interpretations. For one thing, the operational definition of household might not be right. Perhaps households as defined for the CHNS89 are not the correct unit of analysis. We have considered throughout this chapter that individuals rather than households make the key decisions about their work. It is also possible that economic decision making spans several households. In urban areas, the functions of daily life may link together geographically distinct household units (Davis and Harrell 1993; Unger 1993). In rural areas, households may cooperate economically, even though from the perspective of the definition we employ they are distinct units. For example, Croll (1987) describes "aggregate families," groups made up of kin-connected households or neighboring households cooperating for economic or political reasons. It is possible that we might see more diversification if we considered these larger units, although Judd (1994), for one, has argued that boundaries between households have hardened as a result of economic reforms—even boundaries between households linked by family ties.

We might also see more diversification if we did not focus on the spanning of major economic divides. In rural areas, farming households can diversify the crops they grow or pursue agricultural sideline businesses as well as cultivate field crops. Such households may be pursuing explicit diversification strategies, but they would appear specialized according to the measures used in this chapter. In urban areas, it is possible that households diversify between different units in the state sector, between the state and collective sectors, between large and small collectives, or between different kinds of private sector activities. Again, such diversification strategies would not be detected in our measures. At the same time, there is no reason to expect that our hypotheses about household size and gender composition should hold differently for diversification within than for diversification between major sectors of the economy.

Possibly, similarities in the characteristics of individuals living in the same household (because of marital selection, intergenerational status transmission, and mutual influence), common locational advantages, some inherited expertise or physical capital, or shared connections might make similar types of economic activity for household members likely, even if there is no attempt by household members to coordinate their activities. This could explain why we find so much household specialization—although if this is the case, it is not clear why larger households would be more likely than small households to specialize when we compare observed and predicted patterns of economic activity.

Another interpretation is that, at least to some extent, household economic pattern is a result of deliberate planning. It might be a household head setting goals and strategies for the entire household. It might be household members discussing and agreeing on these goals and strategies (Moen and Wethington 1992). In either case, in this interpretation the observed pattern is a matter of intent, a matter of choice. In rural areas, one can imagine explicit labor allocation decisions being made by the household head, perhaps in consultation with others (M. Wolf 1985). In urban areas, one can imagine household members with desirable jobs using their influence to get similar jobs for other household members. It appears that if these patterns do reflect coordinated activity, whenever possible households prefer not to diversify but rather to specialize in some type of economic activity. Such specialization is often correlated with industrialization and economic development (Boserup 1970).

APPENDIX

Using the example of mode of production, the probability that a household will be diversified but not specialized within is simply the probability that any member works inside as well as outside the household. This is calculated using the binomial formula, which simplifies to:

$$1 - q^n$$

where q is the probability that no individuals in the household do household and nonhousehold activities and n is the number of household members. The probability that a household is diversified and specialized is calculated by:

$$\sum_{l=1}^{n-1} \sum_{k=1}^{n-l} \frac{n!}{k!\,l!\,(n-k-l)!}\, p^k q^l r^{n-k-l}$$

where p is the probability that an individual does household-based activity, q is the probability of doing non-household-based work, and r is the probability of doing neither. The household has n members, of whom k do household-based activity, and l do non-household-based activity. Finally, the probability of not being diversified is necessarily the probability of each type of diversification subtracted from one.

NOTES

This research was supported by National Institute for Child Health and Human Development (NICHD) grant P01-HD28076. We also owe a considerable debt to the China Health and Nutrition Survey. Funds for parts of the survey design, data collection, and computerization were provided by the Chinese Academy of Preventive Medicine and the Carolina Population Center. The National Science Foundation (#37486) and the Ford Foundation funded collaborative training and development work. The survey is a collaboration between the Chinese Academy of Preventive Medicine (Ge Keyou as principal investigator, and Zhai Fengying and Jin Shuigao as coprincipal investigators) and a group from the University of North Carolina at Chapel Hill (Barry M. Popkin as principal investigator, and John S. Akin and Gail E. Henderson as coprincipal investigators). We thank Gail Henderson, Nan Lin, and an anonymous reviewer for helpful comments on an earlier draft, and Grant Izmirlian for his assistance with probability computations.

1. In fieldwork conducted during 1993 in Shandong Province and again in 1995 in Hubei Province in CHNS sampling units, we encountered urban neighborhoods that had been villages incorporated by the growing town. Households in these neighborhoods still farmed plots of land and engaged in other agricultural pursuits.

2. Measures of economic pattern are based on data for 11,584 household members ages 15 and older. We restrict age because we are interested in the organization of household labor and want to include only those most eligible for income-producing activities.

3. A small minority (5%) of households containing only retired persons and others not engaged in any type of income-earning activity are also considered specialized households.

4. The CHNS sampled equal numbers of households in county towns as in cities. In the absence of weighting, the urban sample disproportionately represents the experience of town households. Further, because of the way the urban sample was drawn, even with weights, it is not representative of the urban population. The sampling frame included all towns, but not all cities.

5. Given the definition of household employed by the CHNS, temporary migrants may still be included as household members if their registration is with the household, or if they remain economically tied to the household.

6. We tested for urban-rural differences in the effects of size and gender composition. The results of this test showed no differences for occupation and mode of production, and were marginal for employment sector ($P^2 = 11.2$ with $4\ df$).

SIXTEEN

Understanding the Social Inequality System and Family and Household Dynamics in China

Nan Lin

The two critical aspects of the analysis of social inequality are: (1) what are the meaningful rewards in a particular society (e.g., housing, income, family and household resources, health and nutrition); and (2) what factors account for the system of social inequality (rewards) and the placement of individuals, households, and families in that system? The former issue concerns dimensions of social stratification and will be touched on lightly here. (See also works by others on China's stratification system, e.g., Bian 1994b; Bian and Logan 1996; Lin and Bian 1991; Nee 1989; Parish 1984a; Walder 1992b; Walder 1995a; Whyte and Parish 1984.) This chapter focuses on the latter—that is, factors leading to the placement or rewards of social actors in a system of social inequality—and suggests that social inequality results from joint and interactive effects of structural constraints/opportunities and choices of social actors. These propositions are universal in that they suggest where researchers might locate variables that affect the placement of actors in a system of social inequality but do not indicate exactly which variables, or how these variables affect the outcome (placement or rewards).

The specification of variables and types of joint and interactive effects, I argue, is particularistic—that is, particular to time and place. For a given society at a given time, certain variables at the structural level are related to constraints and/or opportunities, and under these constraints/opportunities different types of households, families, or individuals formulate and respond with meaningful choices to attain placement and rewards in the social inequality process. One can imagine these constraints/opportunities along a continuum. At one extreme, structural constraints are so complete as to render choices meaningless. In a total war regime, for example, state policies dictate that every actor is assigned a place in the social hierarchy. At the other extreme would conceivably be a system that has absolutely no

284

structural constraints (total laissez faire), where actors are free to make all choices in maximizing their rewards—perhaps, a utopian liberal capitalism. In actuality, rationalized needs for social stability and social mobility mean that placement and rewards in a social inequality system are based on some combination of constraints and opportunities. Structural constraints are exercised to maintain social order, while structural opportunities are provided so that actors gain or feel rewarded for their choices (efforts). For a given society and time, the researcher must identify structural constraints/opportunities and meaningful choices that explain, as much as possible, the placement or mobility of actors in that social inequality system. Such valued resources can be identified through research on the opinions of the actors themselves. Hypotheses derived from a particular society and time can then be subjected to analysis and verification. This process is open-ended; only through multiple hypotheses can we assess the relative credibility of the variables and hypothesized effects. Nonetheless, alternative and even competing hypotheses are also meaningful as long as the specific placement or rewards are seen as valued resources for the actors under study.

I propose here a particular causal model to examine the process by which structural and choice factors jointly and interactively determine the returns for actors in a social inequality system. This model (fig. 16.1) can be illustrated more concretely with specific hypotheses based on the empirical Chinese situation.

MODEL OF CAPITALIZATION

In the case of China, at least up until the mid-1990s, the state imposed a broad range of constraints on household, family, and individual locations in the society. These included constraints on residential location (whether a household was registered as urban, county, or rural), work location (whether a person worked in the state, collective, or private sector), industrial location of labor (especially whether the work was in the agricultural or nonagricultural sector), and family size (the one-child family policy). Each placement had consequences for income; access to social, cultural, and economic resources (quality of schools; quality and price of goods; access to utilities; access to transportation and communication facilities; quality of environments; access to tickets to sports and entertainment events, bath houses, etc.); and benefits for family and household members (quality of jobs, finding marriage partners, etc.).

Under these structural constraints, can choices by actors (whether households, families, or individual actors) make a difference? Research suggests that indeed they can. Actors in China invest in and mobilize a variety of resources to gain better placements in the social inequality system, either by increasing their chances for more legitimate placements (e.g., actors transferring to a higher-ranked work unit) or by circumventing the structural constraints for better rewards (e.g., rural laborers working in urban areas).

We may define the process of investing in and mobilizing resources as *capitalization*. The invested and mobilized resources become *capital* in the process of gaining better placements or rewards. Two types of capital can be identified: *human capital* and *social capital*. Human capital results from capitalization of time, efforts, and resources (individual and family) to acquire skills and knowledge useful for better placement (occupation, industry, work unit, and income). Typically, human capital includes education, training, and work experiences (Becker 1993; Mincer and Higuchi 1988; T. W. Schultz 1961). Social capital results from capitalization of time, efforts, and resources to cultivate and use other actors who are better placed or positioned for information and influence (Bourdieu 1980; Burt 1992; J. Coleman 1988, 1990; Lin 1982, 1995, 2000). In the Chinese context, social capital typically includes social connections *(guanxi)* and networks (including indirect ties) and the embedded resources (Lin 1995, 2000).

Human capital and social capital not only are important factors in their own right, but also interact reciprocally: human capital promotes social capital, and social capital increases human capital. As an actor gains human capital (e.g., education), it increases his or her chance to be linked to other actors with better human capital. Through these links, the human and social capital of these others become the social capital of the original actor. Further, an actor's increased human capital increases the chances of other family/household members to gain human capital (e.g., a sibling or child going to a better school) (Becker 1991; T. P. Schultz 1995; T. W. Schultz 1974). Increased human capital of other family/household members becomes part of the family/household human capital, and their increased social capital becomes part of the family/household social capital.

Likewise, social capital broadens the pool of capital available to an individual and creates opportunities to gain better human capital (J. Coleman 1988) (e.g., through the help of his or her boss, an individual is able to attend a training program or study abroad). Social connections and their resources are indeed very important in the development of all human capital: they help in getting into better schools (e.g., for children of alumni or big donors) and in getting better jobs (e.g., with chances for promotion).

The development of human and social capital is not entirely the result of choices and actions. In fact, to a large extent, their development is constrained by the structure. In China this is quite apparent. Urban families, for instance, are subject to stricter implementation of the one-child family policy. On the other hand, rural residents are denied many opportunities that are available to urban residents. Their children cannot go to better ("key") schools; their health services are less adequate; adults are not likely to work in state-owned work units; they have fewer on-the-job training opportunities, and so forth. Similar constraints and opportunities differentially exist in political, religious, economic, social, and other spheres. Once located in a particular segment of the population, certain constraints and opportunities almost automatically apply. Thus for a long time children of "bad elements" (e.g., former Nationalist Party members [Guomindang], former capitalists) were denied opportunities to compete for better schools, jobs, or Communist Party membership.

These constraints, however, set boundaries rather than eliminate choices. Within a set of constraints, options and choices remain. For instance, rural youths may break through the urban-rural divide by competing for entrance into urban colleges or joining the army officer corps. These channels legitimize possible relocation to jobs in urban areas (official migration) so that their skills and knowledge are better applied and their achievements rewarded. In recent years, unofficial or temporary migration has also become increasingly available as an option for rural residents. (See part 3 of this volume.)

In any event, structural opportunities/constraints, human capital, and social capital are expected jointly and interactively to lead to the development of another type of capital—institutional capital (Lin 1994). Institutional capital is the capital of mobilizable resources embedded in work units, organizations, party apparatus, work sectors, and occupations. Institutional capital reinforces the dominant values and rules of the society. Capturing it requires entering and becoming part of these organizations, and the chance of entering these organizations depends on a combination of human and social capital. As described above, human capital and social capital provide the skills and knowledge for performing specific jobs and tasks, and also the recognition (or "misrecognition") and acceptance of the society's dominant values (Bourdieu and Passeron 1977). Under the current regime in China we expect that degrees and diplomas from better schools and colleges as well as better social connections will increase the likelihood of entering into better work units (state-owned work units, higher-ranked work units, institutes and agencies rather than enterprises, etc.), better jobs, authority positions, and places in the Party apparatus. Thus, human capital, social capital, and institutional capital jointly and interactively lead to better *returns* in areas such as income, housing arrangements, physical and mental health, and other family and household resources.

ENGAGING THEORY AND RESEARCH

This capitalization model incorporates concepts and propositions quite salient in current intellectual debates in sociology, economics, anthropology, and political science. Various neocapital theories (such as human capital, cultural capital, social capital, and institutional capital) have borrowed the original macrolevel concept of capital from classical Marxist theory and applied it to individual actors (Lin in press [chap. 1]). In its original definition, capital is what is produced when surplus value is appropriated from one class for the benefit of another. The newer view argues that all actors can make choices to generate capital and keep it for their own benefits. This reconceptualization makes it possible to construct propositions that are more consistent with many contemporary empirical systems. Thus, for instance, "labor" can expect to extract and keep salaries and benefits so that they can also enjoy leisure and pleasure, as is evident in most societies.

Neocapital theories do not assert that everyone can capitalize equally, nor do they claim that everyone benefits equally from capitalization. In fact, every neocapital theory recognizes the salience of a social structure as a system of social inequality. Individuals are differentially placed in the system to receive unequal rewards. "Structural" effects—the constraints and opportunities differentially given to different segments of the population—may be political (orchestrated by the state), economic (imposed by the capitalist), or social (enforced by the caste, the belief system, or related to ethnicity, gender, etc.). Yet, each theory assumes that actions by actors remain meaningful so that mobility in the social inequality system is possible. In fact, mobility is essential for a society to survive as a stable system, for the lack of it is the necessary and, some would say, sufficient condition for the formation of class consciousness and class conflict leading to the society's demise (Lin 1982).

If this line of theorizing has some validity, the question then becomes: how does a society balance "stability" with individual choices and rewards?[1] The model proposed in figure 16.1 suggests places to look for relevant variables and possible relationships among them. The remainder of this chapter draws from material in chapters 8, 14, and 15 in this book as well as my own work to illustrate how the model integrates empirical findings.

STRUCTURAL AND SOCIAL CAPITAL EFFECTS ON HOUSING DECISIONS

In chapter 14 Davis presents two arguments: (1) that household size is very much driven by family size, and (2) that this relationship is constrained by state policies (regimes) on housing as well as on family size. Thus, when state policies restricted housing construction and household size for a family, there was little opportunity for individual family members to influence their household sizes. When the policy changed so that the housing market became somewhat privatized and state- and collective-owned housing could be purchased by individuals below market values, then members of a family gained the opportunity to determine household size.

However, the relaxation of the housing restrictions was juxtaposed with the imposition of the one-child policy, which restricts family size at the next generation. On the surface, this would add freedom to the determination of household size, since declining family size would reduce the need for larger households. With emerging availability of more and better housing units and less pressing demand of family size, it seems that housing would no longer be a critical issue for a family. Using the model in the appendix, structural factors (policies regarding housing) of the past constrained the returns (housing arrangements for families); when such factors changed, opportunities became available for reconfiguring housing arrangements.

Yet Davis shows in her case that another factor, the desire to reside with married sons rather than married daughters, often creates tension among family members faced with the need to reconfigure households. She shows that sons remain the ones who will "inherit" (or purchase) their parents' homes. Parents also are very concerned about equity in household divisions among sons (but not daughters). For example, if family were of no concern, the parents in case 1 in Davis's chapter would not be distressed; they would present no option to their second son, but simply ask him to take the housing in Pudong. The second son pushes his parents to move precisely because he realizes that his parents want to be equitable to both their sons. The entire narrative reflects family dynamics and family strategizing, not individual strategizing. In case 2, the father refuses to even consider moving in with his daughter's mother-in-law because of the traditional concern about losing face by not living with one's sons. Again, son preference and family pressure are clearly at work.

Davis shows, first, that structural factors have a direct effect on family size (itself a structural factor, but at a more micro level) in urban China. Second, family size has a direct effect on household arrangements and decisions—a measure of distribution of household/family resources. Finally, yet another important force, social capital, intervenes in the process in the form of the traditional valuing of the male line. This factor distorts the expected effects of state policies on housing decisions. Despite the opportunities allowed by relaxed state policies on housing and smaller family size, the decision about housing remains a collective (family) decision-making process rather than an individual choice.

STRUCTURAL EFFECTS ON THE DEVELOPMENT
OF HOUSEHOLD HUMAN CAPITAL

Chapter 15 by Entwisle, Short, Zhai, and Ma deals with the economic dimensions of household division of labor. Two concepts guide the analysis: diversification (different household members engage in different sectors) and specialization (all household members work in a single sector). The authors find that households tend to diversify less (household members are likely to work in the same sector) and specialize more (each member is likely to confine his or her work to the same sector). This model in effect argues that structural constraints/opportunities (urban/rural, agricultural/nonagricultural, and gender factors) have an impact on the development of household human capital (specialization and diversification).

The findings illustrate the impact of structure (state policies), including (1) segmented household registrations and restricted work mobility between urban and rural areas, (2) agricultural versus nonagricultural segmentation in rural areas, and (3) concentration of state-owned agencies, institutes, and enterprises in urban areas. Because of the lack of mobility between urban and rural areas, residents in urban areas tend to concentrate on getting and staying in jobs in the state sector, for the sake of security and benefits (housing, for example). On the other hand, rural residents are trying to move to the nonagricultural sector to increase their income (see chap. 8). It is not surprising, therefore, to find more specialization and less diversification in urban household work activities and less specialization and more diversification in rural household work activities. These are rational choices made within the constraints of the state policies.

If we follow the model in the appendix, we should expect returns to the differential development of household human capital. That is, we would expect this model to extend to the next causal sequence: differential household capital (specialization and diversification) should generate differential returns (e.g., household incomes). Further, we would expect this relationship to be contingent on the structural context (differential effects of household capital on returns for urban versus rural households, agricultural versus nonagricultural households, etc.). Thus, this sort of model not only places an empirical work in a conceptual framework, but also points out directions where the empirical work should be extended.

GENDER AS A STRUCTURAL CONSTRAINT

The model in the appendix can also be used to study and understand the differential interplay between structural constraints/opportunities and actions (capitalization) for different segments of the population. In the case of gender, we ask: Do structural constraints/opportunities differ for males and females? If so, how? What are the consequences for men and women in their development of human and social capital, in their acquisition of institutional capital, and finally, in the returns of their capital? To my knowledge, no single study conducted in China provides answers to all these questions, but we can piece together data from various studies to begin to understand these processes.

THE SOCIAL INEQUALITY SYSTEM

Evidence from chapter 8 by Michelson and Parish, based on data from rural areas, suggests that women are more likely to be working on farms as men seek out nonagricultural work. Is this a choice or a structural constraint? My own fieldwork suggests that structure in part explains this differentiation (Lin 1995; Lin and Chen 1999). Many new enterprises, while employing a significant number of women workers, are run almost exclusively by men. In many villages married women are sent home when they have children, even if they have been working in the factories. Given these structural barriers, women resort to taking care of the land assigned to their families to continue to be productive. In urban areas, many work units are just as blatant in excluding women workers. The work units can and do publicly announce that they will not hire women because their careers will be interrupted when they become pregnant and mothers, because they are physically not strong enough, and because they do not have the necessary stamina or attention or commitment. As a result, women tend to concentrate in work units that are not at the top of the authority hierarchy (the institutes, the service industries) and undertake professional (scientist, technician, nursing) or clerical (sales) jobs. These jobs do not offer many chances to move in the hierarchical system, and without opportunities to move to authority positions that permit delayed retirements, women tend to leave or retire earlier than men—a self-fulfilling prophecy. (See chap. 7 for data from Tianjin that demonstrates the importance of different age at retirement for gender differences in wages.)

How do men and women differ in acquiring human capital and social capital? Studies have shown that in urban areas, men and women have achieved equity in educational attainment (Lin 1994). In rural areas, while men stay in school longer than women, the gap is fairly small (chap. 8). This is a result not of structural support for women, but of men's response to better opportunities to generate returns—going into private enterprise or becoming entrepreneurs.

Assuming men and women have attained educational equity, do they acquire institutional capital likewise equally? The answer is no. Using 1991 data from Beijing, Shanghai, and Tianjin, I found that men are more likely to enter higher-ranked work units, gain authority positions, and become Party members after controlling for human capital (Lin 1994). When seeking jobs, men seem to be able to find better social connections to help them (social capital) than women (Lin and Bian 1991). This differentiation appears to result from a combination of factors: (1) parents tend to locate better helpers to find jobs for their sons than for their daughters (a selective investment in social capital), and (2) helpers seem to work harder for a male job-seeker than a female job-seeker (helpers with similar resources tend to find better jobs for men than for women). This selective investment in social capital by the helper may be because help on behalf of a son is more appreciated than on behalf of a daughter, incurring greater social debt for the job-seekers' parents to the helper. The ultimate consequences are that capitalization generates unequal returns for men and women.

INSTITUTIONAL TRANSFORMATION AND ITS CONSEQUENCES

The model in the appendix helps guide the research plan, design, identification and measurement of variables, and analyses. It can also guide analysis of the effects of institutional transformations. As China undergoes policy changes toward a market economy and more decentralized relationships between the central government and enterprises, how might these changes impact the development of human and social capital? Would they increase the value of human capital, if we assume that a stronger effect of human capital is expected on returns in the social inequality system guided by market principles? Would they decrease the value of social capital, if we assume a weakened effect of connections on returns in such an emerging system? And most important, how might these changes affect the investment in and return on institutional capital? Would the emergence of nonstate, noncollective enterprises based on market and competition principles erode the values of existing institutional capital? And how would these changes affect the investment of human capital and social capital on institutional capital (e.g., less likelihood of entering state-owned work units, joining the Party, etc.)?

With data from surveys of representative samples of adults from three cities (Beijing, Tianjin, and Shanghai) in 1991, I conducted cohort studies for those entering the labor force during 1949–65, 1966–77, 1978–81, and 1982–91 (Lin 1994). Assuming that urban policy changes took place after 1982, we should expect to find different patterns among human capital, institutional capital, and returns (monthly earnings) between the last cohort (1982–91) and the previous three cohorts. (I did not have measures for social capital in this study.) The results show that for the last cohort, as compared to previous cohorts, educational attainment was influenced more by parental education than by characteristics of parental work unit and Party membership. Gender differentiation on educational attainment decreased for the last cohort. This suggests that education is becoming an investment by parents in the development of human capital rather than institutional capital. Also of interest was the finding that while education remained a significant factor in attaining a position for the last three cohorts, the impact of Party membership, salient in the first two of these three cohorts (1966–76 and 1977–81), disappeared for the last cohort (1982–91). Gender remained a significant factor for attaining authority positions throughout, however. Regarding current wages, education became a significant factor for the last cohort, while gender, important for the previous three cohorts, disappeared. Party membership remained an important factor for getting better wages as each cohort first entered the labor force (measured as wage for the first job).

Thus there is evidence of institutional capital eroding somewhat in the last period examined. Of special interest is the possible "decoupling" of Party membership and authority positions. While this trend is consistent with institutional transformation, persistent gender differentiation suggests that the different institutions may undergo changes at different rates, or even undergo different changes. One possible hypothesis is that the institutional transformations observed in the current era in China apply to political and economic spheres, while institutions of a sociocultural nature (gender) have not kept pace. This study illustrates how the model in the appendix guides analysis for consequences of structural changes but, more importantly, sheds light on where such changes are and are not taking place.

CONCLUDING REMARKS

As many of the chapters in this volume demonstrate, family and household are important social contexts for studying what choices are available and what actions are possible in the changing context of contemporary China. This chapter employs a general model to guide discussion and analysis of social inequality in China: In the attempts of actors in families and households to invest in and mobilize a variety of resources as human and social capital, and to gain institutional advantages and better returns, which structural factors impose constraints and which afford opportunities? It is clear that state policies have differentially influenced the ability of population groups to make appropriate capitalization and gain returns under prevailing institutions. As these policies change, not only will the types and extent of structural constraints and opportunities change, the social context will likewise change its meaning for individuals attempting to capitalize resources and generate returns.

At the same time, an individual is also bound by social—especially familial—resources and obligations. With regard to investing resources and capital, action will be taken and choices made in the context of these more enduring social relations and networks. Under changing policies, the aim will be to optimize gains for individual actors and, equally important, to maintain returns to these social units as well. How these changes will affect the social construction and meaning of households is an important key to understanding social inequality as China enters the next century.

APPENDIX

A Model of Capitalization to Generate Returns
in a Social Inequality System

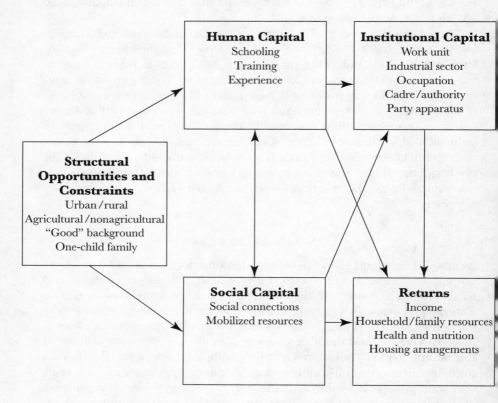

NOTE

1. C. H. Tung, the designated chief administrator of Hong Kong, made it clear in a January 1997 press conference that he was in favor of "social order" over "individual freedom" in formulating new policies and abolishing other policies as Hong Kong prepared to return to China. The structural reality is such that for him to say or do otherwise would lead to loss of his capitalization and rewards in the forthcoming new order of social inequality.

Conclusion

Re-Drawing Boundaries

Barbara Entwisle and Gail E. Henderson

In all societies, boundaries serve critical cognitive and practical functions as people attempt to make sense of the world, yet for China boundaries have always had a particular resonance. One thinks of the Great Wall, or the characters for "China," *zhongguo* ("middle kingdom"), which include a pictograph of a rectangular boundary drawn around a mouth and a halberd. Cultural expressions from China's earliest civilization to the present day, including the architecture of cities, temples, and homes, have impressed observers with the importance given to creating and maintaining divisions between groups of people (e.g., invaders and defenders, family and non-family). China's earliest written records describe rituals of religion and state that were used to "demarcate the fundamental boundary between stability and instability" and to highlight the boundaries of both space and status (Hay 1994, 9). Our attention to boundaries thus echoes the writings of many scholars who have remarked on the Chinese penchant for assigning people and things to their proper places.

Yet boundaries are also elusive. When they are very familiar, we take their existence for granted. But no matter how familiar or unfamiliar it is, a boundary is never really fixed. Even China's best-known boundary, the Great Wall, was not the boundary that many believe it was. The wall that we see now is primarily the result of defensive fortifications undertaken during the Ming Dynasty (1368–1644). It did not prevent invasions by nomads from the north, and rather than being a symbol of strength, it in fact represented the defeat of foreign policy (Waldron 1990). Its salience to present-day politicians lies less in its physical reality than in what it represents about China's place in the world.

It is not surprising that a book on work, household, and gender in China should feature boundaries. Though less tangible than physical boundaries like the Great Wall, definitional, conceptual, social, and spatial boundaries are central to an understanding of work, household, and gender. Boundaries are implicit in the questions that were the original motivation for the papers in this volume: What is work? How have gender inequalities in work changed over the course of recent history in China? How do families and households influence, and how are they influenced by, the organization of work? How has migration affected the work-household-gender nexus? Boundaries set an interpretive context for social comparison and for measuring change. They reflect and instruct about the way things are and the way they ought to be. But boundaries are flexible, permeable, mythic—they are themselves social constructions. This concluding chapter explicates these points, drawing on the other chapters in the volume for evidence and examples.

WORK

In the past decade China has undergone enormous structural change in its economic institutions, both urban and rural. These changes have produced a rapidly expanding and diversifying private sector, complicating and at times obfuscating the distinctions between public and private, foreign and Chinese, and even household-based and non-household-based work. These changes create practical as well as conceptual problems for understanding the nature of work in China today. How should activities be classified? How are they regarded? Where is work taking place? How do contemporary work patterns compare with those of the socialist era, particularly with regard to gender differences in labor force participation, occupation, and level of remuneration? Boundaries are implicit in these motivating questions.

Boundaries are explicit in the framework Rosenfeld (chap. 3) proposes to organize the answers. She defines a two-by-two classification of work activities according to remuneration (yes or no) and location (household or not). Remunerated work outside the household is viewed as work everywhere, whereas unremunerated work inside the household is virtually never seen this way (see also chap. 2). Activities can change classification; for instance, agricultural fieldwork has shifted from mainly an "outside" to mainly an "inside" activity over the past 50 years. The degree to which people engage in particular activities and activity types can also change. In the 1950s and 1960s, for example, women were drawn into the formal labor force in China (Andors 1983; K. Johnson 1983; Stacey 1983; Whyte and Parish 1984), and China continues to have one of the higher female labor force participation rates in the world.

Indeed, many of the chapters in this volume reflect upon the meaning of work, and the boundaries between different tasks. Mann (chap. 1) tells us that historically, work as defined by labor *(lao)* was part of a collective responsibility owed to one's household and to society. Everyone was supposed to labor at gender-, age-, and status-appropriate activities, although certain tasks were more highly regarded than others (mental over manual, for example). Some tasks were carried out in the home, others outside, and when work moved across this boundary, the gender of the worker might also change. Thus the meaning of work was derived from its intrinsic nature, where it was done, and who was doing it. Highlighting the importance of meaning as an independent factor, Zhang writes in chapter 10, "It is not work per se but the value of what is perceived as work that defines gender equality" (p. 184). Rosenfeld echoes this view: "It is not just the site where an activity takes place but also the meaning associated with that site that influences who does the work, in what way, and for what value" (p. 62). It is noteworthy that pay was not a factor in Mann's historical account, although it clearly is in China today (chap. 2).

The nature of boundaries related to work is revealed most clearly when an economic system is in flux. The massive changes instituted by the regime after 1949 and again after 1978 provide ample illustration. When work was collectivized, private activities disappeared for some time in China. This was a problem for women, whose activities by definition were "private" and "inside," especially in rural areas. As a result of state-initiated policies, many women did go outside to work, and in the process redefined gender-appropriate activities. Others got around this in different ways, demonstrating how boundaries can be redrawn. One solution was to redefine the task. Sidelines, for instance, which were forbidden as private activities, became housework and therefore an invisible part of the household (M. Wolf 1985). Child care, seen as a barrier to women's full participation in production, became a collectivized, compensated activity, notably in urban areas but also intermittently and partially in rural areas. In the process, the social meanings of the household shifted as well.

Similar events characterize the post-1978 period, when private enterprise was reinstituted. At the height of the Maoist era, work (gongzuo) was defined as "paid, outside work," or "something that gives you a benzi," an official identification card, in a state work unit (chap. 4). Work in collectives had lower status, while farming, even though collectivized, was never regarded as "real" gongzuo. Following the reforms, there was "no longer a clear line between gongzuo and household-based work; both can bring in money. And there [was] no longer a clear line between gongzuo and farmwork, especially since farmwork is increasingly commercialized" (Harrell, chap. 4, p. 76). Chapter 2, on the meaning of gongzuo, focuses precisely on the unstable boundaries between different kinds of work—agricultural and nonagricultural, household-based and based outside of the household, work for remuneration and work for household consumption. It shows that the meaning of gongzuo changes according to the nature of tasks and who is performing them. Yet equally important, it also shows that there is no clear agreement on what work or a job is.[1]

Despite varying understandings of what counts as work and what does not, data collection in censuses and surveys generally relies on a single question, for example: Does this person have work? Follow-up questions about occupation, sector of employment, and other job characteristics are generally restricted to respondents who have answered yes to this question. Several authors in this volume use these kinds of data, and thus for them, the meaning of work per se is not the focus of their investigation. In chapter 7, for example, Bian, Logan, and Shu define work in their urban sample simply as "work for wages." Others include employment sector (state, collective, private), occupation or industry, or mode of production (e.g., Entwisle, Short, Zhai, and Ma in chap. 15). Boundaries between work and nonwork are built into the response categories. If the concept of work is unclear and the activities to be classified are ambiguous in some way, responses may be misleading. For example, Entwisle and others (1994) note that the work of women in household businesses is underreported. The focus group interviews analyzed by Henderson, Entwisle, Li and associates in chapter 2 suggest why: the location of these businesses "inside" the household and the unpaid nature of the work. The lack of visibility of household-based work may be one explanation for the finding by Goldstein, Liang, and Goldstein (chap. 12) that a great many rural-to-urban female migrants are housewives. One of Zhang's male informants (chap. 10) described his wife's contribution to clothing production as "helping out and looking after things when needed," even though she and her young female workers often spent more than 12 hours a day on this household-based work. This is just one example of how the combination of qualitative and quantitative data approaches featured in this volume helps piece together a more complete picture of the interconnections between work, household, and gender.

HOUSEHOLDS

Households are fundamental to an understanding of gender and work in China. Traditionally, households are thought to divide "inside" work from "outside" work, private from public, and work that is performed by women from that done by men. The malleable character of this boundary emerges as we look again at who tills the fields. As Mann describes in chapter 1, Confucian orthodoxy dictated that men should farm while women should engage in various household sideline ("inside") activities. This changed in the 1950s. In essence, the regime attempted to take economic control away from households by collectivizing as much work as possible, even the "private" and "inside" work of households like child care and cooking. As noted above, women were encouraged to take on new roles outside the household, although they were less likely than men to do the actual fieldwork. Those who did, like Cao Zhuxiang, featured in Hershatter's chapter 5 about rural women in the 1950s, were held up as model labor heroines. After 1978, economic reforms promoted return of the control and location of work to the household, particularly in rural areas. The effect of this was, oddly, to make "outside" and "inside" work both more visible and lucrative, and more private. Furthermore, another kind of "outside" work appeared, as industrialization expanded opportunities outside of the household. When men began to leave agriculture entirely for wage work, women took over more of the heavy farming tasks. In the process, space was again redefined and the classification of fieldwork shifted from "outside" to "inside" work.

How did the boundaries change? The answer depends in part on the causal ordering of gender and the "inside/outside" classification. Was fieldwork associated with men because it took place outside the household, or was it labeled "outside" work simply because men did it? Is it possible that in response to men taking jobs quite far away from the household (that is, traveling to jobs both beyond the local area and away from agricultural into industrial employment), the fields became redefined as part of the household, and thus as the province of women? The answer will be revealed at least partially by future trends, especially by whether or not women follow men into wage employment. This is the trend that Michelson and Parish (chap. 8) expect, for example.

In considering these issues, it is important to remember that the household is both a physical and social location. Traditionally, a household (*hu* or *jiating*) was often surrounded by a wall, the interior geography marked off to provide spaces for various functions, such as worship of ancestor tablets, and for the inner spaces for women, who included the "inside person" (*neiren*) or wife. But the physicality of the household cannot be readily separated from its social role of providing a place for people to live and a site and context for their activities. It is the social aspect of the household that allows its boundaries to move. This is illustrated in Hershatter's story in chapter 5 of Cao Zhuxiang, who, when the need arose, extended the umbrella of "inside" work all the way to marketing towns. It is also vividly represented in chapter 10 by Zhang on migrant workers in Zhejiangcun, whose households stretch across several provinces during their sojourn in Beijing. When such arrangements fall within the official household registration system, they are given administrative validity. One consequence of the differences between physical, social, and official household boundaries is difficulty in labeling different kinds of migrants—temporary versus longstanding versus permanent, official versus unofficial (see chaps. 12 and 13).

In fact, the boundaries between work and household are often fluid. Many kinds of work (sideline activities, retail businesses, and factory production, for example) can take place both inside and outside households.

The apartments of Zhejiang migrants living in Beijing are transformed into clothing production sites, and private living rooms can become public office space when the need arises. For some urban households, work is segregated away from the household, as Davis reports in chapter 14 on Shanghai families. The re-drawing of boundaries between home and workplace, public and private has implications for the visibility and social recognition of different kinds of work, of course, as Rosenfeld explains in chapter 3.

In addition to boundaries within households, there are also boundaries between households. The collective era sought to minimize these in the pursuit of common public interests; the reverse is true of the reform era. The reinstatement of households as units of economic production in the reform era, distinctive to China, may have reinforced boundaries between households there. Of course, whether households really are meaningful units of planning and decision making is an open question that is not easy to answer. In chapter 15 Entwisle, Short, Zhai and Ma show that with respect to work, at least in rural areas, households may be more than the aggregation of their members. Without data over time it is difficult to interpret the level of interdependence or the trend. Boundaries may also weaken and harden over the combined life course of family members, as Davis describes for Shanghai. In urban areas, increased rural-to-urban migration has prompted a defensive response about household boundaries as urban governments strengthen barriers that keep migrants outside of the official urban domain—even going so far as to bulldoze Zhejiang migrants' temporary housing.

Finally, there is an important conceptual distinction to consider: the distinction between household and family. Some researchers see households as secondary to family, indeed, as dependent on negotiation among family members (e.g., Davis, chap. 14); others see a different balance (e.g., Judd 1994). Of course both are relevant, but as a location and site of daily activity as well as a social construction, households have particular importance to an understanding of gender and work. There are practical considerations as well. Survey and census data are almost always collected from households, and most of the chapters in this volume are based on household data. Moreover, the Communist household registration system *(hukou)*, following the imperial system that registered and taxed households *(hu)* as fiscal units (Bray 1997, 93), plays a critical role in the story of work in China—and that system is obviously based on the household.

GENDER

The introduction to the book *Engendering China* describes both the complex meanings that gender embodies and the social forces that influence where the boundary line between male and female is drawn: "Gender signifies that the categories female and male—the meanings assigned to them, the behaviors expected of them, the sense of self associated with them, and the relations among and between those female and male selves—are cultural constructions. . . . [B]ehaviors that are thought to transgress gender boundaries can be understood only if we know how a particular society has mapped those boundaries."[2]

The rhetoric and legal reforms of the Communist regime raised expectations that a utopian socialist world was being created, one that blurred the distinction between male and female, even eradicating gender altogether. Of course this was a utopian vision, and when the gap between rhetoric and reality was exposed, it generated considerable frustration among Western feminists who had hoped and believed that this experiment would succeed (e.g., see M. Wolf 1985). The legacy of sparse and unreliable data from the socialist era, in combination with this utopian vision, creates substantial ambiguity regarding the starting point for understanding trends in various aspects of gender inequality over the past several decades (Whyte, chap. 9).

This ambiguity is some of the context in which our examination of gender in relation to work in China is situated. The chapters in this volume explore two interrelated aspects of this relation: work as infusing meaning into gender, and gender as affecting the work in which people engage. Both types of discussions were produced in response to the same motivating question: How have gender inequalities in work changed over the course of the post-1949 period? For some scholars the question inspires quantitative analyses of how gender affects life chances: schooling, job placement, pay, job mobility and the like (e.g., Bian, Logan, and Shu in chap. 7 and Michelson and Parish in chap. 8). For others, the question raises issues of representation and meaning, best explored in the life stories of individuals (e.g., Hershatter in chap. 5 and Honig in chap. 6).

As Mann shows in chapter 1, work activities were central to the definition of gender in traditional China. This may be partly related to the agricultural economy. Men and women, properly, did different things: "man tills, woman weaves." Women's sphere was "inside," and men's "outside," yet each was seen as critical to the maintenance of the household economy. Entwisle, Short, Zhai and Ma (chap. 15) explore these complementarities in terms of specialization and diversification of work activities in contemporary households. "Man tills, woman weaves" implies specialization by gender within households. The authors of chapter 15 find that households with more women are also more likely to be internally specialized than households with more men.

These historical and contemporary examples bracket the period of flux in the boundary between men's and women's work. The rhetoric of the early 1950s advocated collapse of the boundary between masculine and feminine. Rural labor heroines, such as those interviewed by Hershatter (chap. 5), were extolled because they were doing the work of men. Hershatter notes:

"What the revolution did for these women was not so much to remove the stigma of 'outside' labor as to change the context and the rewards associated with it" (p. 83). Cao Zhuxiang "broke the old habit of believing that women could not do farmwork" (p. 85). Of course, the truth about Cao, as the chapter details, is that she had often worked "outside" before that time, though she might not have called it that. Work previously invisible when performed by women became socially recognized. The relation between gender and work changed in the early 1950s for this reason, as well as because of the actual movement of women into agricultural fieldwork.

Did this represent the erasing of gender differences, or were women expected to become "like men"? Honig's chapter 6 on the Iron Girls of the Cultural Revolution argues that in moving from the cities to the countryside and eschewing the traditional tasks of rural women, the girls had no option other than to become like men. Often it was the sent-down youth who challenged rural beliefs about women's roles. As outsiders, these young women could establish a new precedent far more easily than local women could. Honig also describes how challenging old beliefs about gender and work could be in the interest of local cadres. But the problem was, when everyone becomes a man, who is left to work at home? Both Hershatter and Honig illustrate how deeply hidden beneath the rhetoric of gender equality the problem of child care was. Venturing over the male-female divide was a dangerous, even deadly, undertaking.

The post-Mao era brought a repudiation of this ideology and the rise of a new feminine identity, separate from men. Although traditional Confucian gender roles differed from those espoused by the Communist state and its organ, the Women's Federation (*Fulian*), both periods were characterized by an authoritarian state discourse. In contrast, in the reform era women began to create their own ideas about gender identity.[3] Through the "discovery" of inequality, the public rhetoric that constructed gender identity was challenged (Croll 1995). What was private and invisible thus became public and visible, and the boundaries between men and women shifted.

These shifts in meaning are inextricably tied to shifts in gender differences in work, although there is no one-to-one correspondence. Michelson and Parish (chap. 8) suggest that in the overall context of economic transformation in rural areas, men move first into nonagricultural activities and into growth areas within the nonagricultural economy, and women eventually follow. The authors develop a picture of change that accommodates sharp gender differences at one point in time (e.g., as documented by Yang in the rural areas of Zhejiang Province in chap. 11), with attenuation at some subsequent point. For Tianjin, by contrast, Bian, Logan and Shu (chap. 7) describe remarkable stability in wage differences between men and women between 1978 and 1993. They attribute much of the difference and its stability to a persisting male advantage in education and Party membership, and in job allocation and mobility practices, and a long-standing requirement that working women retire ten years earlier than working men. There is no simple answer to the question of how gender inequalities have changed over the course of the course of the post-1949 period.

CONCLUSION

As we have tried to show, concepts of work, household, and gender presume the drawing of boundaries, and in addition to movement across boundaries, the boundaries are themselves of interest. Further, gender, household, and work that is carried out by men and women inside and outside their households are not three separable and independent dimensions; they are interrelated. An exploration of any one leads inevitably to the other two. The familiar "inside/outside" dichotomy encapsulates this interconnectedness spatially and socially. The space that is set off as the household, distinguishing it from the world beyond it, and the arrangement of space within the household embody cultural concepts of family, work, and gender (Bray 1997, 53, 91). Contemporary social scientists writing about China have not tired of the inside/outside dichotomy and use it to interpret various aspects of gender and household relations. For us, though, the inside/outside boundary is a starting point. The boundary is not a given, but rather is problematized as one among many potential influences on social arrangements.[4]

NOTES

1. This is illustrated by the fact that the same reasons were given to justify why an activity is "not work" and why it is (e.g., "sidelines are not *gongzuo*" "sidelines are *gongzuo*," or "running a household business *[getihu]* is not *gongzuo*," "if you have a *getihu*, you have *gongzuo*").

2. Gilmartin et al. 1994, 1.

3. Women began to create their own ideas about gender identity, using terms consciously outside state discourse, as Barlow (1994, 339) describes. For example, *funü* was discarded for *nüren* or *nüxing*.

4. See Bray's (1997) study of gender and work in late Imperial China for a highly nuanced treatment of these issues.

GLOSSARY OF CHINESE TERMS

baomu	nanny
chengshi hukou	urban household registration
chu	division rank, in the government bureaucracy; the next lower level is department (ke), the next higher is bureau (ju)
dagongmei	young female migrant worker
dahu	rich household
danwei	work unit
dayuan	large residential compound
dingti	officially replace a parent with a child in employment
fenjia	division of family property and residence
Fulian	Women's Federation
geti	individual
getihu	private individual or household business
gongzuo	work, a job
guanxi	connections
Guomindang	Nationalist Party, also called KMT
hu	household
hukou	household registration
jia	family
jin	weight measure (1 jin = .5 kilogram)
kang	a heatable brick bed
lao	labor
laoban	boss
laodong	labor, work
laogong	laborer
mahjong	game played with small tiles
mu	unit of area (1 mu = .0667 hectares)
nongcun hukou	rural household registration

Renmin Ribao	People's Daily
siying	privately owned
siying qiye	private enterprise
waidiren	migrant
Wenzhou	city and prefecture in southern Zhejiang Province, a coastal province south of Shanghai
yuan	basic monetary unit in China
Zhejiangcun	Zhejiang village, name of migrant community in Beijing
zhong-xiao hu	middle income household

REFERENCES

Abu-Lughod, Lila. 1990. "The Romance of Resistance: Tracing Transformations of Power through Bedouin Women." *American Ethnologist* 17: 41–55.

All-China Women's Federation. 1991. *The Report of the People's Republic of China (PRC) on the Implementation of the Nairobi Forward-Looking Strategies for the Advancement of Women.* Beijing.

Anderson, K. L. and W. R. Allen. 1984. "Correlates of Extended Household Structure." *Phylon* 45: 144–57.

Andors, Phyllis. 1983. *The Unfinished Liberation of Chinese Women, 1949–1980.* Bloomington, Ind.: Indiana University Press; Brighton, Sussex, England: Wheatsheaf Books.

Angel, Ronald and Marta Tienda. 1982. "Determinants of Extended Household Structure: Cultural Patterns or Economic Need?" *American Journal of Sociology* 87: 1360–83.

Arkush, R. David. 1984. "'If Man Works Hard the Land Will Not Be Lazy': Entrepreneurial Values in North Chinese Peasant Proverbs." *Modern China* 10: 461–79.

Ban Gu. 1983. "Shihuo zhi, shang" (Treatise on the economy, chapter 1). In *Han shu* (History of the former Han Dynasty). Wenyuange Siku quanshu edition. Taipei: Taiwan shangwu yinshu guan. Vol. 249: 531–545.

Banister, Judith. 1987. *China's Changing Population.* Stanford, Calif.: Stanford University Press.

———. 1992. *Urban-Rural Population Projections for China.* Washington, D.C.: Center for International Research, U.S. Bureau of the Census.

Barlow, Tani. 1994. "Politics and Protocols of Funü: (Un)Making National Woman." Pp. 339–59 in *Engendering China: Women, Culture, and the State,* edited by Christina K. Gilmartin, Gail Hershatter, Lisa Rofel, and Tyrene White. Cambridge: Harvard University Press.

Barrett, Jane. 1973. "Women Hold Up Half the Sky." Pp. 193–200 in *Women in China: Studies in Social Change and Feminism,* edited by Marilyn Young. Ann Arbor: University of Michigan Center for Chinese Studies Press.

Barrett, Richard E., William P. Bridges, Moshe Semyonov, and Xiaoyuan Gao. 1991. "Female Labor Force Participation in Urban and Rural China." *Rural Sociology* 56: 1–21.

Bauer, John, Wang Feng, Nancy E. Riley, and Zhao Xiaohua. 1992. "Gender Inequality in Urban China: Education and Employment." *Modern China* 18: 333–70.

Becker, Gary S. 1981. *A Treatise on the Family.* Cambridge: Harvard University Press.

———. 1991. *A Treatise on the Family.* Enlarged ed. Cambridge: Harvard University Press.

———. 1993. *Human Capital: A Theoretical and Empirical Analysis, with Special Reference to Education.* 3d ed. Chicago: University of Chicago Press.

Beijing Review Staff. 1983. "Female Infanticide: Punishable by Law." *Beijing Review: A Chinese Weekly of News and Views* 26(17): 9.

———. 1995. "Women March into the 21st Century Together with Men." *Beijing Review: A Chinese Weekly of News and Views* 38(36): 3–33.

Bell, Lynda S. 1994. "For Better, for Worse: Women and the World Market in Rural China." *Modern China* 20: 180–210.

Benería, Lourdes and Shelley Feldman, eds. 1992. *Unequal Burden: Economic Crises, Persistent Poverty, and Women's Work.* Boulder, Colo.: Westview Press.

Benjamin, Dwayne and Loren Brandt. 1995. "Markets, Discrimination, and the Economic Contribution of Women in China: Historical Evidence." *Economic Development and Cultural Change* 44: 63–104.

Bernstein, Thomas P. 1977. *Up to the Mountains and Down to the Villages: The Transfer of Youth from Urban to Rural China.* New Haven, Conn.: Yale University Press.

Besteman, Catherine. 1989. "Economic Strategies of Farming Households in Penabranca, Portugal." *Economic Development and Cultural Change* 38: 129–43.

Bian Yanjie. 1990. "Work-Unit Structure and Status Attainment: A Study of Work-Unit Status in Urban China." Ph.D. dissertation, State University of New York at Albany.

———. 1994. *Work and Inequality in Urban China.* SUNY Series in the Sociology of Work. Albany: State University of New York Press.

———. 1998. "Getting a Job through the Web of Guanxi." Pp. 255–77 in *Networks in the Global Village: Life in Contemporary Communities,* edited by Barry Wellman. Boulder, Colo.: Westview Press.

Bian Yanjie and John R. Logan. 1996. "Market Transition and the Persistence of Power: The Changing Stratification System in Urban China." *American Sociological Review* 61: 739–58.

Bian Yanjie, John Logan, Hanlong Lu, Yunkang Pan, and Ying Guan. 1996. "Danweizhi yu zhufang shengpinhua" (Unit-ism and the Commercialization of Housing). *Shehuixue yanjiu* (Sociological research) 61(1): 83–95.

Bielby, Denise D. and William T. Bielby. 1988. "She Works Hard for the Money: Household Responsibilities and the Allocation of Work Effort." *American Journal of Sociology* 93: 1031–59.

Bilsborrow, Richard E., ed. 1993. *Internal Migration of Women in Developing Countries.* ST/ESA/SER.R/127. New York: United Nations.

Bilsborrow, Richard E. and United Nations Secretariat. 1993. "Internal Female Migration and Development: An Overview." Pp. 1–17 in *Internal Migration of Women in Developing Countries,* edited by Richard E. Bilsborrow. ST/ESA/SER.R/127. New York: United Nations.

Blau, Francine D., Marianne A. Ferber, and Anne E. Winkler. 1998. *The Economics of Women, Men, and Work.* 3d ed. Upper Saddle River, N.J.: Prentice-Hall.

Blau, Peter M., and Danqing Ruan. 1990. "Inequality of Opportunity in Urban China and America." *Research in Social Stratification and Mobility: A Research Annual* 8: 3–32

Blossfeld, Hans-Peter and Catherine Hakim. 1997. *Between Equalization and Marginalization: Women Working Part-Time in Europe and the United States of America.* New York: Oxford University Press.

Bose, Christine E. 1984. "Household Resources and U.S. Women's Work: Factors Affecting Gainful Employment at the Turn of the Century." *American Sociological Review* 49: 474–90.

Boserup, Ester. 1970. *Woman's Role in Economic Development.* New York: St. Martin's Press.

Bourdieu, Pierre. 1977. *Outline of a Theory of Practice,* translated by Richard Nice. Cambridge Series in Social Anthropology, 16. Cambridge: Cambridge University Press.

———. 1980. "Le Capital Social: Notes Provisoires." *Actes de la Recherche en Sciences Sociales* 3: 2–3.

Bourdieu, Pierre and Jean-Claude Passeron. 1977. *Reproduction in Education, Society, Culture,* translated by Richard Nice. Sage Studies in Social and Educational Change, 5. Beverly Hills, Calif.: Sage.

Bray, Francesca. 1986. *The Rice Economies: Technology and Development in Asian Societies.* Oxford: Blackwell.

———. 1997. *Technology and Gender: Fabrics of Power in Late Imperial China.* Berkeley: University of California Press.

Brinton, Mary C. 1993. *Women and the Economic Miracle: Gender and Work in Postwar Japan.* California Series on Social Choice and Political Economy, 21. Berkeley: University of California Press.

Brinton, Mary C., Yean-ju Lee, and William L. Parish. 1995. "Married Women's Employment in East Asia." *American Journal of Sociology* 100: 1099–30.

Brokaw, Cynthia J. 1991. *The Ledgers of Merit and Demerit: Social Change and Moral Order in Late Imperial China.* Princeton, N.J.: Princeton University Press.

Buck, John Lossing. 1937. *Land Utilization in China: A Study of 16,786 Farms in 168 Localities, and 38,256 Farm Families in Twenty-Two Provinces in China, 1929–1933.* Chicago: University of Chicago Press.

Burt, Ronald S. 1992. *Structural Holes: The Social Structure of Competition.* Cambridge: Harvard University Press.

Byerly, Victoria. 1986. *Hard Times Cotton Mill Girls: Personal Histories of Womanhood and Poverty in the South.* Ithaca, N.Y.: ILR Press, New York State School of Industrial and Labor Relations, Cornell University.

Cao Zhuxiang huzhu lianzu danxing cailiao (Individual material on the Cao Zhuxiang united mutual aid group). 9 April 1953. (178–209–009). Women's Federation archives held in the Shaanxi Provincial Archives, Xian.

Cao Zhuxiang huzhuzu mofan shijian danxing cailiao (Individual material on model incidents in the Cao Zhuxiang mutual aid group). February-December 1952. (178–27–025). Women's Federation archives held in the Shaanxi Provincial Archives, Xian.

Cao Zhuxiang mofan shiji danxing cailiao (Single material on the model activities of Cao Zhuxiang). 1957. (Handwritten ms.) In records of Hongxing village, Weinan.

Chan, Anita, Richard Madsen, and Jonathan Unger. 1984. *Chen Village: The Recent History of a Peasant Community in China*. Berkeley: University of California Press.

Chan Kam Wing. 1994. *Cities with Invisible Walls: Reinterpreting Urbanization in Post-1949 China*. Hong Kong: Oxford University Press.

Chao, Kang. 1986. *Man and Land in Chinese History: An Economic Analysis*. Stanford, Calif.: Stanford University Press.

Chavez, Leo R. 1988. "Settlers and Sojourners: The Case of Mexicans in the United States." *Human Organization* 47: 95–108.

Chayanov, A. V. 1966. *The Theory of Peasant Economy,* edited by Daniel Thorner, Basile Kerblay, and R. E. F. Smith. Homewood, Ill.: Richard D. Irwin for the American Economic Association.

Chen Benli and Feng Guilin. 1996. "Minggongchao yu Zhongguo nongcun nüxing" (Rural labor migration waves and Chinese rural women). Paper presented at the International Conference on China's Internal Labor Migration, Beijing, 25–27 June.

Ch'ên, Kenneth K. S. 1973. *The Chinese Transformation of Buddhism*. Princeton, N.J.: Princeton University Press.

Cheng Tiejun and Mark Seldon. 1994. "The Origins and Social Consequences of China's Hukou System." *The China Quarterly* 139: 644–68.

China Daily (Beijing ed.). 1988a. "Abuse of Women Workers." 2 April.

———. 1988b. "Capital's Population Reaches 10 Million." 3 November.

Chinese Academy of Social Sciences. 1996. *Zhongguo dagongmei* (Chinese migrant sisters). Unpublished book manuscript. Beijing.

Chinese State Administration and Regulation Bureau of Independent Economy. 1987. *Geti gongshangye zhengce fagui huibian, 1957–1986* (Collection of policies and legal rules regarding independent industry and commerce, 1957–1986). Beijing: Jingji kexue chubanshe (Economic science publisher).

Christiansen, Flemming. 1990. "Social Division and Peasant Mobility in Mainland China: The Implications of the Hu-k'ou System." *Issues and Studies: A Journal of China Studies and International Affairs* 26(4): 23–42.

———. 1992. "'Market Transition' in China: The Case of the Jiangsu Labor Market, 1978–1990." *Modern China* 18: 72–93.

Ch'ü, T'ung-tsu. 1957. "Chinese Class Structure and Its Ideology." Pp. 235–50 in *Chinese Thought and Institutions,* edited by John K. Fairbank. Chicago: University of Chicago Press.

———. 1972. *Han Social Structure*. Vol. 1 of *Han Dynasty China,* edited by Jack L. Dull. Seattle: University of Washington Press.

Coale, Ansley J. and Judith Banister. 1994. "Five Decades of Missing Females in China." *Demography* 31: 459–79.

Cohen, Myron L. 1970. "Developmental Process in the Chinese Domestic Group." Pp. 21–36 in *Family and Kinship in Chinese Society,* edited by Maurice Freedman. Studies in Chinese Society. Stanford, Calif.: Stanford University Press.

————. 1976. *House United, House Divided: The Chinese Family in Taiwan.* Studies of the East Asian Institute, Columbia University. New York: Columbia University Press.

————. 1994. "Cultural and Political Inventions in China: The Case of the Chinese 'Peasant.'" Pp. 150–170 in *China in Transformation,* edited by Tu Wei-ming. Cambridge: Harvard University Press.

Cole, James H. 1986. *Shaohsing: Competition and Cooperation in Nineteenth-Century China.* Association for Asian Studies Monograph, no. 44. Tucson: University of Arizona Press for the Association for Asian Studies.

Coleman, Gould P. and Sarah Elbert. 1983. "Farming Families: 'The Farm Needs Everyone.'" Unpublished manuscript, Department of History, Cornell University, Ithaca, N.Y.

Coleman, James S. 1988. "Social Capital in the Creation of Human Capital." *American Journal of Sociology* 94: S95–S120.

————. 1990. *Foundations of Social Theory.* Cambridge: Harvard University Press.

Confucius. 1938. *Confucius: Analects.* Edited and translated by Arthur Waley. London: G. Allen & Unwin.

————. [1893–95] 1960. *Confucian Analects, the Great Learning, the Doctrine of the Mean.* Vol. 1 of *The Chinese Classics: With a Translation, Critical and Exegetical Notes, Prolegomena, and Copious Indexes,* edited and translated by James Legge. 3d edition, with a biographical note by Lindsay Ride. Hong Kong: Hong Kong University Press.

————. (1979). *The Analects.* Translated by D. C. Lau. Harmondsworth, England: Penguin Books.

Connelly, Rachel. 1992. "Self-Employment and Providing Child-Care: Strategies for Mothers with Young Children." *Demography* 29: 17–29.

Costello, Cynthia. 1989. "The Clerical Homework Program at the Wisconsin Physicians Service Insurance Corporation." Pp. 198–214 in *Homework: Historical and Contemporary Perspectives on Paid Labor at Home,* edited by Eileen Boris and Cynthia R. Daniels. Urbana: University of Illinois Press.

Croll, Elisabeth J. 1980. *Feminism and Socialism in China.* London: Routledge & Kegan Paul, 1978. Reprint, New York: Schocken Books.

————. 1983. *Chinese Women since Mao.* London: Zed Books; Armonk, N.Y.: M. E. Sharpe.

————. 1987. "New Peasant Family Forms in Rural China." *Journal of Peasant Studies* 14: 469–99.

————. 1994. *From Heaven to Earth: Images and Experiences of Development in China.* London: Routledge.

————. 1995. *Changing Identities of Chinese Women: Rhetoric, Experience, and Self-Perception in Twentieth-Century China.* Atlantic Highlands, N.J.: Zed Books.

Dalby, Michael T. 1979. "Court Politics in Late T'ang Times." Pp. 561–681 in *The Cambridge History of China. Vol. 3, Sui and T'ang China, 589–906, part 1,* edited by Denis Twitchett. Cambridge: Cambridge University Press.

Davin, Delia. 1979. *Woman-Work: Women and the Party in Revolutionary China.* Oxford: Clarendon Press.

————. 1996. "Migration, Women, and Gender Issues in Contemporary China." Paper presented at the International Conference on Migration in China, Cologne, Germany, May.

Davis, Deborah. 1989. "My Mother's House." Pp. 88–100 in *Unofficial China: Popular Culture and Thought in the People's Republic,* edited by Perry Link, Richard Madsen, and Paul Pickowicz. Boulder, Colo.: Westview Press.

———. 1990. "Urban Job Mobility." Pp. 85–108 in *Chinese Society on the Eve of Tiananmen: The Impact of Reform,* edited by Deborah Davis and Ezra F. Vogel. Harvard Contemporary China Series, 7. Cambridge: Harvard University Press.

———. 1992. "Urban Families and the Post-Mao State." Pp. 1125–50 in *Family Process and Political Process.* Taipei: Institute for Modern History, Academia Sinica.

———. 1993. "Urban Households: Supplicants to a Socialist State." Pp. 50–76 in *Chinese Families in the Post-Mao Era,* edited by Deborah Davis and Stevan Harrell. Studies on China, 17. Berkeley: University of California Press.

———. 1995. "Inequality and Stratification in the Nineties." Pp. 11.1–11.5 in *China Review 1995.* Hong Kong: Chinese University Press.

Davis, Deborah and Stevan Harrell. 1993. "Introduction: The Impact of Post-Mao Reforms on Family Life." Pp. 1–22 in *Chinese Families in the Post-Mao Era,* edited by Deborah Davis and Stevan Harrell. Studies on China, 17. Berkeley: University of California Press.

Davis, Deborah and Julia Sensenbrenner. 1997. "Bourgeois Childhoods in Working Class Shanghai." Paper presented at the conference "Urban Consumers and Consumer Culture in Contemporary China," New Haven, Conn., 9–12 January.

Davis-Friedmann, Deborah. 1983. *Long Lives: Chinese Elderly and the Communist Revolution.* Harvard East Asian Series, 100. Cambridge: Harvard University Press.

———. 1991. *Long Lives: Chinese Elderly and the Communist Revolution.* Expanded ed. Stanford, Calif.: Stanford University Press.

Deng, Xian. 1992. "Zhongguo zhiqing meng" (The Dream of China's educated young). *Dangdai* (Today's times) 5 (May).

Diamond, Norma. 1975. "Collectivization, Kinship, and the Status of Women in Rural China." Pp. 372–95 in *Toward an Anthropology of Women,* edited by Rayna R. Reiter. New York: Monthly Review Press.

Dixon, Ruth B. 1982. "Women in Agriculture: Counting the Labor Force in Developing Countries." *Population and Development Review* 8: 539–66.

Ebrey, Patricia Buckley, trans. 1984. *Family and Property in Sung China: Yüan Ts'ai's Precepts for Social Life.* Princeton Library of Asian Translations. Princeton: Princeton University Press.

———. 1993. *The Inner Quarters: Marriage and the Lives of Chinese Women in the Sung Period.* Berkeley: University of California Press.

Einhorn, Barbara. 1993. *Cinderella Goes to Market: Citizenship, Gender, and Women's Movements in East Central Europe.* London: Verso.

Elman, Cheryl and Peter Uhlenberg. 1995. "Co-residence in the Early Twentieth Century: Elderly Women in the United States and Their Children." *Population Studies* 49: 501–17.

Elvin, Mark. 1973. *The Pattern of the Chinese Past.* Stanford, Calif.: Stanford University Press.

Emerson, John Philip. 1971. "Manpower Training and Utilization of Specialized Cadres, 1949–68." Pp. 183–214 in *The City in Communist China,* edited by John Wilson Lewis. Studies in Chinese Society. Stanford, Calif.: Stanford University Press.

————. 1982. "The Labor Force of China, 1957–80." Pp. 224–67 in *China under the Four Modernizations; Selected Papers Submitted to the Joint Economic Committee, Congress of the United States,* Part 1. 97th Congress, 2d Session, Joint Committee Print. Washington, D.C.: U.S. Government Printing Office.

Engels, Frederick. 1891. *The Origin of the Family, Private Property, and the State.* 4th edition. Moscow.

England, Paula and George Farkas. 1986. *Households, Employment, and Gender: A Social, Economic, and Demographic View.* New York: Aldine.

England, Paula, Marilyn Chassie, and Linda McCormack. 1982. "Skill Demands and Earnings in Female and Male Occupations." *Sociology and Social Research* 66: 147–68.

Enloe, Cynthia H. 1983. "Women Textile Workers in the Militarization of Southeast Asia." Pp. 407–25 in *Women, Men, and the International Division of Labor,* edited by June C. Nash and María Patricia Fernández-Kelly. SUNY Series in the Anthropology of Work. Albany: State University of New York Press.

Entwisle, Barbara, Gail E. Henderson, Susan E. Short, Jill E. Bouma, and Zhai Fengying. 1995. "Gender and Family Businesses in Rural China." *American Sociological Review* 60: 36–57.

Entwisle, Barbara, Fengying Zhai, Jill E. Bouma, and Barry M. Popkin. 1994. "The Multidimensional Nature of Women's Work Roles: A Study of Contemporary China." Unpublished manuscript, Carolina Population Center, University of North Carolina at Chapel Hill.

Fernández-Kelly, María P. 1983. *For We Are Sold, I and My People: Women and Industry in Mexico's Frontier.* SUNY Series in the Anthropology of Work. Albany: State University of New York Press.

Fink, Deborah. 1986. *Open Country Iowa: Rural Women, Tradition, and Change.* SUNY Series in the Anthropology of Work. Albany: State University of New York Press.

Fligstein, Neil. 1991. "The Structural Transformation of American Industry: An Institutional Account of the Causes of Diversification in the Largest Firms, 1919–1979." Pp. 311–36 in *The New Institutionalism in Organizational Analysis,* edited by Walter W. Powell and Paul J. DiMaggio. Chicago: University of Chicago Press.

Gadgil, D. R. 1965. *Women in the Working Force in India.* Kunda Datar Memorial Lectures, 1964. New York: Asia Publishing House.

Gao, Xiaoxian. 1994. "China's Modernization and Changes in the Social Status of Rural Women," translated by S. Katherine Campbell. Pp. 80–97 in *Engendering China: Women, Culture, and the State,* edited by Christina K. Gilmartin, Gail Hershatter, Lisa Rofel, and Tyrene White. Cambridge: Harvard University Press.

Gates, Hill. 1996. *China's Motor: A Thousand Years of Petty Capitalism.* Ithaca, N.Y.: Cornell University Press.

Gerber, Theodore P. and Michael Hout. 1998. "More Shock than Therapy: Employment and Income in Russia, 1991–1995." *American Journal of Sociology* 104: 1–50.

Giddens, Anthony. 1979. *Central Problems in Social Theory: Action, Structure and Contradiction in Social Analysis.* Berkeley: University of California Press.

Gilmartin, Christina K., Gail Hershatter, Lisa Rofel, and Tyrene White, eds. 1994. *Engendering China: Women, Culture, and the State.* Cambridge: Harvard University Press.

Glenn, Evelyn Nakano. 1992. "From Servitude to Service Work: Historical Continuities in the Racial Division of Paid Reproductive Labor." *Signs: Journal of Women in Culture and Society* 18: 1–43.

Goldin, Claudia Dale. 1990. *Understanding the Gender Gap: An Economic History of American Women.* NBER Series on Long-Term Factors in Economic Development. New York: Oxford University Press.

Goldstein, Alice and Sidney Goldstein. 1996. "Migration Motivations and Outcomes: Permanent and Temporary Migrants Compared." Pp. 187–212 in *China: The Many Facets of Demographic Change,* edited by Alice Goldstein and Wang Feng. Brown University Studies in Population and Development. Boulder, Colo.: Westview Press.

Goldstein, Alice, Sidney Goldstein, and Shengzu Gu. 1993. "Determinants of Permanent and Temporary Mobility in Hubei Province, PRC." Pp. 85–101 in *International Population Conference/Congres international de la population, Montreal, August 24–September 1, 1993.* Vol. 2. Liège, Belgium: International Union for the Scientific Study of Population.

Goldstein, Sidney and Alice Goldstein. 1985. "Population Mobility in the People's Republic of China." Papers of the East-West Population Institute, no. 95. Honolulu: East-West Center.

———. 1990. "China." Pp. 63–83 in *International Handbook on Internal Migration,* edited by Charles B. Nam, William J. Serow, Jr., and David F. Sly. New York: Greenwood Press.

———. 1991. "Permanent and Temporary Migration Differentials in China." Papers of the East-West Population Institute, no. 117. Honolulu: East-West Center.

Goode, William J. 1963. *World Revolution and Family Patterns.* New York: Free Press of Glencoe.

Greenhalgh, Susan. 1985. "Sexual Stratification: The Other Side of 'Growth with Equity' in East Asia." *Population and Development Review* 11: 265–314.

———. 1988. "Fertility as Mobility: Sinic Transitions." *Population and Development Review* 14: 629–74.

———. 1994. "Controlling Births and Bodies in Village China." *American Ethnologist* 21: 3–30.

Griffin, Keith B., and Renwei Zhao, eds. 1993. *The Distribution of Income in China.* Houndmills, Basingstoke, Hampshire, England: St. Martin's Press.

Guo, Fei. 1996. "China's Internal Population Migration since the 1980s: Origins, Processes, and Impacts." Ph.D. dissertation, University of Hawaii at Manoa.

Guthrie, Douglas. 1997. "Between Markets and Politics: Organizational Responses to Reform in China." *American Journal of Sociology* 102: 1258–1304.

Hajnal, John. 1982. "Two Kinds of Preindustrial Household Formation Systems." *Population and Development Review* 8: 449–94.

Hall, Richard H. with Robert T. Buttram 1994. *Sociology of Work: Perspectives, Analyses, and Issues.* Pine Forge Press Social Science Library. Thousand Oaks, Calif.: Pine Forge Press.

Hare, Denise. 1995. "Gender and Wages in Rural China." Paper presented at the Triangle East Asia Colloquium, University of North Carolina at Chapel Hill, February.

Hareven, Tamara K. 1991. "The History of the Family and the Complexity of Social Change." *American Historical Review* 96: 95–124.

Harrell, Stevan. 1985. "Why Do the Chinese Work So Hard? Reflections on an Entreprenuerial Ethic." *Modern China* 11: 203–26.

———. 1993. "Geography, Demography, and Family Composition in Three Southwestern Villages." Pp. 77–102 in *Chinese Families in the Post-Mao Era*, edited by Deborah Davis and Stevan Harrell. Studies on China, 17. Berkeley: University of California Press.

Hay, John, ed. 1994. *Boundaries in China*. London: Reaktion Books.

Henderson, Gail E. 1990. "Increased Inequality in Health Care." Pp. 263–82 in *Chinese Society on the Eve of Tiananmen*, edited by Deborah Davis and Ezra F. Vogel. Harvard Contemporary China Series, 7. Cambridge: Harvard University Press.

Henderson, Gail E. and Myron S. Cohen. 1984. *The Chinese Hospital: A Socialist Work Unit*. New Haven: Yale University Press.

Henderson, Gail E., Barbara Entwisle, and Zhai Fengying. 1996. "'We Are Happy Even in Our Exhaustion: Women and Family Businesses in Shandong." Unpublished manuscript, Department of Social Medicine, University of North Carolina at Chapel Hill.

Hershatter, Gail. 1986. *The Workers of Tianjin 1900–1949*. Stanford, Calif.: Stanford University Press.

———. 1997. *Dangerous Pleasures: Prostitution and Modernity in Twentieth-Century Shanghai*. Berkeley: University of California Press.

Ho Ping-ti. 1962. *The Ladder of Success in Imperial China: Aspects of Social Mobility, 1368–1911*. Studies of the East Asian Institute, Columbia University. New York: Columbia University Press.

Hochschild, Arlie Russell. 1983. *The Managed Heart: Commercialization of Human Feeling*. Berkeley: University of California Press.

Hochschild, Arlie Russell with Anne Machung. 1989. *The Second Shift: Working Parents and the Revolution at Home*. New York: Viking.

Honig, Emily. 1986. *Sisters and Strangers: Women in the Shanghai Cotton Mills, 1919–1949*. Stanford, Calif.: Stanford University Press.

———. 1992. *Creating Chinese Ethnicity: Subei People in Shanghai, 1850–1980*. New Haven, Conn.: Yale University Press.

Honig, Emily and Gail Hershatter. 1988. *Personal Voices: Chinese Women in the 1980's*. Stanford, Calif.: Stanford University Press.

Howe, Christopher. 1971. "The Level and Structure of Employment and the Sources of Labor Supply in Shanghai, 1949–57." Pp. 215–34 in *The City in Communist China*, edited by John W. Lewis. Studies in Chinese Society. Stanford, Calif.: Stanford University Press.

Hsiao Kung-chuan. 1979. *A History of Chinese Political Thought*. Vol.1, *From the Beginnings to the Sixth Century A.D*, translated by Frederick W. Mote. Princeton Library of Asian Translations. Princeton, N.J.: Princeton University Press.

Hsü Cho-yün. 1980. *Han Agriculture: The Formation of Early Chinese Agrarian Economy, 206 B.C.–A.D. 220*. Vol. 2 of *Han Dynasty China*, edited by Jack L. Dull. Seattle: University of Washington Press.

Huang Liu-hung (Huang Liuhong). 1984. *A Complete Book Concerning Happiness and*

Benevolence (Fu-hui ch'üan-shu): A Manual for Local Magistrates in Seventeenth-Century China, translated and edited by Chu Djang. Tucson: University of Arizona Press.

Huang, Lucy Jen. 1963. "A Re-evaluation of the Primary Role of the Communist Chinese Woman: The Homemaker or the Worker." *Marriage and Family Living* 25: 162–66.

Huang, Philip C. C. 1990. *The Peasant Family and Rural Development in the Yangzi Delta, 1350–1988.* Stanford, Calif.: Stanford University Press.

Huang Shu-min. 1989. *The Spiral Road: Change in a Chinese Village through the Eyes of a Communist Party Leader.* Development, Conflict, and Social Change Series. Boulder, Colo.: Westview Press.

Huang Wei. 1991. "Crackdown on Abduction of Women and Children." *Beijing Review* 34(30): 24–27.

Huang Xiyi. 1990. "Zhongguo dangdai shehui bianyizhong nongcun funü jingji shenfen de zhuanhuan" (Transformations in the economic status of rural women in contemporary social changes in China). *Shehuixue yanjiu* (Sociology research) 6.

Hui Lan. 1991. "Gan dache" (Driving a cart). In *Caoyuan qishi lu* (Record of the grasslands). Beijing: Gongren chubanshe.

Ikels, Charlotte. 1996. *Return of the God of Wealth: The Transition to a Market Economy in Urban China.* Stanford, Calif.: Stanford University Press.

Jacka, Tamara. 1990. "Back to the Wok: Women and Employment in Chinese Industry in the 1980s." *Australian Journal of Chinese Affairs* 24, 1–23.

Jefferson, Gary H. and Thomas G. Rawski. 1992. "Unemployment, Underemployment, and Employment Policy in China's Cities." *Modern China* 18: 42–71.

Johnson, Graham E. 1993. "Family Strategies and Economic Transformation in Rural China: Some Evidence from the Pearl River Delta." Pp. 103–36 in *Chinese Families in the Post-Mao Era,* edited by Deborah Davis and Stevan Harrell. Berkeley: University of California Press.

Johnson, Kay Ann. 1976. "Women in the People's Republic of China." Pp. 62–103 in *Asian Women in Transition,* edited by Sylvia A. Chipp and Justin J. Green. University Park: Pennsylvania State University Press.

———. 1983. *Women, the Family, and Peasant Revolution in China.* Chicago: University of Chicago Press.

———. 1996. "The Politics of the Revival of Infant Abandonment in China, with Special Reference to Hunan." *Population and Development Review* 22: 77–98.

Johnson, Marshall, William L. Parish, and Elizabeth Lin. 1987. "Chinese Women, Rural Society, and External Markets." *Economic Development and Cultural Change* 35: 257–77.

Judd, Ellen R. 1994. *Gender and Power in Rural North China.* Stanford, Calif.: Stanford University Press.

Kalleberg, Arne L. and Rachel A. Rosenfeld. 1990. "Work in the Family and in the Labor Market: A Cross-National, Reciprocal Analysis." *Journal of Marriage and the Family* 52: 331–46.

Kamo, Yoshinori and Min Zhou. 1994. "Living Arrangements of Elderly Chinese and Japanese in the United States." *Journal of Marriage and the Family* 56: 544–58.

Kanjanapan, Wiliwan. 1989. "The Asian-American Traditional Household." Pp. 539–

56 in *Ethnicity and the New Family Economy: Living Arrangements and Intergenerational Financial Flows,* edited by Frances Goldscheider and Calvin Goldscheider. Boulder, Colo.: Westview Press.

King, Franklin Hiram. [1911] 1973. *Farmers of Forty Centuries, or, Permanent Agriculture in China, Korea and Japan.* Emmaus, Penn.: Rodale.

Knodel, John, Werasit Sittitrai, and Tim Brown. 1990. "Focus Group Discussions for Social Science Research: A Practical Guide with an Emphasis on the Topic of Aging." Comparative Study of the Elderly in Asia Research Reports. University of Michigan Population Studies Center Research Reports no. 90–3. Ann Arbor: Population Studies Center, University of Michigan.

Kondo, Dorinne K. 1990. *Crafting Selves: Power, Gender, and Discourses of Identity in a Japanese Workplace.* Chicago: University of Chicago Press.

Kriedte, Peter, Hans Medick, and Jurgen Schlumbohm. 1981. *Industrialization before Industrialization: Rural Industry in the Genesis of Capitalism,* translated by Beate Schempp. Studies in Modern Capitalism. Cambridge: Cambridge University Press.

Kuhn, Dieter. 1988. *Science and Civilisation in China,* edited by Joseph Needham. Vol. 5, *Chemistry and Chemical Technology,* part 9, *Textile Technology: Spinning and Reeling.* Cambridge: Cambridge University Press.

Kung, Lydia. 1983. *Factory Women in Taiwan.* Studies in Cultural Anthropology, no. 5. Ann Arbor, Mich.: UMI Research Press.

Lasch, Christopher. 1979. *Haven in a Heartless World: The Family Besieged.* New York: Basic Books.

Lau Siu-kai et al., eds. 1994. *Inequalities and Development: Social Stratification in Chinese Societies.* Hong Kong: Institute of Asia-Pacific Studies, Chinese University of Hong Kong.

Lavely, William. 1990. "Industrialization and Household Complexity in Rural Taiwan." *Social Forces* 69: 235–51.

———. 1991. "Marriage and Mobility under Rural Collectivism." Pp. 286–312 in *Marriage and Inequality in Chinese Society,* edited by Rubie S. Watson and Patricia Buckley Ebrey. Studies on China, 12. Berkeley: University of California Press.

Lee Ching-kwan. 1994. "Women Workers and Manufacturing Miracle: Gender, Labor Markets, and Production Politics in South China." Ph.D. dissertation, University of California at Berkeley.

———. 1995. "Engendering the Worlds of Labor: Women Workers, Labor Markets, and Production Politics in the South China Economic Miracle." *American Sociological Review* 60: 378–97.

Levy, Marion. 1949. *The Family Revolution in Modern China.* Cambridge: Harvard University Press.

Leyda, Jay. 1972. *Dianying: An Account of Films and the Film Audience in China.* Cambridge: MIT Press.

"Li Shuang-shuang." 1963. *Chinese Literature* 5 (May): 105–10.

Liang Heng and Judith Shapiro. 1983. *Son of the Revolution.* New York: Alfred A. Knopf.

Liang Jianmin and Chen Shengli, eds. 1993. *Quanguo shengyu jieyu chouyang diaocha fenxi shujujuan.* (Data volumes of the National Fertility and Birth Control Survey). Beijing: Zhongguo renkou chubanshe.

Liang Zai. 1996. "Market Transition, Foreign Investment, and Temporary Migration: The Case of Shenzhen Special Economic Zone, China, 1979–1994." Paper presented at the annual meeting of the Population Association of America, New Orleans, 9–11 May.

Liang Zai and Michael J. White. 1996. "Internal Migration in China, 1950–1988." *Demography* 33: 375–84.

Lim, Linda Y. C. 1983. "Capitalism, Imperialism, and Patriarchy: The Dilemma of Third-World Women Workers in Multinational Factories." Pp. 70–91 in *Women, Men, and the International Division of Labor,* edited by June Nash and María P. Fernández-Kelly. SUNY Series in the Anthropology of Work. Albany: State University of New York Press.

————. 1990. "Women's Work in Export Factories: The Politics of a Cause." In *Women Workers and Global Restructuring,* edited by Kathryn Ward. Cornell International Industrial and Labor Relations Report no. 17. Ithaca, N.Y.: ILR Press, School of Industrial and Labor Relations, Cornell University.

Lin Nan. 1982. "Social Resources and Instrumental Action." Pp. 131–45 in *Social Structure and Network Analysis,* edited by Peter V. Marsden and Nan Lin. Sage Focus Editions no. 57. Beverly Hills, Calif.: Sage.

————. 1994. "Institutional Capital and Work Attainment." Department of Sociology, Duke University, Durham, North Carolina.

————. 1995. "Local Market Socialism: Local Corporatism in Action in Rural China." *Theory and Society* 24: 301–54.

————. 2000. *Social Capital: A Theory of Social Structure and Action.* New York: Cambridge University Press.

Lin Nan and Yanjie Bian. 1988. "Status Attainment and Social Resources in a Chinese Labor Structure." Paper presented at the annual meeting of the American Sociological Association, Atlanta, 9–13 August.

————. 1991. "Getting Ahead in Urban China." *American Journal of Sociology* 97: 657–88.

Lin Nan and Jay Chih-jou Chen. 1999. "Local Elites as Officials and Owners: Shareholding and Property Rights Transformation in Daqiuzhuang Industry." Pp. 145–170 in *Property Rights and Economic Reform in China,* edited by Jean C. Oi and Andrew G. Walder. Stanford, Calif.: Stanford University Press.

Liu Bohong. 1995. "Zhongguo nüxing jiuye zhuangkuang" (Situation of women's employment in China). *Shehuixue yanjiu* (Sociology research) 56: 39–48.

Liu Shouzhi and Luo Yafu. 1953. "Nongye laomo Cao Zhuxiang daitou xuexi xianjin jingyan" (Agricultural labor model Cao Zhuxiang takes the lead in learning from advanced experience). *Xibei funü huabao* (Northwest women's pictorial) (Xian), 1 May.

Liu Xiang. 1983. *Gu lienü zhuan* (Biographies of women). Wenyuange Siku quanshu edition. Taipei: Taiwan shangwu yinshu guan. Vol. 448: 1–73.

Lobao, Linda and Katherine Meyer. 1995. "Economic Decline, Gender, and Labor Flexibility in Family-Based Enterprises: Midwestern Farming in the 1980s." *Social Forces* 74: 575–608.

Loefgren, Ovar. 1984. "Family and Household." Pp. 446–70 in *Households: Comparative and Historical Studies of the Domestic Group,* edited by Robert McC. Netting, Richard R. Wilk, and Eric J. Arnould. Berkeley: University of California Press.

Loh Wai-fong. 1984. "From Romantic Love to Class Struggle: Reflections on the Film *Liu Sanjie.*" Pp. 165–76 in *Popular Chinese Literature and Performing Arts in the People's Republic of China, 1949–1979,* edited by Bonnie S. McDougall. Berkeley: University of California Press.

Mann, Susan. 1991. "Grooming a Daughter for Marriage: Brides and Wives in the Mid-Ch'ing Period." Pp. 204–30 in *Marriage and Inequality in Chinese Society,* edited by Rubie S. Watson and Patricia Buckley Ebrey. Studies on China, 12. Berkeley: University of California Press.

———. 1992. "Household Handicrafts and State Policy in Qing Times." Pp. 75–95 in *To Achieve Security and Wealth: The Qing Imperial State and the Economy, 1644–1911,* edited by Jane Kate Leonard and John R. Watt. Cornell East Asia Series, no. 56. Ithaca, N.Y.: East Asia Program, Cornell University.

———. 1997. *Precious Records: Women in China's Long Eighteenth Century.* Stanford, Calif.: Stanford University Press.

McDermott, Joseph P. 1990. "The Chinese Domestic Bursar." *Ajia Bunka Kenkyû* (November): 15–32.

Mencius. *The Works of Mencius.* [1893–95] 1960. Vol. 2 of *The Chinese Classics: With a Translation, Critical and Exegetical Notes, Prolegomena, and Copious Indexes,* edited and translated by James Legge. 3d edition, with a biographical note by Lindsay Ride. Hong Kong: Hong Kong University Press.

Mincer, Jacob and Yoshio Higuchi. 1988. "Wage Structures and Labor Turnover in the United States and Japan." *Journal of the Japanese and International Economies* 2: 97–133.

Mintz, Sidney W. 1985. *Sweetness and Power: The Place of Sugar in Modern History.* New York: Viking Press.

Moen, Phyllis and Elaine Wethington. 1992. "The Concept of Family Adaptive Strategies." *Annual Review of Sociology* 18: 233–51.

Moore, Sally Falk. 1978. *Law as Process: An Anthropological Approach.* London: Routledge & Kegan Paul.

Morris, Morris D. 1965. *The Emergence of an Industrial Labor Force in India: A Study of the Bombay Cotton Mills, 1854–1947.* Berkeley: University of California Press.

———. 1983. "The Growth of Large-Scale Industry to 1947." Pp. 553–676 in *The Cambridge Economic History of India.* Vol. 2, *c. 1757–c. 1970,* edited by Dharma Kumar. Cambridge: Cambridge University Press.

Munn, Nancy D. 1986. *The Fame of Gawa: A Symbolic Study of Value Transformation in a Massim (Papua New Guinea) Society.* Lewis Henry Morgan Lectures, 1976. Cambridge: Cambridge University Press.

Nash, June and María Patricia Fernández-Kelly, eds. 1983. *Women, Men, and the International Division of Labor.* SUNY Series in the Anthropology of Work. Albany: State University of New York Press.

Nee, Victor. 1989. "A Theory of Market Transition: From Redistribution to Markets in State Socialism." *American Sociological Review* 54: 663–81.

———. 1991. "Social Inequalities in Reforming State Socialism: Between Redistribution and Markets in China." *American Sociological Review* 56: 267–82.

———. 1992. "Organizational Dynamics of Market Transition: Hybrid Forms, Property Rights, and Mixed Economy in China." *Administrative Science Quarterly* 37: 1–27.

———. 1996. "The Emergence of a Market Society: Changing Mechanisms of Stratification in China." *American Journal of Sociology* 101: 908–49.

Nee, Victor, and Rebecca Matthews. 1996. "Market Transition and Societal Transformation in Reforming State Socialism." *Annual Review of Sociology* 22: 401–35.

Nee, Victor and Frank W. Young. 1991. "Peasant Entrepreneurs in China's 'Second Economy': An Institutional Analysis." *Economic Development and Cultural Change* 39: 293–310.

Nishijima, Sadao. 1986. "The Economic and Social History of Former Han." Pp. 545–607 in *The Cambridge History of China. Vol. 1, The Ch'in and Han Empires, 221 B.C.–A.D. 220*, edited by Denis Twitchett and Michael Loewe. Cambridge: Cambridge University Press.

Nuo Yi. 1995. "Lüse de chengnuo" (The green promise). Pp. 59–71 in *Wushige Beijing nüzhiqing de zishu* (Accounts by fifty female Beijing sent-down youth), edited by Liu Zhongluo, Zang Jian, and Tian Xiaoye. Beijing: Beijing daxue chubanshe.

Odgaard, Ole. 1992. *Private Enterprises in Rural China: Impact on Agriculture and Social Stratification.* Aldershot, Hants., England; Avebury, Brookfield, Vt.: Ashgate.

Ong, Aihwa. 1987. *Spirits of Resistance and Capitalist Discipline: Factory Women in Malaysia.* SUNY Series in the Anthropology of Work. Albany: State University of New York Press.

Oppenheimer, Valerie Kincade. 1970. *The Female Labor Force in the United States: Demographic and Economic Factors Governing Its Growth and Changing Composition.* Population Monograph Series, no. 5. Berkeley: Institute of International Studies, University of California.

Ortner, Sherry B. 1974. "Is Female to Male as Nature Is to Culture?" Pp. 67–87 in *Women, Culture, and Society,* edited by Michelle Z. Rosaldo and Louise Lamphere. Stanford, Calif.: Stanford University Press.

Ostrander, Susan. 1984. *Women of the Upper Class.* Women in the Political Economy. Philadelphia: Temple University Press.

Pan Yun-kang and Nan Lin. 1987. "Contemporary Family Models in Urban China." *Shehuixue Yanjiu* (Sociology research) 3: 54–67.

Papanek, Hanna. 1990. "To Each Less Than She Needs, from Each More Than She Can Do: Allocations, Entitlements, and Value." Pp. 162–81 in *Persistent Inequalities: Women and World Development,* edited by Irene Tinker. New York: Oxford University Press.

Parish, William L. 1981. "Egalitarianism in Chinese Society." *Problems of Communism* 30 (January-February): 37–53.

———. 1984a. "Destratification in China." Pp. 84–120 in *Class and Social Stratification in Post-Revolution China,* edited by James L. Watson. Contemporary China Institute Publications. Cambridge: Cambridge University Press.

———. 1984b. "The Family and Economic Change." Pp. 222–42 in *China: The 80s Era,* edited by Norton Ginsburg and Bernard A. Lalor. Westview Special Studies on East Asia. Boulder, Colo.: Westview Press.

Parish, William L., Chonglin Shen, and Chi-hsiang Chang. 1997. "Family Support Networks in the Chinese Countryside." USC Seminar Series, no. 11. Hong Kong: Institute of Asia-Pacific Studies, Chinese University of Hong Kong.

Parish, William L. and Ethan Michelson. 1996. "Politics and Markets: Dual Transformations." *American Journal of Sociology* 101: 1042–59.

Parish, William L. and Martin King Whyte. 1978. *Village and Family in Contemporary China*. Chicago: University of Chicago Press.

Parish, William L. and Robert J. Willis. 1993. "Daughters, Education, and Family Budgets: Taiwan Experiences." *Journal of Human Resources* 28: 863–98.

Parish, William L. and Xiaoye Zhe. 1995. "Education and Work in Rural China: Opportunities for Men and Women." Population Research Center Discussion Paper Series, no. 95–5. Chicago: Population Research Center, National Opinion Research Center, University of Chicago.

Parish, William L., Xiaoye Zhe, and Fang Li. 1995. "Nonfarm Work and Marketization of the Chinese Countryside." *The China Quarterly* 143: 697–731.

Pavalko, Eliza K. and Glen H. Elder, Jr. 1993. "Women behind the Men: Variations in Wives' Support of Husbands' Careers." *Gender and Society* 7: 548–66.

Pedraza, Silvia. 1991. "Women and Migration: The Social Consequences of Gender." *Annual Review of Sociology* 17: 303–25.

Peking Review Staff. 1978. "Mobilizing Women for the New Long March." *Peking Review* 21(39): 3.

Peng Xizhe. 1995. "New Urban Residents: Vulnerable Migrant Women Bolster China's Economic Development." *China Population Today* 12 (December): 4–5.

Peng Yusheng. 1992. "Wage Determination in Rural and Urban China: A Comparison of Public and Private Industrial Sectors." *American Sociological Review* 57: 198–213.

People's Republic of China. *Quanguo Renmin Daibiao Dahui*. 1983. *Fifth Session of the Fifth National People's Congress (Main Documents)*. Beijing: Foreign Language Press.

Pepper, Suzanne. 1990. *China's Education Reform in the 1980s: Policies, Issues, and Historical Perspectives*. China Research Monograph 36. Berkeley: Center for Chinese Studies, Institute of East Asian Studies, University of California at Berkeley.

Perkins, Dwight. 1994. "Completing China's Move to the Market." *Journal of Economic Perspectives* 8: 23–46.

Polivka, Anne and Thomas Nardone. 1989. "On the Definition of 'Contingent' Work." *Monthly Labor Review* 112 (12): 9–16.

Portes, Alejandro and Saskia Sassen-Koob. 1987. "Making It Underground: Comparative Material on the Informal Sector in Western Market Economies." *American Journal of Sociology* 93: 30–61.

Portes, Alejandro and Min Zhou. 1996. "Self-Employment and the Earnings of Immigrants." *American Sociological Review* 61: 219–30.

Potter, Sulamith Heins and Jack M. Potter. 1990. *China's Peasants: The Anthropology of a Revolution*. Cambridge: Cambridge University Press.

Presser, Harriet B. 1989. "Can We Make Time for Children? The Economy, Work, and Child Care." *Demography* 26: 523–43.

Pruitt, Ida. 1967. *A Daughter of Han: The Autobiography of a Chinese Working Woman. From the Story Told Her by Ning Lao T'ai-t'ai*. Stanford, Calif.: Stanford University Press.

Putterman, Louis. 1995. "The Role of Ownership and Property Rights in China's Economic Transition." *China Quarterly* 144: 1047–64.

Quan Hansheng. [1935] 1979. "Songdai nüzi zhiye yu shengji" (Occupations and livelihood of women in the Song Dynasty). Pp. 193–204 in *Zhongguo funüshi lunji* (Collected essays on the history of Chinese women), edited by Bao Jialin. Reprint. Taipei: Daoxiang chubanshe.

Quataert, Jean H. 1985. "Combining Agrarian and Industrial Livelihood: Rural Households in the Saxon Oberlausitz in the Nineteenth Century." *Journal of Family History* 10: 145–62.

Ran Maoying. 1988. "Women's Employment Challenge." *Beijing Review* 13(28): 29–30.

Rapp, Rayna. 1979. "Examining Family History: Household and Family." *Feminist Studies* 5: 175–81.

Renmin ribao (People's daily). (Beijing.) 1983. "Female Infanticide in China." 7 April.

Reskin, Barbara F. and Irene Padavic. 1994. *Women and Men at Work.* Sociology for a New Century. Thousand Oaks, Calif.: Pine Forge Press.

Reskin, Barbara F., and Patricia A. Roos. 1990. *Job Queues, Gender Queues: Explaining Women's Inroads into Male Occupations.* Women in the Political Economy. Philadelphia: Temple University Press.

Riley, Nancy. 1994. "Interwoven Lives: Parents, Marriage and Guanxi in China." *Journal of Marriage and Family* 56: 791–803.

Ritchie, Mark A. 1994. "Hybrid Classes and Diversification: Household Strategies and Interpenetration in Rural Northern Thailand." Paper presented at the Northwest Regional Consortium for Southeast Asian Studies Conference, Seattle.

Roberts, Kenneth D., and Wei Jinsheng. 1996. "The Floating Population in Shanghai." Paper presented at the annual meeting of the Population Association of America, New Orleans, 9–11 May.

Rodenburg, Janet. 1993. "Emancipation or Subordination? Consequences of Female Migration for Migrants and Their Families." Pp. 273–89 in *Internal Migration of Women in Developing Countries,* edited by Richard E. Bilsborrow. ST/ESA/SER.R/127. New York: United Nations.

Rofel, Lisa. 1999. *Other Modernities: Gendered Yearnings in China after Socialism.* Berkeley: University of California Press.

Rosenfeld, Rachel Ann. 1985. *Farm Women: Work, Farm, and Family in the United States.* Chapel Hill: University of North Carolina Press.

———. 1993. "Women's Part-Time Employment: The Influence of Country Context." Paper presented at the meeting of Research Committee no. 28 of the International Sociological Association, Durham, North Carolina.

———. 1996. "Women's Work Histories." Pp. 199–222 in *Fertility in the United States: New Patterns, New Theories,* edited by John B. Casterline, Ronald D. Lee, and Karen A. Foote. Supplement to *Population and Development Review* 22. New York: Population Council.

Rosenfeld, Rachel A. and Gunn E. Birkelund. 1995. "Women's Part-Time Work: A Cross-National Comparison." *European Sociological Review* 11: 111–34.

Rosenfeld, Rachel A., Mark E. Van Buren, and Arne L. Kalleberg. 1998. "Gender Differences in Supervisory Authority: Variation among Advanced Industrialized Democracies." *Social Science Research* 27: 23–49.

Rosenzweig, Mark R. 1980. "Neoclassical Theory and the Optimizing Peasant: An Econometric Analysis of Market Family Labor Supply in a Developing Country." *Quarterly Journal of Economics* 94: 31–55.

Rozelle, Scott and Leying Jiang. 1994. "Survival Strategies and Recession in China's Agricultural Economy." Paper presented at the annual meeting of the Association for Asian Studies, Boston.

Rublee, Maria Rost. n.d. "Gender Inequality in Pre- and Post-Reform China: Assessing the Trends." Unpublished paper, Department of Sociology, George Washington University, Washington, D.C..

Rural Economy Research Center of China's Ministry of Agriculture. 1996. "Zhongguo nongcun laodongli liudong yanjiu: Waichuzhe yu shuchudi" (Research on China's rural labor out-migration: Out-migrants and origins of migration). Paper presented at the International Conference on Rural Labor Migration in China, Beijing, June.

Sabin, Lora. 1994. "New Bosses in the Workers' State: The Growth of Non-State Sector Employment in China." *The China Quarterly* 140: 944–70.

Sachs, Carol. 1983. *The Invisible Farmers*. Totowa, N.J.: Rowman and Allanheld.

Sacks, Karen. 1974. "Engels Revisited: Women, the Organization of Production, and Private Property." Pp. 207–22 in *Women, Culture, and Society*, edited by Michelle Z. Rosaldo and Louise Lamphere. Stanford, Calif.: Stanford University Press.

Salaff, Janet W. 1981. *Working Daughters of Hong Kong: Filial Piety or Power in the Family*. Arnold and Caroline Rose Monograph Series of the American Sociological Association. Cambridge: Cambridge University Press.

Sangren, P. Steven. 1984. "Traditional Chinese Corporations: Beyond Kinship." *Journal of Asian Studies* 43: 391–415.

———. 1996. "Value Transformation/Appropriation and Gender in Chinese Local Ritual Organization and Practices." Paper presented at the annual meeting of the Association for Asian Studies, Honolulu, 11–14 April.

Schneider, Jane. 1985. "Trousseau as Treasure: Some Contradictions of Late Nineteenth-Century Change in Sicily." Pp. 81–119 in *The Marriage Bargain: Women and Dowries in European History*, edited by Marion A. Kaplan. Women in History, no. 10. New York: Institute for Research in History and Haworth Press.

Schultz, T. Paul, ed. 1995. *Investment in Women's Human Capital*. Chicago: University of Chicago Press.

Schultz, Theodore W. 1961. "Investment in Human Capital." *The American Economic Review* 51(1): 1–17.

———, ed. 1974. *Economics of the Family: Marriage, Children, and Human Capital: A Conference Report of the National Bureau of Economic Research*. Chicago: University of Chicago Press for the National Bureau of Economic Research.

Shanghai tongji nianjian 1995 (Statistical yearbook of Shanghai 1995). 1996. Shanghai: Shanghai renmin chubanshe.

Shanghai tongji ziliao (Shanghai statistical materials). 1980–1983.

Shen, Conglin and Shanhua Yang. 1995. *Dangdai Zhongguo chengshi jiating yanjiu* (Research on contemporary Chinese urban families). Beijing: Zhongguo shehui kexue chubanshe.

Sheng Fengluan. 1991. "Shei shuo funü buneng jin changyuan?" (Who says women cannot enter the threshing ground?) In *Caoyuan qishi lu* (Record of the grasslands). Beijing: Gongren chubanshe.

Short, Susan E. and Zhai Fengying. 1996. "Household Production and Household Structure in the Context of China's Economic Reforms." *Social Forces* 75: 691–716.

Siu, Helen F. 1989. *Agents and Victims in South China: Accomplices in Rural Revolution*. New Haven, Conn.: Yale University Press.

———. 1993. "Reconstituting Dowry and Brideprice in South China." Pp. 165–88 in *Chinese Families in the Post-Mao Era,* edited by Deborah Davis and Stevan Harrell. Studies on China, 17. Berkeley: University of California Press.

Skinner, G. William. 1964–65. "Marketing and Social Structure in Rural China: Part 1." *Journal of Asian Studies* 24: 3–43.

———. 1965. "Marketing and Social Structure in Rural China: Part 2." *Journal of Asian Studies* 24: 195–228.

———. 1976. "Mobility Strategies in Late Imperial China: A Regional Systems Analysis." Pp. 327–64 in *Regional Analysis.* Vol. 1, *Economic Systems,* edited by Carol A. Smith. Studies in Anthropology. New York: Academic Press.

Smith, Arthur Henderson. 1894. *Chinese Characteristics.* New York: Fleming H. Revell.

Smith, Thomas C. 1959. *The Agrarian Origins of Modern Japan.* Stanford Studies in the Civilizations of Eastern Asia. Stanford, Calif.: Stanford University Press.

Solinger, Dorothy J. 1993. "China's Transients and the State: A Form of Civil Society?" *Politics and Society* 21: 91–122.

———. 1995a. "China's Urban Transients in the Transition from Socialism and the Collapse of the Communist 'Urban Public Goods Regime.'" *Comparative Politics* 27: 127–46.

———. 1995b. "The Chinese Work Unit and Transient Labor in the Transition from Socialism." *Modern China* 21: 155–83.

———. 1995c. "The Floating Population in Cities: Chances for Assimilation?" Pp. 113–39 in *Urban Spaces in Contemporary China: The Potential for Autonomy and Community in Post-Mao China,* edited by Deborah Davis. Woodrow Wilson Center Series. Washington, D.C.: Woodrow Wilson Center Press; Cambridge: Cambridge University Press.

———. 1999. *Contesting Citizenship in Urban China: Peasant Migrants, the State, and the Logic of the Market.* Berkeley: University of California Press.

Sørensen, Annemette and Heike Trappe. 1995. "The Persistence of Gender Inequality in Earnings in the German Democratic Republic." *American Sociological Review* 60: 398–406.

Stacey, Judith. 1983. *Patriarchy and Socialist Revolution in China.* Berkeley: University of California Press.

Stark, David. 1996. "Recombinant Property in East European Capitalism." *American Journal of Sociology* 101: 993–1027.

State Statistical Bureau. 1987. "High Employment Rate among Urban Women." *Beijing Review: A Chinese Weekly of News and Views* 30(41): 23–24.

———. 1992. *Zhongguo tongji nianjian 1991* (Statistical yearbook of China 1991). Beijing: Statistical Publishing House of China.

———. 1993. *Zhongguo tongji nianjian 1992* (Statistical yearbook of China 1992). Beijing: Statistical Publishing House of China.

———. 1995. *Zhongguo tongji nianjian 1994* (Statistical yearbook of China 1994). Beijing: Statistical Publishing House of China.

———. 1996. *Zhongguo tongji nianjian 1995* (Statistical yearbook of China 1995). Beijing: Statistical Publishing House of China.

Stewart, David W. and Prem N. Shamdasani. 1990. *Focus Groups: Theory and Practice.* Applied Social Research Methods Series, vol. 20. Newbury Park, Calif.: Sage.

Stichter, Sharon. 1990. "Women, Employment and the Family: Current Debates." Pp. 11–71 in *Women, Employment, and the Family in the International Division of La-*

bor, edited by Sharon Stichter and Jane L. Parpart. Women in the Political Economy. Philadelphia: Temple University Press.

Stockard, Janice E. 1989. *Daughters of the Canton Delta: Marriage Patterns and Economic Strategies in South China, 1860–1930.* Stanford, Calif.: Stanford University Press.

Stockman, Norman. 1994. "Gender Inequality and Social Structure in Urban China." *Sociology* 28: 759–77.

Summary of World Broadcasts (Asia Pacific). 1997. FE 2966 P.G/3. 9 July.

Sun, Lena H. 1992. "Abduction, Sale of Women Reemerges from China's Past." *The Washington Post* (21 June): A-1.

Survey of the China Mainland Press (Hong Kong). 1951a. "31 Girls Trained as Tractor Operators in Peking Suburbs." No. 78 (5 March).

———. 1951b. "Women Crew of 'March 8th' Locomotive Take Up Challenge of Society Sisters." No. 139 (20 July): 11.

———. 1953. "Chinese Women in Construction Work." No. 609 (11 July): 9.

———. 1962. "Women Tractor Drivers and Technicians in China's Rural Communes." No. 2692 (1 March): 20.

———. 1970. "Woman Turbine Generator Operator in Shanghai." No. 4618 (12 March): 100.

———. 1971a. "Chinese Women Electricians Conduct Free Live-Line Operation." No. 4862 (11 March): 25.

———. 1971b. "Iron Girls' Oil Extracting Team in Tach'ing." No. 4876 (1 April): 77.

———. 1972a. "Workers' Wives in Northeast China City Take Part in Socialist Construction." No. 5088 (25 February): 125.

———. 1972b. "Chinese Women Start an Oil Refinery." No. 5095 (6 March): 180.

———. 1972c. "Housewives Start Factory from Scratch in Central China Province." No. 5096 (7 March).

———. 1972d. "Housewives Co-op in Shanghai Makes Tele-Communication Equipment." No. 5097 (9 March).

———. 1972e. "Policewomen in Shanghai." No. 5267 (21 November): 212.

———. 1973a. "More Women in Shanghai Engaged in Productive Work." No. 5341 (14 March): 17.

———. 1973b. "Women Electricians on Southwest China Plateau." No. 5405 (19 June): 213.

Survey of People's Republic of China Press. 1975a. "Steerswomen on Yangtze River Liner." No. 833 (6 April): 126.

———. 1975b. "Wives of Workers Run Farms at Northwest China Oilfield." No. 5615 (5 May): 97.

———. 1976. "More Peking Housewives Join Productive Labor." No. 6085 (19 April): 250.

Szelényi, Iván. 1978. "Social Inequalities in State Socialist Redistributive Economies: Dilemmas for Social Policy in Contemporary Socialist Societies of Eastern Europe." *International Journal of Comparative Sociology* 19: 63–87.

Szelényi, Iván and Eric Kostello. 1996. "The Market Transition Debate: Toward a Synthesis?" *American Journal of Sociology* 101: 1082–96.

Tang Wenfang and William L. Parish. 2000. *Market Transition in Urban China: The Changing Social Contract.* Cambridge: Cambridge University Press.

Tang Yan. 1965. "Qixiannü chayang shensu rufei" (The seven fairy maidens transplant rice seedlings as if they were flying), *Zhongguo funü* (Chinese women) 7 (April): 3–4.

Tausky, Curt. 1984. *Work and Society: An Introduction to Industrial Society.* Itasca, Ill.: F. E. Peacock.

Tawney, Richard Henry. 1932. *Land and Labour in China.* London: Allen & Unwin.

Taylor, Jeffery R. 1988. "Rural Employment Trends and the Legacy of Surplus Labour, 1978–1986." *The China Quarterly* 116: 736–66.

Tefft, Sheila. 1994. "Abduction of Women, Children Rises in China." *The Christian Science Monitor* (24 May): 13.

Thøgersen, Stig. 1990. *Secondary Education in China after Mao: Reform and Social Conflict.* Aarhus, Denmark: Aarhus University Press.

Thorne, Barrie with Marilyn Yalom, eds. 1982. *Rethinking the Family: Some Feminist Questions.* New York: Longman.

Tiano, Susan. 1990. "Maquiladora Women: A New Category of Workers?" Pp. 193–223 in *Women Workers and Global Restructuring,* edited by Kathryn B. Ward. Cornell International Industrial and Labor Relations Report, no. 17. Ithaca, N.Y.: ILR Press, School of Industrial and Labor Relations, Cornell University.

Tiefenthaler, Jill. 1997. "The Productivity Gains of Marriage: Effects of Spousal Education on Own Productivity across Market Sectors in Brazil." *Economic Development and Cultural Change* 45: 633–50.

Tinker, Irene. 1990. *Persistent Inequalities: Women and World Development.* New York: Oxford University Press.

Tomaskovic-Devey, Donald J. and Barbara J. Risman. 1993. "Telecommuting Innovation and Organization: A Contingency Theory of Labor Process Change." *Social Science Quarterly* 74: 367–85.

Topley, Marjorie. 1975. "Marriage Resistance in Rural Kwangtung." Pp. 67–88 in *Women in Chinese Society,* edited by Margery Wolf and Roxane Witke. Studies in Chinese Society. Stanford, Calif.: Stanford University Press.

Trappe, Heike and Rachel A. Rosenfeld. 1998. "Gender Inequality at Work in the Early Adult Life Course: A Comparison of Job Shifting Patterns in the Former East Germany and the Former West Germany." *European Sociological Review* 14: 343–68.

Tsui Ming. 1989. "Changes in Chinese Urban Family Structure." *Journal of Marriage and Family* 51: 737–47.

Tung Mei. 1974. "She's Walked across China." *China Reconstructs* 23 (July): 44–45.

Unger, Jonathan. 1993. " Urban Families in the Eighties: An Analysis of Chinese Surveys." Pp. 25–49 in *Chinese Families in the Post-Mao Era,* edited by Deborah Davis and Stevan Harrell. Studies on China, 17. Berkeley: University of California Press.

U.S. Bureau of Labor Statistics. 1995. *Contingent and Alternative Employment Arrangements.* Report 900. Washington, D.C.: Bureau of Labor Statistics, United States Department of Labor.

U.S. Bureau of the Census. 1993. *Statistical Abstract of the United States. The National Data Book.* 113th ed. Washington, D.C.: Bureau of the Census, Economics and Statistics Administration, U.S. Department of Commerce.

———. 1998. *Statistical Abstract of the United States. The National Data Book.* 118th ed.

(online). Available: http://www.lexis-nexis.com/statuniv/Statistical Abstracts. (18 October 1999).

Vermeer, Eduard. 1988. *Economic Development in Provincial China: The Central Shaanxi since 1930.* Contemporary China Institute Publications. Cambridge: Cambridge University Press.

Walder, Andrew G. 1984. "Communist Neo-Traditionalism, and 'The Remaking of the Chinese Working Class: 1949–1981.'" *Modern China* 10(1): 3–48.

———. 1986. *Communist Neo-Traditionalism: Work and Authority in Chinese Industry.* Berkeley: University of California Press.

———. 1992a. "Markets and Political Change in Rural China: A Property Rights Analysis." Paper presented at the annual meeting of the Public Choice Society, New Orleans.

———. 1992b. "Property Rights and Stratification in Socialist Redistributive Economies." *American Sociological Review* 57: 524–39.

———. 1995a. "Career Mobility and the Communist Political Order." *American Sociological Review* 60: 309–28.

———, ed. 1995b. *The Waning of the Communist State: Economic Origins of Political Decline in China and Hungary.* Studies on China, 21. Berkeley: University of California Press.

———. 1996. "Markets and Inequality in Transitional Economies: Toward Testable Theories." *American Journal of Sociology* 101: 1060–73.

Waldron, Arthur. 1990. *The Great Wall of China.* New York: Cambridge University Press.

Wang Feng. 1997a. "The Breakdown of a Great Wall: Recent Changes in Household Registration System in China." Pp. 149–165 in *Floating Population and Migration in China: The Impact of Economic Reform,* edited by Thomas Sharping. Hamburg: Institute of Asian Studies.

———. 1997b. "Invisible Walls within Cities." Paper presented at Harvard University, May.

Wang Feng and Xuejin Zuo. 1996. "Rural Migrants in Shanghai: Current Success and Future Promise." Paper presented at the International Conference on Rural Labor Migration in China, Beijing, June.

Wang Sheng Jin. 1995. "Industrial Transformation and Population Migration in China." *Asian People and Cities* (Newsletter of the Urban Information Center of Kobe) 20: 7–14.

Wang Sijun. 1994. "A Review of Population Development." Pp. 1–38 in *The Population of China towards the Twenty-First Century: Zhejiang Volume,* edited by Changde Ye, Yuanzhong Ding, Sijun Wang, and Peiyun Dong. Beijing: China Statistics Publishing House.

Wank, David L. 1995. "Symbiotic Alliance of Entrepreneurs and Officials: The Logics of Private Sector Expansion in a South China City." In *The Waning of the Communist State: Economic Origins of Political Decline in China and Hungary,* edited by Andrew G. Walder. Studies on China, 21. Berkeley: University of California Press.

Ward, Kathryn B. 1988. "Women in the Global Economy." *Women and Work: An Annual Review* 3: 17–48.

———. 1990a. "Introduction and Overview." Pp. 1–22 in *Women Workers and Global Restructuring*, edited by Kathryn B. Ward. Cornell International Industrial and Labor Relations Report, no. 17. Ithaca, N.Y.: ILR Press, School of Industrial and Labor Relations, Cornell University.

———, ed. 1990b. *Women Workers and Global Restructuring*. Cornell International Industrial and Labor Relations Report, no. 17. Ithaca, N.Y.: ILR Press, School of Industrial and Labor Relations, Cornell University.

Watson, James L. 1980a. "Slavery as an Institution: Open and Closed Systems." Introduction (pp. 1–15) to *Asian and African Systems of Slavery*, edited by James L. Watson. Berkeley: University of California Press.

———. 1980b. "Transactions in People: The Chinese Market in Slaves, Servants, and Heirs." Pp. 223–50 in *Asian and African Systems of Slavery*, edited by James L. Watson. Berkeley: University of California Press.

Weinan diqu nongye hezuo shi bianweihui bian. 1993. *Weinan diqu nongye hezuo shiliao* (Historical material on agricultural cooperation in Weinan district). Chief editor: Li Xiyuan. Xian: Shaanxi renmin chubanshe.

Weinan xian Baiyang gongshe Hongxing shengchan dadui dang zhibu shuji Cao Zhuxiang mofan shiji danxing cailiao (Single material on the model activities of Party branch secretary Cao Zhuxiang, Red Star production brigade, Baiyang commune, Weinan county). 1962. (Handwritten ms.) In records of Hongxing village, Weinan. 3 March.

Weinan xian minzhu Fulian hui. 1952. *Weinan xian di wu qu liu xiang Cao Zhuxiang pingwei xian mianhua fengchan hu danxing cailiao* (Material on Cao Zhuxiang of the sixth township, fifth district, Weinan county, being chosen as a bumper cotton crop household). (178–27–026). Women's Federation Archives held in the Shaanxi Provincial Archives, Xian. February-December.

Weiner, Lynn Y. 1985. *From Working Girl to Working Mother: The Female Labor Force in the United States, 1820–1980*. Chapel Hill: University of North Carolina Press.

Whyte, Martin King. 1974. *Small Groups and Political Rituals in China*. Berkeley: University of California Press.

———. 1978. *The Status of Women in Preindustrial Societies*. Princeton, N.J.: Princeton University Press.

———. 1984. "Sexual Inequality under Socialism: The Chinese Case in Perspective." Pp. 198–238 in *Class and Social Stratification in Post-Revolution China*, edited by James L. Watson. New York: Cambridge University Press.

———. 1990. "Changes in Mate Choice in Chengdu." Pp. 181–213 in *Chinese Society on the Eve of Tiananmen*, edited by Deborah Davis and Ezra Vogel. Cambridge: Harvard University Press.

———. 1993. "Wedding Behavior and Family Strategies in Chengdu." Pp. 189–218 in *Chinese Families in the Post-Mao Era*, edited by Deborah Davis and Stevan Harrell. Berkeley: University of California Press.

———. 1996. "The Chinese Family and Economic Development: Obstacle or Engine?" *Economic Development and Cultural Change* 45: 1–30.

Whyte, Martin King and William L. Parish. 1984. *Urban Life in Contemporary China*. Chicago: University of Chicago Press.

Wiens, Mi Chu. 1980. "Lord and Peasant: The Sixteenth to the Eighteenth Century." *Modern China* 6(1): 3–39.

Wilbur, C. Martin. 1943. *Slavery in China during the Former Han Dynasty, 206 B.C.–A.D. 25.* Field Museum of Natural History Publication 525. Anthropological Series, vol. 34. Chicago: Field Museum of Natural History.

Wilson, Jeanne L. 1990. "Labor Policy in China: Reform and Retrogression." *Problems of Communism* 90 (September-October): 44–65.

Witke, Roxanne. 1977. *Comrade Chiang Ch'ing.* Boston: Little, Brown and Co.

Wolf, Arthur P. and Chieh-shan Huang. 1980. *Marriage and Adoption in China, 1845–1945.* Stanford, Calif.: Stanford University Press.

Wolf, Diane L. 1990. "Linking Women's Labor with the Global Economy: Factory Workers and Their Families in Rural Java." Pp. 25–47 in *Women Workers and Global Restructuring,* edited by Kathryn B. Ward. Cornell International Industrial and Labor Relations Report, no. 17. Ithaca, N.Y.: ILR Press, School of Industrial and Labor Relations, Cornell University.

————. 1992. *Factory Daughters: Gender, Household Dynamics, and Rural Industrialization in Java.* Berkeley: University of California Press.

Wolf, Margery. 1985. *Revolution Postponed: Women in Contemporary China.* Stanford, Calif.: Stanford University Press.

Woo, Margaret. 1994. "Chinese Women Workers: The Delicate Balance between Protection and Equality." Pp. 279–98 in *Engendering China: Women, Culture, and the State,* edited by Christina K. Gilmartin, Gail Hershatter, Lisa Rofel, and Tyrene White. Cambridge: Harvard University Press.

Woon, Yuen-Fong. 1993. "Circulatory Mobility in Post-Mao China: Temporary Migrants in Kaiping County, Pearl River Delta Region." *International Migration Review* 27: 578–604.

World Bank. 1994. *World Development Report, 1994: Infrastructure for Development.* Oxford: Oxford University Press for the World Bank.

Wu Naitao. 1995. "Employment and Chinese Women." *Beijing Review* 39(10): 6–12.

Xiang Biao. 1993. "Beijing you ge 'Zhejiangcun'" (There is a "Zhejiang village" in Beijing). *Shehuixue yu shehui diaocha* (Sociology and social investigation), no. 3–5.

————. 1996. "How to Create a Visible 'Non-State Space' through Migration and Marketized Traditional Networks: An Account of a Migrant Community in China." Paper presented at the International Conference on Chinese Rural Labor Force Mobility, Beijing, 25–27 June.

Xiang Hong. 1965. "Dazhai tieguniangdui" (The Iron Girl team of Dazhai). *Zhongguo funü* (Chinese women) 3 (March): 14.

Xie Shusen and Bing Chen. 1990. "Nongye renkou liudong tan yuan yu duice" (The cause and countermeasures of the flow of the agricultural labor). *Renkou yanjiu* (Population research) 5: 7–13.

Xie Yu and Emily Hannum. 1996. "Regional Variation in Earnings Inequality in Reform-Era Urban China." *American Journal of Sociology* 101: 950–92.

Xu Huiying. 1991. "18 sui de huanmie" (Eighteen years vanishing into thin air.) In *Caoyuan qishi lu* (Record of the grasslands). Beijing: Gongren chubanshe.

Xu Xinwu. 1981. *Yapian zhanzhengqian Zhongguo mianfangzhi shougongye de shangpin shengchan yu ziben zhuyi mengya wenti* (Commercial production in China's cotton spinning and weaving protoindustry before the Opium War and the problem of the sprouts of capitalism). Yangzhou: Jiangsu renmin chubanshe.

Yan Yunxiang. 1995. "Everyday Power Relations: Changes in a North China Village."

Pp. 215–41 in *The Waning of the Communist State: Economic Origins of Political Decline in China and Hungary,* edited by Andrew G. Walder. Studies on China, 21. Berkeley: University of California Press.

———. 1996. *The Flow of Gifts: Reciprocity and Social Networks in a Chinese Village.* Stanford, Calif.: Stanford University Press.

Yanagisako, Sylvia J. 1984. "Explicating Residence." Pp. 330–52 in *Households: Comparative and Historical Studies of the Domestic Group,* edited by Robert McC. Netting, Richard R. Wilk, and Eric J. Arnould. Berkeley: University of California Press.

Yang, Dennis Tao. 1997. "Education and Off-Farm Work." *Economic Development and Cultural Change* 45: 613–32.

Yang Lien-sheng. 1961. "Schedules of Work and Rest in Imperial China." Pp. 18–42 in *Studies in Chinese Institutional History.* Harvard-Yenching Institute Studies, no. 20. Cambridge: Harvard University Press.

———. 1969. "Economic Aspects of Public Works in Imperial China." Pp. 191–248 in *Excursions in Sinology.* Harvard-Yenching Institute Studies, no. 24. Cambridge: Harvard University Press.

Yang Liuzhi. 1992. "The Current Status and the Trend of Change of the Employed Labor Force in China." Pp. 602–12 in *Dangdai Zhongguo Renkou* (Contemporary Chinese population), edited by Jinxin Sun, Huaiyang Sun, and Weimin Zhang. Beijing: China Census Bureau and State Statistics Bureau.

Yang, Mayfair Mei-hui. 1994. *Gifts, Favors, and Banquets: The Art of Social Relationships in China.* The Wilder House Series in Politics, History, and Culture. Ithaca, N.Y.: Cornell University Press.

Yang Quanhe and Fei Guo. 1996. "Occupational Attainments of Rural to Urban Temporary Economic Migrants in China, 1985–1990." *International Migration Review* 30: 771–87.

Yang, Rae. 1997. *Spider Eaters.* Berkeley: University of California Press.

Yang Xiushi. 1993. "Household Registration, Economic Reform and Migration." *International Migration Review* 27: 796–818.

———. 1994. "Urban Temporary Out-Migration under Economic Reforms: Who Moves and for What Reasons?" *Population Research and Policy Review* 13: 83–100.

———. 1996. "Patterns of Economic Development and Patterns of Rural-Urban Migration in China." *European Journal of Population* 12: 195–218.

Ye Shi. 1961. "Liugengtang ji." In *Ye Shi ji* (The collected works of Ye Shi). Vol. 1. Beijing: Zhonghua shuju.

You Yunzhong. 1993. "Volume and Characteristics of Migration in China in the 1980s." *China 1990 Population Census Papers for International Seminar.* Beijing: China Statistical Press.

Yuan Fenglan. 1991. "Zouchang" (Entering the yard). Pp. 408–13 in *Caoyuan qishi lu* (Record of the grasslands) Beijing: Gongren chubanshe.

Zhai Zhenhua. 1992. *Red Flower of China.* New York: Soho Press.

Zhang Li. 1998. "Strangers in the City: Space, Power, and Identity in China's 'Floating Population.'" Ph.D. dissertation, Cornell University.

Zhang Ning. 1992. "A Conflict of Interest: Current Problems in Educational Reform." Pp. 144–70 in *Economic Reform and Social Change in China,* edited by Andrew Watson. London: Routledge.

Zhang Yue. 1995. "Napian lüzhou" (That green place). Pp. 218–24 in *Wushige Beijing nüzhiqing de zishu,* (Accounts by fifty female Beijing sent-down youth) edited by Liu Zhongluo, Zang Jian, and Tian Xiaoye. Beijing: Beijing daxue chubanshe.

Zhejiang Provincial Statistical Bureau (ZPSB). 1993. *Zhejiang tongji nianjian* (Zhejiang statistics yearbook). Beijing: China Statistical Publishing House.

Zhonghua quanguo funü lianhehui yanjiusuo and Shaanxisheng funü lianhehui yanjiushi (Research Institute of All-China Women's Federation and Research Office of Shaanxi Provincial Women's Federation). 1991. *Zhongguo funü tongji ziliao 1949–1989* (Statistics on Chinese women 1949–1989). Beijing: Zhongguo tongji chubanshe.

Zhou Zhengyuan and Yaode Gu. 1994. "Migration and Moving of Population." Pp. 270–308 in *The Population of China towards the Twenty-First Century: Zhejiang Volume,* edited by Changde Ye, Yuanzhong Ding, Sijun Wang, and Peiyun Dong. Beijing: China Statistics Publishing House.

CONTRIBUTORS

Yanjie Bian is associate professor of sociology at the University of Minnesota. His areas of research interest are economic sociology, social networks, social stratification and mobility, and contemporary Chinese society. He is the author of *Work and Inequality in Urban China* (1994) and editor of *Market Transition and Social Stratification: American Sociologists' Analyses of China* (2000). His most recent project involves social networks and labor markets in China.

Deborah S. Davis, professor of sociology at Yale University, studies contemporary Chinese society. Her most recent edited volumes are *Urban Spaces* (1995) and *The Consumer Revolution in Urban China* (1999).

Barbara Entwisle is professor of sociology and fellow of the Carolina Population Center at the University of North Carolina at Chapel Hill. Her current research focuses on work patterns, childbearing, and child rearing in China; the demography of social networks; integrating quantitative and qualitative approaches; and population dynamics and changes in the landscape in Northeast Thailand. Recent publications include "Gender and Family Businesses in Rural China," *American Sociological Review* (1995); "Geographic Information Systems, Spatial Network Analysis, and Contraceptive Choice," *Demography* (1997); and "Spatial Arrangement of Social and Economic Networks among Villages in Nang Rong District, Thailand," *Social Networks* (1999).

Alice Goldstein is research associate (emeritus), and *Sidney Goldstein* is professor (emeritus) at the Population Studies and Training Center, Brown University. She studies internal migration in relation to women's status and fertility. His research focus is on internal migration in relation to urbanization and economic development. Recent joint publications include "The Relation of Migration to Changing Household Headship Patterns in China," *Population Studies* (1997); "Migration, Fertility, and State Policy in Hubei Province, China," *Demography* (1997); and "Permanent and Temporary Migration in Vietnam during a Period of Economic Change," *Asia-Pacific Population Journal* (2000).

Stevan Harrell is professor of anthropology; curator of Asian ethnology, Burke Museum; and fellow, Center for Studies in Demography and Ecology at the University of Washington in Seattle. He studies family organization, demography, ethnicity, religion, material culture, and education in China and Taiwan. He is editor of *Chinese Historical Micro-Demography* (1996) and co-editor of *Chinese Families in the Post-Mao Era* (1993).

Gail E. Henderson is professor of social medicine at the University of North Carolina School of Medicine. Medical sociology, health care in China, and research ethics are her main areas of academic interest. Recent publications include "Gender and Family Businesses in Rural China," *American Sociological Review* (1995); "Preventive Health Care in Zouping: Privatization and the Public Good," in *Zouping in Transition: The Political Economy of Growth in a North China County* (1998; edited by Andrew G. Walder); and "Trends in Health Care Utilization in Eight Chinese Provinces, 1989–1993," *Social Science and Medicine* (1998).

Gail Hershatter is professor of history and co-director of the Center for Cultural Studies at the University of California, Santa Cruz. Her most recent book is *Dangerous Pleasures: Prostitution and Modernity in Twentieth Century Shanghai* (1997), and her most recent co-edited volume is *Guide to Women's Studies in China* (1999). Her current research project is titled "The Gender of Memory: Rural Chinese Women and the 1950s."

Emily Honig, professor of women's studies and history at the University of California, Santa Cruz, is the author of *Sisters and Strangers: Women in the Shanghai Cotton Mills, 1919–1949* (1986) and the co-author of *Personal Voices: Chinese Women in the 1980s* (1988). Gender in modern China is her main area of academic interest.

Li Ying, associate researcher at the Institute of Nutrition and Food Hygiene at the Chinese Academy of Preventive Medicine, is interested in nutrition and nutrition education with particular reference to conditions in China. Recent publications include "The Changing Trend of Children's Malnutrition and Calculation in 2000," *The Chinese Journal of Health Education* (1998); "Developing Nutrition Education Activities for Rural Children's Parents in China," *Journal of Hygiene Research* (1998); and *Key Message on Infant Feeding* (1995).

Zai Liang, associate professor of sociology at City University of New York–Queens College, studies internal and international migration and race and ethnic relations. Recent publications include "Market Transition, Government Policies, and Interprovincial Migration in China, 1983–1988," *Economic Development and Cultural Change* (1997); "Intermarriage of Asian Americans in the New York City Region: Contemporary Patterns and Future Prospects," *International Migration Review* (1999); and "The Age of Migration in China," *Population and Development Review* (1999).

Nan Lin is professor of sociology and director of the Asian/Pacific Studies Institute at Duke University. His interests include social networks, social stratification and mobility, stress and coping, and transformations of Chinese society. Recent publications include "Local Market Socialism: Rural Reform in China," *Theory and Society* (1995); "Stress in Urban China," *Social Science and Medicine* (1995); "Chinese Rural Enterprises in Transformation: The End of the Beginning," *Issues and Studies* (1998); and "Local Elites as Official Owners: Shareholding and Property Rights in Daquizhuang Industry," in *Property Rights and Economic Reform in China* (1999; edited by Jean C. Oi and Andrew G. Walder).

John R. Logan is professor of sociology and director of the Lewis Mumford Center for Comparative Urban and Regional Research at the University at Albany, SUNY. He has conducted several studies of housing allocation, income inequality, and family relations in China. They include: "Market Transition and the Persistence of Power: The Changing Stratification in Urban China," *American Sociological Review* (1996); "Housing Inequality in Urban China in the 1990s," *International Journal of Urban and Regional Research* (1999); and "Family Values and Co-Residence with Married Children in Urban China," *Social Forces* (1999).

Ma Linmao is deputy director of the Department of Health Statistics, Center for Public Health Information, Chinese Academy of Preventive Medicine, Beijing. Among his articles are "Dietary Factor Correlates of Hypertension and Nutritional Status in China," *Beijing Science and Technology Press* (1998), and "Logistic Regression Analysis of Risk for Type II Diabetes Mellitus," *Chinese Journal of Diabetes* (1999).

Susan Mann is professor of history at the University of California, Davis. The history of late imperial China and family and gender relations are her research interests. Her most recent book is *Precious Records: Women in China's Long Eighteenth Century* (1997), and her most recent co-edited volume is *Guide to Women's Studies in China* (1999).

Ethan Michelson, a Ph.D. student in the Department of Sociology at the University of Chicago, studies social change and the sociology of law. He is writing his dissertation on the emergence and development of the legal profession in China. Recent publications include "Tradition in the Shadow of Modern Legal Practice: Continuity and Change in the Delivery of Justice in China" (in two parts), *Chinese Law and Government* (1998).

William L. Parish is professor of sociology at the University of Chicago. Social change in East Asia is the focus of his scholarly work. His most recent book is *Urban Life in China: The New Social Contract* (1999).

Rachel A. Rosenfeld is professor of sociology at the University of North Carolina at Chapel Hill. She studies social stratification, work and careers, and gender. Recent articles include "Gender Inequality at Work in the Early Adult Lifecourse: A Comparison of Job-Shifting Patterns in the Former East Germany and the Former West Germany," *European Sociological Review* (1998); "Gender Differences in Supervisory Authority: Variation among Advanced Industrialized Democracies," *Social Science Research* (1998); and "Employment Flexibility in the United States: Changing and Maintaining Gender, Class, and Ethnic Work Relations," in *Reconfiguring Class and Gender,* edited by Mark Western and Janeen Baxter (forthcoming).

Susan E. Short, assistant professor of sociology at Brown University, specializes in the study of families and households, social demography, and social change and development. Recent publications include "Looking Locally at China's One Child Policy," *Studies in Family Planning* (1998); "Household Production and Household Structure in the Context of China's Economic Reforms," *Social Forces* (1996); and "Gender and Family Businesses in Rural China," *American Sociological Review* (1995).

Xiaoling Shu is assistant professor of sociology at the University of California, Davis. Social stratification, quantitative research methods, life course studies, social demography, comparative studies, and the sociology of gender are her areas of interest. Recent publications include "Gender-Related Change in Occupational Aspirations," *Sociology of Education* (1998), and "Characterizing Occupations with Data from the Dictionary of Occupational Titles," *Social Science Research* (1996).

Wang Feng, associate professor of sociology at the University of California, Irvine, studies comparative demographic regimes and social transitions in formerly socialist societies. His recently co-authored publications include *One Quarter of Humanity: Malthusian Mythology and Chinese Realities* (1999). He also co-edited *China: The Many Facets of Demographic Change* (1996).

Martin King Whyte is professor of sociology and international affairs and chair of the Department of Sociology at George Washington University. His areas of interest include contemporary Chinese society, the sociology of the family, the sociology of development, and social stratification. He is particularly interested in the social consequences of market reforms in formerly centrally planned economies. Recent publications are "The Fate of Filial Obligations in Urban China," *The China Journal* (1997); "Human Rights Trends and Coercive Family Planning in the People's Republic of China," *Issues and Studies* (1998); and "The Changing Role of Workers" in *Paradox of China's Reforms: Dynamic Economy, Declining Party-State* (1999; edited by Merle Goldman and Roderick MacFarquhar).

Xu Siyuan is assistant professor at the Hubei Anti-Epidemic Disease Station in Wuhan. He is editor of *Hygienic Management of Modern Food Processing* (1995) and author of *A Guide to Field Work in Public Nutrition* (1993). Nutrition and food hygiene are his main interests.

Yang Mingliang is professor at the Hubei Anti-Epidemic Disease Station in Wuhan. He co-edited *Dietary Nutrition and Physical Development of Residents in Hubei Province in the 1990s.* He also wrote "Influence of Economic and Regional Factors on the Nutritional Status of Adults," *Journal of Hygiene Research* (1996).

Xiushi Yang, associate professor of sociology at Old Dominion University, studies migration, urbanization, and international demography. Recent publications include "The New Economic Policy and Permanent Migration in Zhejiang Province, China," *Asian and Pacific Migration Journal* (1997); "Economic Reforms and Spatial Mobility" in *China: The Many Facets of Demographic Change* (1997; edited by Alice Goldstein and Wang Feng); and "Determinants of Temporary Migration: A Multilevel Analysis," *International Migration Review* (1999).

Zhai Fengying is professor and deputy director of the Institute of Nutrition and Food Hygiene at the Chinese Academy of Preventive Medicine. She is co-investigator of the China Health and Nutrition Survey (1989–2000) and co-investigator of a collaborative project with UNICEF on nutrition education, surveillance and intervention. Recent articles include "The Dietary and Growth Status of Preschool Children in Eight Provinces of China," *Acta Nutrimenta Sinica* (1998); "The Nutritional Status and Dietary Pattern of Chinese Urban Residents," *Journal of Hygiene Research* (1996); and "Evaluation of the 24-Hour Individual Recall Method in China," *Food and Nutrition Bulletin* (1996).

Li Zhang is an assistant professor in the Department of Anthropology at the University of California, Davis. Her research interests include culture, power, and space; postsocialist transformations; gender and modernity; migration, identity, and citizenship; and cities and mass consumer culture. She is currently working on a book that examines the reconfigurations of space, power, and social networks within China's floating population.

INDEX

community action work, 55, 71
Confucianism, 25, 302; Confucian classics,
    16–20
Confucius, 17–18, 99
Connelly, Rachel, 58
conscripted labor, 21, 30n8, 31n14
"contingent" work, 53
contractual jobs, 208
corvée labor, 21, 24, 26, 55, 69
Costello, Cynthia, 57
Croll, Elisabeth J., 280
Cultural Revolution (1966–76), 2; and gen-
    der equality, 97–110, 112, 115, 302;
    labor models during, 3, 7, 97–110

dagongmei (young female migrant workers),
    172, 190–93, 194, 235–36, 237
dahu (wealthy households), women in, 176–
    84, 193
danwei (work unit), 272; establishment of, 2,
    71; gender differences in, 123–24; mean-
    ing of work in, 35, 38, 45, 48, 49, 186
danwei hukou (work-unit household registra-
    tion), 76n3
Davis, Deborah S., 63, 288–89, 300
Deng Xiaoping, 113, 115
diversified households, 265–70, 273, 289–
    90, 301
division of labor: as gendered, 6, 67–76,
    184–89; within households, 5, 15–32;
    occupational, 16, 20–21, 69
domestic violence, 181, 238
Dong Zhongshu, 21
Du Ailian, 84
Du Jingjie, 86

Ebrey, Patricia Buckley, 23–24, 25, 68
education: and career entry, 117, 144, 292;
    enrollment rates, 140–41, 155n7,
    241n1; gender differences in, 2, 7–8,
    117, 132, 139–43, 150, 151–52, 158,
    164, 291, 302; and migration, 206–8,
    212, 224, 234; and wages (remunera-
    tion), 292–93
Eighth Route Army, 80
Elbert, Sarah, 62
employment. *See gongzuo* (work, a job); occu-
    pations; work
employment opportunities: gender differ-
    ences in, 2, 7–8, 128–29, 143–48; mi-
    gration effects on, 236–39

Engels, Friedrich, 79
Enloe, Cynthia H., 59
Entwisle, Barbara, 55, 56, 59, 64, 113, 289,
    298, 300, 301
equal pay for equal work (*tonggong tongchou*),
    239

family planning policy, 164, 246, 285, 289
family values, Confucian, 25
farms, 2; decollectivization of, 3, 262, 264;
    gendered labor on, 6–7, 9, 144, 210–12,
    213, 239. *See also* agricultural labor
female infanticide, 4, 8, 163–64
feminism, denunciation of, 98. *See also*
    "proto-feminism"
Ferber, Marianne A., 55
Fernández-Kelly, María P., 191
Fink, Deborah, 58
floating population. *See* migration
Fulian. See Chinese Women's Federation
    (*Fulian*)

Gansu province, migrants in, 203
gender, definition of, 300–301
gender differences: assessing trends in, 8,
    157–67; classical (traditional), 19, 301,
    302; in division of labor, 6, 67–76; in
    education, 2, 7–8, 117, 132, 139–43,
    150, 151–52, 158, 164, 291, 302; in em-
    ployment opportunities, 2, 7–8, 128–29,
    143–48; in household-based produc-
    tion, 54–55, 186–87; imperial, 20–28;
    in meaning of work, 47–49; in migra-
    tion, 9, 202–10, 214–30, 231–42; in
    occupations, 119–23, 150; in Party
    membership, 7, 117, 132, 158, 159, 164,
    302–3; in retirement, 7, 52, 124, 132,
    158, 303; in rural China, 7–8, 103–9,
    134–56; in Shaanxi province, 6–7,
    79–96; in Shanghai, 28–29; in Tianjin
    province, 7, 28, 111–33; in wages (remu-
    neration), 7, 111–33, 148–50, 159, 302–
    3; in work location, 145–47
gender equality: achievement of, 2–3; in
    post-Maoist China, 3, 97. *See also* "Iron
    Girls"
Gerber, Theodore P., 130
getihu (individual businesses), 33, 34, 35,
    144, 153, 196n6, 261
Goldstein, Alice, 234, 298
Goldstein, Sidney, 234, 298

"opening up" (*kaifang*) policy, 183–84
oral history, as documentary evidence, 161

Padavic, Irene, 57
Parish, William L., 136, 137, 291, 299, 302
patriarchy, impact of economic development on, 7, 134, 135–36, 150–51
patrilineal succession, 10
Polivka, Anne, 53
Portes, Alejandro, 53
private home ownership, 246–48, 253
privatization, 3, 33
prostitution, 26, 183–84
"proto-feminism," 161, 164
public goods regime, 246, 248
public works projects, 21, 30–31n10

Qin dynasty, 21
Qing dynasty, 25
Qingming shanghe tu (Going upriver at the Qingming festival), 25
Quan Hansheng, 24

Rapp, Rayna, 175
Red Detachment of Women (ballet), 100–101
redistribution, 264
remuneration, 195n5; determination of, 125–28; and education, 292–93; gender differences in, 7, 111–33, 148–50, 159, 302–3; and meaning of work, 44–45, 46, 48; and Party membership, 292–93; and work location, 6, 51–66
Reskin, Barbara F., 57
retirement, gender differences in, 7, 52, 124, 132, 158, 303
Rosenfeld, Rachel A., 48, 57, 67, 296, 297, 300

Salaff, Janet W., 135
salary. *See* remuneration
Sassen-Koob, Saskia, 53
"scar literature," as documentary evidence, 102
scholars (*shi*), 20
Second National Housing Reform conference (1991), 253
sericulture (*sang*), 19, 136
Shaanxi province, 203; gendered labor in, 6–7, 79–96
Shandong province, 138, 173, 265
Shanghai, 70, 257; gender differences in,

28–29; household configuration in, 10, 245–60, 300; housing reform in, 247–48; migrant community in, 215, 228, 235, 237, 242n6
Shanghai Temporary Migration Survey (1984), 215
shenfen zheng (identity cards), 71
Shenzhen Special Economic Zone, 234, 235, 238
Short, Susan E., 289, 300, 301
Shu, Xiaoling, 298, 302
Sichuan province, 173, 235
silk production. *See* sericulture
siying qiye (private enterprise), 33–34, 153, 261, 297
slavery, 21
social capital, 8, 134, 137–38, 143, 148, 150–51, 152, 286–87, 291–92. *See also* *guanxi* (social connections)
social inequality, 284–94
social status, of workers, 17, 188
social stratification, 284
socialism, 1, 72
Socialist Transformation (1956–58), 114, 115
Solinger, Dorothy J., 173
Song dynasty, 23–24
South Korea, women's employment opportunities in, 151
Special Economic Zones, 228. *See also* Shenzhen Special Economic Zone
specialized households, 265, 270, 273–79, 280, 281, 289–90, 301
State Family Planning Commission of China, 231
Stockard, Janice E., 136
subjective information, problems in evaluating, 157–58
superstitions, 106–7
Szelényi, Iván, 137, 153

Taiwan, women's employment opportunities in, 135, 136, 151
Tang dynasty, 22
Tang Shulian, 84
Tang Yuying, 84
Tang Zhuzhen, 84
Tawney, Richard Henry, 27
temporary jobs, 208
Tianjin province, wage and job inequalities in, 7, 28, 111–33

Designer:	Ina Clausen
Compositor:	G&S Typesetters, Inc.
Text:	10/12 Baskerville
Display:	Baskerville
Printer and binder:	Thomson-Shore, Inc.

3775034